Animal Oppression
and Capitalism

Animal Oppression and Capitalism

Volume 2: The Oppressive and Destructive Role of Capitalism

David Nibert, Editor
Art by Sue Coe

PRAEGER™

An Imprint of ABC-CLIO, LLC
Santa Barbara, California • Denver, Colorado

Library of Congress Cataloging-in-Publication Data

Names: Nibert, David Alan, 1953- editor.
Title: Animal oppression and capitalism / David Nibert, editor.
Description: Santa Barbara, California : Praeger, [2017] | Includes bibliographical
    references and index.
Identifiers: LCCN 2017003395 (print) | LCCN 2017021198 (ebook) | ISBN 9781440850745
    (ebook) | ISBN 9781440850738 (set : hbk : alk. paper) | ISBN 9781440850752
    (vol. 1 : hbk : alk. paper) | ISBN 9781440850769 (vol. 2 : hbk : alk. paper)
Subjects: LCSH: Animal welfare. | Animal rights. | Capitalism—Moral and
    ethical aspects.
Classification: LCC HV4708 (ebook) | LCC HV4708 .A5486 2017 (print) |
    DDC 179/.3—dc23
LC record available at https://lccn.loc.gov/2017003395

ISBN: 978-1-4408-5073-8 (set)
978-1-4408-5075-2 (vol. 1)
978-1-4408-5076-9 (vol. 2)
EISBN: 978-1-4408-5074-5

21 20 19 18 17   1 2 3 4 5

This book is also available as an ebook.

Praeger
An Imprint of ABC-CLIO, LLC

ABC-CLIO, LLC
130 Cremona Drive, P.O. Box 1911
Santa Barbara, California 93116-1911
www.abc-clio.com

This book is printed on acid-free paper ∞

Manufactured in the United States of America

For Beata

Contents

Cross Your Heart and Hope to Die, *Sue Coe 100*

Unwanted, *Sue Coe 115*

Triumph of Capitalism, *Sue Coe 200*

Workers of the World, *Sue Coe 251*

Cruel. (Copyright © 2011 Sue Coe. Courtesy Galerie St. Etienne, NY)

1

Capitalism and Speciesism

John Sanbonmatsu

Speciesism, or the system by which human beings dominate, exploit, and kill other conscious beings for their purposes, precedes capitalist development by thousands of years. Humans hunted or fished nonhuman animals for a variety of communal purposes for countless generations, killing them for food, for clothing, for art, or to propitiate hidden gods. However, for all their brutality toward the other beings, humans by and large did not kill the latter indiscriminately, and they viewed other animals not merely as things but as powerful beings in their own right—as entities who possessed spirits and were integral to the cosmological order. Human power was thus held partially in check by religious and metaphysical beliefs that set limits on human practices and rituals of killing.

With the advent of capitalist relations, however, beginning around the sixteenth century in Europe, the last cultural and practical fetters to total human dominion fell away. On the one hand, the scientific and technological revolutions—themselves largely artifacts of capitalism—vastly amplified humans' powers of dominion over other natural beings. On the other hand, the emergence of a profit-based system of economic development created vast new global markets for nonhuman products. By the end of the twentieth century, speciesism under advanced capitalist conditions had at last reached its zenith as a totalitarian, global system of surveillance, technological control, and mass murder without moral, spatial, temporal, biological, or ontological limits. Today, nonhuman animals born into the industrialized agriculture system spend their whole lives in entirely artificial environments where their bodies, behaviors, and minds are forced to conform utterly to the needs of the administered world of capital. Chickens, for example, are treated not as conscious, feeling beings but as matter to be shaped according to the needs of the system. As Karen Davis observes, quoting from a "poultry" industry manual entitled *Commercial Chicken Meat and Egg Production*:

> . . . . the "technology built into buildings and equipment" is "embodied genetically into the chicken itself." Physical characteristics and behavioral attributes deemed "necessary for commercial performance objectives" should enable a "continued adaptation of chickens to the housing systems and management used by commercial producers." As Michael Watts writes . . . "What is striking about the chicken is the extent to which the 'biological body' has been actually constructed physically to meet the needs of the industrial labor process." (Davis 2012, 15–16)

Nonhuman animals born into such infernal conditions suffer existentially, not merely bodily. Chickens, writes Davis, "are alienated from surrounding nature, from an external world that answers intelligibly to their inner world. There is nothing for them to do or see or look forward to, they are permitted no voluntary actions and are deprived of any opportunity for joy or zest of living. They just have to *be*, in an excremental, existential void, until we kill them" (Davis 2012, 37). Rendered "unable to die," such beings are forced to "become extinct under conditions equivalent to their eternal rebirth in a bottomless pit" (Davis 2012, 41).

The treatment of chickens in the "poultry" industry, however, as bad as it is, is no worse than the treatment experienced by many other species of nonhuman animals caught up in the modern mechanized agricultural system. Cows and horses are routinely skinned alive, pigs are scalded to death in hair-removal tanks, calves in the "veal" industry are raised in utter darkness inside tiny fetid stalls, unable to move or to stand, before being driven to the slaughterhouse to have their throats cut—the list goes on and on. Such practices are so violently cruel that one might suppose they were designed with the specific intention of tormenting their victims. In reality, however, virtually all of the violence inflicted by humans on other animals today stems not from intentional cruelty but from the objective features of our economic system—that is, from capitalism.

Both speciesism and capitalism can be characterized as *modes of production*, in the sense of that term used by Karl Marx and Friedrich Engels to describe "a definite form of activity of . . . individuals, a definite form of expressing their life, a definite *mode of life* on their part" (Marx and Engels 1970, 42). Capitalism is a mode of production insofar as the bulk of human economic or productive activity is organized around the private accumulation of wealth, and because capitalist values, beliefs, and norms come to condition the entirety of society, top to bottom. Speciesism, too, may similarly be viewed as a mode of production, insofar as we are beings who maintain our lives chiefly by dominating, controlling, and killing the other sentient beings. Of the two modes of life, speciesism is undoubtedly the more fundamental one. This is so not only because domination and control of other species is the precondition for all capital accumulation but because our species life, our identity *as* a species, is organized around this dominion. Speciesism, we might say, is the *"Ur"*-modality or most primordial of all modes of human life, of human productive activity.[1] Some 40 percent of the entire land mass of the Earth is now cultivated for agriculture, with some three-quarters of all such land utilized directly or indirectly to raise other animals for slaughter, making nonhuman animal agriculture the most extensive human artifact on the planet and its most salient cultural expression as a species. If it is true, as Marx and Engels wrote, that as "individuals express their life, so they are," then speciesism is the means of human life and perhaps even, in some sense, the meaning of human life.

It took centuries for full-fledged capitalist relations to take hold in Europe and eventually everywhere else; however, once those relations were firmly established, nonhuman animal life suffered a precipitous fall. From the period of industrial capitalist development we can date, among other calamities, the mass extinction of species, the torture of nonhuman animals in laboratories, the creation of zoos and aquaria, and, by the early twentieth century, the intensive "factory" confinement and mechanized mass killing of other animals. The scale and the ferocity of human violence against nonhumans today is without historical precedent: some 50 billion land mammals and avians and as many as 100 billion or more sea animals are slaughtered each year by commercial industries. Meanwhile, we are living through the greatest mass species extinction event in 60 million years. There have been many destructive human cultures and civilizations through the ages, but only capitalism has proved truly *omnicidal*, revealing itself as inimical to all nonhuman animal life as such, everywhere. Simply put, capitalism is the highest form of speciesism, the "ideal," or most fully realized—and therefore most destructive—of the myriad forms that speciesism could conceivably take.

THE COMMODITY SYSTEM

Long before nonhuman animals are obliterated physically, they are destroyed conceptually. From the perspective of capital, other animals are not conscious individuals, beings with experiences, lives, and interests of their own, but exchangeable units—things to be manipulated and disposed of at will. Individual nonhuman animals are never given names by the scientists who vivisect or poison them in their laboratories, nor by the farmers who raise them for slaughter, because they are viewed not as unique persons, but as *quantities*, as abstractions within a system of abstractions. They exist for the capitalist only as inputs within a system of control and extermination—"pork belly futures," lots to be auctioned, "subject 913," and so on. This obliteration of nonhuman subjectivity or "personhood" is a direct effect of the system of commodity production.

When people think of capitalism, they typically think of businesses selling useful products to individuals who need them. However, such a picture misses capitalism's complex, destructive nature as a system of social dominance, exploitation, and coercion. Two features of capitalism in particular render it both a uniquely destructive and a historically distinctive form of economic and social life, distinguishing it from all earlier modes of economic and social life. First, under capitalist relations, the means of human economic and social life—including the labor (or labor power) of human workers—are privately owned by a small clique or class of individuals. Second, goods are manufactured not to meet particular human or social needs but solely in order to generate profit for the owning class. Together these two aspects of capitalism—ownership by a single class and production of goods for exchange rather than for use—are the twin pillars of the modern speciesist system.

The English word *capital*, from which we get the word *capitalism*, derives from the Old French, *caput*, for "head of cattle," reminding us that domesticated nonhuman animals served as one the earliest forms of private property and wealth, hence too of inequality and hierarchy in human culture (Nibert 2002). However, it is not other animals' status as *property*, as such, that seals their doom under capitalism but rather their status as *commodities*. If we wish to understand the reason for the horrific plight of nonhuman animals today, therefore, it is necessary to inquire at some length into the nature of the commodity system.

Prior to the emergence of full capitalist relations, humans produced goods chiefly in order to satisfy the wants and the needs of their societies. Economic activity was useful activity, and production was subordinated to communal values and norms. Ancient peoples hunted, harvested beets, wove baskets, made ceremonial masks, etc., not chiefly in order to sell the goods they produced—maize, olives, "livestock," and so on—but in order to sustain a form of life that was meaningful to them. Neither the emergence of the first markets nor the introduction of money as a means of exchange changed the fact that the things humans produced were intended, first and foremost, to maintain their existing ways of life.[2] As a consequence, per capita human consumption of nonhuman animals remained relatively constant for thousands of years, due partly to the inconstancy and the insecurity of food production, but more importantly to the fact that economic production was organized around the reproduction or simple continuance of the structures of daily human life. In most human cultures, people subsisted chiefly on plant matter, with nonhuman animals' flesh, their milk, the cheese derived from their milk, playing a subordinate role in human diets.

The advent of capitalism, however, changed all this. Production of goods for the first time became severed from direct satisfaction of human wants and needs and instead became organized around what Marx termed *exchange value*, or the value that commodities could command on a market. Perverse as it may seem—and is—goods today are produced not in order to be *used*, but solely in order to be *sold*, in order to generate profit for the owning class. Among other things, this oddity explains why after five centuries of capitalist development more than half the human race still lives on just $2 per day or less, while the richest 62 people on Earth today own more wealth than the poorest 3.5 billion people (Oxfam 2016). Though it is commonly believed that world poverty is due to scarce resources, there is more than enough food, clothing, and shelter to meet the needs of every human being on Earth. Inequality arises not from scarcity but from the fact that the entirety of our species (or nearly so) is made to labor and sweat to enrich a handful of powerful individuals who produce goods for sale rather than for use.

This dynamic has profound implications for nonhuman exploitation. Though it is widely assumed that farmers and agribusinesses reproduce, raise, and kill nonhuman beings so that humans will have something to eat or something to wear, the truth is quite otherwise. Like any other commodity, nonhuman beings are in fact brought into the world not *in order* to be eaten or be worn but in order to be *sold*. This explains why, when market prices for some nonhuman animal product suddenly fall due to overproduction, farmers and agribusinesses deliberately destroy their stocks of the good to stabilize prices. In the first six months of 2015, for example, "dairy" producers in the northeastern United States dumped 31 million pounds of cow's milk into giant manure pits rather than to sell or give it away, after prices for the commodity weakened. At the time, Eric Meyer, president of HighGround Dairy (a capitalist broker of "dairy" products in Chicago), commented, "The world needs less milk" (Mulvany 2015). As this statement suggests, however, *need* is an altogether relative concept under capitalism, since at the time of Meyer's remark over 40 million North Americans were living below the poverty line, while tens of millions more people throughout Central and South America were even worse off. What Meyer meant, then, was not that the world needed less milk, but that the "dairy" industry needed less of it so that corporate profitability in the "dairy" sector might thereby swiftly be restored.

Hence the strange disjuncture under capitalism between need and value, or between what is useful for life and what is merely useful for generating more wealth for those who already possess more than their rightful share of it. Were agriculture organized with the aim of providing everyone with nutritious and sustainable food, rather than with the aim of maximizing private profit, then we would all presumably be vegans, since raising billions of other animals for consumption is unequivocally the most inefficient, ecologically harmful, and unethical form system of food production extant. Instead, under the present capitalist system of production, we find continual increase in the quantity and diversity of nonhuman animal products. Between 1950 and 1970 alone, for example, per capita "meat" consumption in the United States increased a staggering 400 percent, and while total consumption of nonhuman flesh fell off in the 1980s and 1990s—as a result of two recessions and increasing public concern over the adverse health consequences of eating "beef" and "pork"—"meat" consumption today is again on the rise, largely as a result of cheaper commodities and the fad for organic animal products.[3] Global demand for "meat" production has meanwhile exploded, due chiefly to the rise of a new middle class in China, where increased "meat" consumption is associated with higher social status.

It is important to understand, however, that demand itself is an effect of capitalism. Though many people are under the impression that the production of goods in our society is driven by something called "consumer demand," which corporations then respond to, such a view of the workings of the economy is erroneous. It is not consumption that drives production but rather the reverse. The desires and the needs of consumers do play a role in the economy, insofar as companies have to manufacture products that people will buy. All commodities must therefore have a perceived *use value*, or they will not find a buyer. But it is capitalist industry, not the consumer, that makes investment decisions about what is to be produced. The iPhone did not arise because people were clamoring to have one, but because the Apple corporation decided to manufacture and create a market for it. Consumers did not hold street protests or focus groups to demand omega-3s (extracted from dead fish) in their orange juice, but because the orange industry was looking for new ways to diversify its products. Capitalists in fact spend nearly as much money manufacturing demand as they do manufacturing goods. They have to, because when consumption slows, as happens during economic downturns, strikes, and so on, capitalists suddenly find themselves unable to pay their bills and are left with surplus goods, factories, and hired workers on their hands. Such disruptions can be not just costly but economically ruinous, whether for individual businesses or industries or even a national or world economy. Business owners must therefore continually find new markets or expand existing ones for their goods and services or perish in the wider market. Expanding the sphere of consumption— by increasing the rate of consumption and increasing the number and diversity of commodities on offer—is thus a structural imperative for capitalists. That is why the number of nonhumans being brought into the world by humans is always increasing, and why nonhuman bodies are rendered into an ever more dizzying array of commodities, from "Chicken McNuggets" and genetically engineered laboratory mice to "bacon"-flavored potato chips, new styles of "fur" coats and "fur-lined" boots, organic bison jerky, and leather bras—literally hundreds of thousands of new animal goods each year.

The key to this continual expansion of the speciesist production system is to be sought again in the nature of the commodity. Marx observed that under capitalist relations, every commodity leads, as it were, a kind of double life. Alone as an object of use, a commodity appears merely as itself, an entity possessing certain material properties and qualities which make it uniquely the sort of thing that it is. A chair, for example, exists as a sensuous and tangible object. It has certain properties (color, mass, and texture) that render it useful for various purposes. The typical *use value* of a chair is to be sat upon. However, a chair might find many other uses as well. For example, a beautifully crafted chair can be an object of aesthetic appreciation; a chair placed on the stage of a theater might be brandished, threateningly, by an actor playing a character in a play; chairs during the Nazi siege of Leningrad were chopped up into firewood. Objects, in fact, have multiple such *use values*, and for many thousands of years, prior to the development of modern markets, that is *all* that artifacts produced by humans and other animals ever had—that is, use values or utilities.

Once money and markets emerged, however, it became possible to compare different kinds of objects to one another as purely quantitative values. Artifacts then began to develop a secret inner life of their own as *exchange* values. Today, as soon as a produced good enters the market, an artifact which first set out in the world humbly as an object with certain uses suddenly develops a most unusual property: it sheds its form as a material thing, taking on the appearance instead of something intangible and even imaginary—namely, a quantitative or abstract value that enables it to be exchanged with other commodities in the market. As a result, things which in reality are not the same sorts of beings are magically rendered into equivalents of one another, through sheer mathematical proportion. A combustible liquid—petroleum—now becomes $3.20 per gallon. A painting by Van Gogh, which began its existence as an expression of one artist's spiritual and emotional life, is magically transformed at auction into $50 million. A cow's milk, produced to nourish her young, becomes $2.50 per carton. A "spring lamb," meanwhile, becomes $18 at the butcher's. As Marx observed, in order for something to appear on the market as a commodity, it is first necessary for "[i]ts existence as a material thing is put out of sight" (Marx 1978, 305).[4] From the point of view of capital, which sees only from the perspective of exchange value, there is no qualitative difference between an automobile, a luxury townhouse, a stand of ancient redwoods, a chimpanzee owned by a zoo, or a pig bred for slaughter: each has value only as a quantity, an abstract value relative to every other. Like a magician who focuses her audience's attention on something extraneous or inessential, to obscure the true nature of an illusion, capital continuously covers over the true nature of the commodities we buy, hiding from view the complex social and ecological relations that go into their production.

Today, the structural imperative of the capitalist market "to nestle everywhere, settle everywhere, form connections everywhere," as Marx and Engels put it in *The Communist Manifesto*, has created a truly globalized system of speciesist exchange. Rainforests in Brazil are burned to graze "cattle" whose flesh will be sold to Japanese, Canadian, and German consumers. Mice genetically engineered by Charles River Labs in Massachusetts may be exported to researchers in laboratories in China, Belgium, or Argentina. "Fur" taken from nonhuman animals brutally killed in Canada or Sweden winds up as "fur" trim on coats sold in Target stores in Minneapolis. This integration of nonhuman animal bodies into global markets has the added "bonus," from the perspective of capital, of shielding the system from criticism. The bewildering array of nonhuman animal products offered on the market, coupled with the complexity of the commodity supply chain—the nesting of diverse corporate and governmental interests and bureaucracies that stand behind every global commodity—makes it difficult to hold specific institutions and stakeholders accountable for their violence. In particular, the mystifying feature of the commodity system makes it difficult for advocates of social change—such as nonhuman animal rights advocates—to educate the public about the true ethical, ecological, and spiritual costs of capitalist production.

Consumers who buy a "hamburger" at Burger King see only a commodity like other commodities—a consumable product—never the labor processes or ecological consequences of their meal. The system shields them from knowledge of the suffering of the impoverished *campesinos* displaced from their land at gunpoint by "cattle" barons, then rehired to tend "cattle" at a miserable wage. It shields them too from any knowledge of the individual cows who died violently so that they could be ground up to become "beef," and from the suffering of the macaque monkeys and other animals who starved to death after their rainforest was burned down. These consumers never become aware of the emotional desensitization of the slaughterhouse workers who were paid an unlivable hourly wage to slit the throats of terrified cows day after day, nor are they ever made aware of the political and legal institutions, corrupt military oligarchies, trade agreements, and so on, that together formed the complex global web that led to the production of the "burger."

By the same token, the fact that dolphins might have feelings, relationships with other dolphins, memories, and so on, is of no importance to the companies in Japan that process and sell dolphin flesh, nor to the fishermen who are hired to kill the dolphins. The fact that pigs are curious, affectionate beings with needs and interests is likewise not of concern to the farmer who raises and sells them, except insofar as their physical well-being impacts what he or she can get for them at auction. And so on down the line with every other animal "commodity." Under capitalism, the actual qualities of nonhuman animals and the aspects of their being that make them who and what they are (conscious individuals) are not merely devalued but obliterated. When commodified nonhumans are deemed no longer to possess commercial value within the system of exchange, they are thus liquidated, in the same way a shoe manufacturer might dispose of last season's shoes by sending them to a landfill.

In 2001, when sheep, pigs, and cows in the United Kingdom became infected with foot-and-mouth disease, the authorities ordered the mass killing and burning of 10 million farmed animals in England, Wales, Scotland, and Ireland in an effort to eradicate all traces of the disease before it could do more commercial damage to nonhuman animal herds. Some farmers wept openly, watching their commercial assets literally go up in smoke. Such *cullings* occur regularly throughout the nonhuman animal industry, as farmers respond to outbreaks of disease with ruthless mass violence. In another case, three years after the foot and mouth crisis in the United Kingdom, an even more terrible slaughter was unleashed throughout Asia when hundreds of millions of chickens, ducks, and other birds were massacred in an attempt to contain an outbreak of avian flu (the H1N1 virus). In some cases, chickens were beaten to death or buried or burned alive, while mobs of humans stood watching the spectacle. In 2015, in the United States alone, some 30 million birds were put to death to contain H1N1 outbreaks. Equally sudden paroxysms of mass violence can be triggered even by simple price fluctuations in national and international markets, as when falling commodity prices create an incentive for agribusinesses to liquidate their surplus nonhuman "stock."

Though the worst atrocities committed against nonhuman animals typically take place in large-scale, intensive confinement facilities, fundamental indifference toward individual nonhuman life is endemic to all forms of nonhuman agriculture. Farmers on small farms lack the incentive or luxury of dwelling on the individual personalities or needs of the beings they raise. They use the cheapest materials available to construct their captives' housing, buy the cheapest feed to maintain them, employ the cheapest human labor they can to herd or slaughter them, and so on. To the farmer, nonhuman animals are effectively matter on its way to becoming value. Consequently, they are permitted to live only so long as their lives are necessary—and not an instant longer. The life of a chicken or a pig on the best of small farms, where nonhuman animals may have access to the outdoors and be allowed to fraternize, rather than be crowded into enormous sheds or confined in gestation crates, may be markedly better than the life of a chicken or a pig raised in intensive confinement. Yet the underlying nature of the relationship between human and nonhuman animals remains one of naked commercial exploitation: even the least callous farmer raises his nonhuman animals to profit by their violent deaths and will kill them moreover at a fraction of their natural lifespans. Slaves in the antebellum South, too, were subjected to varying degrees and conditions of cruelty, depending on such factors as the size of the plantation operation, the local cultural norms, and the individual temperament of masters and overseers. Ultimately, though, the underlying relation between slaves and slave-holders remained one of exploitation, violation, and violence, and slaves' status as commodities left them entirely at the caprice and mercy of their individual owners. It is the same today with the billions of nonhuman beings entangled in the agriculture system.

Food expert and journalist Michael Pollan and other proponents of the *locavore* and organic foods consumer movements have suggested that the corporatization of agriculture can be reversed by the proliferation of small, family-owned, organic farms. However, market forces are in fact pulling in the opposite direction, placing irresistible pressure on many small farmers to cede management and ownership of their farms to bigger corporate entities. In 2016, for example, agribusiness interests formed an alliance with struggling family farmers in North Dakota as part of their strategy to overturn a 1932 law prohibiting all but resident families from owning farms in the state. Local proponents sought to overturn protections for family farms on the grounds "that the farming and ranching business in North Dakota needs to evolve to stay competitive: Dairies and pig farms have declined in recent years, prompting many people to argue that the industries could use a boost." Katie Heger, a rancher who supported the bill, told one reporter: "We have this picture in our head of the Hollywood farm, with the dairy cows, a couple of pigs, a couple of chickens. . . . There are very few farms that are like that. Farming and ranching is a business. So if we're looking at sustaining agriculture in the state of North Dakota, we need to look at how we can build business" (Bosman 2016).

"Organic" and "humane" nonhuman animal products will no doubt continue to appeal to a segment of the middle and upper classes. But the "brand" of "humane meat" neither can compete nor is meant to compete with cheaper nonhuman animal commodities produced through intensive factory farming methods, where the "brand" is cheapness or affordability. Meanwhile, because factory farming is in fact more efficient than raising nonhuman animals on pasture or on smaller farms, the same pressures that drove capitalists to adopt industrialized nonhuman animal farming techniques in the first place will likely only intensify in the future, as increasing global demand for "meat" and other nonhuman animal products comes up against growing resource scarcity.

Regardless of whether they are raised in a concentrated feed lot operation or on a small family farm, however, farmed animals only have value insofar as they can be sold. This same principle extends to other commercial industries—aquaria, zoos, laboratories, the horse racing industry, puppy mills, and so on—where nonhuman beings find themselves just as fatally vulnerable to the vagaries of the free market. In 2011, the parent company of a small company in British Columbia named Outdoor Adventures, which had supplied "sled dogs" for the Iditarod during the 2010 Winter Olympics, ordered the company to liquidate its now unneeded stock of "sled dogs." The company complied by ordering one of its employees to massacre them. As *The New York Times* reported:

> The killing went on for two days, and several of the deaths were grisly, the compensation board's report said. When an initial shot failed to kill a dog that was the mother of the employee's family pet, she ran around with her "cheek blown off and her eye hanging out" until she was felled by a rifle with a scope, according to the report. The bullet also penetrated another dog, which was not supposed to be part of the kill and which suffered for about 15 minutes before dying.
>
> Another dog, left for dead for 20 minutes, emerged from a mass grave only to be shot again, the report said. The employee said he eventually wrapped his arms in foam padding after the frightened dogs began attacking him. (Austen 2011)

Viewed as investments, and hence as *liabilities*, commodified nonhumans thus find themselves entirely at the mercy of the market and the whim of their owners.

ECOLOGICAL DESTRUCTION, CAPITALISM, AND THE STATE

Given the staggering levels of violence suffered by nonhuman animals trapped in industry today, in factory farming, the "fur" industry, and so on, one might think that nonhuman animal death and trauma at human hands occurs mostly in slaughterhouses, laboratories, and other artificial environments where living beings are turned into lifeless commodities. In reality, free or "wild" animals suffer and die in probably equal or greater numbers through loss of habitat, pollution, or the collateral damage of the fisheries and nonhuman animal agriculture industries. Capitalism strips natural beings everywhere of their means of life. So all-encompassing and indiscriminate is this process, which Marx termed *primitive accumulation*, that it is leading today to the extermination of many species of animal life on Earth.

On Marx's usage *primitive accumulation* referred originally to the historical process in early modern Europe by which human beings were stripped of their connection to the land and their traditional modes of communal life so that capitalist relations could be established and consolidated. For thousands of years, humans had lived in relatively stable communities closely tied to the land; social roles were sharply defined and heritable. However, this very *organicism* to human culture—the continuity of social roles and occupations from generation to generation, the connection humans had to nature—proved an impediment to the development of the new system of production in Europe. Human beings thus were forcibly separated from their prior means of life. Far from being a peaceful process, Marx emphasized, primitive accumulation required violent "expropriation . . . written in the annals of mankind in letters of blood and fire." Formerly communal lands in England were privatized and turned into parcels for commodified nonhuman animals to graze upon, throwing thousands of people off the land. Meanwhile, in the Americas, Africa, and Asia, European colonial powers, funded by mercantilists and banks, murdered and enslaved millions of indigenous people.

Dispossession and displacement were necessary for capitalist development for two reasons. First, it was necessary that peasants and indigenous people be incorporated directly into the capitalist labor process, initially as slaves, later as wage laborers. As Marx wrote, the laborer "could only dispose of his own person"—that is, be forced to sell his labor power at an hourly wage—"after he had ceased to be attached to the soil and ceased to be the slave, serf, or bondsman of another" (Marx, 1978a). So long as people had been able to produce their own lives—to sustain themselves through subsistence farming, hunting, and fishing, or by keeping a portion of what they otherwise had to yield up to the nobility—they had no need to sell themselves or their labor power to others. However, once freed from traditional structures, laborers could be exploited by the new class, in order to turn simple commodities into more complex ones.

Second, the new commodity system required capitalists to lay hold of and control the stuff of the natural world—land, water, forests, mountains, and other animals. Primitive accumulation thus required the dispossession of *other species*, as well as the systematic theft of their means of life. Though Marx did not discuss the fact, the forcible estrangement of other animals from their habitats and thus from their conditions of life—dissolution of their metabolic relations with the natural world—was and remains the fundamental basis of all forms of capitalist development. At the same time Europeans were engaged in genocidal *racial cleansing*, emptying the

African, American, and Australian continents of much of their indigenous human life, they were also engaging in *species cleansing*—the destruction and dispossession of other species through hunting, trapping, fishing, and colonization. Tens of millions of beavers and other animals were slaughtered for their pelts; billions of passenger pigeons were hunted into outright extinction; countless coyotes, wolves, kangaroos, and others were slaughtered as perceived threats to nonhuman animal agriculture and human habitation. Wherever capitalism has since extended its reach, one similarly finds the razing of forests, the draining or the depletion of bodies of fresh water, the extermination of "pest animals," and so on.

Though Marx was chiefly concerned to show how primitive accumulation served as the precondition for capitalist relations, it must be emphasized that the process of dispossession—the violent separation of humans and nonhuman animals from their respective means of communal life—remains an ongoing process. Humans burn down forests in order to graze cows or grow palm oil. They build superhighways through nonhumans' ancestral homes. They pour gasoline into rabbit warrens or down the tunnels of prairie dogs and groundhogs to burn or suffocate them. Ranchers shoot wolves and "wild" pigs from helicopters using assault rifles. Fishing fleets deploy ocean nets the size of office buildings to ensnare countless millions of fish, crustaceans, and sea mammals. As David Harvey observes, "the wholesale commodification of nature in all its forms" today has led to "escalating depletion of the global environmental commons (land, air, water) and proliferating habitat degradations that preclude anything but capital-intensive modes of agricultural production" (Harvey 2004, 75). *Habitat*, let us be clear, means the home, the world of other living, conscious beings—it is the *inorganic body* of the other beings, the means by and through which they produce their characteristic species lives, their unique modes of existence.

What must be emphasized is that capitalism is inherently expansionary, swallowing up ever greater portions of the natural world. Today's widening global ecological crisis is thus a direct consequence of primitive accumulation, as multinational corporations plunder the natural world of its last resources, displacing, poisoning, commodifying, and exterminating other species as they go. There is no ecological problem today that cannot be traced, directly or indirectly, to the commodification of nonhuman animals, to the expropriation of other animals' lands and homes, to the enslavement of once free species and their direct incorporation into the capitalist production process itself. Nonhuman animal agriculture is the second leading cause of global warming, as well as the greatest threat to biodiversity. Effects of the depredations of capitalist production are sloughed off onto nonhuman populations in the form of starvation (from diminished food sources and ruined ecosystems), pollution and despoilment (abandoned fishing lines and nets, the Pacific plastic patch, and urban smog), impaired sexual reproduction, increased birth defects, and on and on. Meanwhile, because of the fiercely competitive nature of capitalism, virtually all of the incentives regarding ecological and interspecies relations run the wrong way. That is, business owners are under continual structural pressure to lower their production costs, which leads them to exploit the natural world and nonhuman animal species as ruthlessly and efficiently as possible. Naturally, however, the suffering experienced by other beings in the course of this accumulation process is deemed wholly irrelevant to the production cycle.

The capitalist war on nature and other animals meanwhile occurs in parallel with the violent disenfranchisement of poor and working people, with the capitalist state serving to ensure both processes. As Harvey writes:

> These [means of primitive accumulation] include the commodification and privatization of land and the forceful expulsion of peasant populations; conversion of various forms of property rights—common, collective, state, etc.—into exclusive private property rights; suppression of rights to the commons; commodification of labour power and the suppression of alternative, indigenous, forms of production and consumption; colonial, neo-colonial and imperial processes of appropriation of assets, including natural resources; monetization of exchange and taxation, particularly of land; slave trade; and usury, the national debt and ultimately the credit system. The state, with its monopoly of violence and definitions of legality, plays a crucial role in both backing and promoting these processes . . . (Harvey 2004, 74)[5]

The role of the state (a term corresponding loosely to the *government* but encompassing not just elected officials but also the totality of departments, civil servants, military and police functions, and so on, that make the state an institution) in promoting and consolidating the capitalist-speciesist system could itself be the subject of an entire book. Under capitalism, the *state* effectively serves to protect the interests of corporations and the wealthy. Though we tend to think of the state as the place where matters of the public interest and public good get decided democratically, in reality the state is a field of battle in which public interests war with private ones, as powerful corporations and wealthy individuals exert outsized influence over legislation and regulatory enforcement. Far from being a neutral arbiter of conflicts in society—between, say, endangered spotted owls and forestry companies, environmentalists and petroleum companies—the state more often than not takes the side of the economically powerful. Because the rich dominate working people in the sphere of civil society, they consequently wield greater influence than working people in the sphere of the state, too. We find that the wealthy tend to get a wider hearing and have more influence than working people. Social power (capital) translates into political power.

Because the state is the institution charged with regulating and smoothing out the contradictions or sources of friction within the capitalist system, by stabilizing markets, preventing certain forms of monopoly, regulating commerce, waging war, etc., the state also plays a pivotal role in regulating and promoting speciesist production. Thus, even in China, a nominally communist country where the Communist Party has nonetheless allowed laissez-faire capitalist development to run amok since the 1980s, the production of nonhumans is closely monitored by the state and woven into long-term plans of national development. In 2014–2015, for example, a massacre of 100 million pigs occurred in China when falling pig prices, following a period of rapid expansion of the "hog" industry, forced thousands of small-scale pig farmers to exit the industry en masse: It was cheaper for the farmers to kill their pigs than to sell them. In the wake of this industry shake up, the Bloomberg news service reported, only a small number of "more modern, efficient businesses"—i.e., large-scale, intensive operations, or factory farms—survived (Singh, 2015). This very result had in fact been encouraged by the Chinese state, as a prelude to the Communist Party's 2015 five-year plan to modernize nonhuman animal agriculture by replacing small-scale farmers with so-called "professionals" (in an effort to create new efficiencies in the production of nonhuman beings) (Ryan 2015).

Everywhere, in fact, we find the state either directly subsidizing domestic nonhuman animal industries, developing lands and waterways for leisure hunters and fishers, funding experimentation on nonhuman animals, requiring such experimentation, or passing and enforcing laws that treat other beings as commercial property. It is true that there has been some very minimal progress towards granting state protections or rights to nonhuman beings, through legislation such as the Endangered Species Act, state reforms of the factory farm system, nonhuman animal cruelty laws, and so on. But the state's main function vis-à-vis nonhuman animals remains one of defending and promoting the interests of industries that exploit them, chiefly through such agencies such as the Department of Defense and Centers for Disease Control and Prevention, state fisheries and "wildlife" departments, the Department of the Interior, the Food and Drug Association, the National Science Foundation, and so on. The U.S. government provides billions of dollars in subsidies and tax breaks to the "meat," "dairy," and chicken egg industries, socializing the costs of nonhuman animal agriculture and privatizing the profits. (U.S. government subsidies for American "dairy" farmers helped boost national cow's milk production from 177 billion pounds in 2005 to a record 208 billion pounds in 2015—a massive increase that had the unintended consequence, mentioned above, of encouraging "dairy" producers to destroy thousands of gallons of milk in order to stabilize prices.) Meanwhile, public monies are spent to clean up the waste, and mitigate the public health costs, of our "meat"-based system of food consumption.

The state also actively promotes, regulates, and profits from the hunting and fishing industries—"stocking" ponds and rivers with nonhuman animals so that they can be "taken" and selling licenses to "sportsmen" who want to engage in blood sports. State officials also cull or indiscriminately slaughter millions of other animals deemed threats (real or imagined) to commercial nonhuman animal interests like "cattle" ranching. In 2015 alone, U.S. government agencies killed an estimated 3.2 million bears, foxes, coyotes, eagles, beavers, and other nonhumans, chiefly at the behest of, and to protect the commercial interests of, "cattle" ranchers (Center for Biological Diversity 2016). The capitalist state meanwhile spends millions of tax dollars on research of direct benefit to nonhuman animal industries, funding basic and applied scientific research, vivisection, and genetic engineering. In the name of public (human) safety, the state indeed requires scientists and corporations to test new drugs and chemical compounds on nonhuman animals before they can go to market, via protocols like the LD-50 test, in which other animals are poisoned with trial compounds until half of them die outright. The U.S. government also funds the U.S. Meat Animal Research Center in Nebraska, which conducts research on how to maximize exploitation of farmed animals. As *The New York Times* reported in 2015, the center has conducted brutal experiments resulting in the extreme suffering and deaths of hundreds of nonhuman animals:

> Pigs are having many more piglets—up to 14, instead of the usual eight—but hundreds of those newborns, too frail or crowded to move, are being crushed each year when their mothers roll over. Cows, which normally bear one calf at a time, have been retooled to have twins and triplets, which often emerge weakened or deformed, dying in such numbers that even meat producers have been repulsed.
>
> Then there are the lambs. In an effort to develop "easy care" sheep that can survive without costly shelters or shepherds, ewes are giving birth, unaided, in open fields where newborns are killed by predators, harsh weather and starvation. (Moss 2015)

Because one of the explicit functions of the state is to ensure the smooth functioning of the capitalist system as such, and because nonhuman animal agriculture is one of the largest and most lucrative sectors of the national economy, the legal and police mechanisms of the government are frequently deployed to shield the industry from critique and to thwart citizens movements for reform. First, the judicial system is set up in such a way as to exclude virtually all commercially reproduced nonhuman animals from meaningful regulatory protection. Second, environmentalists and nonhuman animal rights activists are subjected to government surveillance and even outright repression.[6] After the September 11 terrorist attacks, a coalition of nonhuman animal industries succeeded in getting the U.S. Congress to pass the

Animal Enterprise Terrorism Act (AETA), a draconian law which, in its initial form, effectively criminalized as an act of terrorism any public protest or action that interfered with a commercial nonhuman animal enterprise. Although the AETA has since been modified to permit nonviolent protests for nonhuman animal advocacy, a coalition of nonhuman animal industries has worked aggressively through state legislatures to pass "ag gag" laws that criminalize undercover documentary investigations of illegal abuses of nonhuman animals in farming operations.

Finally, it is because the state is itself one of the leading promoters of speciesism and capitalism as the dominant modes of human life that so little decisive action has been taken by the international community of states to grapple with such ecological crises as global warming or the mass extinction of nonhuman species. For the state to take climate change seriously, for example, it would have to challenge nonhuman animal agriculture, because the latter is the second biggest source of carbon emissions (as well as the biggest threat to global biodiversity). However, the state has no enthusiasm for such an enterprise, and understandably so. Capitalism by its nature entails a perpetual war against other species, perpetual human colonization of the living spaces of other species. Thus, for the state to act to protect nonhuman animals and their habitats would essentially put it into conflict with capitalism—which is to say, in conflict with itself as the main institutional prop for capitalism.

REIFICATION: THE MIDAS EFFECT

If we were to put a name to the cultural process under capitalist relations that objectifies nonhuman animals and causes them to be treated as mere things, that word would be *reification*. Though few people have even heard of the term, reification is perhaps the single most destructive feature of the capitalist system. Derived from the Latin, *res*, for "thing," reification in its broadest sense can be thought of as the "thingification" of the world. It is the process by which, on the one hand, living beings are transformed into *things*, and on the other, lifeless commodities are given the (false) appearance of living subjects or persons.

To explain this process, it is perhaps useful to begin here with a familiar story, the ancient Greek myth of Midas. In the story, King Midas is rewarded by the god Dionysus with the ability to turn whatever he touches to gold. At first, Midas is delighted by his new ability and sets about turning rocks, trees, clothing, and so on, into gold. However, Midas begins to have second thoughts when he picks up a bunch of grapes and watches them turn to gold before he can eat them, and when he brings a chalice to his lips and discovers that the wine has turned to gold before he can quench his thirst. On some tellings of the story, when the king's own daughter appears at his side, Midas unthinkingly embraces her, turning her, too, instantly into lifeless gold. Now unable to eat or drink and bereft a daughter, the king returns to Dionysus and begs him to revoke the spell. The god grants Midas's wish, but the dead daughter cannot be restored to life. Hence, the moral of the Midas fable: greed is a destructive passion, and wealth is a false idol whose worship leads to the neglect of the things that matter most in life.

Like Midas, capitalism as a system of reification transforms whatever it touches—a river, a rainforest, the labor of landless peasants, a pig, or a sea turtle—into a lifeless thing, both figuratively and, in many cases, literally.[7] According to Georg Lukàcs, the Hungarian Marxist who first developed the theory of reification in the 1920s, the origins of this "thingifying" process are to be found in the nature of work activity or labor under capitalism. On the one hand, the minute specialization of labor under capitalism unquestionably propelled human civilization to a more advanced stage of material development, unleashing vast new powers of economic efficiency and productivity. On the other hand, however, specialization fragmented both the worker's laboring activity and by extension her consciousness as well. In stark contrast to the experience of labor in traditional agrarian societies, that is, where a farmer or a peasant would have been engaged in a wide variety of kinds of activity, each one requiring a special form of knowledge—breeding and tending nonhuman animals, understanding the weather and seasons, creating and repairing tools, constructing dwellings, and so on, all in metabolic exchange with the land with other peasants—the modern wage laborer engages in only a single specialized activity, working under the control and the surveillance of an employer or a boss.

Torn from the land and nature and from the tissue of communal bonds, relationships, and rituals that once attached him to other human beings, the wage worker became treated merely as a thing among other things. Today, whether laboring for 12 hours at a time inside a deadly mine or sitting in front of a desk inside a tiny office cubicle, processing forms, workers find themselves thrust into a hostile world over which they can exert little control but to which they must nevertheless perpetually bend their will and effort if they do not wish to starve in the streets. In a word, the organization of society around commodity production has had the effect of *alienating* human beings from their work and even from life itself.

Marx described several related kinds of alienation experienced by workers under capitalist relations (Marx 1978, 66–105). Workers are first of all alienated from the product of their labor. A woman working a Nike assembly line in Indonesia, for example, is not allowed to own the shoes that she helps manufacture. She experiences the fruits of her labor—in this case, the Nike sneakers on the assembly line—as a hostile force, as objects over which she has no control and whose appearance in the world seems to come, and indeed does come, at the expense of her own well-being. The worker thus finds herself alienated from the creative powers of her own mind and body, her own life-activity. Meanwhile, this experience of alienation extends to the worker's experience of other human beings. On one side, she finds herself locked in perpetual conflict with the owner or the boss, since increases in workers' wages come at the expense of the owner's profits—a structural feature of capitalism. On the other side, she finds herself pitted as well against other workers and is forced to compete with them for scarce jobs (unemployment is a permanent fixture of the capitalist economy). Finally, she finds herself alienated from her own nature as a human being. Though born with *human* intellectual and creative potentials, she is unable to realize these powers, whether as an individual person or as a member of a thriving and harmonious species community, because the narrow circumstances of her life thwart their development.

Rather than flourishing as part of a universal community of equals, the laborer is treated instead as a mere thing, an instrument. Workers are exploited for their labor and then tossed aside when they are no longer useful to their employers. Many are denied a livable wage or are forced to endure dangerous conditions in their workplace. Moreover, their alienation extends to the rest of their dealings with society. They receive unfair treatment in the courts and housing market, and they lack the political influence of the rich, even in the so-called democracies. They are the first to be used as cannon fodder in their nation's foreign wars. Though we frequently hear that capitalism encourages innovation and entrepreneurialism, from the vantage point of capital, few things are in fact more suspect or threatening than genuinely free humans expressing their own creativity. The worker is viewed by capital not with love or as a spontaneous source of thought or expression, but with suspicion, as a "potential source of 'error'" (Lukàcs 1972, 89). The need to control the laborer only becomes more acute over time, as the forces of capitalist development intensify. There is a "continuous trend," Lukàcs wrote, "towards greater rationalization, [and towards] the progressive elimination of the qualitative, human, and individual attributes of the worker" (Lukàcs 1972, 88). By rationalization, Lukàcs meant the supremacy of impersonal bureaucracy, scientific control and surveillance of workers in the workplace, as well as a general privileging of scientific technique and logics of mathematical calculation in society over more organic, naturalistic ways of being human and "animal." Reification unites this feature of capitalism—the relentless drive toward efficiency, predictability, control of outcomes—with *commodification*, or the process for turning of all nature and life itself into a series of commodities for exchange.

Consider a simple commodity like a chair handcrafted by a Shaker artisan in the nineteenth century. Though the Shakers, a Christian religious sect in the United States, produced furniture for the market as well as for their own direct use, their objective was not to accumulate wealth but to support their pious way of life. As a consequence, because the Shakers did not subordinate the form and function of their works to *exchange value*, each piece of furniture they made was unique, and each embodied the spiritual sensibilities of the Shaker community. The result was furniture so well made and beautiful that Shaker pieces today are routinely displayed in museums. By contrast, a mass-manufactured lawn chair produced today for a retail giant like Wal-Mart exists for the sole purpose of being sold for profit. Gone from the modern production process are the intimate relations that once bound members of a community of producers to one another. Now the outcome of a complex, impersonal, globally dispersed production process requiring marketing specialists, automated machinery, industrial designers, accountants, assembly line workers, and so on, the modern commodity is notable only for the degree to which every trace of the human personality has been effaced from its surface. The typical mass-produced item is standardized, "cookie-cutter," graceless.

However, it isn't just our artifacts that lose their uniqueness as they get subjected to a fragmented and fragmenting process. *Human workers* themselves, through their fragmented work, also become homogenized, standardized, quantified, and stamped out in cookie-cutter fashion. The reorganization of human economic or material life—the organization of production, factories, labor, and so on—requires the reorganization of the worker too. The worker becomes merely another cog in the corporate machine—like the factory worker in Charlie Chaplin's satirical film, *Modern Times*, who, driven mad by his repetitive labor on an assembly line, suddenly plunges headlong into the machinery, becoming part of the gear-work. As Lukàcs (1972, 90) observed, as the worker becomes incorporated into the apparatus of production, his "personality can do no more than look on helplessly while its own existence is reduced to an isolated particle and fed into an alien system." The worker's mind and body become imprinted with the technological features of the production system. A man employed in sales at a clothing store may be told to conform his affect (outward presentation of emotions) to the needs of his employer's business, smiling warmly at potential customers whether he in fact is feeling happy and sociable or not. Women working in sweatshops and "free trade" zones perform the same actions hundreds of times a day on the assembly line, their bodies made to conform to the production process, causing them in some cases to suffer carpal tunnel syndrome or other repetitive stress injuries.

Driven by capital, which strives to overcome all barriers to accumulation, the technosciences meanwhile become more deeply embedded in daily life, and more total in their capacity to absorb society and nature alike into their structures. As Lukàcs (1972) observed, reification becomes more advanced over time, becoming in effect the "universal structuring principle" of society as a whole (85), as "the process of transformation must embrace every manifestation of the life of society" (95). Like a parasite, capitalism must seize hold of and transform the metabolic activity of its "host," society, if it is to satisfy its conditions of survival and growth. The state, laws, culture, media, and science thus get continually shaped and reconfigured to accord with the needs of capital, so that everything is found "corresponding to its needs and harmonizing with its own structure" (Lukàcs 1972, 95). The human individual too must be made to "harmonize" with the wider structure, must be treated as merely one more object to be manipulated, a bundle of instinctual desires which can and must be molded to conform to the objective needs of the system (Horkheimer and Adorno 2002). As nothing is to be left to chance, advertising culture must inscribe itself upon every available surface of society, from magazines and the Internet to the sides of public buses and even at times the sky itself, using skywriting planes, in order to implant false "needs" in the population. Subjected from birth to an endless barrage of ads and behavioral manipulations, the individual over time becomes accustomed to thinking of himself or herself as a passive *consumer*, rather than as an engaged *citizen* or a reasoning, feeling, moral being with the power to initiate political or social reforms.

In this one-dimensional society (Marcuse 1964), consumer culture reassures us at every turn that what matters more than truth, justice, or moral reason is the individual's "freedom of choice." In premodern societies, the Earth, sky, water, and the living beings of creation all "spoke" to humans, in gestures that contained hidden meanings. The artifactual world that surrounds us today only speaks to itself, in the language of the commodity. Consumer goods effectively "propagandize" for one another, telling the consumer that, since everything has a price, there is no fundamental difference, ethical or otherwise, between any given commodity and any other. Every retail store, every TV commercial functions as a kind of public rhetoric or argument that tells us that the individual self-interest of the consumer trumps all other concerns. Whether I choose to buy a "chicken sandwich" or a vegan burger, it's my "choice." I have a "right" to buy what I like, and a corresponding "right" to not to be criticized for my "lifestyle."

The prevalence of this fallacious and morally pernicious line of private reasoning helps to explain, in part, why nonhuman animal industries and the political right have found it so easy to mobilize broad segments of the public against the environmental and animal rights movements. The spread of libertarian ideology is itself a symptom of reification. It becomes ever harder to think outside the dominant system; as Lukàcs (1972, 93) wrote, "the structure of reification progressively sinks more deeply, more fatefully and more definitively into the consciousness of man."

Such are the myriad ways in which alienation leads to the reification of human consciousness and life, as humans find themselves treated more and more in an instrumental or "thinglike" fashion under capitalism, and are viewed with suspicion as potential sources of "error" in the accumulation process. What though of nonhuman animals caught up within the system of reification?

Like human laborers, who are treated like "isolated abstract atoms whose work no longer brings them together directly and organically," beings whose only intercourse with one another is "mediated . . . exclusively by the abstract laws of the mechanism which imprisons them" (Lukàcs 1972, 90), nonhuman beings too are isolated from one another and from nature. Millions of nonhuman animals are forced to labor: mules, horses, oxen, and elephants are whipped, prodded, or beaten to pull loads, furrow the Earth, and carry humans on their backs. Those raised on factory farms are deprived of any access to air, fresh water, or the Earth, they live their entire lives in entirely artificial conditions and are permitted only those behaviors that conform to the needs of capital. Any spontaneous or free action by the individual animal, any exertion of an independent will, any assertion of an unproductive need or preference is either ignored, if deemed harmless to production, or is brutally suppressed. "Good animals" are thus ones who passively accept the lab technician's brutal procedures, or who go without complaint to the butcher; "bad animals" are ones who resist or try to escape (Lynch 1988). So fundamental to the speciesist system is enforcing "right" behavior in nonhumans that there is a huge secondary market just for the thousands of commodities used to control and punish them: whips, electric prods, cages, electrified fences, bits and blinders, and restraint devices.

As Karen Davis (2012, 36) writes, nonhuman "animals on factory farms are imprisoned in a world from which their psyches did not emanate and which they accordingly do not understand and do not psychologically resemble." The nonhuman being's *self* or *person* becomes wholly enmeshed within a totalitarian structure of violence and domination.[8] While human workers experience isolation and fragmentation through their labor, nonhuman animals experience isolation and fragmentation far more directly— by being cut literally into pieces. Though human workers may be abused and subjected to dangerous workplace conditions, they are not, for all that, stabbed, cut, boiled, burned, decapitated, skinned, disemboweled, or dismembered alive routinely as part of the production process, whereas billions of nonhumans are. Nonhumans trapped in the commodity system are in fact treated far less like laborers than as slaves, prisoners of war, and victims of genocide.

Contemporary advocates of organic nonhuman animal agriculture maintain that smaller-scale, sustainable and artisanal forms of rearing and killing nonhuman animals can eventually replace intensive "factory farming" operations. In reality, though, the neopastoralist or "locavore" longing for a return to supposedly more authentic, less technologically mediated relations between humans and nonhumans is little more than a form of nostalgia for a mode of production long ago destroyed by capitalism. Not only aren't impersonal, mechanized forms of nonhuman control and slaughter disappearing, but the structural imperatives of capitalism are on the contrary demanding ever *more* ruthless and *more* invasive controls, particularly as companies struggle to meet rising demand for nonhuman flesh in China, India, and other developing markets. Factory farming operations are expanding around the world. Meanwhile, some companies are moving to fully automate slaughter as part of the rationalization process, meaning that nonhuman victims will in future be killed by robots.[9] They will scream, bleed, and die without the touch of human hands and outside the hearing of human ears or the seeing of human eyes.[10] Even in the boutique "organic meat" sector, totalitarian controls have become a must. On some organic farms, it is not unusual for sheep or other nonhuman animals to have electronic chips implanted under their skin, to enable farmers to monitor their health as they fatten for market; on other organic farms, farmers raise genetically engineered "organic" chickens, killing them en masse in gas chambers. Driven by capital, which strives to overcome all barriers to accumulation, the technological sciences become more and more deeply embedded in daily life, more total in their capacity to absorb society and nature alike into their structures.

If capitalism, as Lukàcs (1972, 85) suggested, refashions the human world after "its own image," it therefore also now refashions other natural beings in its own image too, commodifying nonhumans at the genetic level to conform their biological natures to the evolving needs of finance capital. Though humans have been manipulating the genome of other species for generations through selective breeding, genetic engineering represents a radical escalation in human powers of controlling the biological destiny of other beings. Genetic changes that once took years or even centuries to cultivate in other species can now be achieved virtually overnight—a "speed-up" of the rate of nonhuman exploitation that reflects the compressed cycle of high-tech commodity production. There are virtually no practical limits today to the kinds of manipulations that scientists can now impose on commodified organisms. Scientists can pick and choose whatever attributes they like, "cutting and pasting" DNA strands from one species, or multiple species, into the embryonic tissue others—even across different evolutionary kingdoms and phyla that may have parted ways hundreds of millions of years ago. *Ontological dispossession*, the theft and mutilation of nonhuman animals' evolutionary natures and "being," is the terrifying result (Weisberg 2013).

Hundreds of new patented organisms, such as Enviropig™—the trademarked name of a pig engineered by splicing pig genes with mouse genes that is "able to digest phosphorous more efficiently and therefore produce less waste and less water pollution than its nongenetically modified counterparts" (Weisberg 2013, 77)—have appeared in recent years. Driving this assault on the ontological integrity of other beings is entrepreneurial capital, which has made the bodies and even the minds of nonhuman beings ground zero for demolishing the last biological limits to wealth accumulation. As one analyst at Fidelity Investments, a high-technology capitalist fund, boasted in an advertisement: "Around the world and across borders, academics, entrepreneurs, and even students are working with over 5,000 DNA sequences called Biobricks™ to explore ideas and invent new organisms." "Within 50 years we could have more life forms invented in the lab than we've ever identified in nature. . . ." (Weisberg 2013, 62). Meanwhile, in a fateful convergence of the biotech industry with the national security state, the Nexia Biotechnologies corporation has partnered with the U.S. Army Soldier and Biological Chemical Command to insert "the dragline silk gene from an orb-weaver spider" into the mammary genes of goats, causing the latter to secrete super-strong fibers in their milk, for producing such commercial products as BioSteel', a material for use in bulletproof vests (Weisberg 2013, 78).

Such grotesque melding of machines and nonhuman animals has now advanced to such a degree that even nonhumans' consciousness is being integrated into machines, through *hybrot* technology. Pigeons, for example, have had computer chips and electrodes implanted in their brains, enabling scientists to steer them around using computer joysticks, while rats on different continents have had their consciousnesses temporarily fused together through an electronic online interface. Scientists have grown rat brain cells and integrated them into computer memory boards and sensing devices. As the mere existence of such infernal experiments suggests, the notion that other animals might have a species integrity of their own—that there might be something profoundly unethical, not to mention obscene, about treating other conscious beings as data sequences, interchangeable parts, or machines—is literally unthinkable within the given paradigm of today's capitalist sciences. This incapacity to tell the difference any longer between a science of life and a science of death, or to distinguish between subjects and objects, persons and things, is itself but a symptom of reification.[11]

CONCLUSION

Barbaric treatment of other sensitive living beings—beings capable of emotions, of forming bonds with others, even of love—is the norm throughout human culture. Capitalism, assuredly, is not the only cause of human oppression of other sentient beings. There are other important cultural forces at work, other systems of power. The dynamics of capitalism, for example, are effected through a wider patriarchal culture that for centuries has subordinated women to men and nonhuman animals to human ones (Adams 1990).[12] Both speciesism and capitalism are artifacts of *patriarchy*, embodying gender norms and behaviors that work against the interests of nonhumans. The continued privileging of masculine ideals of domination and violence in our culture over traditionally feminine emotions and ideals such as compassion, care for others, selflessness, and so on, has, for example, played a crucial role in perpetuating the popularity of blood sports (hunting and fishing), and in blunting the public appeal of the animal rights movement's message of empathy for nonhuman suffering. Acts of sadism and torture directed toward other animals—widespread in nonhuman animal agriculture, circuses, and other industries—are meanwhile typically enacted by working class men, suggesting a link between gender socialization of boys and men, labor exploitation, and speciesism. Because speciesism and patriarchy are closely entwined forms of oppression that have reinforced one another for generations, there seems little prospect of overcoming human dominion over other beings in the absence of full women's equality and the dissolution of the most toxic forms of masculinity.

However, notwithstanding patriarchy, racism, and other structures of power that intersect with and help constitute speciesism, the chief propulsive mechanism of speciesism today remains the capitalist world system. Though capitalism did not create speciesism, it removed the last of the cultural and technical barriers to nonhuman animal exploitation which in previous epochs had set at least some limits to the scale and intensity of speciesist exploitation. The advent of the commodity system engendered both new powers of control and new markets for nonhuman animal products. European colonization—the private funding of overseas expeditions for the plundering of the Third World and the enslavement of foreign peoples—led to, among other things, the establishment of the "cattle" industry in the Americas and the true globalization of markets in nonhuman animal products.[13] Industrialization and with it technical innovations in the sexual reproduction, confinement, transportation, killing, and storage (via refrigeration) of nonhuman animals made possible entirely new scales of exploitation and slaughter. Above all, it was the emergence of new capitalist relations— monopolization of corporate industry, the creation of mass consumer markets, and the intervention of the capitalist state in subsidizing nonhuman animal industries—that made possible the extraordinary proliferation in nonhuman animal products that we see in the twentieth and twenty-first centuries.

There is no need for us to romanticize past forms of exploitative human-nonhuman animal relations in earlier epochs to observe that under modern capitalist relations the Earth's other beings have suffered a truly calamitous fall. The consolidation of capitalism has led to a worldwide system of production that is inimical to all animal life on Earth. Capitalism is inimical to animal life (including human animal life) because it reduces living beings to the status of commodities; because it cannibalizes the ecological order, destroying the conditions necessary to the survival and flourishing of life itself; because it engenders a "machinic" civilization, a technologized system of production, in which vulnerable beings—including human beings—are viewed as mere matter to be disposed of at will by capital; because it corrupts democracy and makes use of the state as a weapon against the powerless; because it aggrandizes and extends the reach of corporate power and influence over human life throughout society; because it alienates human beings from one another and from the other beings; because it conflates or blurs the distinction between subjects and objects, persons and things; because it creates a "second," artifactual nature that alienates us from other natural beings and leads us to mistake cultural and historical constructions for immutable, self-evident facts; because it "interpellates" or molds us, psychologically and behaviorly, into self-interested, isolated consumers, thus thwarting the emergence of new, alternate forms of culture and development, ones more compatible with an image of ourselves as free beings capable of compassion, moral deliberation, and public reason.

The question arises of whether such a system of total violence might be overcome, and whether a postcapitalist or socialist system would necessarily be any kinder to other animals. The fact that the tens of billions of other animals being exploited in capitalist industry have been summoned into existence not to meet human needs or wants but to produce profit suggests some grounds for hope, though perhaps not optimism. Were the speciesist system merely the outcropping of genuine human needs, the expression of our necessary requirements of life, then it would be in vain to resist or to question it, like opposing the breathing of air or the drinking of water. Since, however, the speciesist system is in reality an artifact of culture, it might in theory be done away with and replaced by another, more just system, in the same way that the institution of slavery, which was long viewed as a natural and immutable feature of human life, has largely been abolished.

But capitalism provides contradictory terrain for social activism and reform. On the one hand, capitalism tends to undermine traditional relations and norms, thus making room for new forms of culture and new values. The nonhuman animal rights movement indeed itself owes its existence, in part, to the emergence of capitalist relations, insofar as the social upheavals unleashed by capitalism swept aside traditional belief systems and forms of government and thus created the (uneven) conditions for mass literacy, rule of law, and representative democracy. On the other hand, however, capitalism undermines democratic institutions, cannibalizes nature, and fosters false, destructive needs and desires in the population. Complicating this picture, the crisis tendencies of capitalism meanwhile create both opportunities and risks. As the ecological problems associated with non-human animal agriculture worsen, we can anticipate new openings for nonhuman animal advocacy—new opportunities to educate members of the public about the true nature of the speciesist system. At the same time, the disintegration of the old capitalist order will continue to push many people into fear and conflict, as natural resources dwindle and the power-ful classes seek to contain the aspirations of an increasingly impoverished human majority. Corporations, the state, and right-wing political move-ments will meanwhile continue to oppose animal rights and seek to pre-vent new, life-affirming forms of culture from taking hold.

As for whether nonhuman animals would necessarily fare better under a post-capitalist or socialist mode of economic and political life, answering such a complex question would depend on the nature of the socialist sys-tem that would replace it and on the ideological and cultural assumptions embedded within such a system. It thus remains the work of social justice scholars and activists everywhere to clarify these questions and to work for the development of an ethically inflected, nonspeciesist system of demo-cratic socialism, one in which all animals, human and nonhuman alike, would be allowed to live in dignity and freedom.

NOTES

1. As I have suggested elsewhere, speciesism is indeed one of the few basic fix-tures of the human condition—an *existential* structure providing human beings with a sense of their identity and "dignity." See Sanbonmatsu (2012).

2. This is not to say that the fruits of labor in the ancient world were equitably distributed—social hierarchy was a feature of all ancient civilizations, with wealth and status determined chiefly by caste and kin. Nonetheless, for many centuries economic activity remained bound closely to the traditional arrangements and needs of society. During the feudal period in Europe, for example, agricultural "products," including nonhuman animals, were either consumed directly by the peas-ant producers themselves, or were taxed or otherwise appropriated by the nobility, in order that the latter might maintain its traditional prerogatives and way of life. Family and clan wealth was heritable, not "entrepreneurial."

3. According to Rabobank (2016), 2015 "showed the largest [annual] increase in U.S. meat consumption since the food scares of the 1970s," a one-year jump of 5 percent.

4. As Marx observed, there is not one jot of exchange value in use value, nor one jot of use value in exchange value. We might say that the two values indeed inhabit different planes of existence.

5. See also Nibert (2002, 2013).

6. Past government efforts to destroy legitimate, nonviolent social movements, including, most notoriously, COINTELPRO, have been well documented. Since the 1980s, the FBI has been particularly interested in monitoring and undermining the more militant wings of the environmental and nonhuman animal rights movements.

7. A powerful illustration of the process of reification can be found in Steve Cutts's short animated film, *Man* (2012), available online. Though the filmmaker conflates capitalist exploitation with "man" as such, the film otherwise captures the terrifying dynamic of reification, which reduces living things to the status of things, leaving the Earth itself less and less capable of supporting many forms of life.

8. "Under capitalism animals have come to be totally incorporated into production technology." Barbara Noske (quoted in Nibert, 2013, 190).

9. According to Sue Coe, a full automation slaughterhouse is in fact already being developed in Abu Dhabi (private correspondence, July 10, 2016).

10. A parallel cultural trajectory toward reified forms of mass killing can be observed in the Pentagon's program to develop autonomous unmanned aerial vehicles (UAVs or drones) and robot soldiers capable of killing without direct human supervision or control. Whether on the automated battlefield or in the automated slaughterhouse, the process of reification is eliminating opportunities for human moral deliberation, moral accountability, and compassion.

11. Throughout public culture, we are seeing the systematic erosion of critical, life-preserving philosophical and ethical distinctions between and among machines, plants, nonhuman animals, and bacteria. Science fiction films such as *Interstellar* and *Her* suggest that we can enjoy far greater intimacy and connection with computers and robots than with nonhuman beings. A variety of writers have recently popularized the erroneous view that plants are sentient and have "intelligence." Meanwhile, cognitive scientists, neuroscientists, and some analytic philosophers have described consciousness itself as an illusion, an "epiphenomenon" of mechanistic processes of the "computer" that is the brain. Such developments only serve to reinforce the dominant perception that nonhuman animals are mere matter, to be shaped at will—or rather, shaped in accordance with the needs of capital itself.

12. As Carol Adams (1990, 47) notes, this "parallel trajectory" results in "a cycle of objectification, fragmentation, and consumption" of both nonhumans and of women.

13. See also Nibert (2002, 2013).

REFERENCES

Adams, Carol. 1990. *The Sexual Politics of Meat: A Feminist-Vegetarian Critical Theory*. New York: Continuum.

Austen, Ian. 2011. "Canadians Outraged After Report of Mass Killing of Sled Dogs," *The New York Times*, February 1. Accessed September 7, 2016, from http://www.nytimes.com/2011/02/02/world/americas/02dogs.html.

Bell, Donald D., and William D. Weaver, Jr. (eds.). 2002. *Commercial Chicken Meat and Egg Production*. Norwell, MA: Kluwer Academic Publishers.

Bosman, Julie. 2016. "North Dakotans Reconsider a Core Value," *The New York Times*, June 13.

Center for Biological Diversity. 2016. "3.2 Million Animals Killed by Federal Wildlife-Destruction Program in 2015." Press release of the Center for Biological Diversity, June 20. Accessed September 7, 2016, from https://www.biological diversity.org/news/press_releases/2016/wildlife-services-06-20-2016.html.

Cutts, Steve, director. 2012. *Man*. United Kingdom. Accessed September 7, 2016, from https://www.youtube.com/user/steviecutts.

Davis, Karen. 2012. "The Procrustean Solution to Problems of Animal Welfare." In John Sanbonmatsu (ed.), *Critical Theory and Animal Liberation*. Lanham, MD: Rowman & Littlefield.

Harvey, David. 2004. "The 'New' Imperialism: Accumulation by Dispossession." In *Socialist Register*. Vol. 40. New York: Monthly Review Press.

Horkheimer, Max, and Theodor W. Adorno. 2002. *The Dialectic of Enlightenment*. Gunzelin Schmid Noerr (ed.); Edmund Jephcott (Trans.). Stanford, CA: Stanford University Press.

Lukàcs, Georg. 1972. *History and Class Consciousness: Studies in Marxist Dialectics*. Cambridge, MA: MIT Press.

Lynch, Michael. 1988. "Sacrifice and the Transformation of the Animal Body into a Scientific Object: Laboratory Culture and Ritual Practice in the Neurosciences." *Social Studies of Science*, 18(2): 265–289.

Marcuse, Herbert. 1964. *One-Dimensional Man*. Boston: Beacon Press.

Marx, Karl, and Frederick Engels. 1970. *The German Ideology*. C. J. Arthur (ed.). New York: International Publishers.

Marx, Karl. 1978. "Economic and Philosophical Manuscripts." In Robert C. Tucker (ed.), *The Marx-Engels Reader*, 2d Ed. Princeton, NJ: Princeton University Press.

Marx, Karl. 1978a. "The Secret of Capitalist Primitive Accumulation." *Capital*, Vol. 1, in Robert C. Tucker, (ed.), *The Marx-Engels Reader*, 2d Ed. Princeton, NJ: Princeton University Press.

Moss, Michael. 2015. "U.S. Research Lab Lets Livestock Suffer in Quest for Profit," *The New York Times*, January 19. Accessed September 7, 2016, from http://www.nytimes.com/2015/01/20/dining/animal-welfare-at-risk-in-experi ments-for-meat-industry.html?_r=0.

Mulvany, Lydia. 2015. "The U.S. Is Producing a Record Amount of Milk and Dumping the Leftovers," *Bloomberg*, July 1. Accessed September 7, 2016, from http://www.bloomberg.com/news/articles/2015-07-01/milk-spilled-into -manure-pits-as-supplies-overwhelm-u-s-dairies.

Nibert, David A. 2002. *Animal Rights/Human Rights*. Lanham, MD: Rowman and Littlefield.

Nibert, David A. 2013. *Animal Oppression and Human Violence*. New York: Columbia University Press.

Noske, Barbara. 1997. *Beyond Boundaries: Humans and Animals*. Montreal: Black Rose Books.

Oxfam. 2016. *An Economy for the 1%* (report), January. Accessed September 3, 2016, from https://www.oxfam.org/sites/www.oxfam.org/files/file_attachments /bp210-economy-one-percent-tax-havens-180116-en_0.pdf.

Rabobank. 2016. "Chickens, Cows, and Pigs . . . Oh My!" August. Accessed September 7, 2016, from https://research.rabobank.com/far/en/sectors/animal-protein/chicken-cows-and-pigs-oh-my.html.

Ryan, Chloe. 2015. "Chinese Five-Year Plan Impacts on Meat Industry. *Global Meat News*, November 9. Accessed September 7, 2016, from http:/www.globalmeatnews.com.

Sanbonmatsu, John. 2014. "The Animal of Bad Faith." In John Sorenson, *Critical Animal Studies: Thinking the Unthinkable.* Toronto, Canada: Canadian Scholars Press.

Singh, Shruti Date. 2015. "China Culling 100 Million Hogs Means Record Pork Imports." *Bloomberg*, August 18, 2015. Accessed September 7, 2016, from http://www.bloomberg.com/news/articles/2015-08-18/china-culling-100-million-hogs-means-record-pork-imports.

Weisberg, Zipporah. 2013. *Animal Dialectics: Towards a Critical Theory of Animals and Society.* Dissertation. York University, Toronto.

2

Property, Profit, and (Re)Production: A Bird's-Eye View

pattrice jones

for Inky[1]
I wish I knew how it would feel to be free.

—Nina Simone

I wish I knew how to think outside of capitalism.

I was born in 1961, on the cusp of the current era of capitalism wherein consumer "goods" multiply at warp speed. I can still remember—barely—the days before there were 37 different varieties of orange juice[2] in a typical U.S. supermarket.

In that year, Rachel Carson must have been putting the finishing touches on *Silent Spring*, published in 1962. Reading it decades later, I gaped at her description of flocks of birds in urban and suburban backyards, the disappearance of which prompted women all over the United States to sound an alarm, eventually leading to the discovery that DDT and other poisons were to blame for the sharp decline in the populations of their feathered friends.

WHAT? THERE WERE MANY MORE BIRDS IN THE SKY ONLY A FEW YEARS BEFORE I WAS BORN?

I can almost imagine an urban skyscape with many more songbirds than when I was a child, but I can't know what effect(s) more color, more sound,

31

more *life* might have had on my developing brain, nor can I change the fact that comparatively barren skies feel normal to me. Two or three times, I have had the good fortune to be among trees in which flocks of migrating birds have stopped to rest, and this has given me a glimpse of the days before deforestation, before billions of birds were shot out of the skies, but *that* felt exceptional to me, while machine-generated transmissions (radio waves, microwaves, and Wi-Fi) occupying airways that once thrummed with birdsong and the beating of wings is what feels usual.

It's similar for me with *late* capitalism, by which I mean the current cultural-economic state of affairs in which those machine-generated transmissions thrum with advertisements for the exponentially expanding swarm of consumer "goods" that have come to seem normal in this era of hyper-(re)production and consumption in which no relationship or idea, no clever phrase or dance craze, escapes commodification. The other day, I counted more than 60 varieties of mints and chewing gum arrayed above the conveyer belt at the grocery store checkout line. Until boredom provoked me to count, that felt normal to me, and I probably wouldn't have been quite so bored by a brief wait were it not for the constant stimulation that the Internet has taught my brain to expect.

All of which is to say that my ability to think about capitalism must be presumed to be compromised. Even if there were some site outside of capitalism from which to stand and survey it, significant features might seem so "normal" as to be unremarkable. I might be unable to imagine alternatives to aspects of the situation that feel natural because they have been ever-present within my own lifetime. I might not ask important questions about capitalism's unspoken assumptions—because I make those assumptions myself.

And so I ask myself: Who might be better able to notice the most salient aspects of capitalism? What might we see from their standpoints?

Animal Standpoints

In its most basic form, feminist *standpoint theory* reminds us that "one's social situation enables and sets limits on what one can know" (Harding 1993, 54–55). Given the degree to which my own colonized and commodified mind may be unlikely to perceive important things about capitalism, it occurred to me to ask: What can nonhuman animals tell us about capitalism?

As Alison Wylie (2003) summarizes it, standpoint theory holds that ". . . those who are subject to structures of domination that systematically marginalize and oppress them may, in fact, be epistemically privileged in some crucial respects. They may know different things, or know some things better than those who are comparatively privileged . . ." (26).

Some nonhuman animals, such as cows held captive on for-profit "dairy" farms, subsist entirely within capitalism, with every aspect of their lives, including their very bodies, shaped by its machinations. Other nonhuman animals, such as free-flying birds, cannot escape the climate change, pollution, and incessant encroachments on their habitat caused by capitalism but are not ensnared by its property relations. Nonhuman animals who might be considered inquilines in relation to humans—rats, raccoons, pigeons, and others who find ways to survive within human homes and communities— have yet another standpoint *vis a vis* capitalism, having carved out their own niches within it even as others of their kind (in the case of rats and pigeons) remain commodified captives.

Sandra Harding, who has perhaps done more than anyone to demonstrate the utility of standpoint theory, argues that "the activities of those at the bottom of such social hierarchies can provide starting points for thought . . . from which humans' relations with each other and the natural world can become visible. This is because the experience and lives of marginalized people, as they understand them, provide particularly significant *problems to be explained*" (Harding 1993, 54).

Could this be true for nonhuman animals as well? Could consideration of capitalism from the vantage point of nonhuman animals fundamentally and fruitfully *change the question?*

Indeed this has been the case for me. When I set out to imagine what nonhuman animals might tell us about capitalism if they could, I ended up with more questions than answers. At first that felt like failure, but then I noticed that these were *different* questions than critics of capitalism usually ask. In seeking to answer *those* questions, I hit upon a few ideas that might be useful foci for future investigations—or, even better, interventions— into capitalism.

The Pigeon Point(s) of View

As related by zoologist John McLoughlin (1978), the story of how pigeons came to be so plentifully among us reminds me of the entanglement of nonhuman animal exploitation, colonization, and capitalism: The rock doves who were the ancestors of modern pigeons lived amidst the people of the Mediterranean for millennia, in one of those mutually beneficial cohabitations so common in nature. But then, here and there, people got the idea to reshape the birds to better meet human wishes and began to deliberately interfere with their reproduction. Some sought heavier birds with bigger breasts. Others wanted lightweight long-distance messengers, and still others wanted feathers of specific colors for aesthetic or symbolic purposes. By the first millennium BCE, Egyptians used specially bred homing pigeons for communication, Hebrews sacrificed specially bred doves by the thousands in temple rituals, and people around the region raised pigeons for their flesh in structures called dovecotes. Roman soldiers picked up these practices and spread the dovecote culture, along with the birds themselves, across Europe, using homing pigeons to report back to Rome on their imperialist adventures. Similarly, the Arabs who took up the task of world conquest upon the decline of the Roman Empire spread the dovecote culture into South Asia, maintaining precise genealogical records of the homing pigeons they used to communicate across their expansive domain. Doves had become soldiers, conscripts in imperial wars.

By World War I, the use of pigeons in warfare was so common that 100,000 birds were used as military tools in the course of that conflict (Wallop 2014). At about that same time, the new science of experimental psychology discovered a new use for pigeons, as subjects of experiments. Meantime, within the United States, raising pigeons for "meat" began to be promoted as both a pastime and a commercial endeavor.

Today, many pigeons remain captive. "Meat" markets around the world sell plump young pigeons as "squab." In the United States, rural communities stage festive "hunts" by releasing captive-born birds to be shot out of the sky during their first real flight. Urban enthusiasts raise racing pigeons on rooftops, using the mates and the offspring of bonded birds to lure partners and parents into exhausting efforts to get back home. Unconstrained by any nonhuman animal welfare laws at all,[3] researchers subject pigeons to every imaginable kind of experimentation. Vendors make money selling pigeons to scientists and hobbyists, and, at least in France, pigeons remain military conscripts, ready to be drafted into conflicts not of their choosing (Parussini 2012).

Therefore, pigeons have had the opportunity to observe capitalism from every angle. What do they see?

First, it seems to me that pigeons might not make such a sharp distinction between capitalism and the practices that paved the way for that particular mode of exploitation and accumulation. Each of the key catastrophes of capitalism—private ownership, production, and profit—were visited upon pigeons by people long before accumulated assets coalesced into a configuration that political economists sprang up to call "capitalism." Understanding these continuities might help critics of capitalism to avoid analytic errors that have led some communist economies to become as heartless and environmentally ruinous as any capitalist endeavor.

Again and again in the process quaintly called "domestication," free-flying pigeons were lured into human-constructed nesting places only to be dispossessed of their offspring or made captives themselves. That is one way that "property" comes into being.

A pigeon considered to be property would know, instinctively if not through some process of cognition that we could understand, that the problem is not *private* ownership but ownership itself. To be owned and exploited by some egalitarian collective of unrelated people would not be less onerous than to be owned and exploited by some person or family of people.

In both cases, reduction to the status of property is the problem, which is then compounded by being utilized as a means of (re)production. The ruthlessness of production—in this case, either having your offspring taken from you to be made into "meat," if not being made into "meat" yourself— remains, regardless of the relations among the various makers, vendors, buyers, and users of the products.

Just as I find it difficult to think outside of late consumer capitalism, champions and critics of capitalism alike find it difficult to conceptualize a culture not centered on production. In *The Mirror of Production*, Jean Baudrillard (1975) notes "the virtual impossibility of thinking beyond or outside the general scheme of production" (18). This difficulty arises, in part, from the entanglement of the ideas of humanity and productivity.

In *The German Ideology*, Marx and Engels (1947) assert that men "begin to distinguish themselves from animals as soon as they begin to produce their means of subsistence" (7). Like me, Baudrillard (1975, 21) wonders, parenthetically, "Why must man's vocation always be to distinguish himself from animals?" More importantly, Baudrillard describes a link between productivity and human identity, as experienced by men—and I do mean "men"—living in cultures centered on the ethos of dominion of nature.

Baudrillard (1975, 19) critiques the way of thinking that "hallucinates man's predestination for the objective transformation of the world," finding in this widespread fantasy a key to the reduction of people to their labor power within both capitalist and communist political economies as well as a source of the reckless exploitation of nature, such that "production subordinates Nature and the individual simultaneously" (Baudrillard 1975, 54). People under the spell of this way of thinking see themselves reflected in the products of their labors, and "through this scheme of production, this mirror of production, the human species comes to consciousness *in the imaginary*" (Baudrillard 1975, 19).

This brings us back to the pigeon point of view. Recall that Europeans often rationalized the forced displacement of Native Americans and other indigenous people by asserting that the original inhabitants had not made productive use of the land. Both as indigenes themselves[4] and as captives brought along on voyages of conquest, members of the extended pigeon family witnessed the migrations of European humans from the lands they had so "productively" deforested to these new environs. Pigeons also have had a bird's-eye view of the accelerated expansion of the population of both people and farmed animals subsequent to the imperialist expansions that led ultimately to the globalization of capitalism. Historian and geographer

Alfred Crosby (2003, 75) imagines that "one who watched the Caribbean islands from outer space during the years from 1492 to 1550 or so might have surmised that the object of the game going on there was to replace the people with pigs, dogs, and cattle."

I'm not so sure what pigeons would have surmised. Surely, native pigeons and doves would have noticed the unfamiliar animals and reshaped landscapes that followed the European invasion. Perhaps they did notice that the people waging wars on forests were lighter-colored and differently ornamented than the humans to whom they were accustomed. Perhaps they thought of the difference in the same way as we distinguish between African and Asian elephants. If so, I wonder which behavioral differences might have seemed salient to them.

Hyper-reproductivity comes to mind. Like indigenous peoples everywhere, the native peoples of the Americas tended to keep their populations well below what the land could support. This makes good social *and* environmental sense, as it allows for there to be enough for everybody, even in the times of comparative scarcity that weather fluctuations sometimes present. The Catholic Iberians who first invaded the Caribbean and the Protestant Northern Europeans who later immigrated into what would become Canada and the United States had different ideas and practices. The flip side of the denigration for nonreproductive sexuality that they famously brought to the Americas was a valorization of profligate reproduction that has subsequently come to seem so normal as to appear natural. They went forth and multiplied as recklessly as they cut down trees. Over the centuries, this irresponsible habit (in combination with the despicable practice of importing captive people as laborers) added up to explosive human population growth.

And then passenger pigeons met profit. These peripatetic pigeons had been hunted, in deliberate moderation, by various Native Americans and thus must have perceived people as among the many predators of which to be wary. Immediately upon their arrival, the firearm-toting European immigrants must have seemed to be a different kind of animal. Over time, the foreigners subjected these avian indigenes to three new injuries: captivity, sport hunting, and (most lethally) commercial hunting. Some settlers converted "wild" birds into property in order to monetize their offspring. Others promoted pigeon killing as a wholesome form of recreation for boys and men. With the coming of refrigerated railroads, high-volume commercial hunting of passenger pigeons became such a lucrative endeavor that tens of thousands of birds were killed at a time. Not long after, the last passenger pigeon died alone in a zoo.

Let's look at that sorry story from the pigeon point of view. We can't! The closest matches, within human experience, are genocides from which there were few if any survivors, and records of these might help us to begin to empathize with the combination of horror and incomprehension surviving birds might have experienced surveying stacks of the dead bodies of their flock mates and family members. This is more like if bears, who sometimes do kill people, suddenly became able to kill people by the thousands, *and did so*, gradually emptying our cities as they spirited the bodies off to some unknown place for some unknown purpose.

I hope that imagining such a scenario can help to make profit seem strange, because this is the question that I think may have reverberated, in whatever way that queries ring in bird brains: Why take so many more than you can eat? Not just a few more, to take home to your nestlings or store for the winter, but more than you could consume in a lifetime? Those of us who have grown up within capitalism may tend to see the wish, or even the perceived need, for profit to be natural. Considering the question from the pigeon point of view, the profit motive becomes something that needs to be explained.

Live "Stock" Looks Back

One day, a cow jumped over a "beef" farm fence to birth a calf in the forest, far from the grasping hands of humans. She and her son then found their way to a friendly person who conveyed them to a sanctuary. The mother's fierceness in protecting her son from perceived threats made them a poor match for a sanctuary offering tours to the public, so they both came to VINE Sanctuary, where they eventually joined the hardy herd in our back pasture. The cows in that community organize their own affairs as they see fit. They often choose to sleep in the forest rather than in the barn and drink from a brook or pond rather than water troughs. Other than eyeballing everybody twice each day, just to ensure that nobody is ill or injured in any way, sanctuary staff stay out of the way.

Jan and her calf Justin have flourished in that setting. As Justin has grown up into a sweet-tempered young adult with a fondness for bird-watching, Jan has made friends with cows her own age. She no longer glares and prepares to charge any person who might dare to look too lingeringly at her son, but she still becomes visibly wary when strangers appear.

I've endured more than a few uncomfortable moments under the searchlight of Jan's gaze, hoping she will see that she need not charge at me to protect herself or her son. At such moments, it seems to me that she is both mad and mystified, angered and confused by what she has seen people do to cows. In Jan's expression when she looks at people, even when she is comparatively relaxed, I perceive a combination of challenge and question, as if she is prepared to fight an enemy she cannot fathom.

Maybe I'm wrong in this, but let's imagine that my empathic imagination is in this case correct. What is Jan mad about? What questions does she have?

I don't know enough about the farm from which Jan escaped to know whether she was artificially inseminated while chained into immobility or placed in a situation from which she could not escape a bull brought in for the purpose of impregnating her. Either way, she was not free to refuse to become pregnant with a child destined to be made into "meat." Depending on whether or not the small-scale farm from which Jan escaped was one of the increasingly common (and ostensibly "humane") slaughter-on-site facilities beloved by locavores, Jan would have either heard the screams as other cows were killed or simply witnessed cows wrestled from the herd and never seen again. Some of the victims were her children; others were her friends.

And for what? A cow or other ungulate who witnesses a herd member taken down by a predator also sees the reason for the attack. However upsetting, the incident makes sense to creatures whose auroch ancestors evolved in relationship to truly carnivorous fellow forest denizens, but wholesale slaughter and dismemberment (or disappearance) of relatives and other community members must shock the minds as well as the hearts of these exquisitely social nonhuman animals whose brains (like ours) evolved to be attuned to the experiences of others in the social group.

So, one question Jan might have is: Why?

Another question Jan might have is: How? What kind of creatures are people that they can do such things?

Yet another question Jan might have is: What *other* horrors might you people be capable of committing?

Cows can't understand capitalism. They feel its effects all too well, and they certainly know that people are the proximate cause of their woes, but it would be difficult for them to imagine the rationales used by people to explain any sort of nonhuman animal exploitation to themselves, much less the preposterous mathematics of an economic system that requires incessant growth to avoid collapse.

Those of us who understand, or *think* we understand, the logic of capitalism can exercise both empathy and solidarity by taking Jan's questions seriously. We can ask ourselves afresh: *Why? How? What else?* Instead of accepting "profit" as an easy answer, we can consider the profit motive a questionable phenomenon requiring some explanation. We can notice the sexual violation at the heart of "meat" and cow milk production, and we can join Jan in wondering what other obscenities might be forthcoming from people accustomed to perpetrating such perversities.

Multiplication and Division

Ecofeminist philosopher Lori Gruen (2015) stresses the importance of empathy as an essential cognitive tool for nonhuman animal advocacy.

Feminist anthropologist June Nash (2001) calls for us to use "peripheral vision" when seeking to understand the machinations of globalized capitalism. Having tried to follow that advice in considering capitalism from the perspectives of pigeons and cows, I end up with questions about several of the foundations of that socioeconomic system: property, profit, and (re)production.

OWNERSHIP AND IDENTITY

Nonhuman animals under the control of people don't experience themselves as property but as captives. Empathizing with this perspective makes property strange and draws attention to the violence implicit in it (jones 2006). Nonhuman animals contest captivity in many ways (Gruen 2014). They flee, fight back against their captors, and sometimes even free other animals (Hribal 2011). Thus, it seems safe to conclude that many nonhuman animals experience captivity as a kind of continuing assault.

The problem for nonhuman animals is not only that they themselves are liable to be violently converted into property (if not hatched or born into that status) but also that their habitats are considered by people to be property. Nonhuman animals also contest this, sometimes exercising notable ingenuity in organizing both individual and collective resistance to "development" (jones 2007), but sit-ins by baboons are no match for bulldozers. Hence, even if nonhuman animals were magically emancipated from the category of property, many misfortunes would remain. Property itself is problematic.

I've often imagined how I would explain property to somebody, like a pigeon, who is unfamiliar with the notion of ownership. Of course, a pigeon might understand very well the notion of exclusive use of a nesting cavity. Many birds who build nests certainly do defend them from interlopers and might well endorse the Lockean idea that mixing your labor with found materials entitles you to claim the resulting object as your own.

Most people think of "property" as things owned, but property theorists within philosophy and legal studies tend to use the word to refer to the relationships among people, codified and enforced by laws regarding ownership. In this way of thinking, property is most frequently conceptualized as a "bundle of rights" enjoyed by owners, along with perhaps some responsibilities (Penner 1997). While there may be some argument about whether this or that tangible or intangible item (such as an amputated body part or an idea) rightly falls under the reign of particular property regulations (Morales 2013), and while scholars will quibble (as scholars do) about whether "bundle" is the best metaphor, we should not miss the central insight: Property is a *relationship among people.* Property is ruthless in relation to nonhuman animals and other entities claimed as possessions because property is, in the minds of people, all about *people*.

Perhaps termites could understand our presumed license to seize a homestead without regard for others who might already be living there, but I wonder whether any nonhuman animal could understand the feeling of violation experienced by some human homeowners when some other-than-human animals happen into their suburban backyards. At first this feeling seems absurd. Nonhuman animals aren't party to the agreements people make with each other in order to establish private property, so it is silly for any person to expect nonhuman animals to respect property boundaries drawn up by people. Still, the *feeling* of trespass is real and tends to occur even when the nonhuman animal in question poses no threat.

Thinking about that leads me to notice two aspects of property that often go unremarked:

1. The affective components of the notion of property are wider and deeper than those usually acknowledged by property theorists, even when the objects of ownership are not of particular sentimental value.

2. Speciesism is implicit in the very notion of property, whether or not nonhuman animals are the property in question.

These aspects are related by the degree to which property ownership figures into "human" identity. While it, of course, makes sense for social nonhuman animals of any given species to make agreements among themselves about how they will share the various essential features of their habitats, people go further than this in the ideas and the practices that constitute property, simultaneously elevating and alienating themselves in the process of claiming ownership.

A pair of Canada geese nests, every year, at the edge of a pond past that I frequently drive. When they are nurturing eggs or nestlings, they certainly do defend themselves and their home from any perceived encroachment. Nonetheless, I've seen nothing to suggest that these geese consider themselves to be anything other than two of the many denizens of the pond. In contrast, the people on whose property the pond sits certainly do consider themselves to be the owners of the pond. In so doing, they set themselves above and apart from the waterfowl, frogs, insects, and turtles (not to mention the marsh grass and the water itself) who co-create the ecosystem that is the pond and thus might be considered to have even more of a claim to it.

I am suddenly reminded of the ranchers who feel furious when wolves consume a cow, considering the natural behavior of a handful of indigenous nonhuman animals to be a crime worthy of the death penalty for the whole species. Why such fury? Is it only the slight decrease in profit associated with the loss of one piece of "stock?" Or do the ranchers recognize the threat as more existential? Like the raccoon who tips over a suburban trash bin while committing the crime of rescuing food scraps from a landfill, those wolves are saying, "we don't recognize your system of property. We do not concede the Earth to you."

When nonhuman animals contest property, they also challenge the very basis of "human" identity. We should join them, however we can, and not only because property is so hurtful to *them*. To the degree to which our identities are bound up with what we own, we are alienated from our animal selves as well as the ecosystems upon which we depend for everything.

THE SUPERFLUITY OF SURPLUS

In currently common parlance, to be "extra" is to behave in an excessive manner. In the preceding exercises in empathic imagination, both pigeons and cows noticed and were mystified by the "extra" character of predation by people. From a human standpoint within capitalism, we can see that some of the people who shot hundreds or thousands of passenger pigeons at a time intended to sell their bodies for a profit. However, this leaves much unexplained, such as superfluous killings in the course of sport hunting. Moreover, why a person should *want* profit, which is just another way of saying excess, remains unclear. To people in profit-seeking cultures, the wish for *more,* if not the willingness to commit injuries up to and including killing for that nonessential pleasure, seems natural, but many other animals (including other humans) are collectively content with *enough.*

If we consider "enough" to mean both, (1) sufficiency of resources necessary for livelihood, including an adequate reserve against hard times, and (2) equity within exchanges, then the impulse to accumulate more than that really does need to be explained. From an ecological standpoint, the incessant alienation and the appropriation of as much surplus as possible from a finite planet seems suicidal, especially given another remarkable habit of the humans who created capitalism: overpopulation.

REPRODUCTION AND DUPLICITY

If the pigeons and doves indigenous to Europe were able to communicate with those elsewhere in the world, then they would collectively be able to tell a birds-eye tale of one group of apes depleting one part of the world, literally shipping off the surplus people that the deforested land could no longer support, and then starting the process all over again in other places.

If the pigeons who first were "domesticated" could shout a warning about into the future, they might say, "Watch out! They seem nice at first, *but then they steal your babies!!"* Both the human population explosion and the process of making other animals into property revolves around forced reproduction, and that brings us to patriarchy.

Ascent of Man

How did some humans become the kind of animals who identify themselves via ownership, monomaniacally pursue a fantasied infinite surplus, and center their cultures on incessant (re)production? To begin to answer the questions nonhuman animals might have about capitalism, we must trace some of the many intersections among sexism and speciesism, noticing the pathways by which patriarchy set the stage for an economics of hyper(re)production in the service of appropriation and accumulation.

From the pigeon point of view, patriarchy might look like the males of one species of ape battling each other—individually and in gangs—for control of females, land, and other animals. Each male fights on several fronts, deploying physical force not only in the competition with other males but also in the subordination of human and nonhuman animals as well as in the never-ending quest to administer the workings of the world. They raze forests, dam or divert waterways, and even sometimes chop the tops off mountains. They also wage war on any nonhuman animals who in any way impede their endeavors.

Why did they start fighting with each other? Did they first subordinate the females of their own kind and then extend that practice to other animals or vice versa? Those are good topics for another day, as are many other aspects of patriarchy that ecofeminists such as Carol Adams and Lori Gruen (2014) have identified as correlates of speciesism, but in order to understand how patriarchy paved the way for capitalism, we need only parse this simple phrase: *man versus man over resources.*

Let's come back to what "man" might be after looking at the other terms.

VERSUS

The centrality of competition to patriarchy can be missed when we (quite understandably) focus on the subjugation of women, nonhuman animals, and "nature" by human males. In addition to contributing to many of the more toxic aspects of masculinity, a combative rather than cooperative approach to the mutual use of material resources tends to create stockpiles and scarcity, both of which increase the likelihood of continuing conflict.

Whether due to insecurity, arrogance, or some combination of the two, males in a social system patterned by fights about property will tend, if they can, to amass weaponry and hoard resources. Hoarding by some creates scarcity for others, heightening the tension if not outright fighting and therefore setting the stage for never-ending warfare. Thus does the competition within patriarchy help to supply one of the keystones of capitalism: desire for surplus.

Surplus means *more*. In order for there to be more, reproduction of many kinds must be fostered or even forced. Thus does the wish for surplus that is a function of patriarchy contribute to the obsessive and coercive focus on reproduction known as *reprocentrism*,[5] which is a central element of capitalism.

Competition itself is, of course, another central element of capitalism. In addition to fomenting divisions of all kinds, cultures based on conflicts over property tend toward a fractured rather than holistic view of the natural world. Seeing forests or islands as made up of divisible entities to be assigned to various owners makes it difficult to think ecologically.

RESOURCES

Within patriarchy, males compete with one another to obtain the kinds of exclusive control over resources that are now codified in property law. Thus does patriarchy pave the way for another central element of capitalism: ownership. The conversion of everybody-other-than-men (or, in subsequent racist cultures, everybody-other-than-men-like-me) into potential property has other important consequences.

Within patriarchy, not only female and juvenile humans but also land and other animals are reduced to the status of resources to be exploited by "mankind." Living beings become mere inventory or "livestock." The violence by which this demotion is accomplished fosters callousness, which then facilitates further violence.

Reprocentrism becomes rape when animals, human or otherwise, are the stock to be accumulated. Repeated violations of the bodies of others both requires and reinforces callousness and a feeling of entitlement to dominion over others. These central aspects of toxic masculinity feed into and are fortified by the competitive aspects of patriarchy described above, forming an ever more vicious circle.

MAN

Within patriarchy, the social identities of adult males depend upon their competent performance of masculinity. Manhood is defined, in part, by participation in the competitions described above. "Real men" demonstrate their ability to control the women and other animals under their dominion. In many patriarchal cultures, *only* men may own property, and only property owners are considered real men.

I've often said that pastoralism and patriarchy may be seen as two sides of the same coin, with that coin being the profits of controlling somebody else's body (jones 2014b). Inherently hurtful to human and nonhuman animals, patriarchal pastoralism also set the stage for two of the most central components of modern-day capitalism: reprocentrism and the entanglement of identity and ownership. Hence, any efforts to undermine capitalism or speciesism must be mindful of the interconnections. Neither self-consciously "militant" nonhuman animal rights activism that embraces toxic masculinity nor vegan consumerism that encourages people to buy their way to liberation of other animals are likely to succeed in undermining either capitalism or nonhuman animal exploitation. Similarly, efforts to improve the standing of other animals within the existing legal framework, which ensnares all of nature in property relations backed up by state firepower, may bring some temporary relief of some forms of oppression but are unlikely to lead to true liberation.

Animality as Antidote

Here are some things that pigeons and cows might or might not have noticed about humans:

They like color. A lot. They decorate themselves and their dwellings, often experiencing such frivolity as absolutely essential. They plant flowers with no food value just for the pretty colors and for their scents, which can have almost intoxicating effects. They like intoxication too, seeking out sensations that feel freeing by an ingenious variety of means, including not only chemistry but also art and music.

While best known (among themselves) for their pronounced tendency to communicate by means of self-generated sound-symbols shaped into words and structured into sentences, these talking apes also use color and other kinds of sound to convey emotions and ideas. Many of them are able to denote sound-symbols visually, thereby increasing the distance across which they can communicate. Tool makers among them have invented various devices that increase that distance even further, so that their exchange networks now encircle the globe.

In other words, these are pleasure-seeking creatures who signal to one another incessantly. This extreme sociality makes sense in the light of their extreme vulnerability as neonates and their comparative lack of muscular strength, relative to other apes, even as adults. Not one of them could survive without some others.

However did such weaklings colonize an entire planet? The fact of that colonization offers a clue. Think of all of the different climates in which these virtually hairless apes abide. Think of all of the different ways they have fed, clothed, transported, and sheltered themselves. Think of all of the different tools, both material and conceptual, they have devised along the way and all of the different practices common in different places.

Quiet as it's kept, this diversity was once much more breathtaking than it is today. For all of the pseudo-variety on ostentatious display on the supermarket shelves of late consumer capitalism, the process of trade globalization has hastened the demise of languages and cultures begun by European imperialism. Nonetheless, the fact remains: Behavioral plasticity is a defining feature of the human species.

Behavioral plasticity refers to changes in behavior arising from an organism's circumstances, including "adaptation, learning, memory and changes in adult behavior as a result of experience during development" (Binder et al. 2008, 372). Animals and other organisms vary in the flexibility of their repertoire of responses to environmental circumstances. Noting that *all* behavior is, to some degree, both innate and learned, Mery and Burns (2009, 571) suggest that we see behavioral plasticity as "an interaction between evolution and experience." Most importantly, for our purposes, Morris (2014) highlights the role of behavioral plasticity in allowing organisms to persist in changing environments as well as colonize new environments.

In colonizing so much of the planet mostly by means of behavior,[6] human beings as organisms have demonstrated a remarkable degree of behavioral flexibility. This accounts for not only the diversity of personalities, abilities, and proclivities among humans as individuals but also for the diversity of cultures that have arisen as groups of people developed cultures in response to varying ecological circumstances.

We're at this juncture, standing amidst the clutter of consumer capitalism as polluted seas rise around us, because certain kinds of cultures—cultures that solve problems with violence, stripping habitats of resources and then moving on to do the same elsewhere—tend to reproduce themselves, but the behaviors encouraged by those cultures are no more (or less) "human nature" than more pacific and sustainable ways of being in the world.

People build concentration camps . . . and nonhuman animal sanctuaries. People amass war profits . . . and divest themselves of all wealth in order to aid others. Most people do a bit of both.

What makes the difference? In every case, a complex conjunction of social and material factors stretching back before birth and continuing throughout the lifespan. Capitalism constricts consciousness, favoring some ways of seeing the world and making others seem impossible, but other ways of thinking and being are not only possible but already present.

In his critique of the concept of "man-the-producer" that inflects both capitalist and communist thought, Baudrillard (1975, 75) asserts that "it is impossible to think this non-growth, this non-productive desire." I respectfully disagree. Lesbians, gay men, and otherwise queer people know all about desire that is not centered on reproduction, and our persistence in pursuing that desire despite social and state repression demonstrates its abiding power (jones 2014a).

People of all sexualities know, at some level, that our most heartfelt desires are not for the 37 varieties of orange juice and 60 kinds of chewing gum that consumer capitalism offers us. Let us tap into those desires. Let us allow Afrofuturists, anarchists, and artists of all stripes to teach us to imagine heretofore unthought-of aims and strategies that take our current social and material ecologies into account. Let's liberate all the animals, including ourselves, from the tyranny of property, profit, and production.

NOTES

1. Inky is an octopus who escaped from a New Zealand aquarium by climbing out of a tank, walking across a floor, and then slipping through a grate into a drain-pipe that led to the sea. Would that we all could be as capable of imagination and action, and therefore as free, as Inky.

2. That's the number that I counted one day in one store. Since the brand Minute Maid alone offers 11 varieties—Premium Original Orange Juice, Pulp Free Orange Juice, Orange Juice with Calcium & Vitamin D, Pure Squeezed No Pulp, Pure Squeezed Some Pulp, Pure Squeezed No Pulp with Calcium & Vitamin D, Country Style, Heart Wise', Home Squeezed with Calcium & Vitamin D; Kids+, and Low Acid—in both liquid and frozen form, and since other brands are similarly prolific in devising variations of the same product, the true total of available varieties of orange juice must be much higher.

3. Pigeons and other birds (along with rodents) are not classified as "animals" under the minimal federal nonhuman animal welfare regulations in the United States, leaving the vast majority of other animals in laboratories entirely unprotected.

4. Collectively, pigeons and doves compose the family *Columbidae*, which includes more than 300 extant and extinct species. (The birds commonly called "pigeons" are member of the "rock dove" branch of that family.) The broader order of *Columbiformes* includes not only pigeons and doves but also the unlucky indigene known to Europeans as the dodo.

5. In their germinal anthology, *Queer Ecologies*, Catriona Mortimer-Sandilands and Bruce Erickson (2010, 11) critique the "repro-centric" logic that presumes reproduction to be the prime aim of all animals. I use the term more broadly, to include not only such misunderstandings of animal behavior but also the mono-maniacal focus on reproduction that is a defining feature of sexism, homophobia, and capitalism alike.

6. In those cases where humans eventually evolved new physical characteristics in response to new environments, this was made possible only by the persistence of people in those environments long enough for those changes to occur. That persistence was due to behavioral plasticity.

REFERENCES

Adams, Carol J., and Lori Gruen (eds.). 2014. *Ecofeminism: Feminist Intersections with Other Animals and the Earth.* New York: Bloomsbury Academic.

Baudrillard, Jean. 1975. *The Mirror of Production.* St. Louis: Telos Press.

Binder, Marc D., Nobutaka Hirokawa, and Uwe Windhorst (eds.). 2008. *Encyclopedia of Neuroscience.* Berlin: Springer.

Carson, Rachel. 1962. *Silent Spring.* Greenwich, CT: Fawcett Crest.

Crosby, Alfred W. 2003. *The Columbian Exchange: Biological and Cultural Consequences of 1492.* Westport, CT: Greenwood Publishing Group.

Gruen, Lori. 2014. *The Ethics of Captivity.* New York: Oxford University Press.

Gruen, Lori. 2015. *Entangled Empathy: An Alternative Ethic for Our Relationships with Animals.* New York: Lantern Books.

Harding, Sandra. 1993. "Rethinking Standpoint Epistemology: What Is 'Strong Objectivity'?" In *Feminist Epistemologies*, edited by Linda Alcoff and Elizabeth Potter, 49–82. London: Routledge.

Hribal, Jason. 2011. *Fear of the Animal Planet: The Hidden History of Animal Resistance.* Oakland, CA: AK Press.

jones, pattrice. 2007. "Sharks Bite Back: Direct Action by Animals Around the World." *Satya Magazine*, April 2007.

jones, pattrice. 2006. "Stomping with the Elephants: Feminist Principles for Radical Solidarity." In *Igniting a Revolution: Voices in Defense of the Earth*, edited by Steven Best and Anthony Nocella, 319–29. Oakland, CA: AK Press.

jones, pattrice. 2014. "Eros and the Mechanisms of Eco-Defense." In *Ecofeminism: Feminist Intersections with Other Animals and the Earth*, edited by Carol J. Adams and Lori Gruen, 91–106. New York: Bloomsbury.

jones, pattrice. 2014. *The Oxen at the Intersection: A Collision.* New York: Lantern Books.

Marx, Karl, and Friedrich Engels. 1970. *The German Ideology.* New York: International Publishers.

McLoughlin, John C. 1978. *The Animals Among Us: Wildlife in the City.* New York: Viking Press.

Mery, Frederic, and James G. Burns. 2009. "Behavioural Plasticity: An Interaction between Evolution and Experience." *Evolutionary Ecology*, 24(3). November 26. 571–583. doi:10.1007/s10682-009-9336-y.

Morales, Francisco J. 2013. "The Property Matrix: An Analytical Tool to Answer the Question, 'Is This Property?'" *University of Pennsylvania Law Review*, 161(4): 1125–1165.

Morris, Matthew R. J. 2014. "Plasticity-Mediated Persistence in New and Changing Environments." *International Journal of Evolutionary Biology.* doi:10.1155/2014/416497.

Mortimer-Sandilands, Catriona, and Bruce Erickson. 2010. "A Genealogy of Queer Ecologies." *Queer Ecologies: Sex, Nature, Politics, Desire*, edited by Catriona Mortimer-Sandilands and Bruce Erickson, 1–47. Bloomington, IN: Indiana University Press.

Nash, June. 2001. "Globalization and the Cultivation of Peripheral Vision." *Anthropology Today* 17(4): 15–22. doi:10.1111/1467-8322.00070.

Parussini, Gabriele. 2012. "In France, a Mission to Return the Military's Carrier Pigeons to Active Duty." *Wall Street Journal*, November 11, page 1. Accessed September 30, 2016, from http://www.wsj.com/articles/SB10001424127887 32443980457810493926157320.

Penner, James E. 1997. *The Idea of Property in Law*. Oxford: Clarendon Press.

Wallop, Harry. 2014. "Animal Soldiers: Hannibal's Elephants to Ukraine's Killer Dolphins." *The Telegraph*. March 31. Accessed September 30, 2016, from http://www.telegraph.co.uk/news/uknews/defence/10734220/Animal -soldiers-Hannibals-elephants-to-Ukraines-killer-dolphins.html.

Wylie, Alison. 2003. "Why Standpoint Matters." *Science and Other Cultures: Issues in Philosophies of Science and Technology*, edited by Robert Figueroa and Sandra G. Harding, 26–48. New York: Routledge.

Circus Train Crash. (Copyright © 2010 Sue Coe. Courtesy Galerie St. Etienne, NY)

3

Slaves to Entertainment: Manufacturing Consent for Orcas in Captivity

Núria Almiron

Scientists tell us that orcas have inhabited the planet's oceans for at least 6 million years—probably longer since they belong to the oceanic dolphin family, which first appeared around 11 million years ago. Considering that the genus *homo* is only about 2.8 million years old and modern humans, *homo sapiens*, emerged around 200,000 years ago—almost yesterday in geologic time—orcas have had much more time to evolve than humans.

In fact, if we assess evolution in intelligence without referring to human-centered criteria (i.e., not only based on human senses and the capacity of abstract thought), then cetaceans in general and orcas in particular would rank as more evolved sentient beings than humans in some important aspects. According to Dr. Lori Marino (2011, 115), a leading researcher in whale and dolphin brain anatomy, the brains of these species have evolved "along a different neuroanatomical trajectory, providing an example of an alternative evolutionary route to complex intelligence on earth." This, in short, means that if self-serving views of intelligence (designed to put humans on top) are discarded, cetaceans show how intelligence—and thus the capacity of feelings, emotions and suffering—can be displayed in different, fascinating ways.

Nowadays, the *Orcinus orca* is second only to humans (and possibly the common rat) as the most widely distributed mammal on Earth. They can be found in all oceans from Arctic and Antarctic regions to tropical seas—widely considered evidence of the success of the species, since this expanded habitat means a huge capacity to adapt to very different natural conditions. As in the case of humans, this adaption to the natural environment has additionally produced different orca cultures, which are mostly defined by food and communication. Depending on the area where they live, different groups of orcas have developed different diets, including fish and/or mammal prey (Ford, et al. 2011) and different hunting practices, including very creative group techniques (Neiwert 2015). Furthermore, each distinct population has its own dialect, that is to say, a set of stereotyped calls they use to communicate with one another (Morton 2004). All of these traits are cultural because they are learned, passed down over the generations, and refined over time.

This may seem basic compared to the behavior developed by humans in relation to diet and communication, yet this could well be a human delusion. The complexity of orca societies may be something that humans lack the cognitive capacity to truly understand, since it is based on brain capacities that we ourselves are missing. The most important of these, to our knowledge, is their echolocation ability—the kind of sonar orcas use to communicate and see, defined by some as a genuine sixth sense. Dolphin-family *echolocation*—an ability that bats also share to some extent—puts orcas among the most acoustically sophisticated animals on the planet, since it not only helps them hear sounds or detect the presence of objects, but it also produces clear and detailed visions of objects that go beyond mere vision, allowing them to see *inside* things (Marino et al 2007; Neiwert 2015). In fact, this is why the military employ dolphins to locate objects that we humans cannot find in spite of all our sophisticated technologies.[1]

However, what strikes scientists most about orcas is a universal trait they all share, regardless of their ecotype (habitat and cultural distinctions). As orca researcher Howard Garrett puts it: "Even though they are capable of extreme forms of aggression [during hunting] the prevailing ethos of their culture keeps them from harming each other and from harming other life forms they choose not to eat," including humans (in Neiwert 2015, 92–93). Indeed, cetaceans not only continue to provide an enormous body of empirical evidence for complex behavior, learning, sociality, and culture, but orcas and other cetacean species may "have achieved a level of social-emotional sophistication not achieved by other animals, including humans" (Marino 2011, 125). Orcas' social life in the wild cultivates empathy to their own species and, moreover, extends empathy to others.[2] Theirs are rich emotional lives organized into matriarchal societies that lack aggressiveness and have instead incorporated cooperation as a major trait. This leads Neiwert (2015, 249) to assert that, "if orcas have established empathy as a distinctive evolutionary advantage, it might behoove a human race awash in war and psychopathy to pay attention."

The latter gives particular pause for thought considering how we humans treat orcas. We pollute their waters with spills (the Exxon Valdez case is still having an impact on the local orca population), with contaminants (mostly through persistent organic pollutants or POP), and with noise (from cargo ship traffic, whale watching tourism, and recreational vessels). We extinguish their food sources (we have wiped out many salmon runs). We kill them (fishermen see them as a threat to their catches). We hunt them for zoological parks or breed them in captivity, where we have forced these fast-swimming, long-lived, intelligent social animals to perform, reproduce, and live in tiny concrete tanks separated from their family members. Even more appallingly, we sometimes forget them in *warehouse pools*—windowless backroom tanks with no daylight, total isolation, and zero stimulation, places where parks store animals that are either on sale, waiting for the legal conditions to allow their exportation, in need of separation (usually calves from mothers), or simply unsuitable for display in the show pool. Junior, an Icelandic orca in Marineland, Ontario, spent up to five years in such an enclosure prior to his death (Diebel 2012).

However, orcas have not been selected for this chapter because they are an apex predator or due to their complex social structure, rather because their capture for exhibition in zoos is a modern phenomenon that allows us to accurately track the linkages between capitalism and speciesism.

THE THEORY OF OPPRESSION

The theoretical framework of this chapter is grounded in the theory of oppression (Noel 1968), as applied by Nibert (2002) to speciesism. This framework does not deny the importance of psychological considerations, but these are situated within the context of structural forces. While I strongly believe that the true battle against oppression can only be fought within each of us, it would be naive to ignore the fact that moral behavior is strongly conditioned by the social environment, that is, by the institutional and economic forces that shape human society. As Nibert (2002) notes, in recent decades a growing number of critical sociologists have recurrently shown that all forms of oppression have historical and social structural causes that are rooted, not only but largely, in an unjust social structure. Stressing the psychological and moral foundations of oppression may lead to relevant individual efforts that challenge oppressive practices. These individual efforts are a necessary condition for social change, but they are not sufficient. As long as oppressive social structures persist, the belief system that prevents the large majority of human beings from changing their behaviors will remain nurtured and thus allow for oppression to be perpetuated.

Comprehending the role played by institutional and economic forces in the exploitation of other animals is useful if we are to understand the entire history of their abuse by humans. However, the emergence of capitalism has made this understanding much more necessary due to the development of a new and much more powerful institution of consent manufacturing: the mass media. They have joined the traditional institutions, or ideological apparatus in Gramscian language, of reproducing hegemony: the state, religion, and education (Gramsci 1992).

Consistent with the theory of oppression, speciesism is not considered here a bias or a prejudice but an ideology that justifies the mistreatment of other animals by humans—in particular, it is a type of anthropocentrism that denies nonhuman interests any moral consideration equal to humans, therefore justifying the exploitation of other animals. This chapter's case study, the abuse of orcas, has been chosen because it clearly demonstrates this point: how speciesist ideology—here the belief that humans have the right to exploit orcas—is not the cause of the abuse but rather an instrument created by the abusers to protect their business. It is not, therefore, a mere prejudice in the minds of humans but rather a set of shared beliefs built to legitimate the social order.

The political economy of orcas in captivity—a relatively new phenomenon with an easily traceable history—perfectly illustrates the three factors deemed necessary for the development and the perpetuation of oppression according to the theory of oppression: 1) competition for resources, 2) economic interest of an elite, and 3) ideological conditioning for obtaining the social rationalization and the legitimization of human actions. This chapter is organized in accordance with these three entangled forces. First, the history of whaling is briefly introduced to show how our perspective of whales, and more particularly orcas, was initially driven by the competition for resources. Second, the business of orcas in captivity is presented as evidence of how orca abuse has been motivated primarily by economic interests. Finally, we describe the ideological conditioning constructed by the industry's public relations and lobbying arms to legitimize the exploitation of orcas.

FROM *ASESINAS DE BALLENAS* TO *KILLER WHALES*

Although many non-Western mythologies have always venerated orcas—mostly as ancient creatures with spiritual powers—Western mythology has always considered them merciless killers that have terrified man on the ocean and on land. Their scientific name, the Latin *Orcinus orca*, also illustrates this perception, roughly translating as "whale belonging to the kingdom of the dead."

Since ancient times, orcas have featured prominently in "marine folklore as bloodthirsty, voracious" predators posing extreme danger to humans (Ford et al. 2000, 11). In the first century AD, in what is probably the first scientific description of orcas, the Roman scholar Pliny the Elder portrayed the orca as "a creature that is the enemy of the other species and the appearance of which can be represented by no other description except that of an enormous mass of flesh armed with savage teeth" (Roberts 2007, 175). Certainly, in Pliny's and later accounts from ancient times, it seems as if orcas' hunting traits and aggressiveness in hunting other mammals could somehow be transferred to how they might potentially treat humans—the myth building upon an expectation stemming from respect and fear. While we can only speculate as to why ancient Western mythology demonized orcas, the reason for their bad reputation over the past three centuries is well documented in the history of human fishing.

For millennia, the coastal communities of North and South America, Siberia, South Africa, New Zealand, Japan, and northern Europe killed whales for their "meat, oil, and blubber"—archaeological evidence suggests that the Inuit practiced whaling as far back as 3000 BCE. Those primitive catches were mostly for subsistence needs and constituted a largely "passive opportunistic enterprise" that did not pose a serious threat to whale populations (Richards 2014, 112). Things changed dramatically with the emergence of capitalism and industrial whaling in the seventeenth century as North American and European whalers organized fleets to actively pursue and hunt whales. Within three centuries, mass commercial whaling—with techniques that included killing both mothers and their calves—led to the extinction of some species in some areas of the world and the dramatic decline in numbers of hunted whales everywhere, reducing the industry to almost nothing by the end of nineteenth century.

From the early days of industrial fishing, orcas were always considered too small to be of interest to commercial hunters, yet they were seen as competitors due to the fact that different populations of orcas hunt some of the same prey as whalers (sea mammals) and fishermen (salmon). It is for this reason that the Basques inhabiting the coastline of the Bay of Biscay, probably the first Europeans to hunt whales commercially (Roberts 2014), labeled orcas *asesina-ballenas*, that is, *whale-killers* or killers of whales (Neiwert 2015). The term was wrongly translated into English as *killer whales*—suggesting a serial killer of all sorts of prey—a version that fitted well with orcas' reputation in Western mythology and, in the process, the interests of their competitors; that is, fishermen and whalers, both in need of justification for their gratuitous slaughter. In the past century, Neiwert (2015, 103) recalls that in Canada "fishermen in the Northwest frequently brought rifles along in their boats for the specific purpose of shooting at killer whales should they encounter them, both out of fear and out of a belief the 'voracious' orcas were competing with them for salmon." The threat fishermen perceived to their livelihood turned into the perception of a threat to their lives, even though orca attacks on fishermen in the wild were, and still are, almost unknown.

During the twentieth century, fishermen's concern regarding economic losses, and therefore their animosity towards orcas, was transferred to governments. In Norway, "it was feared that killer whales were decimating herring stocks, so the government encouraged hunting of the species by whalers, even subsidizing this hunt in some years. Between 1938 and 1980, an average of 57 killer whales were taken each year" (Ford et al 2000, 12). Ford et al. also report how in 1960 pressure applied to the Canadian government by sport-fishing lodges on Vancouver Island led to the Federal Fisheries Department developing a program to reduce the number of killer whales by shooting them from a land-based machine gun. Fortunately, the whales had moved out of the area by the time the culling program was about to begin. Viewing orcas as competitors for salmon in the Vancouver region, whether for industrial or sports fishing, is not devoid of irony, given how human populations have overfished, blocked rivers, and destroyed salmon habitat in that region and throughout the globe over recent centuries.

This negative reputation awarded to orcas due to the fishing industry seeing them as competitors for resources remained intact until late into the second half of the twentieth century, when the economic interests of a more contemporary industry—marine parks with captive orcas—promoted an image of orcas as "cuddly water-going pandas" (Neiwert 2015, 117). Neither the old narrative nor the new were true. However, it was precisely orcas' lack of aggressiveness towards humans in the wild that allowed for their capture, imprisonment, and training to perform in the billion-dollar business of the new marine circuses.

THE BUSINESS OF *AQUAPRISONS*

Aquatic zoos or *aquaprisons,* as they are referred to by Dunayer (2001)— also advertised as aquariums, oceanariums, or marine parks by the industry—first flourished in the United States in the late 1930s when Florida-based businessmen discovered that dolphins could be trained to perform stunts. By the 1950s, shows featuring dolphins had spread across the country, and from 1960 onwards, they reached Europe and the rest of the world. These spectacles were not limited to exhibiting marine animals but also forced them to perform like a circus act, an activity unambiguously driven by profit under the pretext of providing entertainment for families. The success of such shows at this time was strongly tied to the media campaign for dolphins promoted by the 1963 *Flipper* movie and subsequent *Flipper* television series, as well as the lack of legislation and concern for the lives of the captured animals during those times.

At first, the dolphin industry had not considered exploiting whales, even smaller ones such as orcas, but in 1964 an orca captured by an artist who had been commissioned to make a statue of one by the British Columbia government, who barely survived three months in captivity, turned into a media sensation. Moby Doll, as she was named, was probably the first orca to receive positive press in the media, and massive public attention triggered a demand for orcas among aquarium owners. The story of how the business of hunting orcas developed from this moment on is explained in full detail by Neiwert (2015).

Interestingly, prior to Moby Doll, another captured orca had been exhibited in the United States in 1961. She was called Wanda and was found disoriented in Newport Harbor, California. Although she died soon after being put in a concrete tank (apparently she was already ill when captured), her captors at Marineland saw a potential business exhibiting orcas and tried to hunt another individual in the months following her death. The difficulties involved in capturing these cetaceans led to the idea being abandoned, and the business, therefore, did not start at that time simply because humans had not yet discovered how benign orcas are. Once they did, and orcas' intelligence and learning capacity were revealed to us, the business took off with the help of a bunch of unscrupulous greedy entrepreneurs who mastered orca hunting and a few aquarium owners ready to take advantage of the fascination these magnificent creatures evoke in humans.

Although marine zoos had captured and bred other sea mammals over previous decades, orcas quickly became the main attraction of the aquariums exhibiting them. Due to this, parks decided to use them as one of their primary advertising strategies, as evidenced in many of their logos.

However, there is clear evidence that orcas in marine parks have always endured a very difficult life since the business first began. Orcas die very prematurely in captivity, having a radically lower life-span than in the wild (Jett and Ventre 2015). This is because in captivity they suffer from a high rate of lethal respiratory infections and severe dental problems, the former mostly due to the pools' water conditions, the latter to their tendency to chew on metal gates and concrete tanks out of boredom and anxiety (Rose 2011). The shallowness of orca tanks also forces them to spend a lot of time at the surface, which leads to prolonged exposure to ultraviolet rays, causing sunburn and retinal damage (Jett and Ventre 2011). Furthermore, there is also a high rate of aberrant behavior among captive orcas who are forced to engage in unnatural behavior, including aggressiveness towards other orcas in captivity and humans—both extremely rare in the "wild." In fact, the only instances of humans being injured or killed by orcas have occurred in captivity. Not to put too fine a point on it, all the years of holding orcas in captivity have clearly demonstrated something that should be common sense: orcas cannot cope with being kidnapped, separated from their families and spending their entire life confined in tiny concrete pools (where, moreover, they are mixed with orcas from disparate social groups). Nor, in the case of orcas born in captivity, do they endure living in such conditions from birth. These extremely social, cultural, and intelligent animals are severely physically and psychologically sickened in aquaprisons, as the documentary *Blackfish* visibly revealed (Cowperthwaite 2013).

The main orca portrayed in *Blackfish*, Tilikum, was involved in the killing of three human beings between 1982 (when he was captured) and 2016. The last attack, which killed SeaWorld trainer Dawn Brancheau in 2010, was even recorded live and broadcasted across the world, generating great public commotion and some changes in regulations protecting trainers in the United States. However, the business has continued despite extensive scientific evidence regarding the miserable life we force these animals to live in captivity, the unnecessary to human risks resulting therefrom, and the increasing public opposition to these parks. The reason for prolonging the experiment of confining marine mammals in tiny concrete tanks can be reduced to one word: business. Despite the growing public sensitivity, the increased regulation, and the impact of the *Blackfish* documentary, 23 million people still visited SeaWorld parks alone in 2015.

In January 2016, there were at least 55 orcas in captivity across the world (46 on display and 9 awaiting exhibition in China) in at least 12 different parks. SeaWorld was by far the largest captor of orcas, with 29 in captivity (six of them on loan to Loro Parque, in Spain[3]) and $1.37 billion in revenues in 2015. The remaining 17 orcas were being exhibited by other companies in France, the United States, Canada, Japan, Argentina, and Russia at the beginning of 2016 (see Table 3.1).

According to the Whale and Dolphin Conservation Society, from 1961 to 2015 at least 150 orcas were captured in the wild, and at least 163 died in captivity (of which 127 were wild-captured), a figure which does not include around 30 miscarried or stillborn calves that died prematurely. An

Table 3.1 Captive Orcas Industry (January 2016)

Owner	Parks owned (year of birth) Visitors per year	Country	Total of orcas confined	Orcas who died in the parks since opening	Visitors per year (last available)	Revenues
Blackstone Group (private equity firm). (SeaWorld Entertainment Inc. is listed on the stock exchange.)	SeaWorld California (1964).	United States.	Corky 2 (wild-caught in 1969). Kasatka (wild-caught in 1978). Ulises (wild-caught in 1980). Orkid (born in captivity, 1988). Shouka (born in captivity, 1993). Keet (born in captivity, 1993). Nakai (born in captivity, 2001). Ikaika (born in captivity, 2002) Kalia (born in captivity, 2004) Makani (born in captivity, 2013) Amaya (born in captivity, 2014)	16	w	SeaWorld Entertainment Inc. (2015) $1.37 B.
	SeaWorld Florida (1973).	United States.	Katina (wild-caught in 1978). Tilikum (wild-caught in 1983). Kayla (born in captivity, 1988). Trua (born in captivity, 2005). Nalani (born in captivity, 2006). Malia (born in captivity, 2007). Makaio (born in captivity, 2010).	12		
	SeaWorld Texas (1988).	United States.	Takara (born in captivity, 1991). Kyuquot (born in captivity, 1991). Tuar (born in captivity, 1999). Sakari (born in captivity, 2010). Kamea (born in captivity, 2013).	9		

Owner	Facility	Country	Orcas	No.	Revenue	Park revenue
Wolfgang Kiessling (private owner).	Loro Parque (1972).	Spain.	Keto (born in captivity, 1995). Tekoa (born in captivity, 2000). Kohana (born in captivity, 2002). Skyla (born in captivity, 2004). Adan (born in captivity, 2010). Morgan (wild-caught in 2010).	1	1 M.	Loro Parque €62 M.
Parques Reunidos (a Spanish-founded amusement park group owned by British investment funds).	Marineland Antibes (1970).	France.	Inouk (born in captivity, 1999). Wikie (born in captivity, 2001). Moana (born in captivity, 2011). Keijo (born in captivity, 2013).	8	1.2 M.	Parques Reunidos total revenue (2014): €0.5 M.
	Miami Seaquarium (1955).	United States.	Lolita (wild-caught in 1970).	1	0.5 M.	
John Holer (private owner).	Marineland Ontario (1961).	Canada.	Kiska (wild-caught in 1981).	17	1.2 M.	-
Granvista Hotels & Resorts (private company).	Kamogawa SeaWorld (1970).	Japan.	Lovey ((born in captivity, 1988). Luna (born in captivity, 2012). Lara (born in captivity, 2001). Earth (born in captivity, 2008).	11	-	-
Nagoya Port Foundation (public aquarium).	Port of Nagoya Aquarium (1992).	Japan.	Stella (wild-caught in 1987). Ran 2 (born in captivity, 2006). Rin (born in captivity, 2012).	2	-	-

(continued)

Table 3.1 Captive Orcas Industry (January 2016) (continued)

Owner	Parks owned (year of birth) Visitors per year	Country	Total of orcas confined	Orcas who died in the parks since opening	Visitors per year (last available)	Revenues
Fundación Mundo Marino (private foundation).	Acuario Mundo Marino (1987).	Argentina.	Kshamenk (wild-caught in 1978).	3	-	-
God Nisanov & Zarakh Iliev (Russian billionaire property developers).	Mosquarium (2015).	Russia.	Narnia (wild-caught in 2012). Nord (wild-caught in 2013). Juliet (wild-caught in 2014).	-	-	-
Chimelong Group (private conglomerate, leader in China's tourism industry).	Chimelong Park (2014).	China.	9 imported; none on display in March 2016 (all wild-caught between 2012–16).	-	-	-

Source: Parks' websites, annual accounts, WDC 2016.

undetermined number of orcas have been born in captivity since 1985 (World and Dolphin Conservation Society 2016).

Regulatory changes have triggered several restructurings of the industry. U.S. authorities banned the capturing of orcas in their waters in 1972,[4] resulting in the business moving to Iceland. The EU also prohibited the wild capture of cetaceans from EU waters and the import of wild-caught cetaceans for commercial purposes at the end of the last century.[5] Cetaceans have still been imported in both cases, ostensibly for education or research purposes, although these individuals have also been displayed in commercial dolphinaria despite neither the United States nor the EU issuing a permit for transferring a "wild orca" to a marine park since 1989. A number of other countries have also banned the capture of orcas, and several have banned keeping dolphins in captivity or introduced such strict regulations that no one is able to meet them. Furthermore, a few countries have banned the captivity of all cetaceans (Costa Rica) or all animals in exhibitions (Bolivia). However, these increasing legal barriers did not bring an end to the industry, but rather made it focus its energies on captive breeding, therefore only adding further reasons for concern over this business.

The ban on capturing orcas in Europe and North America meant that they suddenly became even more valuable to the parks based there—not just because of the limitations restrictions placed on the supply of "wild orcas" but also because of breeding programs, which turned captive males into priceless semen producers.[6] The aim of these programs was to spawn a surplus of animals that could be shipped back and forth between parks, whenever necessary, with no intention of ever releasing them to the wild, yet the genetic pool of captive orcas is very limited, and the breeding programs have, therefore, already resulted in heavy inbreeding (Cronin 2014). Furthermore, marine parks impregnate females at too early an age, a very disturbing practice that literally means raping adolescents due to the fact that artificial insemination is common business. Thus, although captures in the wild ended for these parks, the ethics of keeping orcas in captivity actually worsened during the same period.

In addition, the capturing of orcas in other regions is still far from over. Between 2012 and 2016, at least 15 orcas were captured in the Sea of Okhotsk. The high prices Russian and Chinese parks are willing to pay for an orca are well known to fishermen and poachers in the region (The Dolphin Project 2015). This does not apply only to orcas: 81 beluga whales were caught in the Sea of Okhotsk in 2013 alone. Thirty-four more were believed to have died as a result of the capture operation, and seven died in temporary holding tanks, according to a 2014 paper presented to the Scientific Committee of the International Whaling Commission in Bled, Slovenia (Gilman 2015). Meanwhile, in the West, SeaWorld's profits and share price have been in clear decline since 2013, the year of the release of *Blackfish* (see Table 3.2).

Table 3.2   SeaWorld Entertainment Inc.—Financial Data (in U.S. $)

	2010	2011	2012	2013	2014	2015
Net revenue	1.20 B	1.33 B	1.42 B	1.46 B	1.38 B	1.37 B
Net income	−45.46 M	14.79 M	74.22 M	51.92 M	49.91 M	49.13 M
Stock price (Last in the year) (1)	-	-	-	28.77	17.90	19.69

(1) SeaWorld Entertainment Inc. began trading on the New York Stock Exchange on April 19, 2013, with a ticker symbol of SEAS.

Sources: SeaWorld SEC 10-K Fillings and Yahoo-Finance.com

There can be no doubt that the cruel industry of aquaprisons is first and foremost a big business based on entertaining the masses. The nature of this business is even clearer if we look at the ownership of some of the largest companies: SeaWorld, Marineland Antibes, and Miami Seaquarium were owned by investment funds in 2016 and the remaining parks, notably the new Russian and Chinese ones, by billionaires or private conglomerates built on property and tourism (see Table 3.1). The story these parks have disseminated about themselves in recent times as being research and education facilities is at odds not only with the reality of the inmates confined in their tanks and cages but also with the nature of the parks' owners, mostly businessmen and speculators. How is it that entertainment facilities clearly promoted by capitalist elites who force "wild animals" into slavery have been able to survive for so long?

OF ADVERTISING, PUBLIC RELATIONS, AND LOBBYING

Of course, the answer to the above question is rooted in the ideological conditioning that marine zoos have consistently created to obtain social rationalization and legitimization for their actions. When they were first opened, these aquariums did not conceal their exclusive aim of making profit from animal shows and exhibitions, yet public sensitivity and regulation progressively forced them to mask entertainment behind a veil of education and scientific research, despite the business—that of exploiting public interest in marine mammals and particularly orcas (as well as the self-indulgence of the masses) to make money—remaining unaltered. Since 2013, however, the industry has been forced to invest more in advertising and public relations to convince the public that their activities are innocuous, belying the dramatic lessons we have learnt in the last three decades regarding both orcas in captivity and in the wild.

The public image of orcas has not remained purely in the hands of aquariums, however. Hollywood has also helped to reshape the reputation of orcas from vicious killers to marine pandas through at least three films that portray a meaningful transformation of their image: *Namu, the Killer Whale* (Benedek 1966), *Orca: The Killer Whale* (Anderson 1977), and *Free Willy* (Wincer 1993). *Namu, the Killer Whale* was the first time that orcas were depicted as not only benign but also smart. The starring orca was one of the first to be captured, and the name Namu was also later used as a show-name for different orcas in SeaWorld shows. *Orca: The Killer Whale*, despite being a terribly low-quality movie, also portrayed orcas as intelligent, even moral, beings, while *Free Willy* sent out the message of captivity being negative for orcas back at the beginning of the 1990s.

The impact of Hollywood films on the industry is unknown, yet from the 1990s onward, all aquariums adopted the traditional strategy of zoological parks to build an image of themselves as great contributors to education, conservation, science, and research in order to justify keeping "wild animals" in captivity. Some of the parks, including the largest players in the market, launched foundations or research centers to strengthen this profile, for instance: Fundación Mundo Marino (1987), Loro Parque Fundación (1994), Foundation Marineland (1998), SeaWorld & Busch Gardens Conservation Fund (2003), or Fundación Parques Reunidos (2011). A closer look at the parks' websites in 2016 showed how far this had gone over the years: education and research saturate every element and are sometimes stressed at an even higher level than entertainment, while words like *endangered species, conservation, rescue, rehabilitation, love, respect,* and *care* are ubiquitous on the majority of these websites. It is revealing that the word *captivity* did not appear one single time in SeaWorld's 2014 annual accounts, while *care*—referring to the animals forced to live in its three parks—appeared up to 32 times. Thus, rather than having orcas in captivity, SeaWorld refers to this as having orcas under *human care,* a blatant display of how marketing and advertising have redefined concepts by using language as a tool for masking reality.

Since the 1970s, the aquarium industry has also intensively created different trade organizations and lobby groups to protect its interests. The European Association for Aquatic Mammals (EAAM) was created in 1972. It was followed in 1992 by the European Association of Zoos and Aquariums (EAZA) and the Alliance of Marine Mammal Parks and Aquariums (AMMPA), the latter under the leadership of the most powerful stakeholder in the industry, SeaWorld.[7] It is interesting to note how the language these organizations use has completely suppressed the reality suffered by the marine animals they exploit—that of captivity and exhibition—to focus on the alleged interest they hold for humans—discovering and enjoying the animals on display—as well as conservation and research. For instance, on the 2016 AMMPA website (http://www.ammpa.org), the lobby group defines itself as an international association representing organizations "dedicated to the highest standards of care for marine mammals and to their conservation in the wild through public education, scientific study, and wildlife presentations." On the same page, the lobby group states that it collectively "represents the greatest body of experience and knowledge about marine mammal care and husbandry." Suppression of the captive reality is notable in the lobby group's narrative, in spite of the fact that the whole justification for its purpose is based on the problems caused by captivity itself. AMMPA also defines itself as an organization "dedicated to the concerns and issues that affect the public display of marine mammals." The orca factsheet on AMMPA's website even adjusts the facts to suit captivity regulations. AMMPA maintains that orcas in the wild and in marine aquaprisons have the same longevity, disregarding the well-known fact that orcas live longer in the wild, where they can survive for several more decades free from the diseases developed in captivity (Jett and Ventre 2015). Reframing the reality of nonhuman animals in parks by means of the education-research-caring tactic has been the main aim of the industry's lobby groups since their creation.

It should be acknowledged that the educational and scientific transformation depicted in the parks' public image is not devoid of truth. Most aquariums are involved in the rehabilitation of "wild animals" and research.[8] However, they also conduct invasive research projects aimed at furthering knowledge about marine animals mostly for human interests. These projects are at the very least controversial due to the fact that they can be seen as rather sterile in terms of species protection and very harmful in terms of the well-being of the individuals involved. The most serious drawbacks of research conducted by aquariums are: (1) the fact that these programs can in no way address the real causes of the problems "wild animals" endure— that is, the growth of the human population, which is decimating ocean life and increasingly polluting the water with waste—and of course (2) that they cannot morally justify keeping sentient beings in captivity (let alone forcing them to exhibit and perform). Furthermore, there is a lack of evidence for the educational effects of zoos. Studies have actually shown the opposite, that is, the serious obstacles to obtaining meaningful learning from zoos (Marino et al. 2010). These ethical contradictions have proven to be too blatant, and the industry's science- and education-washing strategy has not been able to prevent a second wave of public attention to orcas, this time much more aggressive.

This new wave of hostile public attention started in 2012 with David Kirby's book, *Death at SeaWorld*; this was followed by the *Blackfish* documentary (2013), Sandra Pollard's book *Puget Sound Whales for Sale* (2014), David Neiwert's *Of Orcas and Men* (2015), and Johan Hargrove's *Beneath the Surface* (2015), all of which focused on revealing the dark side of the industry and the captivity business. Simultaneously, an endless list of websites protesting orcas in captivity and marine parks emerged promoted by animal activists, former trainers, animal protection organizations, and concerned individuals.[9] This time the industry, led by SeaWorld, did not limit itself to defense via the science-washed image but went on the attack. SeaWorld was itself the focus of *Blackfish* and reacted angrily to the documentary by launching an unprecedented advertising campaign in the traditional media and through its websites. This included a new SeaWorldcares.com site, which opposed the "lies" portrayed in the documentary and provided the "truth about *Blackfish*," labeled as "propaganda." The campaign, which was said to have spent $10 million on marketing (Titlow 2015), offered news media a list of eight points to rebut the film's content. A quick review of these points makes it easy to agree with Neiwert (2015, 127) when he states that "in reality, [they] were all distortions or factually false themselves, including the assertion that we don't really know how long orcas live in the wild." For instance, SeaWorld claimed that it does not separate mothers from their calves, which is only true if one defines a calf as one-year-old or younger, as SeaWorld does.

After the science and education rebranding and the verbal belligerence of the campaign against *Blackfish*, the SeaWorld public relations team adopted a third tactic, a sort of "let's join the public outcry" for orcas. It was, however, conveniently redefined to adapt to SeaWorld's needs. In 2015 and 2016, the company announced plans to phase out performances by orcas and breeding programs, and orcas would from then on be exhibited in new tanks allowing for more "natural behavior." The reason put forward for this was that the company "needed to move where society was moving" (Kay, Schneider and AP 2016). This tactic expanded on the core message from its previous campaigns of "we also care" in an attempt to look as if SeaWorld was adapting to the terms of the public outcry. Yet this tactic left its main strategy unaltered—continuing to exploit orcas for economic reasons—and concealed the fact that concrete tanks, regardless of improvements, can never provide a natural environment for orcas. Furthermore, the public relations tactic of "we also care" has always been at odds with the industry's much less visible lobbying actions. While the industry's public relations and advertising campaigns persistently appeal to its commitment to the well-being of the marine mammals confined in its parks, it has simultaneously been lobbying hard against any regulation trying to improve the life of orcas in captivity and, most importantly, against liberating them. AMMPA, in particular, has focused from the beginning on proving the impossibility of successfully liberating an orca into the wild even in the face of excellent results, as was the case with Keiko in 2002. Keiko was an outstanding example of how not to liberate a captive orca (without identifying her home pod and giving her a real chance to reunite with her family) and at the same time was successful in spite of the tragic ending (she was clearly happier in the open ocean but died the following year from a lung infection common in captive orcas). The role of the aquariums' lobbying in this episode, determined as they were to prove that the Keiko experiment was a failure in spite of the clear improvement in the orca's quality of life, is explained in detail by Neiwert (2015, 208–220).

The public relations campaigns also conceal the fact that the industry has not made a single change on its own. Cruel orca-capture techniques were banned in the United States, as was the import of animals captured in the wild in North America and the European Union,[10] and the exhibitions and breeding programs had been made increasingly difficult by legislation,[11] let alone the pressure of activists and, more recently, of some news media with increasingly well informed journalists. In the meantime, the single real act that would show a true commitment to the orcas and other marine mammals in confinement—liberation—has been systematically opposed and hindered by the industry.

ENTANGLEMENTS OF OPPRESSION

Zoological parks emerged in the early nineteenth century to exhibit the living trophies of imperial conquest. In the beginning, they displayed human and nonhuman animals, demonstrating how connected imperialism was to racism and speciesism. Zoos eventually stopped exhibiting members of our own species in cages and rebranded themselves as main actors in species preservation and public education, yet both are fallacies that research and common sense have already unveiled. As Marino, Bradshaw, and Malamud (2009, 25, 27) put it, "by definition, confinement subordinates its captives and gives the viewer complete power over them . . . We are out here; they are in there" while "a zoo filled with empty cages might be a more realistic way to convey the impending loss of species." Even worse, the message sent out by zoos of any kind is that captivity is normal, concealing the fact that forced confinement is cruel and forced exhibition simple slavery.

As has been evidenced throughout this chapter, the human abuse of orcas perfectly exemplifies the three factors of the theory of oppression: they were first seen as competitors for resources and demonized, then exploited for economic interests as fascinating majestic beings, and communication tactics were used by the elites to manufacture consent for both narratives. Beyond the elites, however, other human beings have also suffered the consequences of our immoral treatment of other species, like whalers—once seen as the worst profession in the world—or orca trainers—who not only risk their lives with these large marine mammals in their tanks but also endure many of the problems that orcas face by spending so much time in intensively chemically treated waters.

Humans are not speciesist, per se; rather interests (mostly economic) make us so. The situation is, therefore, reversible and can be undone at any time with huge benefits for all. As the lobby groups clearly see and panic about, acknowledging that orcas must be liberated will automatically lead society to realize that all captive animals in zoos and aquariums should not be there.

At the time of writing this chapter, the two oldest orcas in captivity are females, Corky and Lolita, having achieved the heartbreaking records of spending 46 and 45 years in a concrete tank, respectively. Corky currently lives in SeaWorld San Diego with several other orcas, and although she has given birth many times, none of her offspring have survived in captivity. Lolita has been living in the Miami Seaquarium since she was captured and is the last surviving whale from the bloody Puget Sound captures of the 1960s and 1970s, the hunting episode that laid the foundations for the captive-orca industry. Lolita is living in the smallest orca pool in North America and has been alone with a few dolphins in her tank since 1980, when Hugo, her male partner, died of a brain aneurysm after years of routinely slamming his head into the walls of the pool.

Both Corky and Lolita are perfect candidates for release, since their home pods in the wild are well known. Once the tactics of manufacturing consent for this cruel industry are visible and no longer accepted, zoos and marine parks have the unique opportunity to fully and ethically reshape their business. The use of digital media allows for the best substitute of real nonhuman animals for educational purposes, while conservation efforts can focus on the protection and restoration of wild habitats, not keeping alive inmates in completely unnatural conditions. Of course, the industry will sooner or later have to take responsibility and show true love and care by releasing its captives into sea pen sanctuaries where they can either be rehabilitated and returned to the ocean or, at the very least, spend the rest of their lives in a setting that is as close as possible to the open ocean.[12]

NOTES

1. For further information, see the U.S. Navy Marine Mammal Program: http://www.public.navy.mil/spawar/Pacific/71500/Pages/default.aspx.

2. Orcas have been seen feeding other members of their groups suffering from problems, taking care of each other, waiting for slower members, and taking care of other species (Neiwert 2015).

3. Recognizing the need for crowd control in their tanks, SeaWorld entered into a financial agreement with Loro Parque to send them their "excess orcas" on breeding loan.

4. The U.S. Marine Mammal Protection Act (MMPA) of 1972 made it illegal to hunt or harass marine mammals in the United States.

5. The Habitats Directive (92/43/EEC) prevents the wild capture of cetaceans from EU waters, and EC Regulation 338/97 prohibits imports of wild-caught cetaceans for commercial purposes.

6. SeaWorld insured Tilikum for several million dollars for this reason (CBS News, 2010).

7. Many other international and regional umbrella professional organizations lobby for aquariums' interests, including WAZA (the World Association of Zoos and Aquariums), AZA (the Association of Zoos and Aquariums), BIAZA (the British and Irish Association of Zoos and Aquariums), ZAA (the Zoo and Aquarium Association), JAZA (the Japanese Association of Zoos and Aquariums), and SEAZA (the South East Asia Zoos Association).

8. It is worth noting that this is all but compulsory by law in the European Union, where a directive introduced in 1999 to strengthen the conservation role of zoos made it a statutory requirement that zoos participate in conservation and education.

9. Some active examples in March 2016 were: savelolita.org, orcahome.de, orca network.org, orcaresearch.org, marinelandindepth.com, orcaaware.org, orcaunited .com, facebook.com/ontariocaptiveanimalwatch, theorcaproject.wordpress.com, miamiseaprison.com, www.freemorgan.org, seaworldofhurt.com.

10. For a description of the methods used by the whalers, see Hoyt (1992).

11. For instance, SeaWorld's announcement of stopping its breeding programme in March 2016 followed the response in October 2015 by the California Coastal Commission to approve plans for a new, expanded orca habitat only if the theme park agreed to end the captive breeding of orcas.

12. Tilikum, the orca whale mentioned earlier in the chapter who was exploited by Seaworld, died on 6 January 2017 while this book was being prepared for publication, after three decades of confinement.

REFERENCES

Blackfish. 2013. Directed by Gabriela Cowperthwaite. United States: CNN Films and Manny O. Productions. Film.

CBS News. 2010. "SeaWorld Called Best Place for Tilikum." Accessed on March 30, 2016, from http://www.cbsnews.com/news/seaworld-called-best-place-for -tilikum/.

Cronin, Melissa. 2014. "5 Reasons Why SeaWorld's Orca Breeding Program Is Seriously Bad News." The Dodo, April 30. Accessed on March 30, 2016, from: https://www.thedodo.com/5-reasons-why-seaworlds-orca-b-531056663.html.

Diebel, Linda. 2012. "Marineland: Readers, Activists Demand Change Regarding Care of Sea Mammals." Thestar.com. Accessed on March 30, 2016, from http://www.thestar.com/news/canada/2012/08/25/marineland_readers _activists_demand_change_regarding_care_of_sea_mammals.html.

Ford, John K. B., Graeme M. Ellis, Craig O. Matkin, Michael H. Wetklo, Lance G. Barrett-Lennard, and Ruth E. Withler. 2011. "Shark Predation and Tooth

Wear in a Population of Northeastern Pacific Killer Whales." *Aquatic Biology*, 11: 213–24.

Ford, John K. B., Graeme M. Ellis, and Kenneth C. 2000. *Killer Whales*. Vancouver, Canada: UBC Press.

Free Willy. 1993. Directed by Simon Wincer. United States: Le Studio Canal, Regency Enterprises, Alcor Films.

Gilman, Azure. 2015. "Orca Capture Trade Has Moved to Russia, China, Activists Say." Al Jazeera America. Accessed on March 30, 2016, from http://america .aljazeera.com/articles/2015/11/14/captive-orca-trade-moves-to-russia -china.html.

Gramsci, Antonio. 1992. *Selections from the Prison Books*. New York, NY: International Publishers.

Hargrove, John. 2015. *Beneath the Surface: Killer Whales. SeaWorld, and the Truth Beyond Blackfish*. New York: St. Martin's Press.

Hoyt, Erich. 1992. *The Performing Orca—Why the Show Must Stop. An In-Depth Review of the Captive Orca Industry*. Plymouth, MA: Whale and Dolphin Conservation Society.

Jett, John, and Jeffrey Ventre. 2011. "Keto and Tilikum Express the Stress of Orca Captivity." Project Orca.

Jett, John, and Jeffrey Ventre. 2015. "Captive Killer Whale (Orcinus Orca) Survival." *Marine Mammal Science*, 31(4): 1362–377. Accessed on March 30, 2016, from https://theorcaproject.wordpress.com/2011/01/20/keto-tilikum-express -stress-of-orca-captivity/.

Kay, Jennifer, Mike Schneider, and Associated Press. 2016. "SeaWorld to Stop Breeding Orcas, Making Them Perform Tricks." ABC News. Accessed on March 30, 2016, from http://abcnews.go.com/Entertainment/wireStory /seaworld-end-killer-whale-breeding-program-37713306.

Kirby, David. 2012. *Death at SeaWorld. Shamu and the Dark Side of Killer Whales in Captivity*. New York: St. Martin's Press.

Marino, Lori, Gay Bradshaw, and Randi Malamud. 2009. "The Captivity Industry. The Reality of Zoos and Aquariums." *Best Friends Magazine*, 25–27.

Marino, Lori, Richard C. Connor, and Ewan R. Fordyce. 2007. "Cetaceans Have Complex Brains for Complex Cognition." *PLoS Biology*, e139. April/May. Accessed on March 30, 2016, from http://journals.plos.org/plosbiology /article?id=10.1371/journal.pbio.0050139.

Marino, Lori, Scott O. Lilienfeld, Randy Malamud, Nathan Nobis, and Ron Broglio. 2010. "Zoos and Aquariums Promote Attitude Change in Visitors? A Critical Evaluation of the American Zoo and Aquarium Study." *Society and Animals*, 18: 126–38.

Marion, Lori. 2011. "Brain Structure and Intelligence in Cetaceans." In Philippa Brakes and Mark Peter Simmonds (eds.), *Whales and Dolphins, Cognition, Culture, Conversation and Human Perceptions*. New York: Earthscan: 115–128.

Morton, Alexandra. 2004. *Listening to Whales: What the Orcas Have Taught Us*. New York: Ballantine Books.

Namu, the Killer Whale. 1966. Directed by Laszlo Benedek. United States: United Artists. Film.

Neiwert, David. 2015. *Of Orcas and Men. What Killer Whales Can Teach Us*. New York: Overlook Press.

Nibert, David. 2002. *Animal Rights/Human Rights: Entanglements of Oppression and Liberation*. Lanham, MD: Rowman & Littlefield.

Orca: The Killer Whale. 1977. Directed by Michael Anderson. United States: Paramount Pictures. Film.

Pollard, Sandra. 2014. *Puget Sound Whales for Sale: The Fight to End Orca Hunting*. Washington, DC: History Press.

Richards, John F. 2014. *The World Hunt. An Environmental History of the Commodification of Animals*. Los Angeles: University of California Press.

Ric O'Berry's Dolphin Project. 2015. "Trouble Brewing at Mosquarium." Accessed on March 30, 2016, from https://dolphinproject.net/blog/post/trouble-brewing-at-mosquarium.

Roberts, Callum. 2007. *The Unnatural History of the Sea*. Washington, DC: Island Press.

Rose, Naomi A. 2011. "Killer Controversy Why Orcas Should No Longer Be Kept in Captivity." Humane Society International and the Humane Society of the United States. Accessed on March 30, 2016, from http://www.hsi.org/assets/pdfs/orca_white_paper.pdf.

Titlow, John Paul. 2015. "SeaWorld Is Spending $10 Million To Make You Forget About 'Blackfish.'" *FastCompany*. April 8. Accessed on March 30, 2016, from http://www.fastcompany.com/3046342/seaworld-is-spending-10-million-to-make-you-forget-about-blackfish.

Whale and Dolphin Conservation Society. 2016. "The Fate of Captive Orcas." Accessed on March 30, 2016, from http://us.whales.org/wdc-in-action/fate-of-captive-orcas.

4

ZooBiz: The Conservation of Business?

Rob Laidlaw

The parking lot was massive, capable of accommodating many thousands of vehicles. Guests parked their cars and then walked to designated waiting areas to catch a shuttle all the way to the main gate. Upon disembarking from the shuttle, they encountered a line of people waiting to buy tickets. The line snaked its way away from the entrance, and I stood at the end of it. Approximately 30 minutes later, I reached the ticket booth and purchased a single-day pass for more than $100. After moving into another shorter line, my pass was checked, and I was at last allowed to enter Disney's Animal Kingdom Theme Park.

Throughout the years, I had heard a great deal about Animal Kingdom. It had routinely shown up on lists of the best zoos in the United States, so I was anxious to finally pay it a visit. I didn't know very much about the zoo, other than they had sent some elephants to a nearby facility called the National Elephant Center, and one of those elephants had died.

The last time I had visited anything Disney was decades ago during a family vacation in Florida when we spent a day at the original Disney Magic Kingdom theme park. The big attraction at the time was the brand-new Space Mountain ride, an indoor outer space-themed roller coaster. Today, there isn't just one Disney theme park in Orlando but several, and Animal Kingdom is the newest. A walkway from the entrance led me past several small "wildlife" displays and then over a bridge to Discovery Island and the

71

base of the Tree of Life, one of Animal Kingdom's most iconic features. A massive artificial sculpted tree 145 feet high and 50 feet wide at its base, the Tree of Life incorporates more than 300 nonhuman animal carvings on its trunk, branches, and roots. The structure is supposed to represent the diversity and interconnectedness of life on Earth. At its base were various live "wildlife" displays featuring flamingos, lemurs, and other living beings.

Beyond Discovery Island were the other main sections of the park—Africa, Rafiki's Planet Watch, Asia, and DinoLand USA. The first on my agenda was Africa. Africa's access point was Harambe, a simulation port town featuring architectural styles from different regions of Africa along with a conglomeration of food stands, restaurants, gift stores, and other outlets where visitors could purchase a variety of goods and services. Several African "wildlife" species could be viewed by following the visitor pathway to their respective cages and enclosures, but most required boarding a truck or train. For example, to view the dozens of savannah species, including elephants, rhinos, hippos, and lions in a subdivided 100-acre compound, visitors were required to board one of the Kilimanjaro Safari trucks, and, of course, there was a line-up.

The line moved slowly, and nearly 90 minutes elapsed before I was at the front ready to board a safari truck. There were so many people in line it was impossible to tell exactly how long it was because it snaked back and forth in irregular ways and was obscured by vegetation, a design strategy often used by amusement parks and other high-traffic facilities to interrupt customer sightlines and help create the impression that things are less crowded than they really are.

The safari trucks were packed with dozens of people, and as soon as one was full, off it went, and another pulled up. The trip into the savannah compound was choreographed, and the narration was simplistic and sometimes a bit corny, being primarily factoids interspersed with the odd joke here and there. It seemed that keeping people moving while at the same time being entertained was the primary concern, understandable because of the sheer volume of visitors, but it didn't allow for relaxed observation of the nonhuman animals. Each time the truck stopped, I barely had time to lift my camera to take a photo before it was on the move again.

The Asia section, called the Kingdom of Anandapur, consisted of two simulated villages, replica temples, monuments, ruins, and a fake mountain with the Expedition Everest ride, buffered by restaurants, food stands, and souvenir shops. Every nook and cranny seemed to provide yet another spending opportunity for visitors. Of course, here and there, real nonhuman animals could be viewed, such as the siamangs on a jungle island or tigers in a simulated temple ruin along the Maharajah Jungle Trek path. As I moved through the area, it almost seemed like the nonhuman animals were incidental to everything else, that the simulated villages, landscapes, and rides were the real attractions.

DinoLand USA was more of a children's amusement park with a dinosaur theme. There was a "prehistoric" midway and rides like the Triceratops Spin. It was a cacophony of movement and color set to a background of loud music. Nestled right in amongst it all was an American crocodile exhibit, presumably there because of the crocodile's somewhat dinosaur-like appearance.

Prior to my visit, I had heard good things about Animal Kingdom. I knew that the Disney theme parks were highly commercialized, but I was still surprised by what I encountered. To me it didn't seem like a zoo, at least not in the conventional sense of the word. It was an amusement park for kids and families, with a nonhuman animal component, and walking through Animal Kingdom seemed more like walking through an elaborate movie set than anything in the real world. The congestion and the noise were startling and something I had only rarely experienced in any other zoo or "wildlife" park anywhere, but what seemed most evident to me was that Animal Kingdom was making money. When I later discovered that the park had 10.4 million visitors in 2014 alone (Walt Disney World 2016), I realized the amount of money was considerable.

Disney's Animal Kingdom is a high-profile example of a private, for-profit zoological facility that, if the crowds were any indication, appeared to be very profitable. It's a capitalist entity, like other private zoos and aquariums, that has built its business and its brand over many years. My visit to Animal Kingdom got me thinking more about the role of capitalism, the free market, and commercialization in the world of zoos and aquariums and how it impacts the other nonhuman animals that are the foundation of this industry. My thoughts went far wider than just the most commercial, privately owned facilities because it seemed to me that a great many public zoos and aquariums are, to one degree or another, pursuing a capitalistic path of quasi-commercialization and the commodification of the nonhuman animals they depend on. That may be manifested in a variety of ways, including but not limited to the makeup of the live collections, how live "wildlife" is used, new attractions, and corporate partnerships. In exploring this topic, however, I also wanted to look at how zoos and aquariums support themselves, what they tell their supporters, how nonhuman animals are used, the conditions they experience, and what all this means for the nonhuman animals themselves.

When I started researching the subject of capitalism, I found entire books devoted to its various theories and philosophies, but for this examination of zoos and aquariums, I decided to choose a broad, simple definition of *capitalism*: an economic system in which a business or industry is controlled by private owners who control the factors of production (e.g., capital, land, and labor).[1] In looking at capitalist systems, synonymous with free market systems, involving industries that also use nonhuman animals, they are often nothing more than commodities with little value except in a monetary sense, and that can lead to normalization and acceptance of widespread cruelty and suffering.

There are many obvious examples, such as the trapping of "wild" nonhuman animals for their "fur." Each year, millions of free-living individuals are caught in antiquated leghold traps or snares, simply so the trapper, wholesaler, buyer, designer, and retailer can all make a profit. There isn't a pretense that trapping benefits "wildlife," although sometimes misleading arguments are presented about how trapping may regulate so-called overabundant species and prevent disease. It is an industry geared toward making a profit, and the nonhuman animal is merely a commodity in the process.

An even more obvious example is the use of nonhuman animals in food and agricultural industries and particularly in mass production, factory farm operations. It is now common knowledge that cows, pigs, chickens, and turkeys, to name just a few domesticated species, may often be incarcerated, sometimes for life, in tiny, barren spaces that spectacularly fail to satisfy their biological, behavioral, or social needs, leading to almost ubiquitous suffering. They may be kept indoors on unyielding concrete surfaces with no chance to run, walk, or even make normal postural adjustments such as standing up or turning around. They may be forced to eat monotonous foods, even their own waste or ground up members of their own species, and breathe putrid air, and because disease is ubiquitous, they may be filled with drugs to prevent catastrophic disease outbreaks. This situation, now endured by billions of nonhuman animals annually, is the result of private businesses maximizing their profits. Each time they decrease the size of space, cheapen the food, or do something else that saves them on production costs, it often means depriving each captive of something they need to ensure even a minimum quality of life.

While it may seem obvious that "fur" trapping or factory farms are manifestations of capitalism at its worst, at least when it comes to nonhuman animals, the effects of capitalism may not be as obvious in other industries, such as in zoos and in aquariums.

A suggestion could be made that many zoos and aquariums are not capitalist in the way that private, for-profit facilities are, primarily because they are publicly owned, and the people that operate them may be accountable, to some degree, to government agencies or officials, but after examining zoos and aquariums for the past three decades, I would suggest that a capitalist philosophy and free market[2] approach permeates much of the zoo and aquarium world; that they are, for all intents and purposes and out of perceived necessity, focused on generating revenue; that they increasingly commodify nonhuman animals and often cause them to suffer because of it.

It should be noted upfront that nearly all zoos and aquariums also claim to have other important nonfinancial goals, including conservation,[3] education, and research. For example, according to the Walt Disney Company website, "Conservation has been at the heart of Walt Disney Corporation since its inception." Between 1995 and 2013 the Disney "wildlife" Conservation Fund provided 1,000 grants totaling $24 million dollars to projects around the world (The Walt Disney Company 2013).

The reality for almost all major zoos and aquariums, however, is that they need to place considerable emphasis on the business side of their operations. They must generate sufficient revenue from wherever they can, on an ongoing basis, just to keep operating. Since zoos and aquariums are largely designed as entertainment facilities, it is no surprise that the most common source of income for the majority of them comes from visitors who pay an admission fee. In fact, many zoos generate 50 percent or more of their income from visitors (Grant 2011). Since visitors are so important to their bottom line, zoos and aquariums often adopt a customer-focused and often commercialized approach that involves trying to create fresh, new, and exciting things to keep people interested and coming. In large institutions, that can mean bigger, more expensive exhibits and attractions, which in turn mean bigger and more expensive facilities and operations that need all those visitors to keep coming just to stay afloat. In other words, the bigger zoos get, the greater their need. While visitors are vital to the financial sustainability of zoos and aquariums, other revenue generation vehicles must also be introduced because visitors are often not enough to keep the zoo machine running.

Zoos and aquariums recognize they are competing with other entertainment institutions and businesses and believe they must meet public expectations and demand for mass-market entertainment if they want people to keep coming (Grazian 2015, 173). But that perception can conflict with their stated nonfinancial objectives of conservation and education. Since zoos and aquariums see themselves as part of the leisure entertainment market and recognize that most of their visitors attend for little more than an enjoyable day out, the conflict can manifest itself in facilities downplaying the severity and urgency of the "wildlife" and environmental crises, so as not to alienate visitors (or existing or potential corporate sponsors, some of whom may directly or indirectly contribute to endangerment and extinction of "wildlife" species). When you are out for a nice family day, discomforting, reality-based conservation messaging is a downer. That's why if you walk through almost any major zoo you'll find vague statements about endangered species in far off places and simple, noncontroversial, throwaway factoids about how to help, like recycle your cellphone, wash your clothes in cold water, or drive your car less. Perhaps not surprisingly, zoos and aquariums are increasingly engaged in efforts to make zoo and aquarium visits even more fun and exciting for visitors, with further sanitizing of conservation messaging. You can see this manifested in both private and public zoos. In fact, it would be reasonable to say that many facilities appear to be devolving into purely entertainment, mass market, amusement park-type venues with shows, rides, concerts, light shows, kid's camps, after-hours events, gift stores selling junk, and lots more. The rule seems to be stay safe, avoid controversies, and don't do anything that might alienate your support base. Despite claims to the contrary, that is not a strategy for conserving "wildlife," but a strategy for economic sustainability.

NUMBERS AND GOVERNANCE

While no one can provide an exact number of zoos and aquariums in the world today, it is thought to be about 10,000, with some 1,200 facilities being core, professional zoos or aquariums which are, or have the potential to be, members of recognized zoo federations or associations (The Zoo Inquiry 1994, 11).

Zoos and aquariums represent a broad range of ownership structures that, for the most part, are either publicly owned and controlled or privately owned and controlled. While the numbers of each can vary considerably from region to region and country to country, in North America, estimates place the number of privately operated zoos at as high as 75 percent (Kenny 2012). In the United Kingdom, 90 percent of zoos are privately owned, while in Germany, about 90 percent are publicly owned (Sheridan 2011, 86).

There may also be variance within each category. For example, public zoos may be operated directly by a municipality or a regional or national government agency or alternatively by a publicly controlled company. Private zoos may be independent, for-profit businesses or nonprofit companies, family owned, or operated by a zoological society or similar entity.

Of course, zoos and aquariums come in a variety of sizes and formats. They sit on a continuum from tiny, mom-and-pop operations to massive public institutions, and within that continuum, nonhuman animal housing and care conditions may range from poor to adequate.

VISITORS MEAN SUSTAINABILITY

Zoos and aquariums of all sizes and types rely on visitors for economic sustainability. In addition to paying an entry fee, visitors may also pay for parking, stroller rentals, food, gifts, shows, rides, feeding sessions, photos, and special tours. The greater the number of visitors, the greater the revenue, and that's why so many zoos seem focused on maintaining or increasing the number of people who come through their gates and in adopting a cus-tomer service approach. Already many major zoos boast of annual visitor numbers in the hundreds of thousands or millions. For example, in 2012, the modest-sized Calgary Zoo received more than 1.3 million visitors,

(Calgary Zoo 2012), while the London Zoo received 1.265 million visitors in 2015 (Association of Leading Visitor Attractions 2015).

From what I saw, Disney's Animal Kingdom seemed to effectively exploit the fundraising potential of their many millions of visitors by providing a wide variety of spending opportunities on site, as do some other zoos as well. The San Diego Zoo and Safari Park, operated by the nonprofit Zoological Society of San Diego, provides a multitude of onsite shopping and food opportunities, as well as special tours that involve additional fees on top of the zoo's rather hefty $50 one-day adult pass ($40 for children). Tours range from the $50 Cheetah Safari to the eight-hour $999 Ultimate Safari, advertised as "your key to off-exhibit areas, animal interaction, and the very best in personalized service" (San Diego Zoo 2016).

Many zoos and aquariums also solicit individual charitable donations, both on site and remotely, or grants from charitable foundations. These funding sources are generally restricted to zoos and aquariums that are already nonprofit or charitable or that have an ancillary support organization that is, since donors often want a charitable tax receipt when they contribute.

KEEPING THE VISITORS COMING

Other strategies that zoos often employ include mega exhibits, special "wildlife" features (such as white lions or giant pandas), rides and amusement park-like attractions, and special events.

Mega Exhibits

Zoos and aquariums spend substantial funds on new attraction exhibits and exhibit complexes that they hope will increase visitor numbers. These "attraction exhibits" often seem more focused on creating a better visitor experience than on providing enhanced space and conditions for the nonhuman animals they contain. The zoo world is littered with these artificial landscapes that only superficially resemble the natural environments inhabited by free-roaming "wildlife." One example is the relatively new Journey to Churchill arctic exhibit at the Assiniboine Park Zoo in Winnipeg, Canada, which I visited in 2014 and 2015.

Reportedly constructed at a cost of more than $45 million, the exhibit complex is the first phase of the zoo's planned $200 million redevelopment (Kusch 2011). At approximately 10 acres in size, Journey to Churchill sounds large (and, for a zoo, it is a rather sizeable exhibit complex), but a substantial amount of space isn't allocated to the nonhuman animals at all. Visitor pathways, viewing stations, galleries, washrooms, bleachers, concession areas, a movie theater, children's play areas, a facsimile of the Town of

Churchill with a gift store and 200 seat Tundra Grill restaurant, keeper service areas, gardens, planted buffer regions, and other such features and infrastructure, consume a substantial portion of that purported 10 acres. Looking at the exhibit map, I guessed that only half or perhaps even a bit less of the exhibit complex's space was actually allocated to the "wildlife," and even that was subdivided into several enclosures and off-exhibit pens in another part of the complex.

Mega-exhibits don't come cheap. The Dallas Zoo's elephant exhibit came in at $32 million (Grant 2011), while the LA Zoo's came in at more than $40 million (Bartholomew 2010). Even temporary exhibits can be costly. Giant panda exhibits generally run about $5 million (Grant 2011) or, in some cases, more, even though they will only house the bears during the term of the loan agreement. In April 2016, media reported that the Calgary Zoo, who will be receiving four pandas from the Toronto Zoo in 2018 as part of their joint panda rental agreement, announced that their panda facility was projected to cost more than $16 million, and they hoped to get half of that from the provincial government (CBC 2016).

In 2010, I collected news items describing new capital projects in zoos, most of them new mega-exhibits for specific species or taxa, such as penguins, great apes, and elephants. In just one month, the total amount for zoo-based capital projects exceeded $1.213 billion dollars, and those were just the ones I learned about. Assuming a significant number of those projects came to fruition, they represent a massive expenditure of time, energy, and resources to house a relatively tiny number of captives.

Zoos claim these kinds of capital projects are necessary and important for conservation and education and are not just there to attract visitors. About their Journey to Churchill exhibit, the Assiniboine Park Zoo says, ". . . visitors experience a variety of naturalistic landscapes and animal viewing areas. Interpretive signage and interactive displays invite visitors to learn about biodiversity, climate change and conservation. It is an educational classroom like no other, inviting exploration, challenging thinking and promoting personal action" (Assiniboine Park Zoo 2015). Lofty claims, but do they have any basis in reality? Zoos say they do, but zoo critics say the new "attraction exhibits" are just that—attractions. Often after a year or two or three, the novelty factor wears off, the new is no longer the new, and zoos and aquariums have to come up with the next big attraction to keep the visitors coming.

Special "Wildlife" Features

Probably the most common special "wildlife" features are babies. Since modern zoos began, it seems that babies, of both common and endangered species, have been valued because they attract visitors. Clearly babies are seen as good for business, and zoos promote them at every available opportunity. While I was writing this chapter, the Toronto Zoo was asking city residents to come out to see a new baby rhino, a polar bear, two African penguin chicks, and two panda cubs (Toronto Zoo 2016). On their New at the Zoo website page, Utah's Hogle Zoo listed lion cubs, a baby titi monkey, infant giraffe, baby burrowing owlets, and other new arrivals and states that "people are always anxious to see any new babies" (Utah's Hogle Zoo 2016), but it's not just babies that zoos believe bring in visitors. Other new, rare, unusual or charismatic "wildlife" species may as well.

Numerous unusual or difficult to obtain species are sought after as temporary attractions, including komodo dragons, koalas, white lions, and, the most sought after of all, giant pandas.

Having a direct, close-up nonhuman animal encounter is also a big attraction and can generate extra income. In March 2015, Sea World announced plans for a new multimillion-dollar dolphin facility at its San Antonio location that will offer swim with the dolphin encounters, including a dorsal fin tow ride (Sea World 2015). At the San Antonio zoo, visitors can pay a fee to walk out onto an elevated platform to hand feed a reticulated giraffe (Davis 2016). At the privately owned Featherdale Wildlife Park in Australia, visitors can cuddle a koala or hand feed a kangaroo (Mercer 2014). Hundreds of zoos and aquariums now offer "wildlife" encounters for a fee, and many smaller operations depend on them. In zoos around the world, you can sit on a tiger, have your photo taken with an orangutan, hold a baby kangaroo, or support a giant python wrapped around your waist, all for a fee, of course, but it comes at a cost to the nonhuman animals involved, including stress, discomfort, pain, injury, or even, in some cases, death.

For example, stingray petting pools have become popular in zoos. Large, elevated, shallow pools allow visitors, who have paid a fee, to touch a stingray when it swims by, but these exhibits have had problems, including a number of die-offs. In 2009, 41 cownose stingrays died due to lack of oxygen while they were at the Calgary Zoo (Canadian Press 2009). As I was writing this chapter, the news media reported that 18 stingrays and three sharks died in a petting pool at the John Ball Zoo in Michigan (Wood 8 TV 2016).

Giant Panda Rock Stars

Giant pandas are the rock stars of the zoo world, and institutions often spend years trying to get them. Typically, pairs of pandas are rented for a 10-year period for a fee of $1 million per year, with zoos incurring additional costs related to negotiation and permitting, construction of new exhibits, and then ongoing care. If cubs are produced during a loan, there can also be an additional one-time hosting fee of up to $600,000 per cub. Despite their appeal, many zoos have lost money on pandas. Three years after acquiring pandas in 2003, Memphis Zoo chief executive Chuck Brady said they expected to lose about $300,000 per year (Goodman 2006a). Scotland's Edinburgh Zoo has had a similar experience with the income generated by pandas unlikely to match the expense of having them (Nichols 2011).

In 2010, while the Toronto Zoo was pursuing plans for pandas, Toronto City Councillor Giorgio Mammoliti said, "There's millions of dollars to be made" (Hains 2014). Two pandas arrived at the zoo in March 2013. In addition to spending millions on a new exhibit, the zoo budgets $550,000 per year to fly in bamboo from the United States, $238,149 in staffing costs, and $150,000 in panda insurance. Even with pandas, however, the Toronto Zoo experienced a major decrease in attendance in 2014, with revenues down by $8.3 million (Pagliaro 2014). The birth of two cubs in 2015 presumably boosted attendance and revenue, but whether or not it evens out on the zoo's total panda expenditures, which now include the cub hosting fee, remains to be seen.[4] Regardless, it's clear that in most cases the number of people coming to see pandas drop off dramatically starting about a year after they arrive and then more with each passing year. According to Chuck Brady, Memphis Zoo chief executive, "Year three is your break-even year. After that, attendance drops off, and you start losing vast amounts of money" (Goodman 2006b). It seems those dreams about pandas producing truckloads of cash are just that—dreams.

Amusement Ride Thrills

While attractions not involving live "wildlife" have been present in zoos and aquariums for as long as they have been around, they seem to be gaining in popularity in recent years. Everything from kid's carousels, boat rides, roller coasters, and adventure courses are becoming more common in zoological facilities throughout the world.

The Toronto Zoo recently opened the TundraAir Ride, adjacent to its Arctic wolf exhibit, where for a $12 fee harnessed visitors can shoot along an elevated cable at speeds of up to 48 km/hr. Not too far away is the Gorilla Climb Ropes Course, situated right next to the zoo's outdoor gorilla enclosure. For $8, visitors can climb, swing, crawl, and balance through the almost 33-foot high climbing structure. The Rhode Island Zoological Society, which operates the Roger Williams Park Zoo, signed an agreement with the City of Providence that will supposedly save the city money and allow the zoo to construct zip-lines and aerial courses at certain sites (Pina 2016). A proposal for the new Baton Rouge Zoo mentions zip-lines, adventure courses, a sky lift, splash pads, ropes course, rock wall, and a carousel (Broussard 2016).

As I was writing this chapter, the Toronto Star newspaper featured a story about a proposed magnetic levitation (maglev) monorail at the Toronto Zoo that would let visitors zip around the zoo for a $12 fee (Sachgua 2016).

Take in a Show at Party Central

Many zoos and aquariums offer up various kinds of shows, probably the best known being the orca, dolphin, and sea lion shows in aquatic facilities. SeaWorld's now defunct Shamu Show[5] is arguably the most famous, but almost every zoo and aquarium has one kind of show or another. They can be simple "wildlife" presentations or big production shows, and they can involve almost every kind of nonhuman animal, from reptiles and birds to big cats and elephants.

Music has long been a part of many zoo experiences, but today some zoos also serve as concert venues for major musical acts. At the Toledo Zoo, performers such as Bob Dylan, Steve Miller, and Alan Jackson are part of the zoo's 2016 summer concert series, while the Oregon Zoo also hosts some big-name entertainers. These events require a separate ticket and will be attended by many thousands of music lovers. Other events include annual galas, seasonal light shows, fireworks displays, and kid's camps, to name just a few. Additional revenue may come from the rental of space for weddings, parties, festivals, and other special functions. Of course, depending on how they are conducted, these events may have the potential to affect nonhuman animals in negative ways, especially when they are loud or intrusive in other ways.

CULTIVATING CORPORATIONS

Displayed prominently at many zoo and aquarium entrances, and often at other locations, visitors may find plaques, signs, and other materials featuring the names of various corporate benefactors. They can include big business sponsors from the fossil fuel, forestry, mining, telecommunications, airline and transport sectors, as well as myriad small businesses. They donate cash or goods and services to help with capital projects, exhibit upgrades, "wildlife" acquisitions and transport, and special events. Generally speaking, businesses contribute something, and in exchange, they receive positive exposure (often including media coverage) and an enhanced public image that they believe may benefit their business. A small business donating food for an event may simply receive mention in a newsletter, website posting, or on signs at the event. Major sponsors may receive a lot more.

As a premium status sponsor of the Toronto Zoo giant panda exhibit and sponsor of transportation services, Federal Express Canada received a considerable package of benefits. According to the zoo's COO, the benefits,

> will provide a solid return on investment, measured in terms of brand building, consumer awareness, consumer favour and heightened interest in Federal Express Canada's services and sales. These benefits include the unlimited use of the Panda Partner designation logo, the right to use the Toronto Zoo intellectual property and markings in partner marketing and category exclusivity at the Premium Partner designation. Federal Express Canada will also receive the ability to have a presence at the Zoo with the ability to distribute items to Zoo guests and initiate on-site activations for the purposes of customer engagement. Additionally, there are a number of marketing, media related (both external and internal) and hospitality related benefits at this partnership level. (Hale 2012)

Significant donations can also result in naming rights to buildings or exhibits. One example is the Dallas Zoo's ExxonMobil Endangered Tiger Habitat, which opened in 1999. The name leaves no doubt as to which company paid for a good portion of it.

While seeking corporate support might seem innocuous enough, by doing so, there is the potential for zoos and aquariums to enhance the profile and the reputations of companies associated with the environmental crisis who are criticized by environmental and nonhuman animal rights organizations. Fossil fuel companies are one example. They may support various environmental and climate change initiatives while simultaneously obstructing them through lobbying or the funding of opposing initiatives (Grazian 2015, 202). If zoos and aquariums accept funds from these kinds of businesses and then publicize and praise the companies involved, they may be providing tacit endorsement of those companies and undeservedly enhancing their environmental reputations, something that is often referred to as *greenwashing*.

PUBLIC PRIVATE PARTNERSHIPS

In North America, there is a strong push for the privatization of public zoos, with many major zoos moving in that direction in recent years. Many individual zoos and their respective zoo industry associations promote the idea of public-private partnerships (PPP) that would see zoo operations more or less independent of government, while at the same time continuing to receive public support from them.[6] That model was promoted by the Toronto Zoo in 2012.

At that time, the Zoo projected a 2013 budget of $53.8 million, with $11.1 million coming from the City of Toronto. The municipality owns the nonhuman animal collection and the hard assets (buildings and infrastructure), while the Toronto Zoo Board of Management appointed by the city operates the zoo business. In their commissioned report *The Future of Toronto Zoo Governance*, the Zoo said they wanted a PPP that would provide independent governance, a community-based board leadership and focus with an arm's length relationship with city government (Toronto Zoo 2012, 6). The report goes on to say, "The City of Toronto would annually allocate resources to pay for capital building maintenance, as the property and buildings will continue to be owned by the City of Toronto" (Toronto Zoo 2012, 6). Essentially, the report proposed that the Zoo be free from city control but continue to receive public funding.[7] To date, the Zoo has not been able to secure a PPP.

Zoos can be expensive businesses to operate, especially the larger, urban zoos that employ the largest numbers of staff and who believe they must maintain or increase visitor numbers and revenues. In the City of Toronto where I live, the Toronto Zoo's 2015 revenues were more than $50 million, with expenditures in that range as well. Revenues at the Vancouver Aquarium, Canada's largest marine facility, were $30.45 million (Vancouver Aquarium 2014, 6). Meanwhile, the San Diego Zoo and San Diego Wild Animal Park is estimated to have an annual operating budget more than $200 million (Bennet 2012).

When you add into the mix the fact that zoos are frequently engaged in ongoing capital works projects and infrastructure improvements/repairs, the amounts involved can be very large.

LINING UP FOR PUBLIC HANDOUTS

Many zoos seek and actively lobby for support from governments, and some have come to rely on it for a portion of their annual operating budget and/or for capital projects. That support can be a direct subsidy, such as the more than $11 million of municipal support the Toronto Zoo receives each year from the City of Toronto, or it can be in the form of tax breaks, levies, or bonds.

In many governments, austerity measures have become entrenched, and many public zoos, art museums, and other cultural institutions are seeing their government support diminish each year. They are told to become more efficient and economically self-sustaining by reducing their dependence on government handouts (Mazur 2001, 190). As government support diminishes, many zoos and aquariums look to increased commercialization as their economic salvation, but that doesn't stop facilities from pursuing whatever public funds they can in the meantime.

Some zoos already receive tax breaks, while others are seeking them. Nebraska Legislative Bill 419, which was introduced by State Senator Heath

Mello in 2015, is one example. The bill would allow accredited zoos, including Omaha's Henry Doorly Zoo, to keep funds they collect in sales tax, estimated at approximately $2.67 million over two years, and use them to upgrade their facilities (Gronewold 2015). The bill was passed in 2015 and came into effect January 1, 2016. The Georgia Aquarium and Zoo Atlanta also received tax breaks in 2015 worth $750,000 and $350,000 respectively when the Georgia Senate voted for tax rebates on construction materials (Williams 2015).

That same year, a bill was proposed that would allow for-profit facilities accredited by the Association of Zoos and Aquariums to deduct the cost of goods sold—expenses related to buying or creating a product to sell customers (Cardona 2015). When nonhuman animal activists protested the bill, the two Dallas legislators removed the bill from consideration.

Zoo levies are also on the radar screen of many major zoos. A *levy* is the act of imposing a tax to raise revenue for a project or initiative. A levy can be initiated by a municipality, county, state, or other body who add an extra tax on property owners within the jurisdiction. Specialized levies usually need to be approved by voters before they come into effect. One such levy was overwhelmingly turned down by voters in 2014.

The Columbus Zoo and Aquarium board asked Franklin County commissioners to consider a permanent 1.25-mill levy[8] on the 2014 ballot and launched a $1 million campaign to promote it. The Columbus Zoological Park Association, a private nonprofit group, and businesses provided the funding. Seventy percent of voters turned down the levy. The zoo took another stab at it the following year, but this time they asked voters to renew their existing 0.75-mill property tax for 10 years. They promoted the zoo as an incredible community asset with huge economic and employment benefits and as a critical player in "wildlife conservation." The levy would continue to cost Franklin County homeowners $21 per $100,000 property value on an annual basis, bringing in just under $19 million a year for the zoo. It worked, and the existing levy was maintained (Gray 2015).

Bonds are yet another way that zoos secure public funds. Bonds are debt, and they may be issued by towns, cities, states, or even businesses. Unlike levies that provide funds over a preset period of time, bonds provide cash almost immediately after they are sold. However, the bond issuer must then pay a certain percentage of interest on the bond to the bondholders. The bond issuer is also required to buy the bonds back from the bondholders, repaying the initial purchase price, once the bond's maturity date has been reached.

The Abilene Zoo was hoping to gain approximately $1 million with the passage of Proposition 5 at the City's May 9, 2015, bond election. The zoo planned to use the funds to improve the onsite hospital facility, create bird flight cages, and expand a cat area to accommodate a breeding pair of jaguars. They claimed that not only would the bond improve facilities and enhance the zoo experience for visitors, but it would help facilitate the zoo's conservation work. Once the bonds were sold, the owner of a $75,000 home would see a tax increase of $1.62, while the owner of a $200,000 home would see an increase of $4.33 (Bethel 2015). The bond passed with 70 percent of the city council vote.

In 2008, a $125 million bond for the Oregon Zoo was approved by voters. The money would be used for various projects, including adding space for primates (approximately $22 million) and elephants ($9.2 million), an off-site elephant reserve with a barn, care facilities, and fencing ($12 million), and improving water and electric systems ($11.5 million). Later the zoo reneged on the promise for the off-site reserve, much to the chagrin of elephant advocates (Casey 2008).

Seeking tax breaks, levies, bonds, and other kinds of initiatives are all in the zoo world's fundraising arsenal and collectively add to up to staggering sums of government (taxpayers) support for zoos and aquariums.

THE CASE FOR ECONOMIC SUPPORT

With intense competition for funds, zoos and aquariums often need to convince the general public, businesses, and elected officials that they are serving several useful functions. For those zoos and aquariums that rely on substantive government support, they need to demonstrate that they are serving a beneficial economic function in the community.[9] That can be providing employment, buying local goods, bringing in tourists who then spend money in the municipality, or even by increasing the profile of the community on a regional, national, or international basis. Second, almost all zoos and aquariums need to convince supporters and visitors that they are humane and are legitimately engaged in conservation, including saving endangered species.[10]

THE CASE FOR GOVERNMENT HAND-OUTS

It should be clear by now that many public zoos require some form of ongoing government subsidy to continue operating, as well as for capital projects, and those subsidies can take many forms. To convince decision-makers and legislators that zoos are a good investment, they utilize a variety of tactics, including the production of economic impact studies (EIS) that extol their economic virtues to the communities in which they are located.

A paper posted on the Association of Zoos and Aquariums (AZA) website talks about the economic impacts of zoos and aquariums and construction spending. It indicates that in 2007, AZA member institutions spent a total of $2.98 billion, of which $2.34 billion went for operations, while $643 million went for capital projects, with AZA's international members spending an additional $363.3 million (Fuller 2009, 1). The paper states that the $2.62 billion spent by their U.S. members contributed a total of $7.6 billion to the U.S. GDP, including supporting 74,332 jobs across all sectors of the economy (Fuller 2009, 1). The paper goes on to conclude that each $1 of direct spending by zoos and aquariums generated $2.84 of total economic benefits to the local economies where the institutions were located (Fuller 2009, 8).

A look at some of the many zoo economic impact studies available online reveals a common refrain, that zoos and aquariums are not just local attractions, but they produce substantive economic benefits. On the Cincinnati Zoo website, an article details the findings of a study by the University of Cincinnati Economic Center indicating the Cincinnati Zoo and Botanical Garden has a total annual economic impact of $143 million (Cincinnati Zoo 2013). The study says the zoo generates 1,700 jobs, is a top attraction for visitors from outside the area (who account for a total economic impact of $60.4 million), and that it is "crucial to replenishing and expanding the Greater Cincinnati economy" (Cincinnati Zoo 2013).

A 2010 report about the Toronto Zoo said it "... generates significant economic impacts in the regional economy, from its operations and its investment in capital assets" (The Toronto Zoo 2010). The report claims that in 2009 the zoo contributed $39 million to Toronto's GDP with a $47 million contribution to Ontario's GDP, while capital investments between 2007–2009 resulted in $15.7 million to Toronto's GDP and a $20.9 million contribution to Ontario's GDP (The Toronto Zoo 2010). The report also states that the zoo delivers other benefits, including "wildlife" conservation, scientific research, public education, and supporting sustainable environments, although no substantive evidence is provided to substantiate those other claims (The Toronto Zoo 2010).

In yet another report, this one prepared by Applied Economics in association with Aegis consulting Australia and titled *Contribution of Taronga and Western Plains Zoos to the Economy of New South Wales*, the economic benefits of the two zoos are stated unequivocally. In 2004–2005, the two zoos had operating and capital expenditures of AUS $78.6 million, with estimated gross income effects for the New South Wales economy of AUS $248.1 million (Applied Economics 2005). Those figures include the estimated flow-on multiplier effects (i.e., the proportion of income generated that is re-spent on NSW economic resources) (Applied Economics 2005).

A review of a significant number of zoo economic impact statements shows that they all have the same conclusion. They all state, from an economic perspective, that zoos are a great investment with a solid return for the communities in which they are located. Of course, it should be noted many of these studies are commissioned by the zoos themselves, and whoever is doing the analysis presumably relies on information supplied by their employers.

Certainly, from the perspective of zoos and aquariums, it makes perfect sense to create the strongest case you can to generate support for what you are doing. In fact, I would suggest that it's almost a requirement of the system that currently exists. If you want support, you have to convince people (and government) that you are worth supporting.

THE CASE FOR RESIDENT SUPPORT

The other claim of zoos, that they are centers for nonhuman animal well-being and are important, even vital, institutions of "wildlife" protection, also deserves scrutiny, especially when one considers that this is a frequent refrain used to attract support, especially from members of the public. In fact, if you ask most people what zoos do or why they should be supported, a significant percentage will answer conservation. That perspective is pervasive, even though the actual conservation role and effectiveness of zoos and aquariums is often grossly overstated.

For example, last year I came across an example of a rather exceptional claim about the value of zoo and aquarium "conservation." In 2012, the Georgia Aquarium and partners proposed the import of wild-caught beluga whales into the United States. The Georgia Aquarium's website contained the statement, "Maintaining a sustainable population of beluga whales in human care is essential to the survival of belugas everywhere" (Georgia Aquarium 2012). There was no mention of the fact that maintaining a population of belugas in captivity doesn't even begin to substantively address the core, immediate challenges that threaten the species in the wild, such as climate change, pollution, and, in some areas, hunting.

Even if there was some kind of benefit to having a tiny population of whales in tanks in the United States, for anyone looking to do the most good and create the biggest bang possible for their conservation dollar, it wouldn't make any sense to support it. The housing and care of whales is enormously expensive, and they have a bad habit of dying. Keeping and trying to breed a small number of large, long-lived (up to 75 years), wide-ranging, deep diving, highly intelligent, and exceptionally social beings who still number more than 100,000 individuals in the wild doesn't make any conservation sense. It makes far more sense to consider the needs of a raft of critically endangered species and vital conservation projects that are starving for funds where even a small influx of support could make a real difference.

Given all the hype and propaganda, one could be forgiven for believing that zoos and aquariums are a conservation panacea. After all, that's the message they've been promoting for many years, especially regarding captive breeding, but in reality, even though there may admittedly be a small role for them to play in the captive propagation of endangered species, their activities and effectiveness in this area have, in my opinion, been ridiculously and dishonestly overstated throughout the years.

According to renowned architect and former zoo director David Hancocks (2012), ". . . zoos [and aquariums] shout loudly about their achievements, ignore or defend their shortcomings, and rarely do much that is in fact useful. Most problematically, they persistently say one thing and do the opposite."

The idea that zoos and aquariums can be arks and zoo-based captive breeding is a legitimate, frontline conservation strategy has been significantly eroded, but that hasn't stopped institutions from continuing to promote it to visitors. They have also started to say they have a major role to play in providing technical, material, and financial support for in-situ conservation work and in conducting various forms of research that they claim will ultimately be of benefit to nonhuman animals in the wild. It is certainly conceivable, but so far, their contribution and effectiveness in that area has been overstated as well.

Certainly, there are a few institutions that do seem to provide substantive financial and other support (in proportion to their annual operating budgets and resources) for field (*in-situ*) conservation work, with two of the best known being the Durrell Wildlife Preservation Trust (Jersey Zoo) and the Wildlife Conservation Society, which operates several zoos, including the Bronx Zoo. Others, such as the San Diego Zoo, also claim to be making substantive real investments in conservation, but it appears that most zoos provide proportionately little, if any, direct financial support to the preservation of "wildlife" in nature or wild spaces, and the bulk of those that do allocate something often don't allocate very much at all.

According to *The New York Times* blog titled *Zoos Raise Money for Faraway Animals* by Leslie Kaufman (2012), ". . . the Association of Zoos and Aquariums [AZA] estimates that its member zoos and aquariums gave less than 2 percent of their operating budgets to field conservation activities for wild animals in 2010—about $134 million." If we accept that number as accurate, it still seems very small compared to the billions of dollars the AZA's members spend each year.

A look at the budget allocation pie charts in some zoo or aquarium annual reports would reasonably lead one to believe that zoological institutions spend considerable amounts on conservation, research and education. For example, the Vancouver Aquarium in their 2014 annual report places that number at $4.059 million or 12 percent of its $33.7 million expenditure total (Vancouver Aquarium 2014). That same year, the Toronto Zoo claimed that expenditures for conservation, research, and education were $14.699 million of its $43 million expenditure total (Toronto Zoo 2014). However, specific details as to what those programs actually include are not outlined in the most accessible reports. Presumably they incorporate a very broad range of internal and external expenses, including nonhuman animal maintenance and staff salaries.

No one, not even the harshest critics of zoos and aquariums, would argue that zoos and aquariums do nothing that is beneficial or worthwhile. With an estimated 10,000 zoos in the world and many of them participating or supporting conservation programs and projects to some degree, such a claim would be absurd. The more pertinent question, however, may be are zoos and aquariums allocating enough of their resources to *in-situ* conservation, especially compared to their overall operating budgets, and are they achieving specific, quantifiable conservation outcomes?

To further illustrate the disparity between the impression created by zoo claims and their actual contribution to *in-situ* conservation, one can look at the issue of elephants in zoos. In North America, the Association of Zoos and Aquariums (AZA) promotes its commitment to the preservation of elephants in the wild, but AZA member facilities often appear to provide only token support to *in-situ* elephant conservation initiatives. It seems that many AZA zoo member contributions are directed to the International Elephant Foundation (IEF), a nonprofit organization supported to a significant degree by members of the zoo and circus industry. According to a January 9, 2012, AZA news release, the IEF and AZA planned to allocate just $225,000 in 2012 to support elephant conservation around the world, raising the IEF's grand total contributed since its creation in 1998 to $2 million (American Association of Zoos and Aquariums 2012). Certainly that $2 million is welcome and every penny is needed, but it doesn't seem like much when you consider that a single new exhibit for a half dozen elephants may cost $10, $20 or even $50 million, and collectively AZA zoos have spent, and continue to spend, in the tens of millions of dollars building or refurbishing their elephant exhibits for the approximately 300 elephants they maintain.

The problems that are endangering "wild elephants" in Africa and Asia are not going to be addressed by spending boatloads of money to keep and breed a small number of them in North American zoos. Elephants are quite capable of breeding successfully on their own when given habitat and protection from poachers. Where money needs to be spent is where the elephants are—in the wild.

Overall, the cold reality is that budgetary limitations don't allow most zoos and aquariums to allocate very much to real conservation at all. That's why the bulk of funding for *in-situ* conservation comes from a tiny number of very wealthy institutions (Grazian 2015, 187–188).

Direct expenditures on *in-situ* conservation programs and projects, the kinds of field activities and initiatives that often come to mind when people think about conservation, such as funding additional ranger staff or aerial anti-poaching patrols, can often be relatively minimal, especially when compared to institutional operating budgets. For example, if we look again at the Toronto Zoo, we see it vigorously publicizing online, in print and onsite their support of a range of conservation projects through their Endangered Species Reserve Fund (ESRF). Reading their material, one is left with the impression that the zoo is driving a global network of important conservation initiatives, when, in reality, the level of financial support provided to each project is minimal. The actual dollar amounts of support provided by the zoo are not posted alongside the project descriptions, so anyone wanting to know how much the zoo provides to each has to do their own research.[11]

The ESRF is made up of funds obtained through coin collection boxes, outside organizations including schools, and individuals making donations plus "wishing well" coin collectors on the zoo site. From the years 2005–2013, the Fund maintained an average balance of $800,851 to be distributed to conservation projects worldwide (Zoocheck 2016). Annually, the zoo provides Toronto City Council a list of projects they wish to fund, which the city typically approves. From 2009–2013, the average approved budget for the ESRF was just $84,940 compared to an average uncommitted balance of $828,611, so the zoo requests access to just 10 to 11 percent of their funds each year, presumably equivalent to the interest accrued on the capital. The amount actually spent on the projects may be even less. Over the same five years, the zoo appears to have only utilized approximately 63 percent of the funds that were approved annually. By my estimate, this reduces the percentage of the ESRF that is going to conservation initiatives to a mere 6.47 percent of the total and yields an average actual expenditure of just $53,340. It was not determined if the reduction in the amount of money used is due to over-estimation of project costs during the initial project funding review phase or for another reason. However, no matter the cause, the financial support provided through the ESRF could quite fairly be described as minimal, at best, and if the selected initiatives do not necessitate using all of the approved funds, other vital, cash-starved conservation initiatives could be provided with support, rather than the funds just being left in an account (Zoocheck 2016).

The ESRF supports both internal projects done at or by the zoo and external projects delivered by other agencies or organizations. From 2010–2015, on average 28 projects were proposed annually, approximately 10 being internal and 18 external. There were consistently greater numbers of external projects proposed than internal. However, more funds were allocated to internal projects, so it would seem that the majority of ESRF allocations have actually been directed back to the zoo itself, leaving little for external projects, many of whom received approximately $1,000 each (Zoocheck 2016).

Presumably the Toronto Zoo would argue that it does a great deal more for conservation, education, and research. It certainly articulates that perspective in its materials, and the ESRF is merely one small facet of their efforts in that regard. However, the ESRF programs are advertised extensively by the zoo and help create the impression that substantial funding is applied directly to *in-situ* conservation work, when that does not seem to be the case.

In the absence of involvement with *in-situ* conservation initiatives, zoos and aquariums may still claim to focus on conservation because they engage in *ex-situ* conservation, which often means participation in zoo industry breeding programs, but the realities and the challenges inherent in zoo-based captive breeding for conservation are rarely conveyed to the public. In fact, captive breeding of endangered species for reintroduction purposes is best done entirely away from public view, such as offsite in nonpublic facilities. With few exceptions, zoos and aquariums just don't have the capacity or resources to do very much for conservation.

ENTERTAINMENT BUSINESSES FOCUSED ON CUSTOMER SERVICE

By now, it should be clear that while there are both private, for-profit and public, nonprofit zoos, and everything in between, and that most of them purport to be primarily institutions of conservation, education, and research, the majority of zoos and aquariums are still, for all intents and purposes, entertainment businesses that focus a great deal of their time, energy, and resources trying to attract visitors and generate revenue just to stay afloat, produce a dividend for shareholders, or to prove themselves worthy of government subsidies. To maintain their public popularity, zoos believe they have to adopt a customer service oriented approach, regularly provide fresh, new, exciting things for visitors to see, including cramming a broad assortment of charismatic "wildlife" species, along with other kinds of attractions, into whatever limited space they have, and coat it all with a veneer of conservation to make it a little more marketable. How does all that affect the living, breathing, thinking beings? Does this capitalist business perspective, free market approach, and commercialization oppress and harm nonhuman animals? I believe it does so in a variety of ways.

HOW ARE NONHUMAN ANIMALS AFFECTED?

The majority of traditional zoos and aquariums maintain substantial, diverse, collections of "wildlife" species from around the world.[12] This menagerie-style format is partly rooted in a history of imperialist exploration and conquest at a time when levels of knowledge of nonhuman animal cognition, ecology, evolution, and rights were nascent at best. It also exists because zoo planners and operators believe they need a diversity of species to attract and maintain public interest. Most zoos still seem reluctant to specialize, so they continue to feature large, charismatic vertebrates, such as tigers, lions, bears, rhinos, giraffes, and elephants, to name just a few of the popular species zoos often feel they must have, but keeping substantial numbers of nonhuman animal species within the limited footprint of most zoos can result in each of them (or each group) being allocated only a small amount of the total available space and resources. This phenomenon is obvious and easy to see in zoos and aquariums around the world, especially when large beings (e.g., elephants in zoos) are kept as they often are in small spaces.[13] They don't get huge amounts of space because it isn't there, or it is already occupied and, therefore, not available.

For the nonhuman animals, all is not well on the ark. Throughout the zoo and aquarium world, one can find grossly undersized cages and enclosures, completely barren environments, lack of shelter and privacy, inadequate heat, poor environmental conditions, no enrichment, low-quality food, overcrowding, physical abuse, and nonhuman animals expressing a broad range of abnormal, often self-destructive behaviors, to name just a sample.[14]

The trend among major and even some minor zoos to pursue costly mega exhibits is also something that can negatively impact the lives of zoo captives. These exhibits frequently provide a veneer of naturalness that may look better to visitors but at the same time may fail to properly address the biological and behavioral needs of the residents themselves. At times, it seems that satisfying the perceived needs of visitors is a major or even the top priority. Mega exhibits might also have the potential to distract or deflect attention away from much needed repairs or improvements to existing zoo exhibits and infrastructure.

The acquisition and promotion of charismatic species can also be costly to zoos, with giant pandas being the most high-profile example. In what is often a financially risky attempt to attract visitors, zoos spend millions of dollars to rent pandas. Meanwhile, work on existing exhibits and infrastructure might be delayed as a result, especially if pandas don't turn out to be as lucrative as expected. When the Toronto Zoo acquired pandas, the zoo had a $90 million backlog of repairs, including much needed refurbishments to existing nonhuman animal enclosures (Alcoba 2011). Perhaps the zoo should have focused on the backlog, instead of the pandas.

"Wildlife" may also be removed from the wild to fill zoo and aquarium displays. Just recently, 18 wild caught African elephants were flown to U.S. zoos (Bekoff 2016). Many of the whales and dolphins in captivity worldwide have been caught from the wild, something that one would be hard pressed to say is in their best interest (Rose, Naomi, and Farinato 2009), especially considering the physical, psychological, and social trauma they may experience when captured, separated from family members, transported, and then incarcerated in tiny pools.

Throughout the zoo world, babies of a multitude of species are used to attract visitors, with many being hand-raised for that purpose. Some small zoos seem to breed nonhuman animals every year to ensure they have babies for the spring and summer seasons, often removing them from their mothers for hand-raising so these appealing beings are comfortable in the presence of people. This practice can negatively impact the individuals involved (Frostic 2013), because mothers generally don't want to give up their offspring, and it may facilitate the production of surplus individuals who may have no acceptable placement opportunities at the end of the season and are offloaded to whoever wants them or, in some cases, are culled (Barnes 2014). The nonhuman animals are commodities, and their value lies in their cuteness and tractability, and once that is gone, so are they.

There are other more obvious manifestations of commercialism and how it affects nonhuman animals in zoos. Hosting loud rock concerts and other musical events or fireworks shows will almost certainly cause discomfort or distress to many zoo captives.[15] Other noisy attractions, such as amusement park-type rides or zip-lines that run adjacent to or over exhibits may also have that effect. Night parties and seasonal light events may also be disruptive to nonhuman animals who have little or no opportunity to retreat from the ruckus and who may perceive ranges of noise and low levels of scent well beyond what is apparent to humans and cause irritation and discomfort in ways we can't perceive. Many "wildlife" species, such as wolves, are by nature shy, retiring and seek to avoid the copiousness of noise, smells, and activity that are so inherent to crowds of people.

The conservation veneer applied to what are essentially entertainment businesses may also be problematic by creating the belief in members of the public that zoos are major players in "wildlife" conservation, that captive breeding is a viable long-term strategy for saving endangered species, and people shouldn't worry about impending extinctions of endangered species because zoos will breed those species and repopulate the wild. Those beliefs appear to be why some zoos generate a significant portion of their support. Conceivably, at least a portion of the funds generated by zoos and aquariums from individual, corporate, and government sources could be diverted to in-situ initiatives instead. Even a small portion could make a world of difference in so many regions where monetary and other resources are scarce beyond what most of us in the industrialized Western world can imagine.

A capitalist perspective, free market approach, and the seemingly inevitable commercialization that results from it permeates the world of zoos and aquariums. The ever-present pursuit of stable or, preferably, increasing visitor numbers and increased revenue influences the way that nonhuman animals are treated and kept and the decisions that are made about them. Mega exhibits, special "wildlife" features, zip-lines, rides, rock concerts, subsidies, tax breaks, and bonds are all manifestations of an entertainment-focused industry.

If capitalist forces were removed from the picture,[16] that would mean the oppressive practices of today would be diminished or in some cases gone altogether. No more menagerie-style collections with large numbers of non-human animals being allocated minimal space and resources. No more keeping big, wide-ranging "wildlife" species such as whales, elephants, and polar bears in small zoos that have no ability to provide them with the expansive environments they need. No more taking "wildlife" from the wild. No more expensive, mega exhibits that are all façade and have little or no real relevance to the nonhuman animals they contain or their conservation. No more producing babies to pull in visitors or shunting spectacular, charismatic species around as special attractions. No more noisy disruptive roller coasters, zip-lines, concerts, fireworks shows, and invasive light events. No more buying, selling, or trading nonhuman animals, breeding and then killing them, or using them in off-site film and television productions, circuses, or special events. Instead of being oppressed and commodified, the nonhuman animals would be treated with respect and compassion and their needs placed as the highest priority.

A capitalist free market economy is one in which business and industry are controlled by private owners who function in a way that is largely unfettered by government oversight, regulation, or interference. It is clearly a driving force in many private zoo and aquarium operations, and it seems to be an insidious, yet powerful influence in public facilities. The drive to function with diminishing oversight and control by government (while still receiving public funds), ever escalating degrees of commercialization, and the commodification of "wildlife" all in the pursuit of revenue are indicative of a capitalist free market approach that doesn't put the interests of nonhuman animals, conservation, or education as the highest priority.

As entertainment facilities, zoos and aquariums have shown they work, but they have not shown that they work as a means to substantively help nonhuman animals, conserve species in the wild, or educate and motivate in the way they claim. As conservation and educational mechanisms, they serve to, just barely, fool noncritical observers into thinking they are effective in those realms, but increasingly, people are learning the truth.

NOTES

1. While publicly owned zoos may not be "controlled by private owners who control the factors of production," this chapter suggests that the people who are controlling public zoos often act in the same way as private owners.

2. For the purposes of this chapter, *free market* is defined as a market economy based on supply and demand with no government control.

3. At its best, the term *conservation* means preserving and protecting free-living other animals and their natural environments. However, pro-hunting organizations use the term to denote the necessary regulation of killing hunted other animals to ensure there will be enough of them for recreational hunting in the future.

4. A potential mitigating factor in the Toronto Zoo panda scenario is the fact that the 10-year lease period is being split between the Toronto Zoo and the Calgary Zoo.

5. At the time of this writing, SeaWorld announced that it will be discontinuing its entertainment format orca shows.

6. It should be noted that many PPPs have a goal of weaning zoos or aquariums off the public purse.

7. In 2011 the City of Toronto received a report from KPMG that examined the financial impact of privatizing the zoo. In addition, the Toronto City Council passed a motion directing the Toronto Zoo to send its three surviving elephants to a sanctuary, leading the Association of Zoos and Aquariums to remove the Toronto Zoo's accreditation, a move they claimed was due to a governance issue. However, many observers believe the action was in response to the elephant move decision by the City.

8. A *mill levy* is a tax rate applied to an assessed property. Jurisdictions determine the mill levy rate by figuring out how much tax revenue they will require from it and then dividing that number by the total value of property in the jurisdiction.

9. Some zoos and aquariums also claim they produce a beneficial social function by providing educational and cultural opportunities for lower incomed citizens, students, etc.

10. There do seem to be some exceptions to this premise. For example, Marineland in Niagara Falls, Canada, does not seem to have organized involvement in conservation initiatives, yet it continues to attract significant numbers of visitors.

11. Toronto Zoo Endangered Species Reserve Fund budgets and figures can be obtained through the City of Toronto website.

12. The Toronto Zoo provides an example of how diverse nonhuman animal collections may be. According to its website, the zoo houses more than 5,000 individual nonhuman animals representing more than 460 species. Most other major zoos have analogous live collections.

13. Traditional elephant yards in many urban zoos are less than one acre in size, and even new elephant exhibits are typically just a few acres, often subdivided among numerous elephants. Currently, the Association of Zoos and Aquariums (AZA) outdoor paddock standard for one adult elephant is 5,400 ft^2 (500 m^2).

14. Numerous reports documenting conditions in zoos around the world have been published by a wide variety of NGOs. An abbreviated list of some of them can be found at https://www.zoocheck.com/resources-3/reports-and-research/.

15. The effects, such as stress and fear, of fireworks on domestic "pets" and "wild" nonhuman animals are well established. Fireworks shows in zoos and marine parks have been the subject of criticism from nonhuman animal welfare groups for many years.

16. This comment is not meant to suggest that zoos in other governing systems, including communism, are any better. Nonhuman animals in many zoos situated in communist regimes share many of the same challenges and issues.

REFERENCES

Alcoba, Natalie. 2011. "Cash Strapped Toronto Zoo Waves Goodbye to Elephants." *National Post,* May 14.

American Association of Zoos and Aquariums. 2012. "International Elephant Foundation Grants Backed by Zoo Donations." Accessed on September 10, 2016, from http://www.aza.org/PressRoom/detail.aspx?id=23204. .

Applied Economics. 2005. "Contribution of Taronga and Western Plains Zoos to the Economy of New South Wales." *Aegis Consulting, Australia.* Accessed on September 12, 2016, from https://file:///C:/Users/David/Downloads/06 _zoos_economic_contribution.pdf.

Assiniboine Park Zoo. 2015. "Journey to Churchill." Accessed September 14, 2016, from   http://www.assiniboineparkzoo.ca/zoo/home/explore/exhibits /journey-to-churchill.

Association of Leading Visitor Attractions. 2015. "Latest Visitor Figures." Accessed September 14, 2016, from http://www.alva.org.uk/details.cfm?p=423.

Barnes, Hannah. 2014. "How Many Healthy Nonhuman Animals Do Zoos Put Down?" *BBC News,* February 27. Accessed on September 15, 2016, from http://www.bbc.com/news/magazine-26356099.

Bartholomew, Dana. 2010. "New $42M Elephant Habitat Opens Thursday, Despite Lawsuit." *Daily News*, December 14. Accessed September 12, 2016, from http://www.dailynews.com/ci_16860068.

Bekoff, Marc. 2016. "The Stolen 18, Swaziland Elephants Secretly Shipped to U.S. Zoos to Avoid Legal Challenge." *Huffington Post*, March 10. Accessed September 10, 2016, from http://www.huffingtonpost.com/marc-bekoff/the -stolen-18-swaziland-e_b_9422486.html.

Bennet, Kelly. 2012. "San Diego Zoo's Vision of What Could Be." *Voice of San Diego.* Accessed September 13, 2016, from http://www.voiceofsandiego.org/all -narratives/balboa-park/san-diego-zoos-vision-of-what-could-be/.

Bethel, Brian. 2015. "Bond Could 'Transform' Zoo, Inside and Out." *Abilene Reporter News,* April 4. Accessed September 15, 2016, from http://www .reporternews.com/news/local/bond-could-transform-zoo-inside-and-out -ep-1013062475-350458001.html.

Broussard, Ryan. 2016. "New Baton Rouge Zoo Could Feature Zip Lines and Sky Lift in Effort to Give Visitors New Views of Park." *Business Report*, March 28. Accessed on September 12, 2016, from https://www.businessreport.com /business/new-baton-rouge-zoo-feature-zip-lines-sky-lift-effort-give -visitors-new-views-park-2.

Calgary Zoo. 2012. "Old Attendance Record Broken After 24 Years." Accessed September 15, 2016, from https://www.calgaryzoo.com/media-releases/old -attendance-record-broken-after-24-years.

Canadian Press. 2009. "Lack of Oxygen Killed Stingrays, Calgary Zoo Admits." Accessed September 14, 2016, from http://www.cbc.ca/news/canada/calgary /lack-of-oxygen-killed-stingrays-calgary-zoo-admits-1.797898.

Cardona, Claire. 2015. "Dallas Legislators Drop Zoo and Aquarium Tax Break Bills." *The Dallas Morning News*, May 19. Accessed September 15, 2016, from http://www.dallasnews.com/news/politics/headlines/20150519-dallas -legislators-drop-zoo-and-aquarium-tax-break-bills.ece.

Carr, N. and S. Cohen. 2011. "The Public Face of Zoos: Images of Entertainment, Education and Conservation." *Anthrozoos*. 24(2) 175–189.

Casey, Jerry. 2008. "Metro's Zoo Bond Passes." *The Oregonian/Oregon Live*. Accessed September 15, 2016, from http://blog.oregonlive.com/elections /2008/11/zoobond.html.

CBC. 2016. "Calgary Zoo Panda Upgrades to Cost $16 M, City Seeks $8 M from Province." *CBC News Calgary*, April 6. Accessed September 15, 2016, from http://www.cbc.ca/news/canada/calgary/calgary-zoo-panda-upgrades -16m-alberta-government-1.3523945.

Cincinnati Zoo. 2013. "Zoo Boosts Local Economy with Big Regional Impact." Accessed September 16, 2016, from http://cincinnatizoo.org/blog/2013/07 /31/zoo-boosts-local-economy-with-big-regional-impact/.

Davis, Vincent T. 2016. "New Zoo Habitat Offers Guests Chance to Feed Giraffes." *San Antonio Express*, March 14. Accessed on September 15, 2016, from http://www.expressnews.com/news/local/article/New-zoo-habitat-offers -guests-chance-to-feed-6889769.php.

Frostic, Anna. 2013. "Petition for Rulemaking to Prohibit Public Contact with Big Cats, Bears, and Nonhuman Primates." *Humane Society of the United States*. Accessed September 15, 2016, from https://www.google.com/search?espv =2&rlz=1C1AOHY_en&q=Petition+for+Rulemaking+to+Prohibit+Public +Contact+With+Big+Cats%2C+Bears%09and+Nonhuman+Primates&oq =Petition+for+Rulemaking+to+Prohibit+Public+Contact+With+Big+Cats %2C+Bears%09and+Nonhuman+Primates&gs_l=serp.3 . . . 54640.55458 .0.56512.2.2.0.0.0.0.119.197.1j1.2.0. . . . 0 . . . 1c.1.64.serp..0.0.0.0 .pCnjyT7wphE.

Fuller, Stephen S. 2009. "Economic Impact of Zoo and Aquariums Operations and Construction Spending." *Association of Zoos and Aquariums*. Accessed September 15, 2016, from http://aza.dev.networkats.com/uploadedFiles /About_Us/aza-economic-impacts-zoos-aquariums-final-2009.pdf.

Georgia Aquarium. "Beluga Whale Research & Conservation at Georgia Aquarium." Accessed September 15, 2016, from http://www.georgiaaquarium.org /conserve/research/beluga-whales.

Goodman, Brenda. 2006a. "Eats, Shoots, Leaves, and Much of Zoo's Budgets." *The New York Times*, February 12. Accessed September 20, 2016 from http:// www.nytimes.com/2006/02/12/us/eats-shoots-leaves-and-much-of-zoos -budgets.html.

Goodman, Brenda. 2006b. "U.S. Zoos Barely Able to Afford China's Giant Fees for Pandas." *The Sunday Register Guardian*, February 12.

Grant, Kelli B. 2011. "10 Things Zoos Won't Tell You." *MarketWatch*. Accessed September 20, 2016 from http://www.marketwatch.com/story/10-things-zoos -wont-tell-you-1306528026434.

Gray, Kathy Lynn. 2015. "Zoo Board Approves Levy for Nov. 3." *The Columbus Dispatch*, June 17. Accessed September 15, 2016, from http://www.dispatch .com/content/stories/local/2015/06/17/zoo-levy-approved-by-board.html.

Grazian, David. 2015. *American Zoo: A Sociological Safari*. Princeton, NJ: Princeton University Press.

Gronewold, Anna. 2015. "World-Ranked Omaha Zoo Would Get State Tax Break Under Bill." *Washington Times*, April 7. Accessed September 15, 2016, from

http://www.washingtontimes.com/news/2015/apr/7/nebraska-senators
-advance-bill-to-exempt-zoos-from/.

Hains, David. 2014. "Pandas Take a Bite out of Toronto Zoo Budget." *The Globe and
Mail*, November 30. Accessed September 20, 2016 from http://www
.theglobeandmail.com/news/toronto/pandas-take-a-bite-out-of-toronto
-zoo-budget/article21840549/.

Hale, Robin D. 2012. "Toronto Zoo, Panda Transportation Partner/Sponsor RFP."
Letter/Briefing Note to Toronto Zoo Board of Management. Accessed September 15, 2016, from http://www.toronto.ca/legdocs/mmis/2012/zb/bgrd
/backgroundfile-50178.pdf.

Hancocks, David. 2012. "The Future of Zoos." Public Presentation, October 16, Buffalo, NY.

Kaufman, Leslie. 2012. "Zoos Raise Money for Faraway Animals." *The New York
Times*, May 28. Accessed September 15, 2016, from http://green.blogs
.nytimes.com/2012/05/28/zoos-raise-money-for-faraway-animals/.

Kenny, Harris. 2012. "Privately Operated Zoos Now Considered the Standard, Reason Foundation." Accessed September 15, 2016, from http://reason.org
/news/show/zoo-privatization-2011.

Kusch, Larry. 2011. "Zoo to Hold World-Class Polar Bear Exhibit by 2013." *Winnipeg Free Press*, March 2. Accessed September 15, 2016, from http://
www.winnipegfreepress.com/local/zoo-to-hold-world-class-polar-bear
-exhibit-by-2013-117223033.html.

Mazur, Nicole. 2001. *After the Ark? Environmental Policy-Making and the Zoo*.
Carlton, Victoria, Australia: Melbourne University Press.

Mercer, Phil. 2014. "Cuddling Koalas Is Big Business for Sydney Private Zoo." *BBC
News*, September 28. Accessed September 15, 2016, from http://www.bbc
.com/news/business-29369091.

Nichols, Henry. 2011. "What Price Captive Pandas?" *The Guardian*, December 2.
Accessed September 15, 2016, from http://www.theguardian.com/commen
tisfree/2011/dec/02/pandas-edinburgh-zoo.

Pagliaro, Jennifer. 2014. "Toronto Zoo Revenues Down by $8.3 Million Despite
Pandas' Arrival." *Toronto Star*, November 23. Accessed September 15, 2016,
from   https://www.thestar.com/news/city_hall/2014/11/23/toronto_zoo
_revenues_down_83_million_despite_pandas_arrival.html.

Pina, Alisha A. 2016. "Zip-Lines, Aerial Ropes Course Possible Under Zoo's 20-Year
Pact with Providence." *Providence Journal*, June 6. Accessed September 15,
2016, from http://www.providencejournal.com/article/20160106/NEWS
/160109586.

Rose, Naomi, and Richard Farinato. 2009. "The Case Against Marine Mammals in
Captivity- The Humane Society of the United States." *World Society for the
Protection of Animals*. Accessed September 15, 2016, from http://www
.humanesociety.org/assets/pdfs/marine_mammals/case_against_marine
_captivity.pdf.

Sachgua, Oliver. 2016. "Toronto Zoo Eyes Monorail After Edmonton Firm's Proposal." *Toronto Star*, April 10. Accessed September 15, 2016, from https://
www.thestar.com/news/gta/2016/04/10/toronto-zoo-eyes-monorail-after
-edmonton-firms-proposal.html.

San Diego Zoo. 2016. "Ultimate Safari." Accessed September 15, 2016, from http://www.sdzsafaripark.org/safari/ultimate-safari.

SeaWorld. 2015. "Sea World Unveils Plans for New Dolphin Habitat Opening In 2016." Accessed September 15, 2016, from https://seaworldparks.com/seaworld-sanantonio/media-room/press-releases/2015/2015-dolphin-expansion-project/?m=1.

Sheridan, Anthony. 2011. *What Zoos Can Do.* Munster, DE: Schuling Verlag.

Toronto Zoo. 2010. "The Toronto Zoo—A Major Asset Economic Impact Analysis." *The Economic Planning Group.* Accessed September 15, 2016, from http://www.torontozoo.com/pdfs/economic%20impact%20analysis.pdf.

Toronto Zoo. 2012. "The Future of Toronto Zoo Governance." Accessed September 15, 2016, from http://www.torontozoo.com/pdfs/Toronto%20Zoo%20Governance_Final%20rev5b.pdf.

Toronto Zoo. 2014. "Annual Report." Accessed on September 15, 2016, from http://www.torontozoo.com/pdfs/ZOO_AR_2014_feb8.pdf.

Toronto Zoo. 2016. Accessed September 15, 2016, from http://www.torontozoo.com/.

Utah's Hogle Zoo. "New at the Zoo." Accessed September 15, 2016, from http://www.hoglezoo.org/zoo_visit/whats_new/.

Vancouver Aquarium. 2014. "Vancouver Aquarium 2014 Annual Report." Accessed September 15, 2016, from http://www.vanaqua.org/annualreport2014/.

Walt Disney Company. 2013. "Disney Worldwide Conservation Fund Awards Its 1,000th Conservation Grant." Accessed September 15, 2016, from https://thewaltdisneycompany.com/disney-worldwide-conservation-fund-awards-its-1000th-conservation-grant/.

Walt Disney World. 2016. "Attendance at the Disney's Animal Kingdom Theme Park (Walt Disney World Florida) from 2009 to 2014 (in Millions)." *Statista.* Accessed September 15, 2016, from http://www.statista.com/statistics/236167/attendance-at-the-walt-disney-world-animal-kingdom-theme-park/.

Williams, Dave. 2015. "Georgia Aquarium, Zoo Atlanta and Fernbank Land Tax Breaks. Accessed September 15, 2016, from http://www.bizjournals.com/atlanta/blog/capitol_vision/2015/03/atlanta-attractions-land-tax-breaks.html.

Wood 8 TV. 2016. "3 Sharks, 18 Stingrays Die at John Ball Zoo After Lagoon Malfunction." July 8. Accessed September 15, 2016, from http://woodtv.com/2016/07/08/3-sharks-18-stingrays-die-at-john-ball-zoo-after-lagoon-malfunction/.

Zoocheck. 2016. "Commentary on Toronto Zoo Endangered Species Reserve Fund." Unpublished paper.

Zoo Inquiry. 1994. "WSPA." *Born Free Foundation.* Accessed September 15, 2016, from http://www.bornfree.org.uk/fileadmin/user_upload/files/zoo_check/publications/The_Zoo_Inquiry.pdf.

Cross Your Heart and Hope to Die. (Copyright © 1998 Sue Coe. Courtesy Galerie St. Etienne, NY)

5

The ABCs of Vivisection: (Nonhuman) Animals, Brutality, and Capitalism

Carol L. Glasser

They administered beatings to dogs with perfect indifference, and made fun of those who pitied the creatures as if they felt pain. They said the animals were clocks ... that the whole body was without feeling. They nailed poor animals up on boards by their four paws to vivisect them and see the circulation of the blood which was a subject of great controversy.

Fontanne 1738 (quoted in Spiegel 1996, 65)

A description from Nicholas Fontanne of vivisection practices in the early 1700s.

You failed to provide adequate pre-procedural and post procedural veterinary care. You noted that the guinea pig identified as P38 was doing well following an operation to insert a catheter in its jugular vein for Protocol 13-088-H. However, when your staff was not observing it, the adhesive holding the catheter failed, causing the guinea pig to bleed to death.

(U.S. Department of Agriculture: Citation and Notification of Penalty 2015).

From a 2014 USDA report on nonhuman animal welfare
violations found in University of Oklahoma laboratories;
guinea pigs "named" P5, P6, P8 and P15 also died
in a similar fashion.

*There are other reasons to be confident about the University's growth
potential . . . Over the last 10 years the University's research portfolio has
increased annually by 6 percent . . . the animal research portfolio
accounts for 35 percent of the research activity, this year totaling more
than $550M total.*

From a 2013 internal University of Washington staff email
detailing justification for building a new nonhuman animal
housing facility and increasing the amount of campus
research on other animals.

Every year an estimated 100 million animals are used in research experiments in the United States. Experimentation on nonhuman animals, or
vivisection, has long been opposed on ethical and moral grounds, and moral
opposition to the practice continues to grow. Increasingly, empirical evidence has come to the consensus that vivisection is not the most efficient
or effective way to conduct research and myriad effective alternative
research methods have been developed. Even so, the practice of vivisection
continues. This is of particular concern in the case of public universities,
which are receiving taxpayer dollars in the form of state and federal funding. In this chapter, I argue that the reason that vivisection continues and
is embraced by public research universities is directly tied to capitalism.
Nonhuman animals and vivisection are commoditized, and so it remains
supported, even when it is not in the public's best interest or the best interest of scientific and medical advancement.

Following, I provide the reader with empirical evidence addressing the
lack of efficacy of vivisection. I then explain the key mechanisms through
which universities institutionalize and monetize vivisection. The focus on
generating revenue is not only bad for the nonhuman animals who are killed
and experience extreme distress in the course of vivisection, but it also
stifles scientific innovation and progress. I argue that, even in the face of
mounting evidence that nonhuman animal research models are not efficient or effective, the intersections of the "animal industrial complex" and
the "academic industrial complex" (problematically) create fertile ground
for using vivisection as a source of revenue.

ANIMALS AS LABORATORY "TOOLS"

There are recorded instances of vivisection for academic learning in
ancient Greece as early as the third century BC when Erasistratus used pigs
to study breathing. In the seventeenth century in France and England, a

strong wave of vivisection emerged. Scholars associated with this tradition were known to nail down live dogs by their paws and cut them open in front of other scholars and audiences to study the circulatory system; they believed that other animals could not feel pain. Today, most people recognize that nonhuman animals feel pain and experience stress, but they continue to be objectified as "tools" of research, without much consideration for their lives or well-being.

Nonhuman animals used in experiments have few legal protections; this is particularly true for smaller animals such as hamsters, mice, and rabbits. There is only one federal law, the Animal Welfare Act (AWA), that protects animals used in experiments. Protections under this law are minimal and do not provide *any* protection to birds, fish, mice, and rats, despite the fact that these species make up over 95 percent of all nonhuman animals used for research purposes.

Vivisection is invasive and painful, and other animals are often not provided any pain relief. In the process, they are also commoditized as any other laboratory tool might be. They are sold and purchased in catalogs through which purchasers can request specific "modifications." Nonhuman animals may be manipulated through breeding, genetic engineering, or being physically altered to remove "undesirable" traits (e.g. other animals are bred to contract certain abnormalities and diseases, dogs' vocal cords are typically cut so they don't bark) or to contract certain conditions (e.g. obesity or tumors). Charles River Labs, one of the largest nonhuman animal dealers, makes it clear on a page of their online catalog that other animals are nothing more than objects of research (e.g. "a model"; "study-ready"), rather than subjects of a life:

> Our preconditioning services can help alleviate the space, time and labor costs involved with refining a model to meet your unique research requirements. Whether you are looking for animals fed a special diet, altered through surgery or reared to a certain age, Charles River has the state-of-the-art animal facilities, professional animal care and robust model selection to deliver study-ready animals right to your door (Charles River).

Nonhuman animals are (ware) housed in conditions that are more often than not cramped, dirty, and crowded, and most will never see sunlight or touch the earth. After all this, they are typically killed, either through the procedures of the experiment or because they are no longer of use at the conclusion of the study.

Opposition to using nonhuman animals in research has been steadily increasing in the United States, with the least amount of support among teens and those in their 20s (Goodman, Borch, and Cherry 2013).[1] Even so, many people still feel that vivisection is a necessary evil. In a 2010 survey of U.S. adults, 56 percent of respondents agreed with the statement that research on animals is necessary for medical advancement. Another

27 percent indicated they "did not know," and only 17 percent disagreed (Faunalytics.org 2010).

Despite peoples' perceptions, there is mounting empirical evidence that nonhuman animals are *not* the most effective or accurate models for research. In the 1950s, there was acknowledgement in the scientific community that vivisection was often unnecessary, overused other animals, and was superfluously cruel. This led to the promotion of the principles of The Three R's: replacement (using methods that do not use other animals), reduction (using methods that require fewer nonhuman animals to be used or that can yield more data with the same number of other animals), and refinement (minimizing the suffering of other animals when they are used). The principle of The Three R's has been widely embraced since that time and has "become embedded in national and international legislation regulating the use of animals in scientific procedures" (National Centre for the Replacement and Reduction of Animals in Research), though this legislation only provides minimal protections for most nonhuman animals.

It is undeniable that vivisection was used to develop a number of medical advancements that we have today, but it no longer remains the best way forward for educational or medical advancement. Initiatives to promote The Three R's and a growing consensus in the scientific community as to the inadequacy and waste of vivisection have encouraged the development of many new and more effective research methods. Computer-based and virtual models of dissection are an effective way to teach dissection (Merchant et al. 2014) and improves learning outcomes compared to nonhuman animal models (Predavec 2001). As of 2011, 93 percent of U.S. medical and osteopathy schools no longer require terminal nonhuman animal labs (Faunalytics.org 2012), further highlighting the lack of necessity or efficacy of dissection as a teaching model. Nonetheless, dissection labs remain common in K-12 and post-secondary education. Experimentation on other animals for the purpose of testing cosmetics can be easily and successfully replaced using various technologies, including cell cultures, human tissue samples, and computer models. In fact, cosmetic testing is so obsolete that it was banned in the European Union in 2013, though it is still widely practiced in the United States. Alternative models for medical and basic research include using computer models, cell and tissue cultures, stem cells, or microorganisms (Doke and Dhawale 2013). Among other resources, Johns Hopkins University runs a "global clearing house for information on alternatives to animal testing," called Altweb (http://altweb.jhsph.edu/), which provides resources to researchers to help them find and utilize efficacious research methods without the use of other animals.

One of the key issues with nonhuman animal models is a lack of *translation* of findings from other animals to humans (van der Worp et al. 2010). Research experiments conducted on different species of animals, including humans, will more often than not yield different results. This has been a particular problem for nonhuman animal-based models in the development of drugs and understanding of disease. The nonhuman animal model that has come under the most scrutiny for a lack of translation is the mouse (Engber 2011), the species most widely used in vivisection. The lack of predictive value between nonhuman animal models and human outcomes has resulted in major setbacks and disasters for human health. Some of the best known tragedies due to the failure of translation from nonhuman animal models to humans include the drug Vioxx, which caused at least 140,000 people to have heart attacks (Bhattacharya 2005); delayed understanding that cholesterol leads to heart attacks because the other animal species used to examine this relationship in the 1950s didn't develop atherosclerosis on high cholesterol diets (Greek and Shanks 2009, 63); extreme limb deformities and other birth defects in babies of mothers who had taken thalidomide (Smithells 1992); a decade-long delay in the release of penicillin because it was "excreted too quickly" in rabbit models (Greek and Shanks 2009, 63).

These examples of failed translation are not peculiar. Rather, a lack of translation from other animals to humans is the norm, as systematic reviews of the scientific literature reveal. Knight (2011, 89), for example, analyzed 20 systematic reviews of nonhuman animal research and only found two instances of successful translation. In cancer research specifically, less than 8 percent of findings using vivisection successfully transfer to clinical cancer trials in humans (Mak, Evaniew, and Ghert 2014). A review of six medical interventions (Perel et al. 2006), which examined 100 studies, found that there were similar outcomes between humans and other animals only half the time. Further, the Perel et al. review also found that that "[t]he animal studies were of poor quality . . . with evidence of publication bias" (2006, 4).

Publication bias refers to a bias both in terms of what is submitted to and accepted for publication. When there is a lack of success for a particular experiment in a nonhuman animal model, it is less likely to be published (Greek and Shanks 2009). Further, "[d]rug companies own their data, and they are . . . under no obligation to release the data to the public" (Greek and Shanks 2009, 60); therefore, many studies are never even submitted for publication. As will be discussed, universities are patenting their faculties' research and collaborating with drug companies and other corporations more than ever, keeping even more research away from the scientific community and out of the public sphere. Publication bias in the reporting of research using nonhuman animals means that there are likely many unpublished studies in which there was a lack of success, making the rate of successful translation and prediction based on vivisection even lower than reported. The reluctance to publish "nonfindings" also increases the overall number of other animals used in vivisection, because without knowledge that such experiments were previously conducted, they may be repeated by other researchers.[2]

RESEARCH AS REVENUE

The university plays an instrumental role in the continued reliance on vivisection. On a very basic level, the presence of vivisection in universities has normalized this as a research practice. Social scientists generally find that support for liberal ideologies increases with education. However, the opposite is true in the case of vivisection; the more education someone has, the more likely they are to support it (Goodman, Borch, and Cherry 2013). This speaks to the institutionalization of vivisection through the educational system. As an individual moves through school, the use of other animals in science becomes more normalized and reified. For example, many students engage in classroom dissections in middle school, high school, and/or college; there are examples of nonhuman animal experiments in text books, even the textbooks of disciplines that don't engage in research based on other animals (e.g. word problems in math texts); college students take classes with professors who use animals in their own research. All of this normalizes the practices of breeding and caging animals, experimenting on them while they are alive, and killing them after they are no longer of use to a particular experiment or research lab.

The question remains as to why the number of other animals used in experiments continues to grow and why universities continue to support the practice of vivisection at all since there are alternative, generally superior, methods of research. One reason for this may be a type of inertia. Many professional researchers and university faculty learned to do research using nonhuman animals, so that is what they continue to do and how they teach their graduate students to do research. Another reason is that some are "true believers" (Greek and Shanks 2009, 96) who deeply trust that vivisection is an effective research method. However, given the evidence to the contrary, these reasons don't explain the systemic support and the prevalence of vivisection in universities, particularly when alternatives and superior research methods are available. The continued reliance on vivisection in university research is most directly explained as being revenue-driven.

The academic industrial complex is characterized by a chokehold of economic interests, supported and propelled by political concerns, over the activities of higher education. This is exemplified by the increase in administrators coming out of the business world rather than with a background in the academy. Further, despite ample evidence that interaction with permanent tenured faculty increases student retention (Jaschick 2010), universities are steering away from tenured faculty in favor of adjunct faculty (American Association of University Professors). At the same time tuitions are increasing (Mitchell and Leachman 2015), and students are taking on more debt.

To understand the role of vivisection in the context of the academic industrial complex, we first have to understand how research can lead to revenue in public universities and how vivisection, specifically, fits into this framework. In what has been dubbed the "military-industrial-academic-complex," we see the strong roots of the ties between corporations and academic science dating back to World War I (Leslie 1993) and strengthening in the wake of 9/11 (Giroux 2016). In the 1980s, the passage of the Bayh-Dole Act allowed U.S. universities to own and patent the products of research resulting from federally funded projects, which strengthened and solidified corporate influence over universities. These relationships between university research and external collaborations influence what is researched, how and where results are presented, and what is eventually published (Abraham 1995).

The tie between research and revenue stream is particularly strong in the public universities. In the 2013–2014 academic year, U.S. private, for-profit universities received 90 percent of their total revenues from tuition and fees, compared to 30 percent at private nonprofits and a mere 20 percent at public universities (National Center for Education Statistics 2016). These vast differences in revenue streams can largely be explained by differences in the way each type of university structures research. While public universities are only receiving 20 percent of revenues from tuition, 42 percent comes from government grants, contracts, and appropriations—much of which is directed toward research. Two of the key ways that research endeavors generate revenue while also increasing support for vivisection is through technology transfers and grants. While these processes generate profits directly, relationships with corporations that are built through technology transfer agreements and grants can also lead to additional revenue-generating activity for the university, such as the funding of endowed chairs and direct donations. These provide a fertile ground for the continuation of nonhuman animal experimentation, even as alternative research technologies prove to be more promising and efficacious.

Research grants are perhaps the most transparent mechanism through which universities financially gain from research using nonhuman animals. Science, technology, engineering, and mathematics disciplines, or STEM disciplines, receive the largest share of financial research and development support from the federal government (Humanities Indicators 2016), often in the form of grants.

These grants bring money not just to the individual projects for which they are awarded, but to the university as a whole through indirect costs that are attached to grants. *Indirect costs* are funds that go directly to the university to contribute to expenses the university incurs to support research, but that is not exclusively tied to the specific project. For example, staff to handle the finances, maintaining labs and buildings, and other operational costs the university may incurs to functionally support research on the campus. These are payments *in addition to* the money that is awarded specifically for the research project. Indirect costs, also called faculty and administration rates (F & A), are set by the federal government and may vary by university. These rates can range but are often over 50 percent of the direct cost of the grant. This means that if the indirect cost rate is set at 50 percent, and a researcher is awarded a grant for $500,000 in direct costs of research, the university receives an additional $250,000 from the granting agency to go toward indirect costs.

Prestige and job security for university faculty, particularly in the STEM disciplines, are often tied to their ability to win grants, especially large grants. Vivisection often simply costs more money than using alternate technologies to perform the same type of research (Doke and Dhawale 2013). Purchasing nonhuman animals who were bred for use in vivisection is often more expensive than purchasing the alternative nonhuman model (Costs of Animal and Non-Animal Testing, 2012). The use of other animals also generates additional continued costs. Machines, computer models, tissues, cells, and other methods can be relatively easy to store and don't need continuous care. To conduct research on other animals, a lot of additional supplies must be purchased, and a lot of additional industries have been created to do this: vivariums are needed to house them, cages to contain and separate them, tools to perform the experiments, implements to restrain them while they are being experimented on, and specialized waste protocols to kill them and dispose of their dead bodies. Further, for many types of research, the technology does not need to be repeatedly replaced, whereas nonhuman animals do because once a nonhuman animal is "used" in an experiment, s/he cannot usually be "reused," and s/he is typically killed after the research has ended. This means that grants are often initially higher for this type of research, providing faculty no direct incentive to use other models nor for universities to encourage transitioning away from nonhuman animal models because larger grants mean more prestige and higher indirect costs.

Since nonhuman animals cannot typically be "used" for multiple experiments, vivisection can also create a higher likelihood of researchers seeking a grant renewal, as more nonhuman animals will need to be purchased if a research study seeks to expand or continue. Grant renewals are often awarded more readily than new grants. One of the largest federal granting agencies to the STEM disciplines is the NIH (National Institutes of Health); in 2015 grant renewals from the NIH were more than twice as likely to be funded than were new applications, with a success rate of about 37 percent compared to 16 percent for new applications (Laurer 2016). This contributes in an important way to the persistence of vivisection because, even as newer more effective research models are being developed, there is no incentive for researchers to embrace them. In fact, they are disincentivized. For scholars whose reputation and job security rely on bringing in money through grants, it may seem a more secure route to seek the continuation of a current study, perhaps just tweaking it slightly at each renewal iteration, rather than taking the risk of proposing a new study.

Another key way that animal research can generate revenue in universities is through *technology transfer* agreements in which universities seek to patent research findings, including research based on vivisection. This process encourages universities to commercialize research rather than disseminating it in the public commons via journal articles and other traditional academic modes of research sharing and distribution.

As mentioned earlier, in 1980 the federal Bayh-Dole Act allowed universities to have control over any intellectual property produced by their faculty if it was supported with federal grants. Universities have restructured over the past few decades to be able to better profit off the Bayh-Dole Act and other changes to the patent system that allow for selling research outputs (Valdivia 2013). Even though technology transfers often don't produce revenue, most research universities play into the "business model of licensing university patents to the highest bidder" (Valdivia 2013) because when they do payoff they can generate a lot of money. For example, Columbia University developed a $790 million patent for inserting DNA into cells, and New York University received $1 billion for patents associated with the development of the drug Remicade (Pérez-Peña 2013).

The increase in technology transfers supports vivisection in an absolute sense because it has supported a general increase in the overall amount of money that universities are spending on research. A study of 86 land-grant and state-funded universities found a positive correlation between the number of technology disclosures and the amount of money a university spends on research; between 2003 and 2012 technology disclosures increased by 60 percent, which was matched by a 65 percent increase in total research expenditure (Anderson 2004).

Notably, research support that comes directly from universities' budgets is also being funneled into those disciplines most likely to be involved in vivisection. University research and development (R&D) spending in the science, technology, and engineering disciplines was more than three times that spent on the humanities and social sciences. In 2014, about $12 billion each was spent funding research in both the biological sciences as well as in engineering, and over $20 billion was spent on research in the medical sciences. This is compared to under $1 billion for research in the humanities and less than $4 billion in the social sciences (Research and Development Expenditures at Colleges and Universities 2016).

While some universities may incubate startups for commercializing these new technologies in-house, they more often develop industry-university collaborations and work with corporations to turn research discoveries into commercial products (Valdivia 2013; Farrell 2008). Many universities have a technology transfer office (TTO), with the explicit purpose of developing such relationships. This in turn further strengthens university and corporate ties. Industry-academic relationships, which are bolstered through university licensing of their faculty's research and institutionalized via technology transfer offices, support the use of nonhuman animals in research. While these relationships might foster an increase in research output, they negatively impact research quality by creating conflicts of interest while also stifling creativity and innovation (Stuart 2004).

Industry-university collaborations have been strengthening, particularly with growth in the biomedical industry. The biomedical industry, which includes pharmaceutical companies, is experiencing growth (Jacobs 2015). Some universities, eager for profits, are creating programs to encourage and fund drug development research. Corporations are leveraging this to cut their costs by relying on university researchers to do early-phase research:

Drug companies and research institutes hope that the new programmers will kill two birds with one stone: replenish the pharmaceutical industry's depleted pipeline of new drugs, and bring money to institutions that face shrinking public funding (Hayden 2012).

The tight partnerships between universities and industry create conflicts of interest by creating a loss of objectivity as corporations and their economic interests come to control research agendas. As Stuart (2004) highlights, this in turn can also influence teaching agendas as it can influence university hiring decisions. Universities may well favor hiring faculty who engage in research practices that support corporate agendas, while other important issues that might be of use to the public (but which are not as profitable) might be left unaddressed.

Notably, many of these companies are pharmaceutical and medical companies which must get FDA (Food and Drug Administration) approval for many of their products. FDA approval of many pharmaceutical and medical products requires that they be tested on other animals. This incentivizes the use of vivisection in the initial development and discovery phase of research; if there is an interest in developing a product for industry, the norms of the industry are more likely to be utilized when producing the product, even if these are not the best methods available. In the same way, corporate relationships can also stifle creativity and innovation because there is a delay of knowledge dissemination and lack of knowledge sharing as contracts and technology disclosures are developed. Importantly, industry-university partnerships promote an overall increase in nonhuman animal experimentation outside of the university context, and many of the products developed in universities will be tested on other animals, again by firms that are not held to the professional (albeit weak) standards that university faculty are supposed to follow.

CONCLUSION

University support of vivisection is undeniable. Faculty and staff who engage in this research are rewarded with increased physical support and minimal oversight of their research or the well-being of the other animals who they are using. Professors within the STEM disciplines make significantly more on average than their counterparts in the social sciences and humanities (Jaschick 2016). Universities often invest a great deal in building infrastructure and physical resources to facilitate vivisection as well.[3] Further, models of research that use nonhuman animals receive minimal oversight as well. University research proposals and protocols involving other animals are reviewed by each institution's IACUC (Institutional Animal Care and Use Committee), groups that are primarily staffed by others who also conduct research on nonhuman animals, and their institutional supporters. Not surprisingly, research proposals are rarely rejected, requested exemptions to the minimalist standards of welfare are frequently granted, and initiatives embracing The Three R's are underemphasized (Hansen, Goodman, and Chandna 2012).

University support of vivisection is driven by motives for profit. It has created an institution that systemically supports and actively encourages vivisection in order to generate revenues through grants, partnerships with corporations, and technology transfers. Vivisection persists in public research universities despite systematic reviews of scientific literature that consistently find a lack of translation from nonhuman animal models to human trials, notwithstanding that there are initiatives to reduce, refine, and replace other animals in experiments, despite better more effective research models existing, and without regard to the fact that millions of nonhuman animals are suffering immensely and dying needlessly in the process. Put simply, vivisection persists in public research universities because it is viewed as a revenue stream.

NOTES

1. Opposition to research on nonhuman animals grew 25 percent among teens and 20-somethings in the 10-year period from 2001 to 2011, with 59 percent opposing testing on other animals in 2011 (Goodman, Borch, and Cherry 2013).

2. Studies that use nonhuman animal models have also been critiqued for failing to comprehensively report research procedures (Kilkenny et al. 2010). This includes, among other issues, not determining the appropriate sample size for the

study (van der Word 2010) and failing to report the number of other animals used (Kilkenny et al. 2010). These mistakes make it difficult to use the studies to predict human outcomes, to evaluate the quality of the studies, and it can lead to the duplication of studies. All of this leads to an absolute increase in the number of other animals who are used in experiments and invalidates the utility of the findings for which they were sacrificed.

3. For example, the University of Washington received a fine of nearly $11,000 from the USDA after they performed unapproved experiments on several nonhuman primates, and another was starved to death (Doughton 2013). Rather than shutting down or limiting their vivisection program, the University of Washington decided to "improve" and expand it and is currently in the process of building a new "animal-research facility" at an estimated cost of $123 million.

REFERENCES

Abraham, John. 1995. "The Production and Reception of Scientific Papers in the Academic-Industrial Complex: The Clinical Evaluation of a New Medicine." *British Journal of Sociology,* 46(2): 167–190.

American Association of University Professors. "Background Facts on Contingent Faculty." *American Association of University Professors.* Accessed on September 28, 2016, from https://www.aaup.org/issues/contingency/back ground-facts.

Anderson, Justin Luke. 2004. "University Technology Transfer Productivity," Master's thesis, Oklahoma State University.

Bhattacharya, Shaoni. 2005. "Up to 140,000 Heart Attacks Linked to Vioxx." *New Scientist.* January 25. Accessed September 22, 2016, from https://www .newscientist.com/article/dn6918-up-to-140000-heart-attacks-linked-to -vioxx/.

Charles River. 2016. "Preconditioned Models." Accessed September 23, 2016, from http://www.criver.com/products-services/basic-research/customized -model.

Doke, Sonali K., and Shashikant C. Dhawale. 2015. "Alternatives to Animal Testing: A Review." *Saudi Pharmaceutical Journal,* 23(3): 223–229.

Engber, Daniel. 2011. "The Mouse Trap." *Slate.com.* Last modified November 2011. Accessed September 20, 2016, from http://www.slate.com/articles/health _and_science/the_mouse_trap/2011/11/the_mouse_trap.html.

Farrell, Maureen. 2008. "Universities That Turn Research into Revenue." *Forbes.* Accessed on September 19, 2016, from http://www.forbes.com/2008/09/12 /google-general-electric-ent-tech-cx_mf_0912universitypatent.html.

Faunalytics.org. 2010. "Animal Experimentation: An HRC Research Primer." Accessed September 30, 2016, from https://faunalytics.org/wp-content /uploads/2015/05/Fundamentals_Animal-Experimentation.pdf.

Faunalytics.org. 2012. "New Updates to HRC's Humane Trends; Things You Should Know." Last modified December 2012. Accessed September 19, 2016, from https://faunalytics.org/new-updates-to-hrcs-humane-trends-things-you -should-know/.

Giroux, Henry A. 2007. *The University in Chains: Confronting the Military-Industrial-Academic Complex*. Boulder, CO: Paradigm Publishers.

Goodman, Justin R., Casey A. Borch, and E. Cherry. 2012. "Mounting Opposition to Vivisection." *Contexts*, 11(2): 68–69.

Greek, C. Ray, and Niall Shanks. 2009. *FAQs about the Use of Animals in Science: A Handbook for the Scientifically Perplexed*. Lanham, MD: University Press of America, copublished by arrangement with Americans for Medical Advancement.

Hansen, Lawrence, Justin Goodman, and Alka Chandna. 2012. "Analysis of Animal Research Ethics Committee Membership at American Institutions." *Animals*, 2(4): 68–75.

Hayden, Erika Check. 2014. "Universities Seek to Boost Industry Partnerships." *Nature.com*. Accessed September 30, 2016, from http://www.nature.com /news/universities-seek-to-boost-industry-partnerships-1.15174#graph.

Houghton, Sandi. 2013. "UW Approves New Animal-Research Facility." *Seattletimes.com*. Last modified November 15, 2013. Accessed September 30, 2016, from http://www.seattletimes.com/seattle-news/uw-approves-new-animal -research-facility/.

Humanities Indicators. 2016. "Research and Development Expenditures at Colleges and Universities." Last modified January 2016. Accessed on September 19, 2016, from http://www.humanitiesindicators.org/content/indicatordoc .aspx?i=86.

Human Society International. 2012. "Costs of Animal and Non-Animal Testing: Humane Society International." Accessed on September 19, 2016, from http://www.hsi.org/issues/chemical_product_testing/facts/time_and_cost .html.

Jacobs, John. 2015. "Biotechnology: One of the Last Great Growth Frontiers for Retail Investors." *Forbes.com*. Accessed September 30, 2016, from http://www.forbes.com/sites/johnjacobs/2015/03/04/biotechnology-one -of-the-last-great-growth-frontiers-for-retail-investors/#6701680734f4 March 2015.

Jaschik, Scott. 2010. "Adjuncts and Retention Rates." *Inside Higher Ed*, June. Accessed September 30, 2016, from https://www.insidehighered.com/news /2010/06/21/adjuncts.

Jaschik, Scott. 2016. "What You Teach Is What You Earn." *Inside Higher Ed*, March. Accessed September 30, 2016, from https://www.insidehighered.com/news /2016/03/28/study-finds-continued-large-gaps-faculty-salaries-based -discipline.

Kilkenny, Carol, William Browne, Innes Cuthill, Michael Emerson, and Douglas Altman. 2010. "Improving Bioscience Research Reporting: The ARRIVE Guidelines for Reporting Animal Research." *Journal of Pharmacology and Pharmacotherapeutics J Pharmacol Pharmacother*, 1(2): 94.

Knight, Andrew. 2008. "Systematic Reviews of Animal Experiments Demonstrate Poor Contributions Toward Human Healthcare." *Reviews on Recent Clinical Trials*, 3(2): 89–96.

Lauer, Mike. 2016. "Grant Renewal Success Rates: Then and Now NIH Extramural Nexus." *U.S National Library of Medicine*, May. Accessed on September 19,

2016, from https://nexus.od.nih.gov/all/2016/05/26/grant-renewal-success-rates-then-and-now/.

Mak, Isabella, Nathan Evaniew, and Michelle Ghert. 2014. "Lost in Translation: Animal Models and Clinical Trials in Cancer Treatment." *American Journal of Translational Research,* 6(2): 114–118.

Merchant, Zahira, Ernest T. Goetz, Lauren Cifuentes, Wendy Keeney-Kennicutt, and Trina J. Davis. 2014. "Effectiveness of Virtual Reality-Based Instruction on Students' Learning Outcomes in K-12 and Higher Education: A Meta-Analysis." *Computers and Education,* 70: 29–40.

Mitchell, Michael, and Michael Leachman. 2015. "Years of Cuts Threaten to Put College out of reach for More Students." *Center on Budget and Policy Priorities,* May. Accessed September 28, 2016, from http://www.cbpp.org/sites/default/files/atoms/files/5-13-15sfp.pdf.

National Center for Education Statistics. 2016. "Postsecondary Institution Revenues." Last modified May 2016. Accessed on September 19, 2016, from http://nces.ed.gov/programs/coe/indicator_cud.asp.

National Centre for the Replacement and Reduction of Animals in Research. "The 3Rs." Accessed on September 22, 2016, from https://www.nc3rs.org.uk/the-3rs.

Perel, Pablo, et al. 2016. "Comparison of Treatment Effects between Animal Experiments and Clinical Trials: Systematic Review." *BMJ,* 1–6.

Pérez-Peña, Richard. 2013. "Patenting Their Discoveries Does Not Pay Off for Most Universities, a Study Says." *The New York Times,* November 20. http://www.nytimes.com/2013/11/21/education/patenting-their-discoveries-does-not-pay-off-for-most-universities-a-study-says.html.

Predavec, Martin. 2001. "Evaluation of E-Rat, a Computer-Based Rat dissection, in Terms of Student Learning Outcomes." *Journal of Biological Education,* 35(2): 75–79.

Spiegel, Marjorie. 1996. *The Dreaded Comparison: Human and Animal Slavery.* New York: Mirror Books.

Stuart, James. 2004. "The Academic-Industrial Complex: A Warning to Universities." *University of Colorado Law Review,* 75(3): 1011–1064.

U.S. Department of Agriculture (USDA): Citation and Notification of Penalty." 2015. Reference Number OK140019-AC, November 5, 2015.

Valdivia, Walter D. 2013. "University Start-ups: Critical for Improving Technology Transfer." *Brookings,* November. Accessed on September 19, 2016, from https://www.brookings.edu/research/university-start-ups-critical-for-improving-technology-transfer/.

van der Worp, H. Bart, et al. 2010. "Can Animal Models of Disease Reliably Inform Human Studies?" *PLoS Med,* 7(3): e1000245. Accessed September 30, 2016, from http://journals.plos.org/plosmedicine/article/authors?id=10.1371/journal.pmed.1000245

Unwanted. (Copyright © 2016 Sue Coe. Courtesy Galerie St. Etienne, NY)

6

"Wild Animals" as Goods, Chattel, and Perpetual Victims in Post-Apartheid South Africa[1]

Michele Pickover

PROLOGUE: THE VANQUISHED

The ingrained notion that "wild animals" only exist at the behest of human exploitation and generally now only as part of managed and fabricated aesthetically appealing landscapes, which are often privately owned and have financial spin-offs, means that in the current market-driven, extractive anthropocene world, their survival, as individuals or as species, is now almost totally dependent on them being categorized as commodities. According to Cock (2014, 39) "underlying all capital's strategies—is the broad process of commodification: the transformation of nature and all social relations into economic relations, subordinated to the logic of the market and the imperatives of profit. The process of financialization means increasing instability of these relations and will lead to a deepening of the crisis in nature." The macroeconomic context in Africa is one based on a heavy dependence on resource-intensive commodity exports mainly through massive exploitation of its so-called "natural resources." This is having a direct impact on the lives of nonhuman animals on the African continent, and it does not matter where the locus of power over "wild animals" lies: they are continuously commodified.

Consequently, in Africa "wild animals" have become merely species and specimens. They have all but lost their agency, individuality, and independence and are no longer "wild" because the spatial, ideological, and economic context in which they live is fashioned and driven by human dominance, greed, and destructiveness.[2] They have been conquered—and the conquered are held in contempt, disrespected, and unrecognized. "Wild animals" have become socially and culturally marginalized and invisible. They do not live parallel or separate lives, but their lives are entangled with ours. This is the prerequisite on which they are allowed to exist. Essentially it is a case of exeunt the "wild animals," unless they are co-opted as aesthetic props in the capitalist production and construction of notions of wilderness.

Simultaneously, the global political economy, the State and "wildlife industry" is actively promoting the notion of "wild animals" and the chimera of wilderness to propel profits, thus paradoxically and concomitantly obliterating and constructing. The perpetually increasing scale of "wild animal" commodification as a result of the nexus between hypercapitalism, globalization, pro- "sustainable use" policy discourse and the growth-dependent, unjust, and ecologically flawed global and local development model should be screaming out alarm bells to those who are concerned about the interests of these tyrannized victims. The commodification of "wild animals" in South Africa takes place against the backdrop of colonialism, apartheid, neoliberalism, a deeply ingrained marginalization of "the Other," and a militarized conservation sector which is still largely in the hands of an Afrikaner elite and a particular social subclass which reflects this.

Concurrent scarcity and abundance, and the stimulation of both, are the order of the day. In addition, according to the *Anthropogenic Allee effect*, a concept coined by Courchamp et al. (2006), "the human predisposition to place exaggerated value on rarity fuels disproportionate exploitation of rare species, rendering them even rarer and thus more desirable, ultimately leading them into an extinction vortex." There is the ubiquitousness of African "wild animals" in the global subconscious as well as in the overt materiality and co-option of "wildlife" images and media characterizations by almost every industry transnationally (whether in Europe, the United States, Asia, or Africa). While "wild animals" are becoming extinct in their natural habitats, on the other hand, they are being commercially bred for killing and profit. Even in their endangeredness, "wild animals"—seen as abundant and limitless—their scarceness makes them even more of a target for trade and slaughter.

During the nineteenth century "wild animals" in South Africa were killed on a vast scale as new hunting parties from Europe were penetrating deep into the interior. "Big-game hunters" were seen as the harbingers of civilization and the symbols of patriotism and expansionism. There was a frenzied, indeed almost manic slaughter of "wild animals" that took place to make way for urbanized humans. By the end of the 1890s, European rule and merchant capitalism had, by their efforts to subjugate nature, brought about the almost complete destruction of "wild animals" on the subcontinent. As a result, the demands of commercialism, which got under way after settlement began, rapidly transformed hunting into a war against animals. Today the slaughter continues, in an updated post-metropolis form, with all its added weaponry, vehicles, comfort, and sophisticated technology, within the current political framework of "development" and the economic context of capitalism, and this ritualized killing is supported and legitimized in our conservation policies.

The South African government is a formidable barrier to those fighting for justice for animals. This is because its power protects and legitimizes the ideological forces of exploitation. Historically, South Africa has always taken a pro-consumptive use stance in relation to "wild animals." In the past, it was so that a few people could benefit and have private hunting grounds. It is now located within the language of development. The current management policy is effectively the "consumptive utilization of resources," which has ushered in an extensive increase in the trade in animals and what is essentially farming "wild animals," in line with the policy of the "sustainable utilization of natural resources." In addition, the "consumptive use of wildlife resources" is promoted as an important economic driver. Nonhuman animal suffering is, therefore, not on the government's agenda, and indeed, it is advocating endless exploitation of nonhuman animals, concealing ethical issues and real suffering behind its raw commercialism. The government is driving and overseeing the burgeoning trade in "wild animals" and is responsible for the way hunting is flourishing. Its neoliberal position on elephant ivory sales and its promotion of the hunting industry are examples of its overt "consumptive use" conservation policies—"wild animals" are viewed as mere commodities who usually "pay their way" with their lives. The government also wants to export their conservation policies to other countries in Africa.

THE MARKET IS BOOMING

The violent geography of the trade in Africa's "wild animals" is extensive, lucrative, and ever expanding. The international trade (legal and illegal) involves millions of nonhuman animals every year and is one of the key drivers of species extinction, population decline, suffering, abuse, and death.

The trade in African mammals, birds, and reptiles has grown dramatically since the early 1990s. Profit-motivated nonhuman animal dealers and middlemen and a seemingly bottomless market drive this trade, which hides behind the vague and misused concept of "sustainable use" to pursue its short-sighted agenda. Hungry for hard export cash, South Africa is Africa's biggest "wildlife" trader, and its market is booming and ever-increasing. The major contradiction, although to be expected within the global context of "othering," is the separation of the illegal trade (trafficking) from the legal trade, despite the fact that the two are naturally and obviously intertwined and part of the same continuum. Allowing a market and having a legal trade in "wild animals" and their body parts is at the root of demand and the conversion of living beings into commodities on the "supply" side. Trade opens the door for abuse, including illegal laundering, the hankering of unlimited profit, and the notion of limitless growth in demand, supply, and sales. Emphasis by international bodies and governments is therefore usually on reducing demand of *illegally* obtained items; awareness-raising; increasing expenditure on enforcement and confiscations of illegally traded "products"; legislative compliance; monitoring and evaluation; and support for "sustainable economic activities benefiting rural communities living in and adjacent to wildlife" (often through trophy hunting). The specific use of desensitized and detached language, by governments, international bodies, capital and conservationists, serves to codify, objectify, control, convert, erase, and disembody living beings. It plays an important role in legitimizing and sanitizing the unspeakable so that there is a deliberate collective forgetfulness about the main actors—who is being traded, where they come from—and the holocaust that is being unleashed on "wild animals" through trade and commercial activities. Hence, sterile scientific terminology such as "game," "wildlife products," "wildlife production," "off-takes," "quotas," "harvest," "high value natural resource," "wild sourced inputs," "specimens," "derivatives," and "derived products" are endlessly used when referring to living beings so that they can be used in global human industrial consumer markets for investment, conspicuous consumption,[3] "exotic pets," trophies, exhibition and entertainment, medicine, food, cosmetics and perfume, and fashion.

It is argued in all publications relating to the estimated financial value of the illegal trade in "wild animals" that its clandestine nature make it difficult to measure and quantify. Curiously however, estimated figures for the illegal trade are much more in evidence and readily available than the statistics for the so-called regulated legal trade in "wild animals." In addition, the term *wildlife* often includes charcoal, plants, and timber, making it impossible to get accurate information in relation to "wild animals" only. Uncovering the mystery of the amount of profits generated from trading in "wild animals" and their body parts as a legally and regulated "commodity" is elusive, untransparent, and obfuscatory. It begs the question: is the focus on the illegal trade by the organizations, states, and institutions that promote sustainable development and trade merely a ruse to divert attention away from the consequences and activities of the legal trade?

According to the Wildlife Trade Monitoring Group (TRAFFIC 2016), during the years 2005 to 2009, the Convention on International Trade in Endangered Species of Wild Fauna and Flora (CITES) "endangered species" trade database recorded an annual average of more than 317,000 live birds, just over 2 million live reptiles, 2.5 million crocodilian skins, 1.5 million lizard skins, and 2.1 million snake skins. In terms of hunting trophies, CITES data shows that 10,000 lions were legally trophy hunted between 2003 and 2013, while between 2003 and 2013, 15,518 African elephants were killed for trophies (Tan 2015). These numbers are a low estimate because most of the countries from where the animals traded originate, are poor record-keepers, and corruption is common. The "exotic pet" trade industry is one of the key drivers of the trade in "wild animals." Countries involved in the "exotic pet" trade—both exporters and importers—do not compile reliable data on the extent but nonetheless, in 2005, Karesh et al. suggested that the magnitude of the global trade for the "exotic pet" trade involves over 350 million live nonhuman animals a year, including primates, birds, reptiles, and fish.

Written evidence submitted by TRAFFIC to a 2012 United Kingdom House of Commons Environmental Audit Committee on Wildlife Crime claims that in the early 1990s the estimated value of "legal wildlife products" imported globally was around $160 billion, while in 2009, it was over $323 billion. TRAFFIC also estimated the legal trade of "wildlife products" into the EU alone was worth an estimated €93 billion in 2005, and this increased to nearly €100 billion in 2009. (United Kingdom Parliament 2012). While in 2013, Hübschle (2014, 46) valued the "global legal trade in wildlife" (excluding fish) to be worth between $22.8 billion and $25 billion per annum. CITES[4] stated that "for **key** commodities of CITES-listed Appendix II animals the monetary value is conservatively estimated to range from $350 to $530 million per year, or almost $2.2 billion over the five-year period 2006–2010" (Scanlon 2012).

According to a 2014 United National Environmental Programme (UNEP) report, environmental crime, which includes the illegal trade in "wild animals," is growing two to three times faster than global GDP, dwarfing the illegal trade in small arms and is the world's fourth largest criminal enterprise after drug smuggling, counterfeiting, and human trafficking (Nellemann et al. 2014). A 2016 report concedes that "given this level of volatility in both the seizure record and what is known about the underlying markets, it is nearly impossible to give an accurate and consistent estimate of the criminal revenues generated by "wildlife" trafficking" (United Nations

Office on Drugs and Crime, 2016, 21). The European Commission argues that "wildlife" trafficking is one most profitable organized crimes in the world, with the illegal elephant ivory trade having more than doubled since 2007, and rhino "poaching" increasing by 7,000 percent in South Africa between 2007 and 2013, "endangering the very survival of this species." (European Union 2016). UNEP argues that the ivory trade has been solely responsible for killing more than a quarter of the world's elephant population in the last 10 years, elephants are being killed at a rate that is growing by more than 25 percent every year (Defense Web 2016), and that the possible number of elephants killed in Africa is in the range of 20,000 to 25,000 per year (5 percent) (Nellemann et al. 2014, 7). Statistics from the Great Elephant Census released on September 1, 2016, show an even more alarming situation. The African savannah elephant population has dropped to about 350,000, with forest elephant numbers as low as 70,000.[5] To put this figure in perspective, approximately 1.3 million elephants inhabited Africa in the 1970s. The pace of the slaughter varies from region to region. Between 2009 and 2015, Tanzania lost half of its elephants, and their population has plummeted from about 109,000 to 51,000, a fall of 53 percent (Sieff 2016).

In 2013, the U.S. government estimated that the monetary value from the illegal trade in "wildlife" was between $45 billion to $120 billion each year, with the illegal trade in "endangered wildlife products" (including elephant ivory, rhino horns, and turtle shells) worth at least an estimated $7 billion to $10 billion annually (Wyler and Sheikh 2013).

Many countries, South Africa being one of them, base their pro- "wild animal" trade policy formulation on a false and discredited market-friendly premise that trade is a conservation solution for so-called "endangered species," and legal markets are a panacea for the illegal trade. For example, in relation to the trade in rhino horn, in March 2013, the South African Minister of Environmental Affairs, Edna Molewa, stated that she believes the legalization of the trade is the right direction to take to curb rhino poaching (Rademeyer 2013), while the Department of Environmental Affairs (DEA) in its Rhino Issue Management Report stated that "banning of the rhino horn trade by CITES and the concomitant moratorium on domestic trade by South Africa has had the unintended consequence of increasing poaching of live animals as there is no other horn available" (Republic of South Africa 2013). The tenet of the pro-trade argument is that trade bans produce high prices and scarcity leading to higher illegal trading, and this can be eliminated by a flow of legal supply through captive breeding (farming), sales of stockpiles, and "culling." In this way, they will be able to out-compete the illegal suppliers and drive prices down, thus making "poaching" unprofitable while ensuring high returns for the legal market. Private ownership and business enterprise are key to this argument, and implicit is the development of expanding demand. A pivotal study by Nadal and Aguayo (2014, 1) reviewed the analytical economic arguments used to support the legal market framework. It powerfully shows that "the literature advocating trade as a conservation solution for endangered species relies on models that are based on simplistic and/or extremely restrictive assumptions. In most cases, these models also rely on conceptual tools that have been theoretically discredited." Nadal and Aguayo argue the belief that markets behave as self-regulating mechanisms that lead to equilibrium, and greater efficiency cannot be substantiated, and "the economic analysis of wildlife trade . . . appears to have been trapped in the backwaters of textbook economics" (3) resulting in "incongruities and misleading conclusions" (4).

THE INTERNATIONAL POLICY FRAMEWORK

The overarching global locale in which all South Africa's policies in relation to "wild animals" are firmly positioned is the notion of "sustainable development," described by Giddens as an oxymoron, (Giddens 2009) à la the Brundtland Report (Brundtland 1987) and the 1992 Rio Declaration on Environment and Development, where humans and development are placed at the center of any concern for sustainability. Sustainable development is also articulated in Chapter 3 (Bill of Rights) of South Africa's Constitution, which espouses ". . . ecologically sustainable development and use of natural resources while promoting justifiable economic and social development." This human *über alles* continuum of discrimination and injustice against the "other" persists in the various UN multilateral environmental programs and treaties to which South Africa is a signatory, states party, or supporter. Two examples are:

1. The United Nations Environment Programme (UNEP) Convention on Biological Diversity (CBD)[6] "which couples environmental objectives to the need for development in developing countries and emphasizes that natural resources are the property of individual countries" (Department of Environmental Affairs and Tourism 1997).

2. The Convention on International Trade in Endangered Species of Wild Fauna and Flora (CITES) which governs the global trade in so-called endangered "wild animals." There are currently 182 states parties to the Convention, including South Africa, which ratified in 1975. CITES appears to be concerned not so much with protecting species as with allowing trade in endangered ones, which makes it almost Orwellian in character. Listing species in a hierarchy of appendices, classified according to their vulnerability to extinction, it operates on the premise that "wild animals," particularly those that are listed as "endangered," have an economic value and can be commercially traded. Because the concept of "sustainable use" is at its core, it regulates rather than prohibits trade.

Trade is only regulated for so-called "endangered species." According to CITES, as of October 2, 2013, roughly 5,600 species of animals are listed as threatened in the CITES appendices (I, II, and III) (Convention on International Trade in Endangered Species of Wild Fauna and Flora 2013). Usually this is as a result of trade or the combination of loss of habitat and trade. This means that there are many other animals that are endlessly traded but are not listed on the three CITES appendices. There are thousands of species of "wild animals" who fall outside of so-called "regulated" international trade yet they are legally traded internationally and accompanied by the appropriate permits and official documents. According to the United Nations Office on Drugs and Crime (2016, 10), permits for about 900,000 legal shipments of protected "wildlife products" are issued annually. These nonhuman animals are often obtained illegally but laundered through the legal regulatory framework, including trophy hunting, live sales, "wildlife" farming and ranching, breeding and captive operations, including zoos. According to a June 2015 CITES press release, their trade database had exceeded 15 million records of trade since the mid-1970s—this would mean many millions more nonhuman animals as each record usually represents more than one individual being (CITES 2015). A recent study that analyzed CITES "wild animal" trade records for Appendix I and II species exported out of Africa (involving 2,337 species), between the years 2003 to 2012 found that 90 percent of the records contained discrepancies across almost every type, including quantity, appendix, origin, purpose, source, term, and year, and records missing an import quantity were the most frequent type of discrepancy, occurring in 63 percent of all trade records. It also found that the 50 African countries included in the study were involved in data discrepancies, with Appendix 1 species having more divergences than the other appendices (Russo 2015).

A number of other additional protocols and frameworks further strengthen the commodification of "wild animals." The Nagoya Protocol on Access to Genetic Resources and the Fair and Equitable Sharing of Benefits Arising from their Utilization is a 2010 supplementary agreement to the CBD, providing a legal framework for the implementation of "the fair and equitable sharing of benefits arising out of the utilization of genetic resources" (UNEP 2010). The Collaborative Partnership on Sustainable Wildlife Management (CPW) was initiated in 2013 in response to the CBD's "Decision XI/25 on sustainable use of biodiversity: bushmeat and sustainable wildlife management" (Convention on Biological Diversity 2012), and is a partnership of 13 international organizations who are pushing for the "sustainable use and conservation of wildlife resources." The mission of the CPW is to "increase cooperation and coordination among its members and other interested parties on sustainable wildlife management to promote the sustainable use and conservation of terrestrial vertebrate wildlife in all biomes and geographic areas, contributing to the conservation and sustainable use of biodiversity, and to human food security, livelihoods and wellbeing" (Convention on Biological Diversity 2016).

Through its 2011 report *Towards a Green Economy: Pathways to Sustainable Development and Poverty Eradication*, the United Nations Environment Programme (UNEP 2011) has also articulated and adopted a framework for 'policy makers' which defines the notion of the green economy as one which improves "human well-being and social equity, while significantly reducing environmental risks and ecological scarcities" through investing in and utilizing "natural capital." By re-packaging neoliberal hypercapitalism as the "green economy" and maintaining that markets are the means of promoting sustainable development, "wild animals" are reduced to "natural capital" and forever coupled to the "green economy" and growth. Embedded within the zeitgeist of this report is not only the commodification of nature (and by implication "wild animals") but also the increase in their transnational flow. According to Cock (2014, 28) we are in an era of new commodification where the market is expanding "into all aspects of the natural world; an attempt by capital—in the name of protection—to affect the last enclosure of the commons—that of Nature itself." Given this context, it is not surprising that Lee Scott, CEO of Wal-Mart is on record as saying "Sustainability . . . the single biggest business opportunity of the 21st century and the next main source of competitive advantage" (Lacour 2009).

Evidence of the support of the South African government for a shift to a green economy and a people-centric approach is clear in key policy documents such as the New Growth Path (2010), the National Development Plan (2012) and State of the Nation addresses, government official speeches.[7] This is all in the context that in South Africa only 11 percent of the land is "under conservation," and according to a 2014 presentation by the chief policy advisor for Strategic Environmental Intelligence of the Department of Environmental Affairs, of the 223 river ecosystem types, 60 percent are threatened with 25 percent of these critically endangered; 50 percent of the wetlands have already been lost, and of the remaining 792 wetland ecosystems, 65 percent have been identified as threatened and 48 percent critically endangered (Lukey 2014). The State is promoting the "wildlife industry" and "sustainable use" as a key strategy for "rapid socioeconomic transformation," the "growth of the wildlife economy" and "economic development." In a 2015 speech, the minister of environmental affairs said that "the sustainable utilization of species, including legal hunting, has historically played a significant role in the growth of populations of species, including lion, elephant and rhino," and the hunting industry, which in 2015 they valued at around R6.2 billion (approximately $500,000,000), "is well-regulated and a source of much needed foreign exchange, job creation, community development and social upliftment" (Modise 2016). In 2015, the government also committed itself to the National Biodiversity Economy Strategy (NBES). A critical element of this strategy is to "empower local communities to become significant players in the wildlife industry through the establishment of wildlife based enterprises . . . we believe local communities must be placed at the heart of conservation because unless local communities receive tangible socioeconomic benefits and become part of the wildlife and related industries, the concept of conservation will continue to be regarded as exclusive and elitist." Part of this endeavor is to mobilize "new emerging wildlife farmers" and "establish benefit asset sharing agreements around bioprospecting applications" (Thomson 2016). In addition, the Department's "Vision 2024 Green Economy: Wildlife Based Land Reform Support Programme" key deliverables include: 60,000 jobs; 2 million hectares of communal land restored and developed for "conservation and commercial game ranching;" equity redress by the provision of R4 billion in "game;" and "300,000 heads of wildlife under black empowered and owned ranches."[8]

Clearly, globally, as Sullivan (2014) points out, nature (and "wild animals") is being seen as money. Hence in 2013, with the backing of UNEP, the World Business Council for Sustainable Development (WBCSD) and the International Union for the Conservation of Nature (IUCN) established the World Forum on Natural Capital. According to their website (http://naturalcapitalforum.com), ". . . there are both serious risks to business, as well as significant opportunities, associated with biodiversity loss and ecosystem degradation" and "the World Forum on Natural Capital . . . see it as a chance to reframe nature as the solution to global challenges, rather than a part of the problem."

In 2015, members of the UN General Assembly adopted the 2030 Agenda for Sustainable Development. The Sustainable Development Goals (SDGs) articulate the "global agenda for improving human living conditions." At the same time, the SDGs advocate "sustainable consumption and production patterns," "conservation and sustainable use of the oceans, seas, and marine resources" for sustainable development, and "the protection, restoration and promotion of sustainable use of terrestrial ecosystems, sustainably manage forests, combat desertification, and halt and reverse land degradation and halt biodiversity loss."[9] Also somewhat duplicitously included in the SDGs is the statement: a world "in which humanity lives in harmony with nature and in which wildlife and other living species are protected."[10]

NEW DISCOURSES, BUT NO JUSTICE FOR NONHUMAN ANIMALS

In addition, community conservation and development projects funded by the World Bank always ensure that they are compatible with "sustainable development," UNEP treaties and the goals of the Convention on

Biological Diversity. The perceived legitimacy of these neoliberal "new conservation" projects is reinforced by the argument that they are in response to, and in opposition with, so-called traditional and authoritarian preservationist/protectionist models, which stemmed from imperial Europe into the colonial states. Access to and use of "wild animals" was characteristically restricted in defense of class hierarchy and which, by definition, excluded ordinary people and communities. The power of defining the value and purpose of "wild animals" and the land they occupied in South Africa was the exclusive purview of white hegemony.

Woven into the fabric of their management practices of "wildlife conservation" was the conquest and dispossession of indigenous black communities. What Death (2014, 1226) calls the "exclusive preservationist approaches to conservation, dominated by white liberals and conservatives who obviously put the interests of charismatic mega-fauna, hunting, and white agriculture ahead of black populations." The subliminal underlying assumption by authors critical of this colonial and apartheid model is that "wild animals" were also the main beneficiaries at the expense of people,[11] despite the fact that "wild animals" were similarly victims of the same expansive and abusive social schemas: purely viewed as things, as commodities, as assets within an aesthetic landscape, within the logic of the market and scientific utilitarianism, to be managed, kept, and killed for a financial return. In this way "wild animals" are perpetually positioned as villains, acting against the interests of poor communities who were/are the targets of unjust systems such as colonialism and apartheid. The "new conservation" paradigm, which speaks to issues of redress, parity, land restitution, benefit-sharing, and ownership, does not represent a shift in sensibilities towards "wild animals." The shift in the locus of power over "wild animals" from colonial and apartheid conservation to "new conservation" may have denoted a change in the rhetoric but not in their exploitation and commodification.

Neoliberal capitalism, which is the official UN position, and which has transfigured "wild animals" into goods and chattel has been adopted, adapted, and articulated by governments across Africa and the world, but it is not only mainstream conservation and the global free market agenda that have subjugated animals. It is also the rhetoric of The Left and environmental justice advocates, who, in their criticism of "conservation-oriented ... dominated character of the ... mainstream environmental movement" (Munnik 2007, 2) and who "positioned themselves in opposition to many forms of conservation as they supported black South Africans in their efforts to claim back land that they had lost to conservation" (Munnik 2007, 3), also subordinate "wild animals" to human development needs, seeing them as "resources" and as having no place in social justice struggles, particularly in the Global South. It is a matter of righting past human rights wrongs, of unequal access to "environmental resources" between the settler community and the majority African population.

South African environmental and social justice activists who supposedly connect the "red," "green" and "brown" issues such as Jacklyn Cock (2011), while arguing that the sustainability discourse has been appropriated by neoliberal capitalism, and the commodification of nature is driving capital's response to the ecological crisis, simultaneously also argue that the discourse of sustainable development is an advance on the earlier protectionist models because it is concerned with "human needs" (Cock 2007). In this context, social justice is not an all-encompassing notion that affirms the value of all forms of life against the interests of wealth, power, and technology. Instead, the demeaning and sweeping euphemistic language of exploitation is used when referring to "wild animals" and their habitats—their priority is ecological sustainability within the context of protecting limited "resources" but ensuring that these "resources" are used for the benefit of all [humans] and not just for the privileged few (i.e., the idea of "benefit-sharing"). In their quest for social justice for the poor and powerless, "other" nonhuman animals are always excluded.

After the death of apartheid, there was a window of opportunity for inclusive justice to be part of the process of building a new society and for the interests of other animals to be included in the new Constitution. This never happened. In relation to "wild animals," this was for two key reasons: the influence of individuals from the environmental justice movement in developing government policy and legislation (what I call the era of white mischief) in the early 1990s; and the ensuing and almost simultaneous co-option and appropriation of the sustainable community livelihoods and development position by mainstream conservation and the "wildlife" industry, who all jumped on the bandwagon in the service of advancing the neoliberal project within government, its agencies, and policies. In the post-colonial and apartheid State, other animals continue to be subjected to a permanent cycle of never-ending domination, marginalization and injustice. They are reduced to squatter status, occupying land at the behest of their less than fair human owners. For them, whether it is under colonial, capitalist, or African nationalist rule, they are subjected to endless conquests, dispossession, displacement, expropriation, eviction and perpetual removal, and relocation. For the "wild animals," who are equally disempowered and disenfranchised victims of colonialism, apartheid, and capitalism, it has resulted in a lethal and abusive commodification cocktail. It has meant that pro-"wildlife utilization" organizations exclusively partner with government and also act as consultants in designing, managing, and developing government policy, training government employees ("capacity building"), writing up and evaluating reports for government, and facilitating government hosted workshops.

An example of such an organization is Africa Resources Trust (now renamed Resource Africa), which was established in 1994[12] and whose main aim is supposedly to alleviate poverty through the "sustainable use" and exploitation by local communities of "natural resources such as wildlife." It has, amongst others, promoted the Communal Areas Management Programme for Indigenous Resources (CAMPFIRE) in Zimbabwe; supported the Southern African Development Community, Regional Community Based Natural Resource Management Projects (SADC CBNRM); and has been funded by the European Union—Conservation and Development Opportunities from Sustainable Development (CODEOSUB) Southern African Project.

Resource Africa favors the trade in elephant ivory,[13] arguing that "elephants and their ivory are immensely valuable, especially to rural communities, who could benefit from a legal trade . . . The only solution resides in establishing a carefully constructed open market for ivory, which is transparent and regulated, and which channels benefits to the communities who live with these elephants. In this way, trade would be a huge benefit to the species and to Africa."[14] Proponents of the "sustainable use" of "wild animals" argue that developing countries want to see fewer, not more, exemptions for environmental purposes and that stimulating trade helps conservation. They agree with the CBD, which focuses on the supply rather than the demand side of biodiversity, and assumes that "extinction is primarily driven by restrictions on supply, such as loss of habitat, rather than unregulated demand," and argue that "these supply side problems require solutions at national policy level, and particularly solutions which focus on increasing the value of wildlife to producers" (Broad 2001). From this point of view, Africa and the nonhuman animals that live here are just one big marketplace. According to Dr. David Lavigne:

> [C]onservation has reached a turning point. It has been hijacked by the so-called 'wise-use' movement. This Orwellian takeover has stolen the mantle of conservation and abused it to promote trade in wildlife under the guise of ecological sustainability . . . We need to scrap conservation as we know it, because it has become part of the problem, not part of the solution. Perhaps both the word conservation, and the movement it inspired, should be abandoned and replaced with something that recognizes humans are a part of nature and that the future of our species and that of others are inextricably linked. (Siggins 2004)

THE SOUTH AFRICAN "SUSTAINABLE USE" POSITION: EXPLOITATION AND CRUELTY

Historically, South Africa has always taken a virulent "consumptive use" stance in relation to "wild animals." The privatization and commercialization of "wild animals" was well advanced by the late 1800s, through trophy (recreational) hunting consumption and the killing of "wild animals" as "vermin" to make way for agriculture and towns. According to Van Sittert (2005, 272):

> European settlement in southern Africa can be read as a process of "bring-ing in the wild," which, in the case of nonhuman animals, involved their conversion from res nullius into private property through the act of capture or enclosure. The process was driven by the insatiable appetite of local and world markets for a wide range of animal products, supplemented by state subsidies targeting certain species with too low or no market value.

It is within the global ideological milieu of capitalist production, and the affiliated international trade and utilization treaties that South Africa is currently conceptualizing and affecting "wild animals," not only reproduc-ing colonial conservation practices but adding the political layers of "sus-tainable development," "benefit-sharing," redress and land reform. This has further subjugated and oppressed "wild animals" and relentlessly exploited other species. More specifically, it is against the sharp edge of the concept "sustainable resource use" that it has honed and entrenched its merciless incentive-driven "conservation" strategies and attitudes toward "wild animals."

The current African National Congress (ANC) government is a formi-dable barrier to those fighting for justice and against the oppression of non-human animals. This is because its power protects and legitimizes the ideological forces of exploitation. It is within the overarching development framework and under the guise of poverty alleviation that the South African government is spearheading an aggressive "consumptive use" and "if it pays it stays" agenda. The prevailing thesis is that species can only be conserved if rural communities become more tolerant of "wild animals," and they will only become more charitable towards them if they receive economic benefits, usually at the expensive of the other animals themselves though trophy hunting of "charismatic megafauna" and other "wildlife species." This stance can be seen in the writings of most South African scientists, as articulated by Selier and Minin: "sustainable utilization of wildlife is . . . a win–win strategy for the expansion of the conservation estate and for gen-erating important economic benefits for local communities."

Bolstered largely by white capital and interests, South Africa's implemen-tation of "sustainable use" is so all-pervasive that its unyielding and vocif-erously outspoken support for this exploitative and cruel patriarchal enterprise, which kills, commodifies, and subjugates every "wild" individ-ual in South Africa through trade, hunting, and tourism, means it is fast becoming a pariah state, even within the omnipotent and dominant pro-use global landscape. The Department of Environmental Affairs (DEA) maintains that "sustainable use" is the cornerstone of its policies in rela-tion to "wild animals." Nonhuman animal suffering is not on its agenda.

Indeed, it is working hand-in-glove with the "wildlife industry" to advance the trade in and killing of "wild animals." It is also acting as a conduit to provide polices and legislation (or lack thereof) for industries to continue unhindered. In addition, there are inadequate policies and legislation; lack of enforcement and implementation; an ill-equipped civil society and an uninformed public; and pressure on government from a strong pro-trade and pro-hunting lobby and strong and well-funded pro-utilization conservation organizations.

Local legislation, guidelines, norms, and standards serve to entrench exploitation and the conversion and re-coding of individual "wild animals" into human assets and resources. One such problematic concept, which remains part of the South African legal framework, is The Roman Dutch law principle of *res nullius*. It has been expediently used as a defense by both "owner" and "poacher," for example:

a. if a "wild" animal escapes from the "owner's" enclosure and is captured by someone else with the intention to "own" and profit from "it," the capturer would argue that they did not steal but rather took abandoned "property;"

b. it is also invoked by "owner's" (including the State) to avoid responsibility and custodianship by arguing that the nonhuman animal had escaped and had therefore become "ownerless."

This position continues to be evoked even though it is an obsolete defense because there have been changes in the law.[15] In terms of South African common law, *res nullius*, "wild animals" cannot be owned, but in 1991, South Africa passed the Game Theft Act (105 of 1991) so as to legalize private ownership by protecting the landowner's rights of ownership of "wild animals" that escape or are lured from the landowner's "sufficiently enclosed" land. *Res nullius* has no place in South Africa—it was first proposed as a political justification for white ownership of land in the Cape in the 1830s and is closely linked to colonial and imperial notions of possession and ownership. It is in conflict with the South African Constitution and is no longer justifiable in a democratic society.

The South African government regularly states that the hunting industry operates in line with the concept of "sustainable utilization of natural resources" as espoused by the International Conservation Union (IUCN) and argues that hunting and allied businesses, which includes breeding; capture and transportation; and taxidermists, contribute significantly to the central revenue *fiscus* and create jobs. In addition, they argue that hunting is in line with conservation practices and is a "nondetrimental" practice. However, an analysis of six African countries—South Africa, Zimbabwe, Zambia, Mozambique, Namibia, and Tanzania—where trophy hunting has been touted by the industry and governments as "an effective conservation tool," unsurprisingly showed that in reality: trophy hunting is causing decline in "wild animal" numbers, having negative impacts on "wild" populations, and causing the loss of healthy individuals that are key for reproduction and social cohesion; there is also an extremely close link between legal hunting and "poaching;" that trophy hunting is fueling corruption; and that trophy hunting encourages the unfair redistribution of the wealth generated (Cruise 2016).

South Africa has the largest hunting industry in sub-Saharan Africa, and it is Africa's most popular destination for foreigners wishing to kill anything from elephants and buffalo to the 4.5-kilogram blue duiker and 1.6-kilogram genet. South Africa also has a large domestic recreational ("biltong" or South African dried "meat") hunting industry. In addition, so-called subsistence or "bushmeat" hunting, usually referred to as "poaching" (with all its cruel implications), takes place in many parts of the country. "Poaching" is on the increase in South Africa because it coincides with poverty, joblessness, and market-driven "wildlife" trade and policies.

The hunting industry is far from under control, with canned hunting officially endorsed and supported by the State. The reality is that most trophy hunting in South Africa is essentially canned to a greater or lesser extent. According to a 2016 report prepared for the Development Bank of South Africa by the Endangered Wildlife Trust entitled *An Assessment of the Economic, Social and Conservation Value of the Wildlife Ranching Industry and Its Potential to Support the Green Economy in South Africa*,[16] during 2014 in South Africa, there were 6,734 private "wildlife" properties with exemption permits and 2,245 open farms ("wildlife" ranches without exemption permits); the total number of live nonhuman animals sold at auctions was estimated to be 225,200; the total number of other animals trophy hunted was estimated to be 130,186; the total numbers of nonhuman animals killed for "meat" was estimated to be 453,996; the total number of herbivores on all "wildlife" ranches across South Africa was estimated to be 5.987 million; and the number of "wild animals" translocated reached almost 250,000.

South Africa remains the world's top destination for the hunting of captive raised lions, and according to the DEA, there are approximately 6,000 lions in captivity (at any given time) held in about 200 facilities (Funston and Levendal 2014). Sixty-eight percent of Africa's "wild animals" that were killed by American trophy hunters between 2005 and 2014 came from South Africa; that is, of the 565,558 African "wild animals" killed during this period, 383,982 came from South Africa (Bale 2016a). A Humane Society International report for the same period showed that out of a total of 5,587 lion trophies, 3,999 came from South Africa (Humane Society International 2016).

Although the situation with regards to lion and rhino hunting has attracted widespread attention and criticism, both locally and abroad, the killing of all species of "wild animals" has increased significantly over the past 10 years. According to DEA, "hunting tourists inject R1 billion into the South Africa economy in the 2013 season" (Neethling 2015). In 2013, 7,638 overseas hunters came to South Africa, killing 44,028 "wild animals" (African Indaba 2015). "Recreational" or "biltong hunting" is also widely undertaken, and a study by pro-hunter and Professor Melville Saayman (2015) estimated that the 200,000 South African "biltong hunters" kill an average of eight nonhuman animals each a year—approximately 1,600,000 "wild animals" annually. Such statistics are not a given and cannot be independently verified. It is worrying that in a country that is aggressively advocating and allowing the killing of other animals for profit that many hunting regulations are poorly enforced, and provincial and national officials do not collect and collate the relevant data—a failing which calls into question the basis on which many decisions in relation to "wild animals" are taken. Many officials, by the government's own admission, either misunderstand or fail to apply national environmental regulations such as the Threatened and Protected Species regulations (TOPS). In addition, despite the scale of the industry, DEA does not have an electronic permit system that allows it to collate the numbers of hunting permits issued nationally. If it requires information, it has to contact the nine provinces individually, and they too do not have electronic permit systems. The consequence of this is that DEA "does not have information on the number of hunting permits issued for a particular species across the country"[17] nor "does not keep a national register of professional hunters, and there is no limit to the number of hunters permitted." The trophy hunting industry in South Africa is not only growing but is also extremely difficult to monitor or police. Official control is poor at best. The national and provincial hunting permit systems have been inefficiently administered, and a national permitting database does not exist, so for the hunting and "wildlife" industry, it is virtually a case of *carte blanche*.

The so-called "new" conservation paradigms that include notions of the well-heeled legal white hunter versus the illegal impoverished black "poacher;" the intense privatization, corporatization, and commodification of "wild animals;" and livelihoods and benefit-sharing, further exclude and entrench antagonistic views of, and alienation from, "wild animals" by local communities. Fixing the relationship between communities and "wild animals" within the construct of "human-wildlife conflict" leads to loss of agency and exploitation of both humans and "wild animals." Private ownership is at the core of the "new conservation" discourse, and thus there is state-capital collusion and "state capture" by capital, particularly the hunting industry when it comes to "wild animals."

The post-apartheid State has played a significant role in supporting and privileging the privatization of "wild animals" for profit by passing enabling legislation to assure private ownership of "wild animals," selling "wild animals" from national and provincial protected areas and parks at lower prices, and poor institutional enforcement and corruption. This has made it complicit in the growth of the lucrative, unrestrained and reprobate "wildlife industry." There is asymmetry and an ideological convergence between the State and the contentious "wildlife industry." This is particularly problematic given that it is about much more than mere issues of enforcement and regulation. It is about perverted states and power arrangements within the state system. Approximately one-sixth of South Africa's total land has been fenced and converted for private "wildlife-based production." Dhoya Snijders (2014, 178) reveals that the "wildlife industry" is organizing politically and using its muscle and resources to influence government policy, importantly in ways that exclude dissenting voices. An example of this is the establishment of the Wildlife Forum in 2005. It deliberately excludes labor, nonhuman animal welfare, and civil society stakeholders. "When asked why these stakeholders were absent, an industry member commented: 'No, no, they are not real stakeholders. They don't own anything; it's [that they are] not hunters, not landowners.'" The Wildlife Forum, which works hand-in-glove with Safari Club International, promotes a discourse alliance that endorses both government's conservation interests and industry's development interests. Thus, in line with neoliberalism, the development of "wildlife" policy in South Africa reveals a strong alliance between the state and capital (in this case the hunting industry) by means of deregulation and public–private partnerships (Snijders 2014). In this way, the South African government is enabling a political milieu where capitalist interests can influence and shape policy so as to continue to access "resources."

The ANC government, through South African National Parks (SANParks), a public entity of the Department of Environmental Affairs, and whose mission is to "develop, manage, and promote a system of national parks that represents the biodiversity and heritage assets by applying best practices, environmental justice, benefit sharing, and sustainable use," operates at a profit and generates 75 percent of its operating revenue (South African National Parks 2016). This includes revenue from the sale of "wild animals" which from 2011 to 2014 amounted to R134 248 173 (Hübschle 2016). In this same period, the sale of rhinos made up the largest percentage. Between January 2010 and June 2014, 354 rhinos were sold and six "given away" for R 81,060,538 (Molewa 2014). These figures exclude the number of rhinos and profit made by provincial conservation authorities. Thus, at the same time that rhinos are being killed at an accelerated rate, the State is not only actively stimulating the trade in rhinos but making a profit as part of the bargain.

National and provincial parks see "wild animals" as lucrative assets and sell them to local private operators and dealers, including for trophy hunting purposes, for onward sale via private auctions, and to overseas destinations such as zoos and other captive facilities. To ensure the protection and survival of "wild animals," they should not be sold off to be killed as hunting trophies, but rather they should only be translocated in order to expand the range of the species. Instead of this precautionary approach, SANParks appears to prefer to rather promote and actively facilitate the trophy hunting of "wild animals" which they supposedly hold in custody and care on behalf of all South Africans, not only through live sales but also by allowing hunting along the Kruger National Park's ever-increasing porous borders. "Wild animals" in and from protected areas in South Africa are not simply government property or a "natural resource" to do with as bureaucrats please. They are sentient creatures deserving of care and respect. Nevertheless, the Internet is littered with boasts of hunters from Europe and the United States who seem to get a perverse thrill from killing "Kruger animals" from what they often offensively refer to as the "Dark Continent," sticking them on their walls as symbols of domination and prowess. So, on the one hand, SANParks says it goes totally against their mandate and legislative regulations to allow hunting in the national parks, but on the other hand, it appears to be smoothing the way and encouraging trophy hunting and the killing of the very beings that are supposed to be under its protection.

Conservation agencies and private hunting and tourism areas, especially those who share boundaries with national and provincial reserves, have been using *res nullius* to argue that "wild animals" belong to no one and therefore can be freely appropriated and used, including by individuals. Although South African conservation legislation champions the notion of ownership of "wild animals," particularly the privatization of "wild animals," it conveniently avoids the issue of "wild animals" who are removed, lured, or escape from protected areas and national parks or who move through areas where the fences have been deliberately removed between the public estate and private reserves. "Wild animals" living in the Kruger National Park (where hunting is not allowed) are moving across unfenced boundaries on the park's western border into the Associated Private Nature Reserves (APNR) and on the park's eastern border into Mozambique where they are commercially trophy hunted by foreign trophy hunters for exorbitant sums. The Protected Areas Act[18] prohibits certain "extractive activities" in national parks, including hunting. Nonetheless, hunting is taking place in the areas that share open boundaries with the Kruger National Park. Trophy hunters are salivating to kill individuals who originate from the KNP because they have big horns and large tusks. The APNR comprises top tourism lodges and privately owned properties. Trophy hunting takes place in the APNR, and over the past 20 years, elephant, lions, buffalo, leopard, rhino, and other nonhuman animals were hunted and sold off. This fact is carefully shielded from tourists visiting expensive tourist lodges in the area. The 1996 agreement between SANParks and the APNR makes no reference to commercial trophy hunting. The South African government approved the killing of the following nonhuman animals in the APNR for 2016: 33 elephants, 223 buffalos, three hippos, one lion, one rhino, 4,648 impala, one zebra, nine waterbuck, 23 warthogs, and one giraffe. In addition, 19 rhinos were also approved for live sales.

RHINOS: AN EXAMPLE OF COMMODIFICATING UNTIL EXTINCTION

In relation to rhino sales in 2014, SANParks spokesperson said that they "had transactions with several businesses and were not at liberty to divulge who they were doing business with" (Wildenboer 2014). There have been several reports of rhinos that had been bought from the State being shot almost immediately, some even in their crates for their rhino horn, or for trophies in canned (so-called "put and take") "hunts," which in relation to rhinos have been described by one provincial government official as ". . . buy rhino, kill it, replace it, kill it . . . [sic]" (Hübschle 2016, 197). The State does not care what happens to the "wild animals" once they leave its custody, and nor does it seem to care who it sells them to, whether the buyers are known criminals or have been formally charged with crimes, including illegal activities relating to "wild animals." For example, since 2004 SANParks, through the Kruger National Park, sold 120 rhinos, "at a massively reduced fee," to white-lion canned hunter Alexander Steyn a notorious "outfitter" for various Vietnamese rhino hunts (Joubert 2015). Perversely, the authorities claim that revenue from sales goes "back into conservation," and these include anti-poaching activities, research, land acquisition, and community beneficiation projects (Molewa 2014).

Trade and trophy hunting has driven rhinos in Africa to the edge of extinction. In the 1960s, there were approximately 100,000 rhinos. In 2015, the number of white rhinos was estimated to be between 19,682 and 21,077 and black rhinos estimated at between 5,042 and 5,455. South Africa currently holds 79 percent of Africa's rhinos.[19] The fact that the population is currently the largest in the world is perversely perceived as "population success." This has been used as a justification, particularly in a country where greed and poverty intersect, for their exploitation, commodification, and killing, particularly through trophy hunting, local auctions, live international sales, and consumption of their horns. Not surprisingly, and in tandem, the illegal killing of rhinos is also growing exponentially, and rhinos are being slaughtered on an industrial scale to meet demand for horn in newly affluent Asian countries. South Africa is at the epicenter of the rhino horn trade. The trade in rhino body parts, specifically their horns, has meant that more rhinos have been killed illegally in South Africa since 2008 than at any other time in the last 90 years, with official statistics for the period 2008 to April 2016 standing at 5,411, that is, more than 25 percent of the total population in South Africa (including those held on private properties and those being farmed specifically for the purpose of stockpiling their horns in the hope that the trade in rhino horn will soon be legalized). This represents 85 percent of all rhinos "poached" in Africa since 2008 (United Nations Office on Drugs and Crime 2016). South Africa, Mozambique, Zimbabwe, and Kenya are the main sources of seized shipments of rhino horn. The United Arab Emirates and European countries (including Slovakia, the Czech Republic, Belgium, Italy, and Germany) are indicated as transit countries. In order of importance, Vietnam, China, Ireland, the Czech Republic, the United States, and Thailand are indicated as destination countries (United Nations Office on Drugs and Crime 2016). Europe is currently a destination market and an in-transit trafficking hub to other regions. (European Commission 2016).

In line with their pro-hunting position, and despite the unconscionable number of rhinos that are dying as a result of the rhino horn trade, South Africa is also the premier market for those wishing to shoot rhinos legally for trophies.[20] Not surprisingly, the trophy hunting industry is also being used to launder rhino horns into the illegal trade and is fast becoming a front for "poaching" and illegal activities, as the current war on rhinos has shown.[21] Using the CITES legal regulatory framework, and therefore with full knowledge of the South African government and the CITES secretariat, the movement and sale of rhino horns as trophies and live rhinos to overseas destinations, including those who consume rhino horn such as Vietnam and China, constitutes not only a convergence of the legal and illegal trade but also a conscious stimulation of the trade—both legal and illicit. According to CITES (Trade Database 2015), the total number of rhino trophies that were exported from South Africa from 2001 to 2014 was 2,693, with 24 percent of these going directly to countries in the East, mainly Vietnam. Between 1995 and 2014, South Africa exported 1,096 live rhinos, of which 35 percent went to countries in the East, mainly China, Vietnam, and Thailand (CITES Trade Database 2015).

The war on rhinos is also being fed by private ownership. Rhinos are killed legally as hunting trophies and their horns laundered into the illegal trade; owners kill their rhinos and sell the horns to criminal networks claiming they were victims of poachers; owners allow criminals to kill their rhinos and then take a portion of the profits; and others dehorn their rhinos and sell the horns to smugglers. The State, through its environmental agencies, has purposefully transformed private "wildlife" ownership into a full-blown agricultural activity. Its conceptualization of "conservation" as utilization and commodification is also actively encouraging and legitimizing criminal and unethical activities. It has literally become a numbers game: the government can argue in international forums for trade, hunting, and live sales by pointing to the growing number of privately owned rhinos as evidence of successful "conservation" despite the fact that what goes on in many of these privately owned farms is the opposite of protection, unethical and illegal, and not adequately scrutinized or policed. CITES banned the international trade in rhino horn in 1977, and as a result, they were listed as Appendix 1 (most endangered), although they could still be trophy hunted "for noncommercial purposes." The ban failed to include stockpiled horns or the destruction of stockpiles, and this provided a major loophole for continued trade. In 1987, CITES acknowledged that trade was the "primary factor responsible for the destruction of rhinos populations" and urged all parties to destroy their stockpiles (CITES 1987). Domestic trade was also outlawed. It is extremely unlikely that South Africa heeded this call, particularly because deeply woven into the fabric of South Africa's apartheid history is the killing of and profiting from "wild animals," whose fates were closely bound to the use of State-sanctioned violence. The apartheid state was deeply involved in the slaughter of tens of thousands of elephants and in the sustained smuggling of ivory, rhino horn drugs, and diamonds through South Africa for resale internationally to support its war machine in Africa in the 1970s and 1980s (Kumleben 1996; Rademeyer 2012). The smuggling trade in "wild animal" body parts was not only allied to the South African security apparatus but protected by them, and as a result, their networks and reach grew unimpeded and into the post-apartheid era (Humphreys and Smith 2014, 803). After the demise of the apartheid state and the dawn of democracy in 1990 when the social and political landscape was being recast and reimagined, the official approach towards "wild animals" remained seamlessly callous and inhumane, certainly no cause to celebrate as far as the other animals were concerned.

At no stage did South Africa destroy its rhino horn stockpile. Clearly it had been stockpiling and trading in rhino horn for years, disposing of it illegally in the apartheid years, and then, post-1990, actively lobbying for the trade to be legalized. The first step in this process was to have their rhino population down listed to Appendix II.[22] In 1992, South Africa proposed to CITES that the trade in rhino horn be allowed. Although this was not accepted by the parties, two years later, not only was South Africa's proposal to down list their population adopted, but the way was opened for the amassing and privatization of rhino horn with the end game being trade. Part of their rationale for trade was that it would "benefit rhino conservation . . . [and that it] results in improved intelligence, as the legal entrepreneur informs on the black-market activities, and that a dependable supply of products depresses black market prices. In addition, it was argued private landowners would be encouraged to invest in rhino populations and protect them as utilizable, economic assets."[23] The 1994 approval also meant that South Africa could legally trade in rhino horn domestically, making it easier to launder. South Africa has been lobbying for the re-opening of the rhino horn trade ever since, and it is a position continuously supported by the ruling ANC and Cabinet. Currently, South Africa's rhino horn stockpile is in the hands of government, approximately 21 tonnes (Sapa 2015) (representing 5,250 dead rhinos) and the private industry, approximately 6 tonnes[24] (representing 1,500 rhinos). Poor stockpile management practices of ivory and rhino horn in South Africa has encouraged leakage into illicit markets. The demand for future profit through market speculation by stockpiling body parts, for example rhino horn and elephant ivory, is one of the key drivers of the trade in "wild animals." The South African government's pro-use, pro-abuse, pro-trade, and pro-private ownership stance towards rhinos, particularly because they are stockpiling rhino horn and encouraging private owners to do the same, means they are actively not limiting supply and in so doing are spurring on the proliferation of rhino deaths, playing a role in stimulating demand and pushing up the price and perceived value for dead rhinos and their body parts (both legally and illegally). Rhinos have become the victims of financial speculation.

Protecting rhinos for who they are is not on South Africa's agenda, but rather it is the disembodied rhino as a highly profitable commodity which has owners (both government and the private industry) salivating and incentivized by the black-market value of rhino horn, even if this means accelerating the poaching crisis, causing pain and suffering and threatening the very existence of rhinos as a species.[25] As Hübschle notes:

> [R]egulatory breaches and the exploitation of legal and regulatory loopholes, including illegal hunting and dehorning of rhinos, as well as the stockpiling and laundering of illegally harvested rhino horn into legal trade flows constitute modes of 'production.' What renders these flows particularly efficient and safe is the early stage conversion of an essentially illegal good to legal status (the laundering of illegally harvested horn into legal trade flows), and contrariwise, the conversion of a legal product (the hunting trophy) into an illegally traded good in consumer markets. (Hübschle 2016, 292)

The United Nations Office on Drugs and Crime (2016, 10) noted that "case studies show that when illegally traded wildlife is introduced into legal commercial streams, criminals have access to a much larger source of demand than they would have had on the black market alone."

In 1993, there were 650 rhinos in private hands, and there are now 6,200 owned privately (Stoddard 2016). South Africa's deliberate promotion of the commodification of rhinos and their ownership by private individuals has not only grown the trade (both legally and illegally) in, and trophy hunting of, rhinos but has also meant that they are being bred and farmed as agricultural products so that they can be continuously de-horned. Rhino farmer John Hume, who is essentially factory farming rhinos, currently owns approximately 1,200 rhinos and is the largest rhino breeder in South Africa and the world. According to Hume, he "harvests" rhino horn to save them (Bale 2016b). Hume also bought hundreds of rhinos directly from the Kruger National Park. The fact that SANParks has chosen to sell so many rhinos to one single buyer, particularly given the increase in the illegal killing of rhinos and the stockpiling of horns by private individuals, reveals much about the State's position. According to Hume, he has five tonnes of rhino horn stockpiled, and he harvests a tonne every year (Laing 2016). Izak du Toit, John Hume's lawyer, is quoted as saying: "We would sell to the poachers to prevent them from killing rhinos," (Crone 2015) so it seems that breeders such as Hume have no problem with selling their stockpiles off to transnational criminal smuggling networks.

CONCLUSION: WHAT TO DO?

Societal injustice, subjugation, the proliferation of violence, and exploitation frame the indifferent "wildlife" industry. Building on this is layer upon layer of systematic victimization, brutality, unimaginable cruelty, violence, greed, selfishness, disrespect, neglect, insensitivity, denial, disconnection, objectification, disassociation, disharmony, mechanization, commodification, and cultural and religious practices and prejudices. It is with individual, community, and ultimately global silence, consensual ignorance, complicity, and avoidance that these fundamentally cruel practices continue to grow, fester, are camouflaged, and ultimately feed upon themselves. This has particular resonance in South Africa because of the serious problem of violence the country has faced and is facing and the tools required to combat it.

The hegemonic construction, economization, and recasting of "wild animals" as disposable commodities which binds them to the economic concepts and structures of advanced capitalism without intrinsic value, is taking place as the Earth is reaching finite limits and "resource use" is intensifying as a consequence. This refiguring of "nature," including "wild animals," as money presents "a massive opportunity for the invigoration of capitalist economic relations" and is happening at the precise "apocalyptic moment of the Anthropocene and the hegemony of global neoliberal ideology" (Sullivan 2014, 31) and within the "contemporary moment of global crisis . . . wherein 'nature' is being consolidated, metaphorically and literally, as 'natural capital'" (Sullivan 2014, 2). Hypercapitalism and the conversion of "wild animals" into "natural capital" and commodities (the cause) is what has to be addressed otherwise; everything else we do in response to the exploitation of other animals (the symptoms) will be for naught.

The idea that capitalism, through sustainable development, endless growth, putting a price on "wild animals," trade and the market, is a panacea for inequality and poverty and will protect and ensure the survival of "wild animals" is clearly fallacious. Capitalism and the concomitant government "wildlife policies" are not only assuring the extirpation of "wild animals" but are deliberately positioning people against other animals and enhancing existing trans-species inequities, and because the ideological framework of "sustainable and resource use" are corrosive activities and concepts, the current economic policies cannot work for "wild animals" and their protection. The existence of "wild animals" is deeply intertwined with structures of power and othering. Add to this the lack of fiscal resources needed for effective institutional capacity and enforcement, private ownership, and corruption to the mix, and it is a lethal situation indeed.

The nonhuman animal rights and liberation movement raises structural, political, and economic questions and of power relations more generally. It is thus fighting to transform social relations by rejecting dominant cultural, religious, and economic structures and challenging sites of power and privilege and is part of a growing international movement for social change working to construct a new political, social, and economic base. It is a branch of the increasing voice against corporate capitalism, which is exploiting human and other life, particularly because the oppression of other animals is primarily motivated, and it is intensified, by economic and industrial interests. It thus shares the same global and local enemies as other progressive social movements. As a fairly young movement, it is still debating its philosophical and theoretical base. It is also apparent that there is a need for much more discussion about the shape and future direction of the movement. It has also been criticized from within for not paying sufficient attention to other social struggles and the effects of the new global economic order on the oppression of other animals (humans). There is confusion on the theory that informs actions and also too little discussion about how compromises happen, which is leading to division. Additionally, it is being censured for allowing itself to be sidetracked and compromised by the reformist nonhuman animal welfare position, which while caring about nonhuman animal welfare is commendable, it simply isn't enough. Globally the nonhuman animal rights and liberation movement can still be characterized by "social shallowness" because it has no connections to mass-based movements, and it has not yet developed into a coherent oppositional force. There are still a range of disparate organizations, groupings, and activists that are tentatively beginning to challenge the hegemonic, hierarchical, and speciesist concepts of oppression and are, in the final analysis, providing an embryonic foundation for the concept and practice of nonhuman animal rights and liberation to grow and develop into a socially cohesive pressure group. The movement remains in the fledgling stage, still needing to be united, develop resistance strategies and philosophical positioning, and seek popular support.

In the South African context, which has rising inequality poverty and unemployment, corruption, poor service delivery, and growing civil unrest, how does the movement cultivate a "politics of equal dignity" (Taylor 1992, 41) and "ecologies of co-existence," make policy interventions where the interests of "wild animals" are respected while at the same time addressing human inequality and poverty within the context of colonial and apartheid redress; connect "the dots between all these various oppressions" (Bond 2011, 17), and read against the grain of the "new conservation" livelihoods paradigm?

The fight on behalf of other animals is also not just a struggle against capitalism and global corporatism but against the dominant, predatory societal framework of "othering," through hierarchy, greed, power, control, intimidation, subjugation, repression, oppression, destruction, duplicity, apathy, and propaganda. The key is to link the oppressions and recognize common aspects and parallels for humans and other animals. To end nonhuman animal exploitation, social arrangements and institutions need to be changed, and this dictates collectivism, sustained alliances, and bridge building both at the global and at a local level, with human rights organizations, other social actors, and emerging social movements.

Additionally, meaningful and far-reaching policy changes both locally and globally cannot occur without heightened public awareness that is galvanized into action, but globally, the nonhuman animal rights movement first needs self-reflection to engage in dialogue with itself (to establish whether differences are merely on a tactical level or if there are more serious ideological factors) so as to develop a consensual position and move forward. Indeed, future strategies and tactics employed by the nonhuman animal rights groups in South Africa can provide important lessons for the rest of the nonhuman animal rights movements and other social movements worldwide.

The questions that remain to be answered are:

1. Given the severe injustices that South Africans and other countries in the South are facing as a result of free-market and state policies, and the focus of organizations, groupings and activists to right these wrongs, will they be able to make the connections, become more inclusive, and broaden their struggle so as to forge alliances outside of their traditional partnerships that focus on jobs, livelihoods, and living standards?

2. Will academics and activists begin to question the language of development and take on board that the same forces of domination, control, and oppression that marginalized and alienated rural communities in South Africa equally marginalize and alienate animals?

3. Will human-focused civil society groupings be able to deconstruct their long-established anthropocentric identities and promote alternative ones?

4. Will nonhuman animal liberation groupings in South Africa be able to develop their policies and campaigns to link the exploitation of other animals into other social justice issues, thereby generating broader support and effecting and transforming political and social practices?

The exploitation of humans and other animals are mutually reinforcing because they are fueled by a common material exploitation. Oppression of animals that are not human often takes place invisibly, and social constructs and economic arrangements that separate people from the means of production has meant that the brutal exploitation and suffering of other animals is becoming increasingly invisible and ignored. We, therefore, need to work for social changes that lead to the liberation of both humans and other animals. Importantly, we need to take a step back from the immediate and short-term to consider the long-term strategy to achieving freedom for other animals. There needs to be a move from the individual to the collective. We need to think and act strategically if we hope to transform society's values and the dominant political, cultural, social, and economic system. On a broader level, we need to:

1. Develop truly liberatory politics (Boggs 2011) that emphasizes inclusive justice.

2. Develop an agenda revolving around the dismantling of neoliberal capitalism.

3. Initiate an ecological model of development and animal-rights consciousness.

The nonhuman animal liberation movement needs to question and challenge the capitalist economic framework of growth-oriented corporatism and current skewed power relations. It needs to engage in transpolitical and transformative extra-legal, extra-parliamentary activism. The struggle against nonhuman animal exploitation must be framed and contextualized within societal political, economic, and social systems and modes of productions. Dominant modes of production and dominant exploitative cultural practices, whether it is industrialized, religious, or traditional, need to be confronted. We can do this by:

1. Establishing global networking structures and undertaking joint campaigns;

2. Creating think tanks to discuss strategies and tactics and promote debate within the movement and beyond;

3. Pushing for intersectional politics (one struggle) and forming alliances with other diverse, anti-globalization, anticapitalist social movements and those opposed to the financialization of nature (including trade unions, feminists, ecological, civil society networks, and gay/lesbian) and getting the agenda of other animals onto the social justice agenda;

4. Encouraging academic research, publishing, teaching, and the establishment of institutes to ensure that the dominant discourse that is represented in peer-reviewed journals is countered and marginalized;

5. Integrating questions of justice for other animals in debates on the environment;

6. Developing public policy and playing an active, tactical, and strategic role in political processes;

7. Engaging with issues around global hunger and poverty alleviation;

8. Campaigning and developing strategies by drawing on lessons from the South and taking cognizance of the issues of concern in the global South as well as drawing lessons from other social movements;

9. Exposing the link between human and nonhuman animal violence.

10. Pressuring governments to put resources into protection and environmental stewardship.

NOTES

1. A portion of this chapter has been adapted from Pickover, Michele (2005) The Environmental Movement in South Africa: An analysis of animal-based issues, campaigns and organizations. *CCS Grant Report*: 1–47. Available online at http://ccs.ukzn.ac.za/default.asp?3,28,10,2379. Used by permission of the Centre for Civil Society, University of KwaZulu-Natal.

2. It is for this reason that I will be using the phrase "wild animals" in quotes in this article.

3. According to findings by the U.K. Environmental Audit Committee in relation to the nature of demand in Southeast Asia and China, "wildlife" crime is driven by investment and conspicuous consumption. (Fourth Special Report, 2012–2013). Accessed September 27, 2016, from http://www.nwcu.police.uk/wp-content/uploads/2013/04/House-of-Commons-EAC-Wildlife-Crime-Govt-Response-to-Committees-3rd-report-of-sessions-2012–13.pdf.

4. Convention on International Trade in Endangered Species of Wild Fauna and Flora

5. A project led by Elephants Without Borders. Accessed September 27, 2016, from http://www.greatelephantcensus.com.

6. Entered into force on December 29, 1993.

7. See New Growth Path (2010). Accessed September 27, 2016, from http://www .gov.za/about-government/government-programmes/new-growth-path. National Development Plan (2012). Accessed September 27, 2016, from https://www.kpmg .com/Africa/en/IssuesAndInsights/Articles-Publications/Press-Releases /Documents/BRICS%20NDP%20handout.pdf.

8. Vision 2024 Green Economy: Wildlife Based Land Reform Support Programme was a presentation prepared by the South African Department of Environmental Affairs. Accessed on September 26, 2016, from https://www.environment .gov.za/sites/default/files/docs/wildlifebasedlandreform.pdf.

9. See "Sustainable Development Goals." United Nations. Accessed September 26, 2016, from http://www.un.org/sustainabledevelopment/development -agenda/.

10. Probably as a result of lobbying from international nonhuman animal welfare organizations such as WSPA and others.

11. As articulated, for example, in the *"Whose Eden? An overview of community approaches to wildlife management"* Report (International Institute for Environment and Development: July 1994). Accessed September 26, 2016, from http://pubs .iied.org/pdfs/8260IIED.pdf.

12. The founder, Jon Hutton, is a British ecologist. He has been the chair of the IUCN Sustainable Use Specialist Group and the director of the UNEP World Conservation Monitoring Centre (UNEP-WCMC).

13. Despite the fact that between 1979 and 1989 when elephant was listed on Appendix II and therefore legally allowed to be traded, their population declined by half.

14. See Executive Director of Resource Africa, Julian Sturgeon's Facebook page—Accessed September 26, 2016, from https://www.facebook.com/julian sturgeon.

15. See Game Theft Act 105 of 1991 and Public Protector Report no.3 of 2014/2015. Common law has evolved to transcend the wide reach of the *res nullius* principle, and statutory law has since imposed obligations that supersede the common law. The interpretation is also at odds with the principles of the National Environmental Management Biodiversity Act.

16. A copy of the report can be viewed at https://www.ewt.org.za/scientific%20 publications/An%20assessment%20of%20the%20economic,%20social%20and%20 conservation%20value%20of%20the%20wildlife%20ranching%20industry%20 and%20its%20potential%20to%20support%20the%20green%20economy%20 in%20SA.pdf. Accessed September 26, 2016.

17. Parliamentary Question No. 305, July 3, 2009. Still remains the situation in 2016.

18. Act 57 of 2003 (as amended by Act 31 of 2004). For background on the Protected Areas Act, see https://www.animallaw.info/statute/south-africa-protected -areas-act-national-environmental-management. Accessed September 27, 2016.

19. Data compiled by the International Union for Conservation of Nature (IUCN) Species Survival Commission's African Rhino Specialist Group (AfRSG). Accessed September 27, 2016, from https://www.savetherhino.org/latest_news /news/1462_iucn_reports_deepening_rhino_poaching_crisis_in_africa.

20. Of the 317 white rhinos killed by American hunters between 2005 and 2014, 308 came from South Africa (Humane Society International 2016).

21. See, for example, https://fightforrhinos.com/2016/05/12/hunting-outfitters-involved-in-poaching/. Accessed May 15, 2016.

22. The nonhuman animal, CITES argues, can withstand the exploitation resulting from the removal of protection.

23. See the CITES document, https://www.cites.org/eng/cop/09/prop/E09-Prop-17_Ceratotherium.PDF. Accessed September 27, 2016.

24. According to the Private Rhino Owners Association estimates, its members have about 6 tonnes. Accessed September 27, 2016, from http://uk.reuters.com/article/uk-safrica-rhinos-idUKKCN0X1178.

25. White rhinos have the heaviest front horns, weighing on average 4 kilograms. In 2015, a kilogram of rhino horn was said to be worth $65,000. Accessed September 27, 2016, from http://www.dailymaverick.co.za/opinionista/2015-12-01-lifting-the-ban-on-rhino-horn-trade-is-no-victory-for-rhino-owners/#.V0cD3DX5j4Y.

REFERENCES

African Indaba. 2015. "General News from Africa: Sustainable Use." Accessed September 27, 2016, from http://africanindaba.com/2015/02/news-from-and-about-africa-february-2015-volume-13-1/.

African Resources Trust and TRAFFIC International. 2000. "Report on the U.K. Workshop on CITES and WTO Trade Rules."

Bale, Rachael. 2016a. "Exclusive: Hard Numbers Reveal Scale of America's Trophy Hunting Habit." *National Geographic,* February 6. Accessed on September 22, 2016, from http://news.nationalgeographic.com/2016/02/160206-American-trophy-hunting- wildlife-conservation/.

Bale, Rachael. 2016b. "An Inside Look at the World's Biggest Rhino Farm." *National Geographic,* January 22. Accessed on September 22, 2016, from http://news.nationalgeographic.com/2016/01/160122-Hume- South-Africa-rhino-farm/.

Boggs, Carl. 2011. "Corporate Power, Ecological Crisis and Animal Rights." In John Sanbonmatsu (ed.), *Critical Theory and Animal Liberation.* Lanham, MD: Rowman & Littlefield Publishers, 71–90.

Bond, Patrick. 2011. "The Politics of Climate Justice." *University of KwaZulu-Natal Press.* Accessed on July 19, 2016, from http://ggjalliance.org/sites/default/files/Bond%20Politics%20of%20Climate%20Justice%20UKZN%20Press.pdf.

Broad. S. 2001. *The Nature and Extent of Legal and Illegal Trade in Wildlife,* Paper presented at the Seminar for Wildlife Trade Regulation and Enforcement, September. Cambridge University: TRAFFIC and African Resources Trust.

Brundtland, Gro H. 1987. "Our Common Future." *World Commission on Environment and Development.* Accessed on September 21, 2016, from http://www.un-documents.net/our-common-future.pdf.

CITES. 1987. "Conservation of and Trade in African and Asian Rhinoceroses." Accessed September 26, 2016, from https://cites.org/eng/res/09/09-14R15.php.

CITES. 2015. "Trade Database Passes 15 Million Records." *Convention on International Trade in Endangered Species of Wilf Fauna and Flora.* Accessed on September 21, 2016, from https://cites.org/eng/cites_trade_db_passes _15million_records.

CITES Trade Database. 2015. Accessed September 22, 2016, from http://trade.cites .org/.

Cock, Jacklyn. 2011. Green Capitalism or Environmental Justice: A Critique of the Sustainability." Accessed on August 3, 2016, from https://ds.lclark.edu /soan498/wp-content/uploads/sites/108/2014/09/Jacklyn-Cock-green -capitalism1.pdf.

Cock, Jacklyn. 2007. "Sustainable Development or Environmental Justice: Questions for labour from the Steel Valley struggle." *Labour, Capital, & Society.* Accessed on August 3, 2016, from https://www.google.com/search?site =&source=hp&q=Sustainable+Development+or+ Environmental+Justice %3A+questions+for+labour+from+the+Steel+Valley+struggle &oq=Sustain ale+Development+or+Environmental+Justice%3A+questions+for+labour+ from+the+Steel+Valley+struggle&gs_l=hp.3 . . . 2445.2445.0.3944.2.2.0.0. 0.0.144.14 4.0j1.1.0. . . . 0 . . . 1c.2.64.hp..1.0.0.0.WK0gQD0oh0k.

Convention on Biological Diversity. 2012. "Decision Adopted by the Conference of the Parties to the Convention on Biological Diversity at its Eleventh Meeting." Accessed September 25, 2016, from https://www.cbd.int/doc/decisions /cop-11/cop-11-dec-25-en.pdf.

Convention on Biological Diversity. 2016. "Subsidiary Body on Scientific, Technical and Technological Advice Twentieth Meeting." United Nations Environment Programme. Accessed September 25, 2016, from https://www.cbd.int/sbstta/.

Convention on International Trade in Endangered Species of Wilf Fauna and Flora. 2013. "The CITES Species." Accessed September 21, 2016, from https://cites .org/eng/disc/species.php.

Courchamp, Franck, et al. 2006. "Rarity Value and Species Extinction: The Anthropogenic Allee Effect." *PLoS Biology,* 4(12). doi:10.1371/journal.pbio.004 0415.

Crone, Anton. 2015. "Lifting the Ban on Rhino Horn Trade Is No Victory for Rhino Owners." *Daily Maverick,* December 1. Accessed on September 22, 2016, from http://www.dailymaverick.co.za/opinionista/2015-12- 01-lifting-the-ban-on-rhino-horn-trade-is-no-victory-for-rhino-owners/#.V- QsY5MrIxd.

Cruise, Adam. 2016. "The effects of trophy hunting on five of Africa's iconic wild animal populations in six countries." *Conservation Action Trust.* Accessed on July 5, 2016, from http://conservationaction.co.za/resources/reports /effects-trophy-hunting-five-africas-iconic-wild-animal-populations-six -countries-analysis/.

Death, Carl. 2014. "Environmental Movements, Climate Change, and Consumption in South Africa." *Journal of Southern African Studies,* 40:6, 1215–1234.

Defense Web. 2016. "Environmental Crime on Increase." Accessed on September 21, 2016, from http://www.defenceweb.co.za/index.php?option=com _content&view=article&id=43 800:environmental-crime-on-the-increase &catid=87:Border%20Security&Itemid=188.

Department of Environmental Affairs and Tourism. 1997. "White Paper on the Conservation and Sustainable Use of South Africa's Biological Diversity." Accessed on September 21, 2016, from https://www.environment.gov.za /sites/default/files/legislations/biodiversity_whitepaper_18163_gen1095 .pdf.

European Commission. 2016. "European Union Action Plan Against Wildlife Trafficking." Accessed on August 7, 2016, from https://ec.europa.eu /transparency/regdoc/rep/1/2016/EN/1-2016-87-EN-F1-1.PDF.

Funston, P. J., and M. Levendal. 2014. "National Environmental Management: Biodiversity Act; Biodiversity Management Plan for African Lion (*Panthera Leo*)." *Department of Environmental Affairs.* Accessed on February 5, 2016, from https://www.environment.gov.za/sites/default/files/gazetted_notices /nemba_africanlion_managementplan_gn351g38706.pdf.

Giddens, Anthony. 2009. *The Politics of Climate Change.* London: Polity.

Hübschle, Annette Michaela. 2016. "A Game of Horns Transnational Flows of Rhino Horn." *Universität zu Köln.* Accessed on August 29, 2016, from http:// pubman.mpdl.mpg.de/pubman/item/escidoc:2218357:5/component /escidoc:2261029/2016_IMPRSDiss_Huebschle.pdf.

Hübschle, Annette Michaela. 2014. "Of Bogus Hunters, Queenpins and Mules: The Varied Roles of Women in Transnational Organized Crime in Southern Africa." *Trends Organized Crime,* 17(1): 31–51.

Humane Society International. 2016. "Trophy Hunting by the Numbers: The United States' Role in Global Trophy Hunting." Accessed on September 22, 2016, from http://www.hsi.org/assets/pdfs/report_trophy_hunting_by_the.pdf.

Humphreys, Jasper, and M. L. R. Smith. 2014. "The 'Rhinofication' of South African security." *International Affairs,* 90(4); 795–818.

Joubert, Pearlie. 2015. "Rhinos Sold to Canned Hunter." *News 24,* June 30. Accessed on September 22, 2016, from http://city- press.news24.com/News/Rhinos -sold-to-canned-hunter-20150627.

Karesh, W. B., R. A. Cook, E. L. Bennett, and J. Newcomb. 2005. "Wildlife trade and global disease emergence." *Emerging Infectious Diseases,* 11:7, 1000–1002.

Kumleben, M. E. 1996. *Report of the Commission of Inquiry into the Alleged Smuggling of and Illegal Trade in Ivory and Rhinos Horn in South Africa.* Accessed September 27, 2016, from http://www.rhinoresourcecenter.com/pdf_files /131/1311074532.pdf.

Lacour, Sebastien. 2009. "'Blended' Value Creation: A Social Capital Perspective." *UCT Graduate School of Business.* Accessed on September 21, 2016, from gsblibrary.uct.ac.za/researchreports/2009/Lacour.pdf.

Laing, Aislinn. 2016. "Why the World's Largest Rhino Farmer Is Cutting Off Their Horns." *The Telegraph,* February 26. Accessed on September 22, 2016, from http://www.telegraph.co.uk/news/worldnews/africaandindianocean /southafrica/12173750/Why-the-worlds-largest-rhino-farmer-is-cutting -off-their-horns.html.

Lukey, Peter 2014. "Introduction to the Environmental Offsetting Discussion Document Project." Department of Environmental Affairs. South Africa.

Accessed September 25, 2016, from https://www.environment.gov.za/sites /default/files/docs/offsetdiscussion_documentproject_presentation.pdf.

Modise, Albi. 2016. "Minister Edna Molewa Welcomes Lifting of SSA Embargo on Hunting Trophies." Government of South Africa. Accessed on September 22, 2016, from http://www.gov.za/speeches/minister-edna-molewa -welcomes-lifting-saa-embargo-hunting-trophies-23-jul-2015-0000.

Molewa, Edna. 2014. "SANParks Have Sold 354 Rhinos Since 2010." Accessed September 27, 2016, from http://www.politicsweb.co.za/documents/sanparks -have-sold-354-rhinos-since-2010—edna-mol.

Munnik, Victor. 2007. "Solidarity for Environmental Justice in Southern Africa: A Report for Groundwork." Accessed on July 23, 2016, from www.groundwork .org.za/specialreports/Solidarity%20for%20EJ%20in%20SA.pdf

Nadal, Alejandro, and Francisco Aguayo. 2014. "Leonardo's Sailors. A Review of the Economic Analysis of Wildlife Trade." The Leverhulme Centre for the Study of Value. Accessed on August 29, 2016, from http://thestudyofvalue .org/wp-content/uploads/2014/06/WP5-Nadal-and-Aguayo-Leonardos -Sailors-2014.pdf.

Nellemann, C., R. Henriksen, P. Raxter, N. Ash., and E. Mrema. 2014. "The Environmental Crime Crisis—Threats to Sustainable Development from Illegal Exploitation and Trade in Wildlife and Forest Resources." United Nations Environment Programme. Accessed on August 7, 2016, from https://www .cbd.int/financial/monterreytradetech/unep-illegaltrade.pdf.

Neethling, Nikki. 2015. "Hunting Brings in Big Bucks for SA." *SARChI,* March 3. Accessed on February 6, 2016, from http://www0.sun.ac.za/sarchi/hunting -brings-in-big-bucks-for-sa/.

Payne, Jill. 1998. "Re-creating Home: British Colonialism, Culture, and the Zuurveld Environment in the Nineteenth Century." Rhodes University. Accessed on August 29, 2016, from http://contentpro.seals.ac.za/iii/cpro /DigitalItemPdfViewerPage.external?id=2109814084643128&itemId =1002404&lang=eng&file=%2Fiii%2Fcpro%2Fapp%3Fid%3D21098140846 43128%26itemId%3D1002404%26lang%3Deng%26nopassword%3Dtrue% 26service%3Dblob%26suite%3Ddef#locale=eng&gridView=true.

Rademeyer, Julian. 2013. "SA Pushes for Legal Trade in Rhino Horn." *Mail & Guardian.* Accessed on September 21, 2016, from http://mg.co.za/article /2013-03-22-00-sa-pushes-for-legal-trade-in-rhino-horn.

Republic of South Africa. 2013. "Rhino Issue Management Report." Department of Environmental Affairs. Accessed on February 2, 2016, from https://www.envi ronment.gov.za/sites/default/files/docs/rhinoissue_managementreport.pdf.

Roche, Chris. 2003. "'Fighting Their Battles O'er Again': The Springbok Hunt in Graaff-Reinet, 1860–1908." *Kronos,* 29: 86–108.

Russo, Alexandra. 2015. "The Prevalence of Documentation Discrepancies in CITES (Convention on the International Trade in Endangered Species of Wild Fauna and Flora) Trade Data for Appendix I and II Species Exported Out of Africa Between the Years 2003 and 2012." Percy FitzPatrick Institute of African Ornithology. Accessed on August 29, 2016, from https:// open.uct.ac.za/bitstream/handle/11427/15685/thesis_sci_2015_russo _alexandra.pdf?sequence=1.

Saayman, Melville. 2015. "TREES: Tourism Research in Economic Environs and Society." *North-West University.* Accessed on September 22, 2016, from http://www.nwu.ac.za/trees.

Sapa. 2015. "Decision Over Sale of Stockpile Rhino Horn Set for 2016." *Mail & Guardian,* February 10. Accessed September 22, 2016, from http://mg.co.za /article/2015-02-10-stockpiled-rhino-horns-sale-decision-will-be-made -in-2016.

Scanlon, John E. 2012. "CITES Trade: Recent Trends in International Trade in Appendix II-Listed Species (1996–2010)." United Nations Environment Programme World Conservation Monitoring Centre. Accessed on September 21, 2016, from https://cites.org/common/docs/Recent-trends-in-inter national-trade-in-Appendix-II-listed-species.pdf.

Selier, S. A. J., and E. Di Minin. 2015. "Monitoring Required for Effective Sustainable Use of Wildlife." *Animal Conservation,* 18: 131–132.

Sieff, Kevin. 2016. "The Largest-Ever Survey of Elephants in Africa Reveals Startling Declines." *Washington Post.* August 31. Accessed September 25, 2016, from https://www.washingtonpost.com/news/worldviews/wp/2016 /08/31/the-largest-ever-survey-of-elephants-in-africa-reveals-startling -declines/.

Siggins, Lorna. 2004. "Conservation Must Be Scrapped, Says Marine Scientist." *Irish Times.* Accessed on September 22, 2016, from http://www.irishtimes .com/news/conservation-must-be-scrapped-says-marine-scientist-1 .1144864.

Snijders, Dhoya. 2014. "Wildlife Policy Matters: Inclusion and Exclusion by Means of Organizational and Discursive Boundaries." *Journal of Contemporary African Studies,* 32(2): 173–189.

South African National Parks. 2016. "Brief History." Accessed on September 22, 2016, from https://www.sanparks.org/about/history.php.

Stoddard, Ed. 2016. "A Species' Fate and $2 Billion at Stake as South Africa Mulls Rhino Horn Trade." *Reuters,* April 4. Accessed on September 22, 2016, from http://uk.reuters.com/article/uk-safrica-rhinos-idUKKCN0X1178.

Sullivan, Sian. 2014. "The Natural Capital Myth; Or Will Accounting Save the World? Preliminary Thoughts on Nature, Finance, and Values." The Leverhulme Centre for the Study of Value. Accessed on August 30, 2016, from http://thestudyofvalue.org/wp-content/uploads/2013/11/WP3-Sullivan -2014-Natural-Capital-Myth.pdf.

Tan, Avianne. 2015. "Beyond Cecil the Lion: Trophy-Hunting Industry in Africa Explained." ABC News, July 31. Accessed September 18, 2016, from http:// abcnews.go.com/US/cecil-lion-trophy-hunting-industry-africa-explained /story?id=32785057.

Taylor, Charles. 1994 (1992). *The Politics of Recognition.* Princeton, NJ: Princeton University Press, 25–74. Accessed on August 30, 2016, from http:// elplandehiram.org/documentos/JoustingNYC/Politics_of_Recognition .pdf.

Thomson, Barbara. 2016. "Ms. Barbara Thomson Tables Department of Environmental Affairs 2016/2017 Budget Vote Policy Statement." Department of Environmental Affairs, South Africa. May 3. Accessed on September 22,

2016, from https://www.environment.gov.za/speech/thomson_tables_2016 _2017budgetvote.

TRAFFIC. 2016. "Wildlife Trade." June 17. Accessed September 27, 2016, from http://www.traffic.org/display/Search?moduleId=19659396&searchQuery =2.1+million+snake.

United Kingdom, Parliament, House of Commons Environmental Audit Committee. 2013. *Wildlife Crime, Third Report of Session 2012–13*, Volume I. Accessed on August 7 2016, from http://www.nwcu.police.uk/wp-content /uploads/2013/04/House-of-Commons-EAC-Wildlife-Crime-Govt -Response-to-Committees-3rd-report-of-sessions-2012-13.pdf.

United Nations Environment Programme (UNEP). 2010. "Biodiversity Is Life." Accessed September 25, 2016, from https://www.cbd.int/iyb/doc/prints /factsheets/iyb-cbd-factsheet-abs-en.pdf.

United Nations Environment Programme (UNEP). 2011. "Towards a Green Economy: Pathways to Sustainable Development and Poverty Eradication." Accessed September 25, 2016, from https://sustainabledevelopment.un.org /content/documents/126GER_synthesis_en.pdf.

United Nations Office on Drugs and Crime. 2016. *World Wildlife Crime Report: Trafficking in Protected Species.* Accessed on August 30, 2016, from https:// www.unodc.org/documents/data-and-analysis/wildlife/World_Wildlife _Crime_Report_2016_final.pdf.

Van Sittert, Lance. 2005. "Bringing in The Wild: The Commodification of Wild Animals in the Cape Colony/Province, 1850–1950." *Journal of African History,* 46(2): 269–291. doi:10.1017/S0021853704009946.

Wildenboer, Norma. 2014. "Questions Raised over Rhino Sale." *IOL,* August 29. Accessed on September 22, 2016, from http://www.iol.co.za/scitech/science /environment/questions-raised-over-rhino-sale-1743202.

Wyler, Liana S., and Pervase A. Sheikh. 2013. "International Illegal Trade in Wildlife: Threats and U.S. Policy." Congressional Research Service Report for Congress. Accessed on August 30, 2016, from https://www.fas.org/sgp/crs /misc/RL34395.pdf.

7

Capitalism and Masculinity: Kangaroo Killing in Australia

Lara Drew

INTRODUCTION

Every year billions of nonhuman animals in Australia are exploited through unwarranted intrusions and abuse. The exploitation of kangaroos in Australia is a damning example of the ways in which nonhuman animals are commodified and viewed as "resources." While the kangaroo is an "iconic" and celebrated Australian symbol featured on coat of arms, trademarks, and advertisements, they also are categorized as "pests" and commodified as "game," "meat," "leather items," tourist "products," and a number of other commercial items. Institutions and systems organize, administrate, and normalize this violence as legitimate, making it an important ethical and political issue in Australia.

This chapter examines how nonhuman animals have long been framed in economic terms as the property of humans. Nonhuman animal lives and bodies are a means of profit creation within capitalism, and this violence is normalized, routinized, and made to appear legitimate. By focusing on kangaroos, this chapter examines the ways in which capital in Australia continues to imprint itself on the bodies of these nonhuman animals in brutal ways. While exploitation can exist without capitalism, the structure and nature of modern-day capitalist relations of production has been deepened (Torres 2007) and fundamentally influenced by the logic of growth and expansion, which continues to exacerbate the domination of nonhuman animals.

Hegemonic masculinity contributes to the routine justification and violence inflicted upon kangaroos. Given masculinity is traditionally intertwined with the killing of nonhuman "wild animals" in general, I critically discuss its inherent relationship to the violence inflicted on kangaroos. I draw on critical animal studies and argue that both capitalism and hegemonic masculinity serve to maintain the routine oppression of nonhuman animals in Australia, with the situation of kangaroos as just one example. The relations of nonhuman animal exploitation are extended, deepened, and maintained through the dynamics of capitalism and hegemonic masculinity, systems of domination that are "mutually reinforcing" (Torres 2007). My intention is to unpack these "mutually reinforcing" forms of domination in order to make them more visible and to highlight their role in the "naturalization" of kangaroo oppression.

Further, while research about kangaroo exploitation exists (Boom et al. 2012; Croft 2005; Garlic and Austen 2012), no research has brought direct attention to capitalism and masculinity in relation to the exploitation of kangaroos in Australia. However, there has been extensive research of the linkage between hunting and masculinity (Kheel 2008; Luke 2007), including research about nonhuman animal exploitation and capitalism (Nibert 2002, 2013; Torres 2007; Wadiwel 2015). Although the chapter is about the exploitation of kangaroos specifically, the basic concepts apply to other nonhuman animals within Australia—and elsewhere—who are routinely oppressed.

Expanding the narrative surrounding the exploitation of kangaroos by addressing capitalism and hegemonic masculinity is crucial for scholars and activists. Many critical theorists have started to point to capitalism and masculinity as key to nonhuman animal exploitation; however, this is most often in regard to nonhuman animal agriculture. The exploitation of "wildlife," in this chapter kangaroos, warrants similar analysis. Scholars and activists must broaden their discourse to elucidate the repressive nature of the kangaroo industry. By bringing critical analysis to bear on the oppression of kangaroos, I hope to help the movement to engage in a stronger liberatory project, one developing in the interests of both human and nonhuman animals.

KANGAROOS

Kangaroos have long been regarded as an iconic symbol in Australia, and Australians have invested their national identity these nonhuman animals. Tall and muscular, they have beautiful slender faces with fine lines.

Sensitive, quiet, present, and observant, kangaroos have long established a presence on the Australian landscape. Australian poet D. H. Lawrence (1994, 23) famously observed the kangaroo in a poem as a "sensitive, long pure-bred face, with full antipodal eyes, so dark. Wistfully, sensitively sniffs the air, and then turns, goes off in slow leaps. On the long flat skis of her legs, steered and propelled by that steel strong snake of a tail. Quiet, remote and inquisitive to look back . . . ." Featured on the coat of arms, major trademarks, advertisements, and a well-known tourist emblem, the kangaroo is *seemingly* "valued" in Australia.

However, the actual life experience of kangaroos is a very different narrative. Kangaroos are commodified as "game meat" and tourist "trinkets." They are advertised as a "healthy red meat" alternative that is framed as "environmentally friendly." In addition to this "game meat" industry, farmers are granted licenses to kill anyone they deem as "pests" or "vermin" on their land. Further, annual government-sanctioned "conservation culls" are granted in the name of "environmental protection" despite that fact that kangaroos are a native species. Kangaroos have been hunted and killed in atrocious ways and have been found disemboweled and in pieces. The act of killing is undeniably violent in itself, but in the cases where kangaroos are killed in particularly ghastly ways, these reports ironically draws the ire of the nation—even though the public supports the killing industry.

The routine killing is often justified through the labelling of kangaroos as "pest" and "vermin." However, according to (THINKK 2015), the think tank or research group that focuses on alternative narratives about kangaroos, the notion of kangaroos as "pests" has been significantly overstated. Current research indicates that kangaroos do not exist in abundance nor in "pest" proportions (Boom et al. 2012). In 2001, kangaroo numbers were estimated to be 57.5 million, but by 2010, the numbers had fallen to just 25 million (Kangaroo Population Estimates 2016), but these numbers are questionable given the counting techniques used by various agents. Further, a "plague" of kangaroos is not biologically plausible given they breed very slowly and only have one joey (a baby kangaroo) per year with one in the pouch at one time. Kangaroo joeys also naturally have very high mortality rates of around 70 to 100 percent depending on species/conditions, further inhibiting their ability to "explode" in numbers as often claimed (Boom and Ben-Ami 2012). Six species of the kangaroo family have become extinct since the European invasion, and some species, such as the brush tailed rock wallaby, have been killed for their "fur" in such numbers that they are endangered (Ramp and Vernes 2015). A country so *seemingly* attached to the kangaroo routinely kills its "valued icon" at 10 times the number of harp seals killed in the Canadian seal hunt (Wicks 2012). Australia is still home to the largest slaughter of land-based "wildlife" on the planet (Boom et al. 2012; Wicks 2012).

The life situation of kangaroos is a routine repertoire of violence, deprivation, suffering, and death. Nonhuman animals should have the basic right to their territory, their selves, their bodies, and their space. They should be free from unwarranted intrusions and/or abuse (Adams and Donovan 2007). Their oppression, normalized and routinized, must be challenged.

THE HUMAN RELATIONSHIP AND ATTACHMENT TO THE "PEST" STATUS

Despite being native to Australia, the perception of kangaroos as "pests" is deeply and widely entrenched (Boom et al. 2012). Kangaroos have long occupied the unusual position as both valued "icon" and "pest." The industry and the government, together with ranchers and farmers, have socially constructed the kangaroo as a "nuisance," thus allowing for the growth of a kangaroo killing industry. This is not surprising given the history of white, colonial Australia that saw "squatters" turn vast tracts of land into ranches for cows, sheep, and horses (known as stations). These invasive enterprises were "driven by the implacable logic of capital accumulation, [as] the squatters inflicted immense damage on the native flora and fauna" (O'Lincoln 2016). Today agriculturalists argue that kangaroo numbers have increased due to the installation of artificial water holes. Kangaroos are regarded as "competitors" within nonhuman animal-based agriculture given they are perceived as "competing" with "livestock" for crops and resources (Boom et al. 2012). The killing of kangaroos is presented as necessity for the protection of agriculture. The killing industry capitalizes on the bodies of dead kangaroos by marketing "products" made from their bodies. In addition, government departments of the environment, national research organizations, and rural corporate enterprises also have declared kangaroos as invasive to grasslands and grassland species throughout the country. The popular opinion of kangaroos as "pests" has meant that they have been lumped into the same stigmatized category as other human-introduced, and consequently devalued, species such as foxes, "wild cats," cane toads, and camels. Kangaroos have long been characterized as a species in "plague proportions" and are represented as a threat to the national economy and to the society.

KANGAROO KILLING AND CAPITALISM IN AUSTRALIA

The Commercial Kangaroo Industry

The public has been encouraged to develop a distant relationship with the "troublesome" kangaroos. From the standpoint of the commercial kangaroo industry, this relationship is framed in economic terms. The "pest" status means that a rather ironic monetary "value" is placed on kangaroos. On one hand, a "pest" is seen as someone of "little value," while on the other hand, "pests" within our economic system are given value because of the "pest" status. The "pest" categorization permits kangaroos to be demonized and to be treated as "resources" without constraint. In the commercial industry, they are deemed a mere commodity for people to kill as they please. Engineering the public to view kangaroos as "pests" serves to normalize the violence.

Thus, capitalist imperatives have legitimated the "pest" status and have shaped the stigmatized identity of kangaroos. The view of the "troublesome" kangaroo, past and present, is cultivated by those whose economic interests are served by kangaroo deaths. These vested interests include the commercial kangaroo-as-food industry. Owners of these businesses promote kangaroo flesh as abundant, environmentally sustainable, and much preferable to the commercial ranching of cows and sheep, which is plagued by concerns about pollution and methane production. Public acceptance of the view of non-human animals as mere resources is not surprising given that, for all their lives, humans have been deeply immersed in a "culture that largely devalues other animals and legitimates humans' self-interested use of their lives and bodies" (Nibert 2002, 15). Resultantly, the killing of kangaroos and the commodification of their body parts are normalized by the capitalist system. Their stigmatized identity naturalizes and preserves their commodification.

Also facilitating the commodification of kangaroos is the fact that their brutal treatment and death are largely invisible to the public. They are not farmed like other nonhuman animals killed to be used as food in Australia. Rather, they are killed within their free-living communities where their killing is more hidden and concealed than that of other nonhuman animals. Kangaroos are killed in the dark, in remote environments and away from public view and camera lens. Young kangaroos are removed from the pouch and either clubbed to death or left to starve after their mothers have been killed. Although the killing of other nonhuman animals on farms is typically hidden as well, the visibility of the sheds and slaughterhouse equipment makes their lives and deaths somewhat more noticeable. In regard to kangaroos, most humans are largely distanced from the realities of this production, with very few photographs and video footage having ever showed the process.

Despite their devaluation, the treatment of kangaroos still arouses some conflicting emotions in Australia. Whether they are a "pest," "resource," or an untouchable native "icon" remains somewhat contentious. Kvinta (2015) describes the relationship between humans and kangaroos as fraught with a strong love-hate bond, but all the while, the bodies of kangaroos, like other nonhuman animals in Australia, are leveraged for profit.

Agriculture and Kangaroos

Kangaroos also are killed in the interest of "protecting" the nonhuman animal-based agricultural industry. As mentioned earlier, in this industry they are demonized and seen as "pests" because they supposedly compete with oppressed cows, sheep, and other ranched nonhuman animals for rangeland. The devaluation and violence against kangaroos occurred early after the British invasion as the demand for the hair of sheep by British textile mills and the growth of the "wool" industry came to be regarded as the foundation of the new nation's economic prosperity (Taylor 2014). The Australian economy was characteristically portrayed as "riding on the sheep's back." Kangaroos were killed, and much of their land was used as sheep stations. (Taylor 2014). For this reason, kangaroos have long been vilified and slaughtered by the millions in rural Australia, especially now in the modern era as the overgrazing of oppressed cows and sheep degrade the landscape. From the perspective of ranchers, every blade of grass eaten by a kangaroo is stolen from the mouth of a profitable "livestock animal" (Taylor 2014). Due to this widespread assumption (despite opposing research by THINKK), ranchers continue to label kangaroos as a threat to the "national economy." Labeling kangaroos a "threat" to the economy shows the privileging of the capitalist economy over the lives of nonhuman animals.

Such oppression of kangaroos is not surprising given the role nonhuman animals—both enslaved and free-living—have been forced to play in the development of capitalism (Torres 2007). To Nibert (2002, 2013), the advent of agriculture, rooted in the oppression of nonhuman animals, led to the creation of hierarchies and the accumulation of privately held wealth. Historically, throughout much of the world, free-living animals were killed in order that land and water were easily available for ranched nonhuman animals whose oppression as food and other resources produced wealth for elites. Continuing this oppressive practice today in Australia, the way to keep the land "free" for agriculture and "development" is to kill kangaroos and related beings, so even though kangaroos are not farmed like other nonhuman animals, they remain victims of violence, which is underpinned by the creation of hierarchy and the accumulation of capital. This economic domination of land and nonhuman animals is justified and made to appear "natural" (Adams and Gruen 2014)—processes necessary for the smooth functioning of the capitalist system. People are conditioned to believe that nonhuman animals, like kangaroos, are inanimate objects that exist only to serve "man's" needs (Kheel 2007). Tashee Meadows (2010, 153) remarks "unfortunately, unlike car parts on an assembly line, these "products" are living beings that move, often causing the shooter to miss his mark. They're dismembered while still alive and conscious . . . these beings resist at every point of their captivity and torture." Kangaroos suffer and are killed merely for the purpose of producing profit. Kangaroos, like other nonhuman animals, should not be considered "objects" or "commodities" as they are living/feeling beings who should have rights to thrive and survive.

Land "Development," Tourism, and Kangaroos

Kangaroos have symbolic worth in that their presence and image are used to "brand" products as Australian and to value-add to capitalist ventures aimed at a tourist market (for example, private kangaroo zoos or tourism in general). There is a clear contradiction between the ways in which kangaroos are publicly embraced and promoted for their use-value as symbolic capital on one hand, but they are also quickly disposed of (out of public eye) when seen to be threatening the profitability of other industries (for example, ranching and the land "development" industry).

In this way, kangaroos are transformed from beings who live for themselves into beings that are exploited for their profit-producing potential. This is not surprising given that people in Western societies are bombarded with ideas of profit and efficiency, and both nonhuman and devalued human animals have been viewed as "resources" or "pests" to be killed in substantial numbers. A world completely tainted by hierarchy and dominance underlie the ways we have been taught to see nonhuman animals—"as objects to be manipulated" (Bookchin 2005, 450) and "objects" to be disposed of in the interest of land "development." Given this, as well as the "pest" status of kangaroos, the public is convinced that this is the "natural order of things" and their oppression is normalized.

MASCULINITY AND HUNTING IN THE AUSTRALIAN LANDSCAPE

Hegemonic masculinity is deeply connected with the oppression of kangaroos. Masculinism is a gendered ideology that is socially constructed and shaped by cultural context (Connell 2005) and in Australia masculinity is grounded in the "macho-Australianism." "Civilization" has been built upon the historical emergence of a masculine ego consciousness that arose in opposition to nature, which was seen as feminine (Ruether 1975). Masculine domination of society—patriarchy—is based upon the imperative to "control" all that is considered "nature." Such male dominance in Australia is deeply rooted in a violent, patriarchal past and over the years the presence of aggressive, controlling males have been "naturalized."

Traditional Australian history tells the tale of the British as "discovers" and how these white men came to settle a strange country and transform it by their science and technology, capital, and labor, thus creating "civilization out of wilderness" (Attwood 2005). Masculinity revolved around the physical mastery of a "hostile environment," tying in with narratives of colonialism, civilization, and "taming" marginalized peoples and nature. Manhood in Australia has been linked to "open rugged spaces of the Australian bush." The "tough," "brave," and "heroic bushman" are popular images in Australian history.

Australian identity and masculinity has been famously examined in Australian literature. This was exemplified by an Australian bush poet, Banjo Paterson (2012, 58), who romanticized the rural Australian male: "The man from Snowy River let the pony have his head, and he swung his stockwhip round and gave a cheer, and he raced him down the mountain like a torrent down its bed." Though these ideals stand in stark contrast to the brutality of "the Australian" also reflected in Australian writings. Bruce Elder (2003), in the famous book *Blood on the Wattle* documented significant painful events of white Australia's past and observed that, "there was no law and no morality on the frontier. It was a shifting territorial cliché where men were men, life was tough. Loneliness was normal, and fortunes were carved out of the virgin bush with bare hands." Kenneth Cook (2012, 31), in the Australian classic *Wake in Fright* encapsulated the masculinity of white Australia in his main character Grant who "killed many kangaroos that night and even once made a disastrous attempt to eviscerate one before he was sure it was dead; and it flopped about with its entrails spilling . . . Everybody laughed, and they laughed again because Grant was covered in blood, and they drank all the whiskey, and all the beer and their shooting became wilder." The masculinization of Australian identity stems from the British invasion of Australia, and it still has a significant hold and impact when looking at how nonhuman animals are treated, particularly kangaroos, and the complex relationship Australia has always had with them.

Despite the high level of urbanization, images of hunting, rurality, and agriculture remain dominant in the Australian consciousness. Traditional hegemonic notions of masculinity play a central role in these images. At center stage is the determined, practical, strong-willed individual—the man of the land—heroic, aggressive, and stoic. Constructs of hegemonic masculinity emphasize rational detachment and emotional stoicism as an ideal (Connell 2005). These images of masculinity in the Australian landscape are reinforced on a daily basis and tend to emphasize and justify behavioral norms in rural culture, which is intent on killing kangaroos. While people in urban areas also hold masculine and macho attitudes about killing kangaroos, the commercial kangaroo industry largely occurs in rural contexts. The practices of hegemonic masculinity often occur in rural spaces and through hunting and agriculture (Luke 2007). Rurality and masculinity within Australia intertwine and play a significant role in the justification of kangaroo killing and categorizing them as a "pest."

The connection between hunting and masculinity is commonly expressed (Kheel 2007). It is mostly associated with male domination, a drive for conquest, and the managing of nature (Kheel 2007). Some feminist theorists have long argued that the killing of "wild" nonhuman animals is an attempt to assert mastery and control over the natural world (Adams and Donovan 2007; Kheel 2007; Luke 2007; Merchant 1980). The method of dominating bodies through hunting is one expression of hegemonic masculinity. Alexis (2015, 117) relates it to "a political-social system that insists that males are inherently dominating, superior to everything and everyone deemed weak, especially females, and endowed with the right to dominate and rule over the weak and to maintain that dominance through violence." Hegemonic masculinity fosters social structures that serve to maintain male advantage over females and the natural world (Kheel 2007). Hegemonic masculinity has been normalized within Australian culture and operates in routinized ways to justify the killing of kangaroos and convince the public that it is the "natural order of things."

Skin and Body Parts: Feeding Masculinity

The manifestation of masculinity is significantly evident in the commercial kangaroo industry. While kangaroos are killed for consumption, parts of the kangaroo's body and skin are made into "products" for tourists. Kangaroo paw backscratchers, scrotum bottle openers, key chains, coin pouches and corkscrews, nipple warmers, and G-strings are produced as Australian souvenirs. These "products" are powerful and significant expressions of masculinity. The nature of such "products" is intentionally vulgar and displays stoic toughness, violence, and aggression, a certain sort of "manliness."

For example, an actual kangaroo paw displaying "the finger" is sold to tourists. The commodity is an example of exaggerated manliness with a display of aggression. Toughness, hostility, and violence are symbolized in this "product." The finger itself resembles macho imagery reflecting dominance and invulnerability. The paw represents not only the defiance of the paw holder but also a defiance toward the kangaroo, a way of proving dominance of the human over the nonhuman animal. It is a prime example of a hypermasculine product intended to a sell a hypermasculine ideology. While consuming body parts of any nonhuman animal is disturbing, these "products" have a particular vulgarness and reinforce a culture defined by violence and objectification. The vulgar "products" are rude, offensive, obnoxious, distasteful, and intertwine with Australian "humor" and its larrikin (a badly behaved young man) character.

Such kangaroo "products" also have a sexual undertone and aggression. The kangaroo scrotums and nipple warmers, for example, feed into objectification and sexualization. The image of the hunter derived from such "products" insinuates a strong, sexual, and "manly" male. The hunter not only asserts his masculinity by successfully killing the kangaroo, but by creating a vulgar product to further demonstrate and reinforce his masculinity. In other words, the hunter has proven that he can "take down" a kangaroo and then produces vulgar "products" to express his own masculinity and dominance. Luke (2007) likens the relationship of the hunter and the hunted to a passionate, yet violently aggressive sexual affair. The nonhuman animal is overcome by the power of hunter and further objectified as his body parts are transformed into sexualized "products." The nature of these "products" feed into the macho-Australian identity. In particular, the kangaroo scrotums perpetuate "Australianness." "Grab them by the balls" is a well-known national slang to impress someone. It implies that, now, one has your testicles they can control you, increasing the aggressor's sense of potency. Given this understanding, successfully killing a kangaroo and to "grab them by the balls" by turning the scrotum into an object for sale is the ultimate domineering and objectifying act toward kangaroos. To "grab them by the balls" could translate to "you're my slave now," and I can objectify and control you any way I like. These "products" resemble forms of entrenched masculinity that is evident within Australian culture.

The macho and competitive relationship that hunters display toward kangaroos is unmistakable. The hunter puts forth his own masculinity through the act of successfully killing/using the body parts of the male kangaroo in particular. Interestingly, male kangaroos will typically display some mannerisms that resemble human male behavior. The largest male may dominate during the mating season, or they may play by kicking and boxing other males in the family group. Additionally, some Australians may see the kangaroo as "competing" with humans because they walk on two legs, have two arms, and have families. The masculinity of the hunter is projected onto kangaroos in such a way that kangaroos are seen as competitors within the cultural landscape. The "products" generated from the bodies of kangaroos reinforces the hunter's own masculinity and sense of dominance.

The commercial kangaroo industry is a prime example of an enterprise in which the oppression of nonhuman animals is used to bolster hypermasculinity. While all forms of hunting and farming are inherently violent, this industry reinforces and fosters a culture of violence in extreme ways. It is violence regarded as "thrilling" and "manly" at the expense of kangaroos. Again, this links back to the fact that "nature" is treated and deemed "inferior," reaffirming masculine values and mindsets that justify violence and exploitation of nonhuman animals.

CAPITALISM AND MASCULINITY: THE INTERSECTIONALIZED NATURE OF DOMINATION

I turn now to a discussion of capitalism and hegemonic masculinity, systems of domination that are "mutually reinforcing." Addressing and analyzing mutually reinforcing logics of domination and drawing connections between power relations is crucial (Adams and Gruen 2014; Cudworth 2015; Eisenstein 1977; Glasser 2011; and Hartmann 2010). Understanding this "interdependence" of hegemonic masculinity and capitalism is essential to the political analysis of the oppression of nonhuman animals and in this case kangaroos specifically. The intersectional nature of these forms of domination reinforces the highly "naturalized" human domination of kangaroos and other nonhuman animals in Australia.

Hegemonic masculinity and capitalism are both founded on notions of authoritarian and hierarchical structures and transactions. Capitalism is grounded in hierarchical and authoritarian class structures, while hegemonic masculinity is underpinned by the hierarchical sexual structuring of society (Hartmann 2010). These hierarchical divisions are intersecting forms of domination that underpin kangaroo exploitation in Australia. At first glance, kangaroos are economically "valued" for the commercial industry. As we live in a society organized around the profit motive, land "development" and agriculture are economic priorities—making kangaroo deaths the basis for the growth of these industries. Given the hierarchical gender divisions, kangaroos and other nonhuman animals are associated with the "feminine." These gendered divisions reflect an ideology that views nonhuman animals as inferior and lacking value, "granting" men the inherent right to objectify and commodify them. This is particularly glaring through the production of the aforementioned grotesque items made from kangaroo bodies that reflect aggression in a particularly hypermasculinist way. Hegemonic masculinity, the domination of females and nonhuman animals, cannot be reduced to economics, while capitalism, as an economic class system driven by the pursuit of profit, feeds off the gendered ordering.

Capitalism drives profit maximization, and devalued humans and other animals are exploited in the process. Nonhuman animals function as property, and the commodification process is writ upon them physically (Torres 2007). Such hierarchy and imposed authority are directly linked to a capitalist mindset, which encourages individualism, competition, and a general lack of concern for other beings (Drew and Taylor 2014). Kangaroos, like other nonhuman animals, become "nothing more than living machines, transformed into beings who live for themselves into beings that live for capital" (Noske 1987; Twine 2012). Not only do they "live for" capital in Australia, but they are born into a country that has long been influenced by and values a stoic toughness and aggression that devalues females and nonhuman animal life. In both systems of domination, the kangaroos are devalued and are perceived as having worth only when their bodies are successfully subject to capitalist and masculinist control.

The kangaroo is seen as a valued "icon,"—a capitalist commodity—yet also regarded as a "wild animal" that must be tamed and controlled by the white Australian bushman. Hence, looking at both hegemonic masculinity and capitalism leads to a fuller understanding of why kangaroos are exploited in Australia. Capitalism and hegemonic masculinity feed into each other and serve to compound the oppression and domination of kangaroos. If the structure of oppression is to be changed, understanding this mutually reinforcing oppressive relationship is fundamental.

However, it is not just capitalism and hegemonic masculinity at play. Race interplays significantly within the Australian narrative. Western culture has justified the killing of "wild animals" to near extinction and the genocidal killing of Aboriginal peoples in countries colonized by the West (Plumwood 2002). The Australian colonizing culture and its treatment of Aboriginal people also has had devastating consequences on the continent and its "wildlife" (Plumwood 2002). The oppression of kangaroos and other free-living nonhuman animals in Australia is deeply entangled with the oppression of Aboriginal Australians. For the white, hypermasculinized Australian male, Aborigines are like women and nonhuman animals—inferior and subject to domination and control. Historically, when white, colonial invaders killed kangaroos and took the land for ranching, they took Aboriginal land too. Aborigines were massacred, repressed, and enslaved on sheep stations and related operations; sexual assault of Aboriginal women was widespread. While each form of oppression is unique, these intersecting elements (race, gender, and species) remain entrenched today and reinforce a cycle of domination that underlies the killing of kangaroos in Australia.

INTERSECTIONAL AWARENESS AS CRITICAL TO RADICAL RESISTANCE

Although some scholars and activists do valuable work in efforts to improve conditions for nonhuman animals, many do not consider the role of capitalism and hegemonic masculinity. Developing powerful critiques of human domination of nonhuman animals is crucial, particularly within the nonhuman animal rights movement and scholarship in Australia. Mainstream literature about kangaroos makes their treatment seem unrelated to the global economic system and disconnected to issues of gender, race, and masculinity. Such critiques tend only to focus on the *morality* of how we treat nonhuman animals. However, the way kangaroos, and all devalued humans and nonhuman animals in Australia, are treated is integrally linked to the nature of capitalist commodity production and the nature of masculinity in Australian society.

However, in Australia, many scholars and activists fail to identify kangaroo exploitation as an expression of capitalism and hegemonic masculinity and as a form of institutionalized domination (Pellow 2014). Calls for more humane treatment of kangaroos should be replaced with calls for total liberation. Moving to an analysis of the multiple forms of domination provides important tools, not only to resist and campaign against kangaroo killing, but to also denounce pro-capitalist and hypermasculinist theories and ideas within existing scholarship and academia in general. This ideological and strategic shift is crucial to expose exploitation and oppression in its many forms. Moreover, when activists and scholars fail to challenge capitalism and the role of hegemonic masculinity, they are complicit in systemic oppression (Drew and Taylor 2014). Challenging the ideologies that makes oppression seem natural and taking action against capitalism and other forces that undergirds oppression are all essential aspects of a liberatory project (Alloun 2015). Understanding the intersectionalized nature of domination can bring liberation movements together and can provide important opportunities for collaboration (Nocella et al. 2014).

CONCLUSION

It has long been argued that nonhuman animals only have value as commodities, and their interests do not matter in any moral sense (Francione 2008). The exploitation of kangaroos in Australia is a powerful case that highlights the ways in which nonhuman animals are commodified and viewed as "resources" for human use and gain. On one hand, the kangaroo is a celebrated Australian symbol. On the other hand, kangaroos are killed every night in remote areas of the Australian outback for reasons of land "development," agriculture, and the commercial industry for their flesh and skin. Capitalist imperatives have shaped the conditions and treatment of kangaroos in Australia and speciesist, sexist and racist ideologies legitimate this exploitation. Capitalism and hegemonic masculinity serve to maintain the routine oppression of nonhuman animals both in Australia and throughout the world. Increasing awareness and understanding of the multiple forms of domination that exist is necessary for the development of an effective movement for liberation for kangaroos and all nonhuman and human animals.

REFERENCES

Adams, Carol, and Josephine Donovan. 2007. *The Feminist Care Tradition in Animal Ethics*. New York: Columbia University Press.

Adams, Carol, and Lori Gruen. 2014. *Ecofeminism. Feminist Intersections with other Animals and the Earth*. New York: Bloomsbury.

Alexis, Nekeisha. 2015. "Beyond suffering: Resisting Patriarchy and Reproductive Control." In Anthony Nocella, Richard White, and Erika Cudworth (eds.), *Anarchism and Animal Liberation. Essays on Complementary Elements of Total Liberation.* Jefferson, NC: McFarland, 108–125.

Alloun, Esther. 2015. "Ecofeminism and Animal Advocacy in Australia: Productive Encounters for an Integrative Ethics and Politics." *Animal Studies Journal,* 4(1): 148–173.

Attwood, Bain. 2005. *Telling the Truth about Aboriginal History.* Crow's Nest, New South Wales: Allen & Unwin.

Bookchin, Murray. 2005. *The Ecology of Freedom. The Emergence and Dissolution of Hierarchy.* Oakland, CA: AK Press.

Boom, Keely, and Dror Ben-Ami. 2011. "Shooting Our Wildlife: An Analysis of the Law and Its Animal Welfare Outcomes for Kangaroos and Wallabies." *Australian Animal Protection Law Journal,* 4: 44–60.

Boom, Keely, et al. 2012. "'Pest' and Resource: A Legal History of Australia's Kangaroos." *Animal Studies Journal,* 1(1):17–40.

Cook, Kenneth. 2012. *Wake in Fright.* Melbourne, Australia: Text Publishing Company.

Connell, Raewyn. 2005. *Masculinities.* 2d ed. Cambridge, UK: Polity.

Croft, David. 2005. "Kangaroos Maligned—16 Million Years of Evolution and Two Centuries of Persecution." In Maryland Wilson and David Croft (eds.), *Kangaroo Myths and Realities.* Victoria, Australia: Australian Wildlife Protection Council, 17–31.

Cudworth, Erika. 2015. "Intersectionality, Species and Social domination." In Anthony Nocella, Richard White, and Erika Cudworth (eds.), *Anarchism and Animal Liberation: Essays on Complementary Elements of Total Liberation.* Jefferson, NC: McFarland Books, 93–107.

Drew, Lara, and Nik Taylor. 2014. "Engaged Activist Research: Challenging apolitical Objectivity." In Anthony Nocella, John Sorenson, Kim Socha, and Atsuko Matsuoka (eds.), *Defining Critical Animal Studies. An Intersectional Social Justice Approach for Liberation.* New York: Peter Lang, 159–176.

Eisenstein, Zillah. 1977. "Constructing a Theory of Capitalist Patriarchy and Socialist Feminism." *Critical Sociology,* 7(3): 3–17.

Elder, Bruce. 2003. *Blood on the Wattle: Massacres and maltreatment of Aboriginal Australians since 1978.* 3d ed. New York: New Holland Publishers.

Francione, Gary. 2008. *Animals as Persons. Essays on the Abolition of Exploitation.* New York: Columbia University Press.

Garlick, Steve, and Rosemary Austen. 2012. "The Emotional Lives of Kangaroos: Rehabilitation, Science and the Environment." Paper presented at Australian Wildlife Rehabilitation Conference. Townsville, Australia.

Glasser, Carol. 2011. "Tied Oppressions: How Sexist Imagery Reinforces Speciesist Sentiment." *Brock Review,* 12(1): 51.

Hartmann, Heidi. 2010. *The Unhappy Marriage of Marxism and Feminism: Towards a More Progressive Union.* London: Palgrave Macmillan.

Kangaroo Population Estimates. 2016. "Australian Government, Department of Environment." Accessed February 8, 2016, from http://www.environment

.gov.au/biodiversity/wildlife-trade/natives/wild-harvest/kangaroo-wallaby
-statistics/kangaroo-population.

Kheel, Marti. 2007. *Nature Ethics: An Ecofeminist Perspective.* New York: Rowman & Littlefield Publishers.

Kvinta, Paul. 2015. "They Shoot Kangaroos, Don't They?" Accessed September 10, 2016, from http://www.outsideonline.com/2037071/overrood-behind-scenes -australias-surprising-kangaroo-conflict.

Lawrence, D. H. 1994. *The Complete Poems of D.H. Lawrence. New Edition.* London: Wordsworth Editions Ltd.

Luke, Brian. 2007. *Brutal: Manhood and the Exploitation of Animals.* Chicago: University of Illinois Press.

Meadows, Tashee. 2010. "Because They Matter." In A. Breeze Harper (ed.), *Sistah Vegan. Black Female Vegans Speak on Food, Identity, Health, and Society.* New York: Lantern Books, 150–154.

Merchant, Carolyn. 1980. *The Death of Nature, Women, Ecology, and the Scientific Revolution.* San Francisco: Harper & Row.

Nibert, David. 2002. *Animal Rights/Human Rights: Entanglements of Oppression and Liberation.* Lanham, MD: Rowman & Littlefield.

Nibert, David. 2013. *Animal Oppression and Human Violence: Domesecration, Capitalism, and Global Conflict.* New York: Columbia University Press.

Nocella, Anthony, John Sorenson, Kim Socha, and Atsuko Matsuoka. 2014. "Introduction: The Emergence of Critical Animal Studies: The Rise of Intersectional Animal Liberation." In Anthony Nocella, John Sorenson, Kim Socha, and Atsuko Matsuoka (eds.), *Defining Critical Animal Studies: An Intersectional Social Justice Approach to Liberation.* New York: Peter Lang, xix–xxxvi.

Noske, Barbara. 1997. *Beyond Boundaries: Humans and Animals.* Montreal: Black Rose Books.

O'Lincoln, Tom. 2016. "The Squatters in Colonial Australia." Accessed March 27, 2016, from http://www.anu.edu.au/polsci/marx/interventions/squatters .htm.

Paterson, Banjo. 2012. *Poems of Banjo Paterson.* New York: New Holland Publishers.

Pellow, David. 2014. *Total Liberation. The Power and Promise of Animal Rights and the Radical Earth Movement.* Minneapolis: University of Minnesota Press.

Plumwood, Val. 2012. *Environmental Culture. The Ecological Crisis of Reason.* New York: Routledge.

Ramp, Daniel, and Karl Vernes. 2015. "Fact Check. Are Kangaroos at Risk." Accessed March 28, 2016, from http://theconversation.com/factcheck-are -kangaroos-at-risk-37757.

Ruether, Rosemary. 1975. *New Woman/New Earth: Sexist Ideologies and Human Liberation.* New York: Seabury.

Taylor, Affrica. 2014. "Settler children, kangaroos and the cultural politics of Australian national belonging." *Global Studies of Childhood,* 4(3): 169–182.

THINNK. 2015. "The Think Tank for Kangaroos." Accessed March 13, 2015, from http://thinkkangaroos.uts.edu.au/publications.html.

Torres, Bob. 2007. *Making a Killing: The Political Economy of Animal Rights.* Oakland, CA: AK Press.

Twine, Richard. 2012. "Revealing the 'Animal-Industrial Complex'—A Concept and Method for Critical Animal Studies?" *Journal for Critical Animal Studies,* 10(1): 12–39.

Wadiwel, Dinesh. 2015. *The War Against Animals.* Leiden, the Netherlands, and Boston: Brill/Rodopi.

Wicks, D. 2012. "Cute Baby Seals and Kangaroo Pests." Accessed September 10, 2016, from https://www.voiceless.org.au/content/cute-baby-seals-and-kangaroo-pests.

8

The Roots of the Sixth Mass Extinction[1]

Julie Andrzejewski

"Humans aren't the only species on Earth, we just act like it"
Popular Slogan—Anonymous

EXTINCTION IS PERSONAL

Extinction is personal! Foremost, it means the personal anguish and deaths of billions or trillions of individual nonhuman animals, birds, or insects. It involves the myriad emotions and distress experienced by the parents and/or communities who have lost their young ones (Safina 2015). If we happen to have access to one of the few media sources that cover the sixth mass extinction of species at all, we might see images of emaciated or dead polar bears who are unable to hunt seals without sea ice (Lawler 2015). We might come across a photo of an orangutan whose forest home was torn down for a palm oil plantation, but we may only read that she "disappeared." We likely won't be made aware that she and her baby burned to death as they clung to their familiar tree homes (Tucker 2014).

We have certainly heard of the "colony collapse" of the honeybees whose deaths have been attributed to the neonicotinoid pesticides used on so many crops, pesticides that still have not been fully banned anywhere. But we are not likely to contemplate what was experienced by the individual bees who became sick and disoriented from the poison and left their hive home never to return. And what were the feelings of the last po'o-uli, the Hawaiian honeycreeper, when there was no answer to his mating call?

We may have heard that amphibian species are vanishing, but have we even noticed that the once frequent frogs, toads, or salamanders are missing in our neighborhoods, local parks, or wilderness areas? What is happening to them? What miseries are they undergoing on their way to extinction? Many people know that Monarch butterflies are becoming scarce, but how many of us know the underlying causes? How and why are they dying? Do we know that bats are dying by the millions of white nose disease? What are the consequences of these deaths for the many nonhuman animals whose lives depend on bats, butterflies, and amphibians?

When we do pursue these stories further and come to understand the interconnections of this massive global agony, it is easy to become overwhelmed. After all, what can *we* do about extinction anyway? Our tendency is to look away, not think about it, avoid information, but *now* is the only time we *can* do something about it, and there are significant actions we can take to make a life-saving difference!

In this chapter, I only have space to highlight key alarming reports about the sixth mass extinction and how the human economic system of capitalism, through pervasive and global exploitation and pollution of the Earth, has created and shaped the driving forces of extinctions. Simultaneously, I will explore why the U.S. public is largely unaware of the severity and consequences of the extinction crisis. Finally, I will present key actions recommended by leading scientists or activist organizations that must be taken immediately if we want to stem the tide of extinctions of other animals and plants and possibly even save ourselves.

WHY ISN'T THE PUBLIC MOBILIZED?

Critical readers must be wary of corporate journalistic reports that sanitize or minimize stories of nonhuman animal extinctions. Our earlier study (Andrzejewski and Alessio 2013) shows a dearth of articles published by corporate media on the topic and how the few that are published promote denial, fragmentation, distancing, and inappropriate relief. Mainstream media frequently make assumptions that foster speciesism. This reporting creates a false sense of being informed among those who rely upon mass media as a primary source for information. The mainstream media distance readers by using terms like *colony collapse, population decline,* or *percentages* of a certain group of living beings that are threatened with *extirpation,* the local or global elimination of a species. In this way, extinctions of particular nonhuman animals, birds, insects, or plants are made to seem remote, less immediate, less catastrophic . . . less personal. Like war victims of some rival country, we are unlikely to hear about their individual lives, personalities, or the particular circumstances of their suffering or deaths, especially since humans and human institutions such as corporations are usually at the root of nonhuman animal deaths and extinctions.

Further, in "the sixth mass extinction of species," the words *mass* and *species* carry a certain quality of alienation, each word signifying an unknown number of beings, possibly hundreds or maybe millions. The nonhuman animals at risk may be endemic (limited) to only one place or span the globe, making it difficult for the public to grasp the enormity of the problem or to empathize with the individual nonhuman animals or their communities. On the other hand, the singularity of the word *extinction* may seem to infer that it is just one event or some natural occurrence rather than referring to the hundreds of thousands of nonhuman animal and plant extinctions that are underway in diverse places as a result of various modes of human exploitation.

Beyond wording, corporate media information about the sixth mass extinction is fragmented, denied, trivialized, distanced, or missing altogether. As a result, people in the United States and other countries under the sway of the Western media are only vaguely aware that such a crisis exists or are lulled into thinking the problem is not that bad, is faraway in time or space, or that science will solve it. Those who are aware of the process of extinction are misinformed about the severity of the problem by media omission or disinformation. In a word, the real extinction story has been *censored* so that the industries profiting from the drivers of extinction can continue to plunder the Earth while decimating other forms of life and/or their means of survival (Andrzejewski and Alessio 2013).

In stressful twenty-first century human lives, words might very well determine whether we pause long enough to consider, even briefly, what extinction means for the beings experiencing it, for the intricate web of life, or for humans. Most people can't conceive that the term extinction could apply to us—the human animals—who have been taught to consider ourselves dominant, superior, rational, technological, or invincible in comparison with other animals or species. In fact, humans are not immune to the extreme events pushing plants and nonhuman animals to extinction.

WHAT *IS* THE SIXTH MASS EXTINCTION?

A mass extinction is when a large number of species become extinct in a relatively short period of time. Based on fossil records, scientists estimate that approximately 99 percent of all species that have ever lived on Earth have become extinct during five previous mass extinctions that occurred at various times millions of years ago. While there is no certainty about the causes of each mass extinction event, various theories suggest that the first one (the Ordovician about 444 million years ago) was the result of glaciation, the middle one (the Permian) was caused by massive lava flows in Siberia that led to global warming (Jamail 2015a), and the most recent (the Cretaceous) occurring 65 million years ago by an asteroid (Kolbert 2014, 16).

Modern humans only appeared on Earth some 200,000 years ago (Sample, 2016). Yet, it is speculated, based on the available evidence, that as humans became established, they began having a negative impact on other forms of life such as mammoths, mastodons, aurochs, and possibly Neanderthals (Kolbert 2014, 238). However, the *rate* of extinctions, meaning how many species became extinct in any given period of time, appeared to remain very low in the nineteenth century, leading Darwin to propose that species went extinct slowly through natural selection. However, Darwin himself noticed "animals which have been exterminated, either locally or wholly, through man's agency," extinctions that were clearly not slow (Kolbert 2014, 68). In hindsight, it became clear to scientists in a number of fields that the number and rate of extinctions of nonhuman animals began increasing noticeably and then exponentially with the advent and spread of industrialization, capitalism, militarism, and imperialism.

Since the 1970s, scientists have studied and documented a contemporary massive decline in species. Further, even where other animals have not been entirely extinguished, their populations have decreased dramatically. Recall that *population decline* means that many individual nonhuman animals, including birds, marine life, and insects, suffered and died or were unable to raise their young because of some serious disturbance. The cumulative results of countless research projects clearly verify that with ever increasing technological sophistication, human activities are causing what is now known as the sixth mass extinction of life on Earth.

While many individual human activities are implicated, and some human individuals contribute significantly to extinctions, it is crucial to differentiate between the impact of individuals and the large-scale corporate projects of global capitalism. Projects such as wars, mines, dams, deforestation, factory farming, chemical monoculture agriculture, nuclear power, extraction and combustion of fossil fuels, commercial fishing, manufacture of chemicals and toxic products, various forms of hunting, and the proliferation of garbage—the list is long—are the types of activities primarily responsible for extinctions. Such corporate ventures seize and/or manipulate excessive amounts of materials from the Earth, destroying ecologies and killing other animals, directly or indirectly, for the purpose of maximizing profits. The resulting extinctions are happening so rapidly that they are disrupting the intricate web of life whereby species rely upon each other in complex ways. As explained by the Center for Biological Diversity (2013):

> Although extinction is a natural phenomenon, it occurs at a natural "background" rate of about one to five species per year. Scientists estimate we're now losing species at 1,000 to 10,000 times the background rate, with literally dozens going extinct every day.

Finally recognizing mass extinction as a problem in 2002, the world's governments agreed to stop the rate of biodiversity loss by 2010. Not only was that goal not met, the rate of extinctions continues to escalate unabated (United Nations Environment Programme, 2010). Indeed, activist, environmental and "wildlife" organizations, not governments, are leading the efforts to study, document, educate, litigate, and demand the immense changes needed to slow or staunch this persistent tragedy. One of these, the Species Alliance (2010), succinctly but dramatically summarizes the research:

> Today, scientists believe that we are entering the 6th Mass Extinction. But unlike the previous five, this one will not take centuries to unfold—in fact, it will take place in our lifetimes. As scientists begin to realize the severity of the crisis and new worldwide assessments are made, the news is difficult to believe. At least half of all plant and animal species are likely to disappear in the wild within the next 30–40 years, including many of the most familiar and beloved large mammals: elephants, polar bears, chimpanzees, gorillas, and all the great apes, all the big cats, and many, many others. Bird species are similarly imperiled, songbird populations have declined by 50% in the last 40 years. One out of every eight species of plant life worldwide and almost one third of the plant species within the United States already face extinction. Populations of large ocean fish have declined by 90% since the 1950s. All around the world, birds, reptiles, mammals, amphibians, fish, and invertebrates, as well as trees, flowering plants, and other flora, are all in steep decline . . . Scientists estimate that tens of thousands of species are vanishing every year, including many that have yet to be discovered or named.

HOW CREDIBLE IS THE EVIDENCE?

While mainstream news outlets and even some research publications may introduce their reports with qualifiers such as "we may be in the beginning" of a sixth mass extinction, in fact, the evidence available demonstrates that the sixth extinction event is well underway. Many thousands of scientists and organizations have conducted painstaking research related to the deterioration of the Earth's ecologies and what is called biodiversity. Many of these scientists, emerging from the traditional Western sciences, are unlikely to subscribe to an animal rights philosophy or engage in a critical analysis of capitalism. Nevertheless, collectively the research they present provides a compelling record of the suffering, deaths, drastic population losses, and extinctions that other animals and plants are now experiencing.

Many organizations are involved in providing the data needed for urgent policy changes. One of the oldest global organizations researching and raising the alarm about the extinction crisis is the International Union for Conservation of Nature (IUCN). In partnership with conservation and environmental organizations and a network of scientists and experts from almost every country, the IUCN produces *The IUCN Red List of Threatened Species,* a report formally updated every four years. The goal of the Red List is "to provide information and analyses on the status, trends and threats to species in order to inform and catalyze action for biodiversity conservation" (IUCN 2015). Although it is likely the most comprehensive and well-known report, IUCN acknowledges that it still identifies only a small portion of the countless thousands of species of nonhuman animals, plants, and fungi.

Another significant report, the biennial *Living Planet Report* is based on the Living Planet Index by the World Wildlife Fund (WWF) in partnership with the Zoological Society of London and the Global Footprint Network. In 2014, they reported this grim news:

> Globally, populations of fish, birds, mammals, amphibians and reptiles measured for the report have declined by 52 percent since 1970, and freshwater species have suffered a 76 percent decline—an average loss almost double that of land and marine species (World Wildlife Fund 2014).

Even though such species are not yet extinct, steep population declines make it much more difficult for a species to recover and maintain a viable presence in an ecosystem. Further, other interconnected nonhuman animals, plants, and insects may be forcefully impacted leading to what is described as cascade and collapse. Once a confluence of significant interconnections is violated, a cascade effect is imminent, and collapse will be sudden and permanent.

The United Nations is aware that 80 percent of the remaining biodiversity of plants and nonhuman animals is located in the 20 percent of land mass occupied by indigenous peoples (First Peoples Worldwide, nd). For this reason, the UN and other organizations working to curtail the loss of animals and plants are beginning to value, learn from, and partner with traditional indigenous peoples to develop policies to protect both the peoples and the other animals (Interagency Support Group on Indigenous Peoples' Issues 2014). This effort is especially important given that corporations have been stealing and patenting indigenous knowledge and the flora and fauna endemic to indigenous peoples' lands for decades (Shiva 1997; Smith 1999).

Intergenerational knowledge and spiritual connections with the Earth and all forms of life generates the strength of resistance within some indigenous communities who have formed a frontline against the destructive practices of industrial extraction and exploitation of nature. The tenacity and courage of indigenous activists, often small in number and facing overwhelming forces, cannot be overstated, and at times result in stunning victories, such as the prevention of the "black death" coal terminal at Cherry Point, WA, where coal would have been exported to China (Mapes 2016). At this writing, 200 tribes and their allies have gathered to support the Standing Rock Sioux who are challenging corporate plans to build a Dakota pipeline that threatens their land and water. Their prayerful peaceful protests, met by police exploiting dogs for intimidation and violence on behalf of the company, have inspired rallies in over 100 U.S. cities (Knight 2016a).

While indigenous knowledge is not widely disseminated, alliances between and with indigenous peoples can generate effective activism for extinction prevention. Further, understanding the worldviews of indigenous peoples may facilitate a change in perspective needed to counter capitalism's exploitive view of the natural world.

WHAT IS CAUSING THE SIXTH EXTINCTION? CAPITALISM VS. NATURAL LAW

With all our hubris, humans around the globe have invented imaginative theories, theologies, and/or realities that may or may not correspond with the physical structures or processes of the natural world. Sociologists call such "realities" *social constructions* (Berger and Luckmann 1966). Many, if not most, socially constructed realities serve those who create and control them, justifying oppressive or destructive activities such as the extraction and human "ownership" of natural "resources," the stratification of classes or castes, hierarchies of importance and power based on race, gender, physical appearance, species, and other identifiable or accusatorial characteristics (Andrzejewski et al. 2009; Alessio 2011).

Such "realities" have been coupled with the twentieth century rise of the field of public relations (PR) that fosters skills in manipulating public opinions through carefully crafted and highly selective messaging using compromised authority figures, skewed or false data, emotional appeals, or the creation of doubt. PR skills, brought into the service of corporations and capitalism, became more powerful with the invention of each new communication technology, greatly stabilizing profit-based false realities. Through a combination of censorship (omission) and propaganda (false information), corporate PR has a corrupting influence on public opinion and undermines democracy.

The beliefs of some societies, however, have long been based on close and astute observations of nature and their local ecosystems. Over millennia, they developed and honed their own sciences of nature based on *natural law*. These perceptive observations, many from oral societies, have been acknowledged in the Western world as indigenous knowledge and/or ethnosciences (Harding 1993; LaDuke 1996; Linden 1991; Shiva 1997; Smith 1999).

The fundamental principle of *natural law* recognized by indigenous sciences refers to the physical properties and processes of nature. As LaDuke (1996) explains, natural law is viewed as pre-eminent in indigenous intellectual thought, a law that takes precedence over all others. While humans can devise their own traditions, beliefs, laws, and policies, natural law dictates the consequences of actions regardless of what beliefs or laws humans have fabricated. For instance, the agreement forged at the Conference of Parties (COP) 21 Paris climate talks allows countries to "postpone making critical cuts to their emission outputs;" however, co-author Patrik Pfister points out that such "leeway" is "more than the climate system allows," meaning that drastic and irreversible changes in the climate will, therefore, continue to escalate (McCauley 2016).

Another tenet of indigenous intellectual thought is "taking only what you need and leaving the rest" (LaDuke 1996). In contrast, capitalist thinking is based on human domination and a utilitarian view of nature as only important for its benefits to humans: trees and forests are viewed as timber, water is viewed as irrigation, a wilderness is viewed as holding exploitable resources such as coal or oil. Capitalism conflicts with natural law because it is based on greed—"taking more than you need and not leaving the rest" (LaDuke 1996). Therefore, according to indigenous intellectual thought, capitalism is inherently out of order with natural law.

As Vandana Shiva (1993, 305), one of the leading global activists for biodiversity points out, "The industrial revolution converted economics from the prudent management of resources for sustenance and basic needs satisfaction into a process of commodity production for profit maximization." Naomi Klein (2014, 21), a global climate activist explains,

> . . . our economic system and our planetary system are now at war. Or, more accurately, our economy is at war with many forms of life on Earth, including human life. What the climate needs to avoid collapse is a contraction in humanity's use of resources; what our economic model demands to avoid collapse is unfettered expansion. Only one of these sets of rule can be changed, and it's not the laws of nature.

There is an essential conflict in capitalism between what is beneficial for the Earth and living beings and maximizing short-term profits. Extreme climate disruption, death and suffering of human and other animals, extinctions, predictions of dire consequences—nothing thus far has disrupted the greed and motivation to make the most money regardless of the natural consequences.

WHAT ARE THE DRIVERS OF EXTINCTIONS?

The Hunting Businesses

Controversy persists about whether human hunting drove many other animals to extinction, especially large species or megafauna, as humans migrated to new regions of the world. Some studies claim that climate change (warming or cooling) is the culprit, and humans came on the scene *after* megafauna were already declining (Balter 2014). However, most evidence seems to support the "overkill" theory, which postulates that humans were the driving force behind the extinctions of nonhuman animals such as the mastodons, mammoths, saber-toothed cats, giant sloths, and the like (Kolbert 2014, 230–235; Stolzenburg 2008). It appears that humans were a lethal force even before capitalism.

Yet, with industrialization and capitalism, hunting and fishing quickly became multibillion dollar businesses with many constituencies seeking a piece of the profit pie. Under capitalism, technologies have been developed to entrap and/or kill vast quantities of nonhuman animals, birds, and marine life with deadly efficiency. Trophy hunting, "wildlife" trade, "bush meat," commercial fishing technologies, and the elimination of competitive species, especially predators, are emptying the forests, prairies, wetlands, and oceans. Mountains too have experienced human pressures, but some other animals have been able to survive, if not thrive, by living in places most inhospitable to humans (Wendle 2015).

Safari Club International (SFI), a hunting advocacy organization, epitomizes the interlocking strategies used to support the business of massive killing by "sport" and trophy hunters. Claiming a mission of "wildlife conservation," SFI fosters a culture of self-aggrandizement through the killing of esteemed or feared other animals. Their website hosts a record book to recognize those "who have achieved exceptional levels of big game hunting . . . These individuals show their *support of wildlife conservation* and management through participating in hunting expeditions" (SFI 2016, italics mine). Boasting over 50,000 members and a $10 million budget, SFI "exercises a substantial amount of lobbying power, shaping anti-wildlife conservation policies that only satisfy trophy hunters' bloodlust, negatively impacting wildlife on a global scale," according to an investigative report by AlterNet (Loki 2016). In Defense of Animals (IDA) describes SFI as promoting:

competitive trophy hunting throughout the world, even of rare species, and not shying away from canned hunts, through an elaborate awards program. SFI continues to create and feed a culture glamorizing death and violence globally, across political lines, international borders, and against wildlife and even people. Fortunes are made on the back of millions of animals . . . (Loki 2016).

SFI offers 15 Grand Slam Awards for killing various combinations of non-human animals (the Big Five of Africa, Cats of the World, "Wild" Oxen of the World, etc.) and a Hunting Achievement Award for killing a total of 125 nonhuman animals. The guide and hunter who killed Cecil the Lion in 2015 were members of SFI.

A second example of rampant hunting/killing is the U.S. government agency misnamed "Wildlife Services." Using taxpayers' money, this agency has for decades poisoned, shot, trapped, bludgeoned, and in other myriad ways slaughtered millions of nonhuman animals, particularly predators, every year. Most victims, even threatened or endangered species, are those other animals considered "pests" by the ranching industry (Predator Defense 2014). Ranchers also receive public subsidies by grazing cows on public lands at a small percentage of the actual value, thus contributing to the loss of habitat and forage for native other animals.

Further, many U.S. state Departments of Natural Resources (DNRs), who collaborate with "Wildlife Services," consider hunters and ranchers to be their primary constituencies. They benefit financially from hunting licenses whether for nonhuman animals killed for consumption or for trophies. Contrary to any mission they may espouse relating to "wildlife" conservation, these state agencies often defy the Endangered Species Act regulations and push for licensed trophy hunts for wolves, grizzly bears, big cats, and other predators (Milman 2016).

Illegal "Wildlife" Trafficking

On another front, in Africa, Asia, and Latin America, the increased opening of forest and wilderness areas to logging, mining, agriculture, and other human activities sets the stage for the decimation of other animals through "bush meat" hunting. "Bush meat" "poaching" has become an international commercial enterprise and "the most significant immediate threat to the future of wildlife in Africa and around the world; it has already resulted in widespread local extinctions in Asia and West Africa" (Bushmeat Crisis Task Force, nd). Elephants, apes, monkeys, reptiles, antelopes, buffalo, birds, tortoises, pangolins, civets, porcupines, bush pigs, and others are targeted. This massive killing of other animals for their flesh has led to what has been dubbed the empty forest syndrome, forests where large nonhuman animals can no longer be found (Vander Velde 2014). Rare and endangered species often bring higher prices. Some are captured and transported alive and thus suffer immensely before they are finally killed (IDA Africa 2013).

Under capitalism, the greatest profits are made by going beyond what is legal while continually lobbying to expand the laws to allow even more favorable conditions for making money (Alessio 2011, 162–164). Thus, in spite of national and international laws for the protection of "wildlife," the illegal "wildlife" trade has burgeoned to become a $20 billion a year industry. In fact, the United Nations has only recently passed a resolution "on illicit trafficking of wildlife, calling for urgent action . . . (by adopting) new sustainable development goals identifying wildlife crime as a global threat . . . (and by urging) member countries to treat wildlife crime as a serious crime under the U.N. Convention against Transnational Organized Crime" (Guynup 2016, 12). Unknown to many U.S. citizens, the United States is one of the key destinations for "poached and smuggled wildlife," most of it coming from Latin America through Mexico and destined to be eaten. Highest in demand is "meat," then "fins, feathers, eggs, shells, and shoes . . . followed closely by small manufactured leather products, such as wallets and belts, and dead animals likely intended for display, consumption or further processing" (Indenbaum 2016, 15).

Investigating for Defenders of Wildlife, Guynup (2016, 12) explains, "Everything imaginable is being illegally hunted and traded, from birds, fish and turtles to frogs, monkeys, and butterflies that come in a pupae." Yet the United States only has 200 inspectors trying to search for tens of thousands of pounds of "illegally" killed nonhuman animals, their body parts, or products made from their bodies coming into the country. The consequences of this decimation of global "wildlife" cannot be overstated. Trafficking "wildlife" around the world is wiping out imperiled species and spreading viruses and disease to "wild" populations, but there are broader impacts. Extracting hundreds or thousands of nonhuman animals from an ecosystem causes inestimable damage, dismantling natural systems that have been fine-tuned over millennia (Guynup 2016, 15).

Nonhuman Animal Agriculture

Nonhuman animal agriculture in all forms, but especially the most extreme form called factory farming whereby billions of sentient other animals are subjected to the most restrictive and filthy type of imprisonment, cruelty, and slaughter every year, is a key driver of extinctions. Drawing from scores of global reports, organizations, and experts, the film *Cowspiracy: The Sustainability Secret* (Cowspiracy The Facts 2015) asserts that, "animal agriculture is the leading cause of species extinction, ocean dead zones, water pollution, and habitat destruction."

The challenging truth about the short- and long-term consequences of nonhuman animal agriculture on humans, other animals, and the environment is not often disseminated by the corporate media or even the independent media in many instances. While the endangerment of human health by the overuse of antibiotics in "livestock" has received some coverage, issues such as the connection between nonhuman animal emissions and anthropogenic climate disruption (ADC), the pollution of fresh and ocean waters by nonhuman animal excrement, the starvation of humans in countries exporting "meat," and the killing of endangered species to protect "livestock" have received little or weak attention.

The data, documented from a wide variety of sources, are compelling. Just a few of the alarming factors gathered by Cowspiracy The Facts (2015) from a variety of credible sources like the Food and Agriculture Organization of the United Nations include:

- *Greenhouse gases:* "Animal agriculture is responsible for 18% of greenhouse gas emissions, more than the combined exhaust from all transportation" (1).

- *Water use:* "Animal agriculture ranges from 34–76 *trillion* gallons annually . . . 5% of water consumed in the US is by private homes. 55% of water consumed in the US is for animal agriculture" (4–5).

- *Land use:* "Livestock or livestock feed occupies 1/3 of the earth's ice-free land" (5).

- *Ocean dead zones:* "Livestock operations on land have created more than 500 nitrogen flooded dead zones around the world in our oceans" (6).

- *Desertification:* "1/3 of the planet is desertified, with livestock as the leading driver" (7).

- *Excrement:* "130 times more animal waste than human waste is produced in the US . . . 5 tons of animal waste is produced per person in the US" (8).

- *Empty oceans:* "As many as 2.7 trillion animals are pulled from the ocean each year" (9).

- *Amazon destruction:* "Animal agriculture is responsible for up to 91% of Amazon destruction . . . Up to 137 plant, animal, and insect species are lost every day due to rainforest destruction . . . approximately 136 million rainforest acres (have been) cleared for animal agriculture" (10–11).

- *Impact on "wild" animals:* "10,000 years ago, 99% of biomass (i.e. zoomass) was wild animals. Today, humans and the animals that we raise as food make up 98% of zoomass" (12).

- *Antibiotic use:* "80% of antibiotics sold in the US are for livestock" (12).
- *Impact on human hunger:* "Worldwide, at least 50% of grain is fed to livestock. 82% of starving children live in countries where food is fed to animals and the animals are eaten by western countries" (13).

And yet, such realities of nonhuman animal agriculture and factory farming are ignored, trivialized, or censored so the consequences of eating "meat" and "dairy"—on oceans, freshwaters, "wildlife," ecologies, climate disruption, human health, extinctions, and the future of our planet, not to mention the other animals themselves—are obscured, denied, or even contradicted.

Global Climate Disruption

Anthropogenic (human caused) climate disruption (ACD) with its related perils, ocean acidification, and sea level rise, is probably the single largest threat to plant and animal species, including human animals. As fossil records indicate, climate change, both warming and cooling, has been implicated in previous global extinction events that occurred millions of years ago. Most previous extinctions transpired over tens of thousands of years or longer. However, the extraction and burning of fossil fuels (coal, oil, gas, and methane) to power industrialization and the machinery to make products for the modern world have—in just a few hundred years— created a warming trend that is unprecedented in the history of the planet.

Climate disruption is a more accurate descriptor than global warming because the changes in the atmosphere from burning fossil fuels are triggering extreme weather events of all kinds—heat waves, droughts, hurricanes, typhoons, tornados, excessive rain and floods, blizzards, and extreme cold. Further, as Guy McPherson, 30-year climate change expert and evolutionary biologist points out, climate disruption is exacerbated by self-reinforcing feedback loops.

> A self-reinforcing positive feedback loop is akin to a "vicious circle": It accelerates the impacts of anthropogenic climate disruption (ACD). An example would be methane releases in the Arctic. Massive amounts of methane are currently locked in the permafrost, which is now melting rapidly. As the permafrost melts, methane—a greenhouse gas 100 times more potent than carbon dioxide on a short timescale—is released into the atmosphere, warming it further, which in turn causes more permafrost to melt, and so on (Jamail 2015a, 2).

McPherson and other scientists have discovered more than 50 such self-reinforcing feedback loops, and new ones continue to be found. Further, these feedback loops interact with each other, increasing their impacts on the climate (Jamail 2015a).

How serious is this for life and biodiversity on planet Earth? Award winning investigative journalist Dahr Jamail, author of the Climate Disruption Dispatches based on mega-analyses of hundreds of studies and notable research think tanks, puts it this way:

> Sixty-three percent of all human-generated carbon emissions have been produced in the last 25 years, but science shows us that there is a 40-year time lag between global emissions (our actions) and climate impacts (the consequences) . . . Since the industrial revolution began, the human species has increased the average global temperature by 0.85 degrees Celsius. In December 2010, the UN Environmental Program predicted up to a 5-degree Celsius increase by 2050. This is a shocking piece of information because a 3.5-degree Celsius increase would render the planet uninhabitable for humans due to collapsing the food chain at the level of oceanic plankton and triggering temperature extremes that would severely limit terrestrial vegetation and, hence, our ability to feed ourselves. (Jamail 2015b)

These new predictions are particularly distressing because scientists have been overly cautious and conservative in their calculations. Such conservatism is not surprising given decades of climate change denial and disputes, with scientists and research coming under concerted attack by politicians and media campaigns. This political environment was created by the unrestrained influence of the fossil fuel corporations over politicians, the revolving door between industries and governmental regulatory agencies, and the money poured into PR campaigns to influence public opinion. These attacks clearly act as powerful disincentives to scientists who otherwise might have felt compelled to make bolder, more accurate predictions.

Indeed, it has only recently been revealed that the American Petroleum Institute and the large oil companies *knew* about the catastrophic impacts of carbon emissions since the 1970s. In spite of this knowledge, they funded politicians and PR disinformation campaigns to foster public doubt in order to continue their profiteering at the expense of life on Earth (McCauley 2015; Negin 2016; Knight 2016).

HOW IS CLIMATE DISRUPTION AFFECTING OTHER ANIMALS AND EXACERBATING EXTINCTIONS?

Because climate disruption is interrelated with so many other disturbances of the Earth's environment, it is not easy to show a direct causality of extinctions. Even when there *is* a clear connection, government agencies, acting in the interests of their corporate friends, impede and delay actions to protect other animals and the earth. For instance, only after a protracted 15-year legal battle by the Center for Biological Diversity and partners,

Greenpeace and the Natural Resources Defense Council, were the U.S. Fish and "Wildlife Services" and Department of the Interior forced to list the polar bear as an endangered species based on climate change. The evidence is clear that the bears' diet of ringed seals is threatened by the melting of sea ice (Center for Biological Diversity 2016).

Jamail (2015b) speaks of the impact on human animals, but if the "food chain" collapses, it will collapse for other animals and other forms of life as well. Climate change already appears to be a major factor affecting the ability of living beings to find food. Even the corporate *Washington Post* reported that mass mortality events (MME[2]) of birds, whales, antelopes, and corals are attributed to major changes in their ecosystems related to weather. In particular, huge numbers of murre seabirds in Alaska died of starvation, "having trouble finding their normal food course—herring and other small fish—because of the region's recent unusual weather and the abnormally high temperature of water in the sound" (Kaplan 2016, 2). Similarly, ACD was implicated as a key component in the decline of butterflies in the United Kingdom.

Plants and trees are also facing die-offs that, in turn, affect the other beings depending upon them for food or shelter. Extremely serious is the impact of ACD on phytoplankton (the base of the food chain), in some cases causing large blooms (NRCNA 2015, 12) in other places a reduction by 20 percent or even changing the timing and species of phytoplankton (Jamail 2016a, 4), thereby causing substantial shifts in the "food chain." These are among the changes that human research is observing. However, whether humans are documenting the consequences of all these changes or not, the lives or deaths of other animals and birds are being impacted profoundly.

The Impact of Sea Level Rise on Other Animals

According to the National Research Council of the National Academies (NRCNA 2015), Arctic temperatures are rising twice as fast as the average global temperature rise. These changes occurring in the Arctic are affecting the environments of living beings over the entire planet. The melting of both land and sea ice is causing sea levels to rise and areas of open water to expand and remain open longer. The NRCNA (2015, 11) reports,

> The Arctic is home to living creatures found nowhere else on Earth. Many are highly specialized, having evolved in response to the unique Arctic environment over millions of years. As ice melts and temperatures change, these species face mounting challenges, including the possibility of extinction.
>
> Some of the most recognizable Arctic animals, such as polar bears, seals, and walruses, rely on sea ice as a platform for resting and hunting. Like the

Arctic's human residents, these animals face the loss of habitat and drastically reduced hunting ranges as sea ice recedes.

Nonhuman animals affected by these changes are attempting to make adaptations. For instance, in 2014, 35,000 walruses crowded onto the shore at Point Ley, Alaska, as there was no sea ice for mothers to raise and nurse their young pups (NRCNA 2015, 11).

ACD in the arctic will affect the weather and environment everywhere. Changes in the jet stream will change the weather substantially in the mid-latitudes including the United States and, "a significant change in the strength of the AMOC (Atlantic meridional overturning circulation) would alter winds, temperatures, and precipitation patterns around the globe" (NRCNA 2015, 17). Further, the Arctic oceans are being flooded with fresh water from the melting. Every change will bring life-altering challenges for other animals, challenges that some will not be able to survive. Each extinction will have ripple effects on still other animals.

In their 2013 report, *Deadly Waters: How Rising Seas Threaten 233 Endangered Species*, the Center for Biological Diversity (CBD) documents the impacts on U.S. coastal nonhuman animals, such as submersion or erosion of habitats, saltwater intrusion of water sources and changes in plants, and destruction of marshes. Highlighting five species most threatened, CBD details how the Key deer, the loggerhead sea turtle, the Delmarva Peninsula fox squirrel, the western snowy plover, and the Hawaiian monk seal will be at great risk of extinction.

The Impact of Ocean Acidification on Other Animals

Acidification is changing the ocean environment in ways too numerous to outline here but will particularly harm any nonhuman animal that builds some type of shell. Beyond clams and oysters, this would include a large number of beings including starfish, sea urchins, barnacles, various worms, snails, and corals.

One of the most destructive results of acidification is the bleaching and death of corals, of which there are hundreds of species. Reefs built by corals create ecosystems within oceans. Kolbert (2015, 130) points out, "Thousands—perhaps millions—of species have evolved to rely on coral reefs, either directly for protection or food, or indirectly, to prey on those species that come seeking protection or food. This co-evolutionary venture has been under way for many geologic epochs." Indeed, it is estimated that 25 percent of ocean species rely on corals (WWF Global nd), and yet, highly endangered by acidification and rising ocean temperatures (Fulton 2016), their demise signifies disaster for the other animals they protect.

LAND USE AND HABITAT LOSS

Human animals now dominate the land and seascapes like no other species. There is virtually no place on Earth untouched or unpolluted by humans where other animals can try to live a "normal" life. Every ecosystem has been shaped by human and corporate projects. Imperialism, the intense global exploitation of the Earth and all forms of life for maximizing profits, has brought living beings to the brink of extinction, yet there seems to be no limit to the destruction that humans will inflict for money. It is not possible to address the damage to habitat and "wildlife" from all the various mining, drilling, agriculture, deforestation, dams, and other projects in this short chapter, but I will highlight a few as examples. Some of the human profit-based projects decimating other animals are:

Mining and Drilling

There are so many types of mining, drilling, and now fracking of the Earth's surface, it would take several volumes to detail the damage they have done and are doing to the Earth, to other animals, and all life. The National Mining Association (2016) lists 40 common minerals. This list doesn't even include various types of oil and gas or even sand and gravel. Some of the well-known minerals include aluminum, clays, coal, cobalt, copper, gold, iron, lead, nickel, platinum, silica, silver, titanium, tungsten, and uranium. The mining of each of these substances causes life-threatening damage to the habitat, water, plants, and other animals living in or near the affected environments, not to mention oil spills, gas leaks, and the longevity of radioactive tailings. Some particularly grievous examples are:

Mountaintop Removal: Appalachia is one of the most biodiverse areas of the United States (Reis, 2009). Yet, since 1970, mountaintop removal (MTR) coal mining has "destroyed some 500 mountains, decimated 1 million acres of forest, and buried an estimated 2,000 miles of streams" (National Wildlife Federation 2016). Coal companies, with the complicity of state and federal government agencies even under the Obama administration, have clear-cut or burned the forests, blown up the top one-third of the mountains, and shoved the "overburden" into valleys obliterating streams "causing permanent and irreversible damage to the landscape" (Curry 2015). There is little to no real reclamation; instead, it consists of planting a monoculture of fast-growing non-native species. Along with the decline of profitable coal in the region, a recent lawsuit by the Center for Biological Diversity succeeded in forcing the U.S. Fish and Wildlife Service to propose the protection of two crayfishes under the Endangered Species Act that could begin a new era to stop mountaintop removal (Curry 2015).

Tar Sands Oil: If you go to the Government of Alberta website and click on Oil Sands (incredulously subtitled Alberta's Clean Energy Story and listed online as Alberta's Oil Sands Wildlife and Biodiversity), you will see an egregious and blatant example of PR greenwashing (another word for a propaganda cover up of environmental devastation). Carefully packaged with claims of operating under "some of the most stringent regulations and standards" and "making operations more environmentally sustainable," these assertions could not be further from the truth (Oilsands.alberta.ca 2014). Compare these claims with the well-documented article, "Alberta's Wildlife Death Toll on the Rise" (Gehrke 2014).

In stark contrast, and making a clear connection to the corporate cause of these other animal deaths, Gehrke (2014, 1) begins,

> Killing in the name of big oil, the tar sands operations happening in Canada will result in a catastrophic death toll of wildlife, this year. Ever since their beginning, the tar sands oil drilling, processing, and distributing have been one of the most alarming environmental issues to face the world ... The negative impacts from the tar sands include: The loss of habitat land, pollutants released into the air and water, loss of water from nearby waterways, decrease in wildlife populations, more tailings ponds, higher cancer rates among indigenous people, and oil spills through the distribution of these refined oils.

Woodland caribou, critically endangered, are most impacted by the loss of their habitat in the boreal forest. In just 10 years, they have lost half of their population with predictions of losing 5 to 15 percent more each year (Gehrke 2014, 2). To counter this loss of caribou by deforestation, the Canadian Fish and Wildlife (CFW) began shooting and poisoning gray wolves. This misguided reasoning will further endanger the Canadian lynx because fewer wolves will allow more coyotes to increase their competition for snowshoe hares, the primary food source of the lynx. In addition, 145 black bears were also gunned down by CFW as they were pushed out of their normal forest habitat into human residential areas (Huffington Post Canada 2012). Migrating birds are poisoned by what are euphemistically called tailings "ponds" but are really large lakes of permanent poison. In combination with the destruction of their breeding grounds, 58,000 to 402,000 bird deaths each year will be related to the tar sands (Gehrke 2014, 2). The numbers don't show the carnage or the agony foisted on these nonhuman animals. Further, in 2016, climate disruption drought caused the Ft. McMurray wildfire that decimated tens of thousands of other animals living in the boreal forest (Rieger 2016). So much for Alberta's Clean Energy Story—a fable for the benefit of the oil companies.

Hydraulic Fracking: The activist organization Food and Water Watch (2014) explains fracking as "an extreme method of oil and gas extraction that involves pumping millions of gallons of toxic fluid deep underground to fracture rocks and release oil and natural gas. The process can't be done safely, and research has shown that fracking pollutes the air we breathe, makes our drinking water toxic, worsens climate change and makes people sick."

Vice President Dick Cheney, former Halliburton CEO, was able to protect this relatively new fossil fuel industry from federal regulations, ensuring that it was exempt from the Clean Water Act, the Safe Drinking Water Act, the Superfund Act, and more (SourceWatch 2012). After more than 10 years and more than 1 million fracking wells, the evidence is accruing that fracking is destroying and fragmenting habitat, interfering with migration routes, creating dangerous noise, water, and air pollution, and creating earthquakes in places such as Oklahoma where they rarely happened previously (Ridlington and Rumpler 2013).

Just one average well and its extensive industrial infrastructure can disturb 30 acres of prairie or forest (Straub 2015). Endangered species that have already experienced extensive disturbances and losses to fracking are lesser prairie chickens, dunes sagebrush lizards, greater sage-grouse, the Indiana bat, and the northern long-eared bat (Straub 2015). The deaths of these individuals are forewarnings for other animals not yet diminished to the point of endangerment by the various dangers of fracking.

Touted as a "cleaner" fossil fuel, power plant companies are seeking to replace coal with natural gas. While activist organizations such as Food and Water Watch have experienced some success getting fracking bans in localities and in the entire state of New York, fossil fuel companies are working hard to stop local and state bans.

Other Corporate Projects: Corporate destruction of the Earth's environments and nonhuman animal habitats are so great and so many, it is not possible to even mention all of them, but the sum total of these assaults constitutes nothing short of the aftermath of a global war—a war for profit over life. Drilling for oil or gas in oceans (shallow or deep), clear cutting for lumber, deforestation and fragmentation of rainforests (Kolbert 2015, 148–192) are only a few of the many corporate projects destroying habitats. Hydroelectric dams, touted as "clean energy," inundate some habitats with water while disturbing and diminishing the natural flow of rivers, threatening one-third of the world's freshwater fish (Winemiller et al. 2016).

POLLUTION: TOXIC CHEMICALS AND MILITARY CONTAMINATION

The pollution of the air, water, and lands with toxic products, chemicals, nanoparticles, GMOs (genetically modified organisms), and radiation is another key driver of nonhuman animal deaths and extinctions. In the

United States, the Toxic Substances Control Act (TSCA) regulates only a quarter of the 80,000 chemicals "encountered daily in electronics, furniture, clothing, toys, building materials, cleaning and personal care products, and much more" (Grossman 2015). Throughout the chain of production process and product use through disposal, these chemicals get into the air, soil, freshwater, and oceans. These chemicals not only affect the humans that make and use them but other animals as well when the chemicals are dispersed into the environment. Toxic chemicals are also disseminated through the explosion of weapons of war and the burning of fossil fuels and garbage. World Wildlife (nd) explains how they affect other animals,

> When toxic chemicals and metals enter the environment, organisms may absorb them through their skin or ingest them in their food or water. Animals higher in the food chain accumulate these toxins in higher and higher concentrations, a process called biomagnification. Top predators—including fish, birds, and mammals—can have much higher levels of these toxins in their bodies, making them more likely to experience the diseases, birth defects, genetic mutations, and other deleterious effects of these poisons.

Capitalism has created a culture of consumerism combined with disposable products. Through planned obsolescence and perceived obsolescence (fashion), people buy products that rapidly break or go "out of style" transforming into garbage (Leonard 2011). Newly discovered products like antibacterials, nanoparticles, and microbeads are immediately allowed into products without oversight or scrutiny only to discover later the damage to the environment and the health of human and other animals they cause.

Pesticides may cause acute or chronic effects, secondary poisoning, or indirect effects on "wildlife." While most pesticides today do not bioaccumulate like DDT, they can greatly alter the nervous system of other animals and can affect their ability to survive. Birds, amphibians, and aquatic other animals are most affected. As estimated by the U.S. Fish and Wildlife Service, "67 million birds die from pesticide poisoning each year and more than 600 million are exposed" Fish are also vulnerable with 6 to 14 million killed every year (Defenders of Wildlife nd, 3–4). Herbicides also take a toll with one study concluding that glyphosate (Roundup) was killing tadpoles (Meadows 2008).

Further, GMOs have been inserted without labeling into crops and food products. When labeling was placed on state ballots, the industries spent millions on PR campaigns to convince people it would be too costly. Finally, when public demands became too insistent and Vermont passed a GMO labeling law, the industries turned to lawsuits and federal legislation in their attempts to prevent labeling. GMOs and nicotinoids were finally banned on "wildlife" refuges in 2014 but continue to be prevalent throughout the United States and other countries where allowed (Barnard 2014).

Plastics have contaminated food, water, and now the oceans. Giant garbage patches of plastic—larger than area of some countries—now exist in every ocean where they break up into tiny pieces and are eaten by marine animals and birds. Thousands of birds continue to die because their stomachs are filled with plastic. For illustration, one estimate suggests that by 2050 there will be as much plastic as fish in the oceans (Wearden 2016).

U.S. Military Pollution: By far the greatest polluter on the planet, however, is the U.S. military (Andrzejewski 2014; Sanders 2009). Besides being the largest emitter of carbon dioxide than any other entity, the short- and long-term effects of chemical, biological, radioactive, explosive, and environmental modification weapons are more destructive and contaminating than ever before. As I discovered in researching nonhuman animals and war, "most United States weapons now contain radioactive depleted uranium with a half-life of 4.7 billion years" (Andrzejewski 2014, 78–79). In an investigative report on the environmental impact of militarism, Sanders (2009, 88) identifies the total long-term consequences as:

> . . . *omnicide*—the destruction of all life, human and animal and vegetable . . . Human beings are not the only victims of this unspeakable poisoning through exposure to uranium. Plants and animals also absorb the radioactive particles, making uranium a permanent part of the food chain.

Further, radioactive weapons require nuclear power plants that can manufacture weapons-grade plutonium and tritium. Nuclear power plants are a necessary first step to developing nuclear weapons—this is why the United States and the small group of "nuclear countries" are reluctant to allow other countries to obtain nuclear power plants.

Nuclear power plants, in themselves, are a deadly nonhuman animal-killing technology. As demonstrated by Three-Mile Island, Chernobyl, and most recently Fukushima, there are no technologies that can mitigate the radiation released by the meltdown of a reactor. Fukushima is an example of a worst-case scenario where tons of radioactive water has been and continues to be released into the Pacific Ocean (Jamail 2016c). Contamination has been found in tuna near the U.S. West Coast (LaForge 2015). Still, new and destructive military schemes are being deployed every year—one of the latest is the testing of electronic warfare on the Olympic peninsula, a project that was discovered to be already "illegally" in progress, even though the required Environmental Impact Statement and public comments with final authorization were not completed.

> "According to Karen Sullivan, former assistant regional director at the U.S. Fish and Wildlife Service's Division of External Affairs and a retired endangered species biologist, the Navy's actions are also illegal. 'They have exempted themselves from disclosing to the public, and even to state and federal agencies, the full scope and nature of their actions, in order to segment

them into smaller pieces that individually may look harmless but cumulatively have big impacts'"

(Jamail 2016b)

DO SOMETHING!

Senator Bernie Sanders has called for a political revolution to make governments work for the people and the Earth rather than the corporations and the top 1 percent. Nowhere is this revolution needed more urgently than to stop the assault on the Earth, on the most vulnerable human animals and all the other animals who are suffering greatly from the profit-making schemes of the richest 1 percent and those who aspire to join that exclusive club.

Citizens from every country must mobilize with no delay to take the actions most relevant in their particular circumstances. Environmental, social justice, peace, and nonhuman animal activist organizations have already been collaborating with one another to take legal action against corporations and governments to stop further damage and enforce the laws. Some lobby local, state, and national governments to enact new laws for the protection of people and other animals, birds, marine life, and insects on a broad range of issues. Whatever environmental hazards befall people, other animals suffer as well or greater, sometimes to the extinction of their entire species.

So what strong actions can individuals and communities take as part of a political and environmental revolution to help save other animals and plants of our localities and the world?

15 POWERFUL AND EFFECTIVE ACTIONS YOU CAN TAKE

1. Read independent media for uncensored, more accurate information to be able to critically analyze the biases of corporate media. Don't look away or avoid information that makes you uncomfortable such as the seriousness of the sixth mass extinction, global climate disruption, or the consequences of eating "meat." Investigate and critically analyze constructions of the western mindset, face the truth, then take action. You will feel better when you can act boldly with accurate information.

2. Join activist organizations working on these issues and support them with your money and your actions. The more an organization tries to change the root causes of the problems, the more challenging the work but the more rewarding are the victories. Just a few examples of the

many remarkable organizations that have made a big difference for human and nonhuman animals and the environment:

Center for Biological Diversity: Winning 93 percent of its lawsuits, the Center has successfully gained protection for 757 species under the Endangered Species Act among other impressive victories. Read "Our Story" for inspiration on what a few committed individuals can do. The Center has also provided leadership in alliances between environmental, nonhuman animal, indigenous, and human rights organizations to press government agencies to take forceful actions to defend human and nonhuman animals and the Earth.

Earthjustice: Originally the legal arm of the Sierra Club, Earthjustice now teams up with other organizations and people to successfully defend the Earth, nonhuman animals, and people in court—"because the Earth needs a good lawyer."

350.org: Formed as recently as 2008 by students and author Bill McKibben, this organization has quickly burgeoned into a global force for arresting climate disruption and put themselves on the line for stopping the KXL pipeline.

3. Support the Endangered Species Act: Passed in 1973 almost unanimously with bipartisan support, this Act has been instrumental in saving species and wild places of the Earth. Such protections foil the best laid plans of the wealthy and corporations to exploit every last inch of the Earth regardless of the consequences to plants, human and nonhuman animals, or future generations.

   In the last five years, Republicans have launched 164 attacks according to the report titled: *The Politics of Extinction: The Unprecedented Republican Attack on Endangered Species and the Endangered Species Act*. Many of these attacks have tried to remove certain other animals from ESA protection, nonhuman animals that "are perceived as threatening the economic profits of powerful special interests, such as the oil and gas industry or big agriculture" (Pang and Greenwald, 2015, 3). In spite of 90 percent support of the American public for the Endangered Species Act, the attacks continue to escalate. In addition, these attacks influence regulatory agencies to weaken their support for endangered species (Pang and Greenwald, 2015, 4). Protections for wolves, in particular, have been weakened substantially, leading to the killing of thousands even though they are nowhere near fully recovered. If awareness can be raised and actions taken, public support and actions can make the difference of life or death for these other animals.

4. Stop the vilification and eradication of predators: Given the recent recognition and documentation that top predators are keystone species in maintaining biological diversity, it is particularly important to stop the

state, national, and global wars on predators. Predators such as big cats, wolves, coyotes, bears, killer whales, and sharks continue to suffer particular animosity and targeting towards a goal of complete eradication in most of the world. The loss of these top predators is hastening the extinction of many other animals and plants in their environments. Even the loss of smaller predators such as sea otters, hunted for their pelts, has an extremely deleterious effect on the kelp forests that support many fish and marine animals (Stolzenburg, 2008).

5. Become politically active. Join organizations that will inform you about local, state, and national legislation that will have an impact (good or bad) on animals and the Earth. Get out of your comfort zone and contact your congressperson, senator, state legislator, local county or city officials. Let them know your position and ask them to let you know their decisions. Even politicians influenced by corporate money realize they must respond when the public is watching. Work to elect people who have a record of supporting nonhuman animals and the Earth against corporate greed. Use the League of Conservation Voters (2015) and Humane Society of the United States (2015) legislative scorecards on the environment and other animals to examine the voting records of Congress and, where available, state legislators.

6. Support indigenous tribes, organizations, and activism. Indigenous peoples from hundreds of nations around the world are putting their lives on the line for nonhuman animals, plants, people, and the Earth. Global Witness (2016) documents the danger they are in as they go up against the world's most powerful corporations (Buncombe 2016). Only a tiny number of movements and people, such as Wangari Maathai and the Greenbelt Movement, have received global recognition by the Goldman Environmental Prize, the Right Livelihood Awards, or rarely the Nobel Peace Prize, but independent media outlets provide information about these incredible movements that will never be covered by the corporate news. Support the efforts of these courageous peoples.

7. Support organizations working for campaign finance reform and to reverse the Citizens United Supreme Court decision that allows wealthy donors and corporations to contribute money without being identified. The five congressmen who have initiated the greatest number of attacks against the Endangered Species Act have received millions of dollars from the oil and gas industry and big agriculture (Pang and Greenwald 2015). Such campaign contributions are nothing but legalized bribery. We, the public, must insist that our elected officials are working for the betterment of other animals, people, and the Earth, not for private profits.

8. Work forcefully to avert disastrous climate disruption. Immediate and drastic shifts in energy use and methods must be made to stop greenhouse gas emissions if we are to save life on Earth. A shift to 100 percent renewable energy is possible (Bergeron 2009; Heinberg 2016). Work for peace and sharing resources with other animals and people around the world. Personally and politically, change your lifestyle and work with organizations on campaigns such as Keep It In The Ground—legislation to stop the extraction and use of fossil fuels.

9. Work to shift military policies and activities toward saving the Earth rather than destroying and contaminating it. Even the Pentagon and CIA recognize that climate disruption, water scarcity, sea level rise, food insecurity, land grabs, and other inequities can quickly lead to conflict and wars, with climate change an immediate and urgent threat to national security (Davenport 2014; CNS News Staff 2015).

10. Support the *enforcement* of nonhuman animal protection laws. Having the Endangered Species Act, the Lacey Act, the Global Anti-Poaching Act, and Obama's Executive Order 13684 to combat "wildlife" trafficking (Loki 2016) on the books is one thing, but there must be funding and agency will for enforcement. Join with organizations to work for enforcement of these laws.

11. Pressure corporations to support nonhuman animal saving policies. After Cecil the Lion was shot illegally in Kenya by the trophy hunting Minnesota dentist, a member of SFI, there was such a public outcry that several airlines decided to ban any cargo containing other animal remains from trophy hunts. Public pressure was brought to bear on airlines that did not voluntarily join the ban.

12. Change your diet and your consumption habits: Become a vegan. Boycott all nonhuman animal products, including products that destroy the habitats of other animals. The United Nations and many food and environmental organizations recognize the connection between nonhuman animal agriculture and climate disruption, habitat destruction, and food production. They strongly recommend that humans move quickly toward a plant-based diet if we want to survive on a planet challenged by shrinking resources and global climate disruption (Carus 2010). As for ivory, skins, "furs," body parts, "meat," "dairy," and other nonhuman animal products, it is clear that if there is no demand, the products will not be made, and other animals are less likely to be killed.

13. Shop knowledgeably. Don't buy or use poisons. Avoid purchasing plastic packaging, bags, and other disposable products. Protect the species

in your yard and community. Avoid lawn and garden toxins and plants that contain neonicotinoids and other pesticides. Ask businesses not to supply products containing toxins. Use organic methods of plant protection. Create nonhuman animal, bird, bee, amphibian, and butterfly-friendly yards.

Support local co-ops, farmers' markets, and independent and small businesses that evaluate the impact of the products they produce and sell. Reduce demand by reusing, using up, wearing out, or going without products that destroy other animals or their habitats.

14. Oppose the killing, trapping, or poisoning of any nonhuman animals whether deer, wolves, coyotes, fox, raccoons, frogs, toads, butterflies, or spiders. Make room to share the world with other species. Take unwanted bees, spiders, and mice out of your house to let them live.

15. Support the increase and the protection of public lands, waters, and oceans: local, state, national, and oceanic. For example, work to stop efforts to drill, frack, strip mine, or remove mountains for fossil fuels, to practice damaging war games or dump toxic waste. Protect neighborhood greenbelts.

CONCLUSION

The assaults and extinctions that other animals are suffering from the cumulative impacts of human capitalist industrial projects are pervasive. Many of these projects have similar impacts on human animals. In most cases, these projects and their consequences are censored, denied, or covered up by PR campaigns through the corporate-owned media. Corporations and wealthy individuals continue their projects through the corruption of politicians who accept their campaign donations or through the revolving door where corporate employees are appointed to government regulatory agencies which then favor corporate policies instead of the public good.

When the global public gains access to accurate information, we can mobilize to have far-reaching impacts. The scientific reports about the sixth mass extinction seem bleak since the consequences of capitalist projects on natural law are becoming impossible to deny. However, when people become active, enormous changes can be made much more quickly than expected. Our challenge is to not look away but rather to seek accurate information and become active in an urgent political and environmental revolution.

Extinction is personal. Every frog, bird, butterfly, wolf, orca, lion, and human is affected by one or more of these injurious human capitalist projects. Even species with large populations can collapse. No animal or species, including humans, is safe, but there are opportunities for major changes. It is up to us to take action individually and collectively.

NOTES

1. Small parts of this chapter have been adapted and updated from Andrzejewski, Julie and John C. Alessio. 2013. "The Sixth Mass Extinction." In Mickey Huff and Andy L. Roth (eds.), *Censored 2014: Fearless Speech in Fateful Times: The Top Censored Stories and Media Analysis of 2012–13,* 365–386. New York: Seven Stories Press.

2. A mass mortality event (MME) is defined as: "removing more than 90 percent of a population, resulting in the death of more than a billion individuals, or producing 700 million tons of dead biomass in a single event" (Fey et al. 2015).

REFERENCES

Alessio, John C. 2011. *Social Problems and Inequality: Social Responsibility through Progressive Sociology.* Farnham, Surrey, England: Ashgate.

Andrzejewski, Julie. 2014. "War: Animals in the Aftermath." In Anthony Nocella, Judy Castles-Bentley, and Colin Salter (eds.), *Animals in War: Confronting the Military Animal Industrial Complex,* 73–100. New York: Lexington Press.

Andrzejewski, Julie, and John C. Alessio. 2013. "The Sixth Mass Extinction." In Mickey Huff and Andy L. Roth (eds.), *Censored 2014: Fearless Speech in Fateful Times: The Top Censored Stories and Media Analysis of 2012–13,* 365–386. New York: Seven Stories Press.

Andrzejewski, Julie, Marta Baltodano, and Linda Symcox. 2009. *Social Justice, Peace, and Environmental Education: Transformative Standards.* New York: Routledge.

Balter, Michael. 2014. "What Killed the Great Beasts of North America?" *Science,* January 28. Accessed April 24, 2016, from http://www.sciencemag.org/news /2014/01/what-killed-great-beasts-north-america.

Barnard, Jeff. 2014. "Wildlife Refuges Phasing Out GMO Crops, Pesticides." *The Seattle Times,* August 6. Accessed March 31, 2016, from http://www .biologicaldiversity.org/news/center/articles/2014/seattle-times-08–06 -2014.html.

Berger, Peter L., and Thomas Luckmann. 1966. *The Social Construction of Reality.* Garden City, NY: Doubleday.

Bergeron, Louis. 2009. "Study: Shifting the World to 100% Clean, Renewable Energy by 2030: Here are the Numbers." *Stanford News,* October 20. Accessed July 12, 2016, from http://news.stanford.edu/news/2009/october19/jacobson -energy-study-102009.html.

Buncombe, Andrew. 2016. "Environmental activists: 2015 was deadliest year for people fighting to protect the planet" *Independent,* June 19. Accessed July 4, 2016, from http://www.independent.co.uk/news/world/americas

/environmental-activists-2015-was-deadliest-year-for-people-fighting-to
-protect-the-planet-a7090891.html.

Bushmeat Crisis Task Force. Nd. "What is the Bushmeat Crisis?" Accessed
March 18, 2016, from http://www.bushmeat.org/bushmeat_and_wildlife
_trade/what_is_the_bushmeat_crisis.

Carus, Felicity. 2010. "UN Urges Global Move to Meat and Dairy-Free Diet." *The
Guardian,* June 2. Accessed July 12, 2016, from https://www.theguardian
.com/environment/2010/jun/02/un-report-meat-free-diet.

Center for Biological Diversity. 2013. *Deadly Waters: How Rising Seas Threaten 233
Endangered Species.* Accessed March 20, 2016, from https://www
.biologicaldiversity.org/campaigns/sea-level_rise/pdfs/SeaLevelRise
Report_2013_print.pdf.

Center for Biological Diversity. 2013. "The Extinction Crisis." Accessed February 20, 2016, from http://www.biologicaldiversity.org/programs/biodiversity
/elements_of_biodiversity/extinction_crisis/.

Center for Biological Diversity. Nd. "Our Story." Accessed July 11, 2016, from http://
www.biologicaldiversity.org/about/story/.

Center for Biological Diversity. 2016. "Saving the Polar Bear." Accessed March 20,
1016, from http://www.biologicaldiversity.org/species/mammals/polar_bear/.

Clarkson, Linda, Vern Morrissette, and Gabriel Régallet. 1992. *Our Responsibility
to the Seventh Generation. Indigenous Peoples and Sustainable Development,*12–14, 19–25. Accessed February 1, 2016, from https://www.iisd.org
/pdf/seventh_gen.pdf.

CNSNews.com Staff. 2015. "CIA Director Cites 'Impact of Climate Change' as
Deeper Cause of Global Instability." *CNSNews.com,* November 16. Accessed
July 12, 2016, from http://www.cnsnews.com/news/article/cnsnewscom
-staff/cia-director-cites-impact-climate-change-deeper-cause-global.

Cowspiracy The Facts. 2015. *Cowspiracy.* Accessed on May 1, 2016, from http://
www.cowspiracy.com/facts/.

Curry, Tierra. 2015. "Two Crayfishes Threatened by Mountaintop-removal Mining in West Virginia, Kentucky, Virginia Proposed for Endangered Species
Act Protection." Center for Biological Diversity press release, April 6.
Accessed April 25, 2016, from https://www.biologicaldiversity.org/news
/press_releases/2015/crayfish-04-06-2015.html.

Davenport, Coral. 2014. "Pentagon Signals Security Risks of Climate Change." *The
New York Times,* October 13. Accessed July 12, 2016, from http://www
.nytimes.com/2014/10/14/us/pentagon-says-global-warming-presents
-immediate-security-threat.html?_r=0.

Defenders of Wildlife. Nd. "The Dangers of Pesticides to Wildlife: A White Paper
by Defenders of Wildlife." Accessed March 31, 2016, from https://www
.beyondpesticides.org/assets/media/documents/pesticidefreelawns/resources
/DWDangers_Pesticides_Wildlife.pdf.

Fey, Samuel B., et al. 2015. "Recent Shifts in the Occurrence, Cause, and Magnitude of Animal Mass Mortality Events." *Proceedings of the National Academy of Sciences,* January 27. 112:4, 1083–1088.

First Peoples Worldwide. Nd. "Who are Indigenous Peoples." Accessed March 21,
2016, from http://www.firstpeoples.org/who-are-indigenous-peoples.

Food and Water Watch. 2014. "Ban Fracking Everywhere." Accessed on April 25, 2016, from http://www.foodandwateractionfund.org/campaign/ban-fracking-everywhere.

Fulton, Deirdre. 2016. "'Red Alert': Great Barrier Reef Severe Bleaching Raised to Highest Threat Level." *Common Dreams.* Accessed March 21, 2016, from http://www.commondreams.org/news/2016/03/21/red-alert-great-barrier-reef-severe-bleaching-raised-highest-threat-level.

Gehrke, Aaron. 2014. "Alberta's Wildlife Death Toll on the Rise." *Iowa Tar Sands Project Blog,* December 19. Accessed March 28, 2016, from https://iowatarsandsproject.wordpress.com/2014/12/19/albertas-wildlife-death-toll-on-the-rise/.

Global Witness. 2016. *On Dangerous Ground,* June 20. Accessed on July 4, 2016, from https://www.globalwitness.org/en/reports/dangerous-ground/.

Grossman, Elizabeth. 2015. "Untested Chemicals are Everywhere, Thanks to a 39-Year-Old U.S. Law. Will the Senate Finally Act? *The Guardian,* February 13. Accessed March 31, 2016, from http://www.theguardian.com/lifeandstyle/2015/feb/13/us-senate-toxic-chemicals-law-health-safety.

Guynup, Sharon. 2016. "Appetite for Destruction: U.S. Consumer Demand Fuels Illegal Wildlife Trade, Jeopardizing Imperiled Species Around the Globe. *Defenders of Wildlife,* (Winter), Vol. 19:2.

Harding, Sandra. 1993. *The "Racial" Economy of Science.* Bloomington, IN: Indiana University Press.

Heinberg, Richard. 2016. "100% Renewable: What We Can Do in 10 Years." *Yes Magazine,* February 22. Accessed July 12, 2016, from http://www.yesmagazine.org/issues/life-after-oil/100-renewable-energy-what-we-can-do-in-10-years-20160222.

Huffington Post Canada. 2012. "145 Black Bears Killed in Alberta Tar Sands." February 22. Accessed July 12, 2016, from http://www.huffingtonpost.ca/2012/02/22/black-bears-wildlife-alberta-oil-sands-tar_n_1293109.html.

Humane Society Legislative Fund. 2015. "Humane Scorecard." Accessed September 28, 2016, from http://www.hslf.org/our-work/humane-scorecard.html.

IDA Africa. 2013. "Bushmeat." *In Defense of Animals Africa.* Accessed March 18, 2016, from http://www.ida-africa.org/bushmeat_7.html.

Indenbaum, Rosa. 2016. "Defender to the Core: A Q & A with a Defenders Expert." *Defenders of Wildlife.* Vol. 19:2.

Interagency Support Group on Indigenous Peoples' Issues. 2014. *The Knowledge of Indigenous Peoples and Policies for Sustainable Development: Updates and Trends in the Second Decade of the World's Indigenous People,* June. Accessed March 21, 2016, from http://www.un.org/en/ga/president/68/pdf/wcip/IASG%20Thematic%20Paper_%20Traditional%20Knowledge%20-%20rev1.pdf.

IUCN 2015. "Overview of the IUCN Red List." *The IUCN Red List of Threatened Species. Version 2015-4.* Accessed March 21, 2016, from http://www.iucnredlist.org.

Jamail, Dahr. 2015. Experts Warn of Cataclysmic Changes as Planetary Temperatures Rise. *Truthout,* April 27. Accessed May 1, 2016, from http://www.truth

-out.org/news/item/30449-experts-warn-of-cataclysmic-changes-as
-planetary-temperatures-rise.

Jamail, Dahr. 2015a. "Mass Extinction: It's the End of the World as We Know It."
Truthout, July 6. Accessed February 20, 2016, from http://www.truth-out
.org/news/item/31661-mass-extinction-it-s-the-end-of-the-world-as-we
-know-it.

Jamail, Dahr. 2015b. "Climate Disruption Dispatches with Dahr Jamail." *Truthout*,
nd. Accessed May 1, 2015. http://www.truth-out.org/news/item/22521
-climate-disruption-dispatches-with-dahr-jamail.

Jamail, Dahr. 2016a. "Freak Storms and Butterfly Die-Offs: This is Your Climate
on Fossil Fuels." *Truthout*, February 1. Accessed February 28, 2016, from
http://www.truth-out.org/news/item/34631-freak-storms-and-massive
-animal-die-offs-this-is-your-climate-on-fossil-fuels.

Jamail, Dahr. 2016b. "Exclusive: Navy Uses U.S. Citizens as Pawns in Domestic War
Games." *Truthout*, January 11. Accessed on April 25, 2016, from http://www
.truth-out.org/news/item/34367-exclusive-navy-uses-us-citizens-as-pawns
-in-domestic-war-games.

Jamail, Dahr. 2016c. "Radioactive Water is Leaking into the Pacific." *Truthout*,
January 27. Accessed July 12, 2016, from http://www.truth-out.org/news
/item/34565-radioactive-water-from-fukushima-is-leaking-into-the
-pacific.

Kaplan, Sarah. 2016. "In Pitiful Animal Die-Offs Across the Globe—from Antelopes to Bees to Seabirds—Climate Change May Be Culprit. *The Washington Post*, January 13. Accessed March 19, 2016, from https://www
.washingtonpost.com/news/morning-mix/wp/2016/01/13/how-climate
-change-could-be-contributing-to-animal-die-offs/.

Klein, Naomi. 2014. *This Changes Everything*. New York: Simon & Schuster.

Knight, Nika. 2016. "New Report Details Big Oil's $500 Million Annual Climate
Obstructionism." April 7. Accessed September 28, 2016, from http://www
.commondreams.org/news/2016/04/07/new-report-details-big-oils-500
-million-annual-climate-obstructionism.

Knight, Nika. 2016a. "Dakota Access Construction Will Continue, Pipeline Corp
CEO Vows." September 13. Accessed September 14, 2016, from http://www
.commondreams.org/news/2016/09/13/dakota-access-construction-will
-continue-pipeline-corp-ceo-vows.

Kolbert, Elizabeth. 2014. *The Sixth Extinction: An Unnatural History*. New York:
Picador.

LaDuke, Winona. 1996. *Native American Land Struggles, Environmentalism, and
Indigenous Women*. February 14. Recorded presentation, St. Cloud State
University, MN.

LaForge, John. 2015. "Fukushima Radiation in Pacific Reaches West Coast." *Coun-
terpunch*, October 14. Accessed July 12, 2016, from http://www.counter
punch.org/2015/10/14/fukushima-radiation-in-pacific-reaches-west-coast/.

Lawler, David. 2015. "Emaciated Polar Bear Pictures Raise Global Warming Concerns." *The Telegraph*, September 15. Accessed March 19, 2016, from http://
www.telegraph.co.uk/news/earth/environment/globalwarming/11865256
/Emaciated-polar-bear-pictures-raise-global-warming-concerns.html.

League of Conservation Voters. 2015. *League of Conservation Voters National Environmental Scorecard.* Accessed on August 25, 2016, from http://scorecard .lcv.org/scorecard.

Leonard, Annie. 2011. *The Story of Stuff: The Impact of Overconsumption on the Planet, Our Communities, and Our Health and How We Can Make It Better.* New York: Free Press.

Linden, Eugene. 1991. "Lost Tribes, Lost Knowledge." *Time,* September 23. 46–54.

Loki, Reynard. 2016. "The Bigger Story Behind the Killing of Cecil the Lion that the Media Overlooked." *AlterNet,* January 14. Accessed February 14, 2016, from http://www.alternet.org/environment/bigger-story-behind-killing -cecil-the-lion-media-overlooked.

Mapes, Lynda V. 2016. "Tribes Prevail, Kill Proposed Coal Terminal at Cherry Point." *The Seattle Times,* May 9. Accessed on May 9, 2016, from http://www .seattletimes.com/seattle-news/environment/tribes-prevail-kill-proposed -coal-terminal-at-cherry-point/.

McCauley, Lauren. 2015. "More than Exxon: Big Oil Companies for Years Shared Damning Climate Research." *Common Dreams,* December 22. Accessed February 24, 2016, from http://www.commondreams.org/news/2015/12/22 /more-exxon-big-oil-companies-years-shared-damning-climate-research.

McCauley, Lauren. 2016. "Act Now, Urges Study, or Planet Faces 10,000+ Years of Climate Doom." *Common Dreams,* February 8. Accessed February 9, 2016, from http://www.commondreams.org/news/2016/02/08/act-now-urges -study-or-planet-faces-10000-years-climate-doom.

Meadows, Robin. 2008. "Common Herbicide Lethal to Wetland Species." *Conservation Magazine,* July 9. University of Washington. Accessed March 31, 2016, from http://conservationmagazine.org/2008/07/common-herbicide -lethal-to-wetland-species/.

Milman, Oliver. 2016. "Jane Goodall's Bid to Save Grizzly Bears as Montana Plans for $150 Hunting Licenses." *The Guardian,* May 6. Accessed August 25, 2016, from https://www.theguardian.com/environment/2016/may/05/jane -goodall-grizzly-bears-yellowstone-endangered-species.

National Research Council of the National Academies (NRCNA). 2015. *Arctic Matters: the Global Connection to Changes in the Arctic.* Washington, DC: National Academy of Sciences.

National Wildlife Federation (NWF). Nd. "Getting Off Coal." Accessed March 28, 2016, from https://www.nwf.org/What-We-Do/Energy-and-Climate /Drilling-and-Mining/Getting-Off-Coal.aspx.

National Mining Association. 2016. Accessed July 12, 2016, from http://www.nma .org/index.php/minerals-publications/40-common-minerals-and-their -uses.

Negin, Elliott. 2016. "ExxonMobil Feels the Heat." *Catalyst,* (Winter). 15: 16–17.

Oilsands.alberta.ca. January 2014. "Alberta's Clean Energy Story." Accessed March 28, 2016, from http://oilsands.alberta.ca/images/CEnergy_Brochure _Jan_2014_Online.pdf.

Pang, Jamie, and Noah Greenwald. 2015. *The Politics of Extinction: The Unprecedented Republican Attack on Endangered Species and the Endangered Species Act,* July. Tucson, AZ: Center for Biological Diversity. Accessed

March 29, 2016, from http://www.biologicaldiversity.org/campaigns/esa_attacks/pdfs/Politics_of_Extinction.pdf.

Predator Defense. 2014. *Exposed: The USDA's secret war on wildlife.* Accessed February 23, 2016, from http://www.predatordefense.org/exposed/index.htm.

Reis, Patrick. 2009. "Are Endangered Species Being Sacrificed for Coal in Appalachia?" *Scientific American,* August 10. Accessed March 28, 2016, from http://www.scientificamerican.com/article/endangered-species-coal-appalachia-mountaintop-removal/.

Ridlington, Elizabeth, and John Rumpler. 2013. *Fracking by the Numbers: Key Impacts of Dirty Drilling at the State and National Level,* October. Environment America Research and Policy Center. Accessed April 25, 2016, from http://www.environmentamerica.org/sites/environment/files/reports/EA_FrackingNumbers_scrn.pdf.

Rieger, Sarah. 2016. "Ft. McMurray Fire May Have Caused 'Massive Destruction' of Wildlife." *Huffington Post Alberta,* May 15. Accessed on July 12, 2016, from http://www.huffingtonpost.ca/2016/05/13/fort-mcmurray-wildlife_n_9957784.html.

Safari Club International (SFI). 2016. Accessed February 23, 2016, from https://www.safariclub.org/what-we-do/record-book/world-hunting-awards.

Safina, Carl. 2015. *Beyond Words: What Animals Think and Feel.* New York: Henry Holt & Co.

Sample, Ian. 2016. "Oldest Known Case of Neanderthal-Human Sex Revealed by DNA Test." *The Guardian,* February 17. Accessed February 18, 2016, from https://www.theguardian.com/science/2016/feb/17/oldest-known-case-of-neanderthal-human-sex-revealed-by-dna-test?CMP=fb_gu.

Sanders, Barry. 2009. *The Green Zone: The Environmental Impact of Militarism.* Oakland: AK Press.

Shiva, Vandana. 1997. *Biopiracy: The Plunder of Nature and Knowledge.* Brooklyn: South End Press.

Shiva, Vandana. 1993. "Colonialism and the Evolution of Masculinist Forestry." In Sandra Harding (ed.), *The "Racial" Economy of Science.* Bloomington, IN: Indiana University Press.

Smith, Linda Tuhiwai. 1999. *Decolonizing Methodologies: Research and Indigenous Peoples.* London: Zed Books LTD.

SourceWatch. 2012. "Fracking." *The Center for Media and Democracy.* Accessed July 12, 2016, from http://www.sourcewatch.org/index.php/Fracking.

Species Alliance. 2010. *Call of Life: Facing the Mass Extinction.* Accessed February 20, 2016, from http://calloflife.org/p-story.htm.

Stolzenburg, William. 2008. *Where the Wild Things Were: Life, Death, and Ecological Wreckage in a Land of Vanishing Predators.* New York: Bloomsbury.

Straub, Lana. 2015. "After the Frack: Habitat Fragmentation." *Earth Island Journal,* July 2. Accessed March 29, 2016, from http://www.earthisland.org/journal/index.php/elist/eListRead/after_the_frack_habitat_fragmentation/.

Torres, Phil. 2016. "Biodiversity Loss and the Doomsday Clock: An Invisible Disaster Almost No One Is Talking About." *Common Dreams,* February 10. Accessed February 10, 2016, from http://www.commondreams

.org/views/2016/02/10/biodiversity-loss-and-doomsday-clock-invisible -disaster-almost-no-one-talking-about.

Tucker, Jessica. 2014. "5 Innocent Animals Suffering at the Hands of the Palm Oil Industry." *One Green Planet,* April 25. Accessed January 31, 2016, from http://www.onegreenplanet.org/animalsandnature/innocent-animals -suffering-at-the-hands-of-the-palm-oil-industry/.

United Nations Environment Programme (UNEP). 2010. *Global Biodiversity Outlook 3: Biodiversity in 2010.* Accessed from https://www.cbd.int/doc /publications/gbo/gbo3-final-en.pdf.

Vander Velde, Bruno. 2014. "10 Things You Didn't Know About Bushmeat in Africa." *Center for International Forestry Research (CIFOR),* September 3. Accessed March 18, 2016, from http://blog.cifor.org/23954/10-things-you -didnt-know-about-bushmeat-in-africa?fnl=en.

Vinik, Danny. 2016. "Why the GOP is Trying to Stop the Pentagon's Climate Plan." *Politico,* June 23. Accessed July 12, 2016, from http://www.politico.com /agenda/story/2016/06/republicans-trying-to-stop-pentagon-climate-plan -000149.

Wearden, Graeme. 2016. "More plastic than fish in the sea says Ellen MacArthur." *The Guardian,* January 19. Accessed July 12, 2016, from https://www .theguardian.com/business/2016/jan/19/more-plastic-than-fish-in-the-sea -by-2050-warns-ellen-macarthur.

Wendle, John. 2015. "Chernobyl and Other Places Where Animals Thrive Without People." *National Geographic,* October 9. Accessed July 12, 2016, from http://news.nationalgeographic.com/2015/10/151008-chernobyl-animals -thrive-without-people-science/.

Winemiller, K. O., et al. 2016. "Balancing Hydropower and Biodiversity in the Amazon, Congo, and Mekong." *Science,* January 8. 351:6269.

WWF Global. Nd. "Coral Reefs." Accessed July 12, 2016, from http://wwf.panda .org/about_our_earth/blue_planet/coasts/coral_reefs/.

World Wildlife Fund. Nd. "Threats and Pollution." Accessed March 31, 2016, from http://www.worldwildlife.org/threats/pollution.

World Wildlife Fund. 2014. *Living Planet Report.* Accessed March 20, 2016, from http://www.wwf.eu/media_centre/publications/living_planet_report/.

Triumph of Capitalism. (Copyright © 2004 Sue Coe. Courtesy Galerie St. Etienne, NY)

9

Toward a Vegan Feminist Theory of the State

Corey Wrenn

Consumption is the lynchpin of capitalist relations. For this reason, women and other animals, who are systematically packaged as consumable objects to be bought and sold in marketplaces, are particularly vulnerable. Consumption is a practice that necessitates inequality: some will consume, and some will *be* consumed. It is a demonstration of control over others.

In her seminal work, *The Sexual Politics of Meat*, Carol J. Adams (1990, 26) writes of anthroparchy[1] and material relations: "People with power have always eaten meat." In a capitalist system, power is concentrated through the exploitation of vulnerable groups, and this vulnerability is exemplified in "meat."[2] "Meat" in this context refers not only to the butchered flesh of Non-human Animals but also the fragmented flesh of human women. In both cases, it holds true that, "consumption is the fulfillment of oppression" and "the annihilation of will" (Adams 1990, 47). Power rests on the consumption of feminized bodies, human and nonhuman alike.

Power is thus defined by access to and control over the feminine, but as this chapter will demonstrate, it is *made possible* by this feminine exploitation as well. Vegan feminism expands traditional analyses of power and identifies an intersection between systemic violence against women and other animals (Adams and Gruen 2014; Kemmerer 2011). It necessitates a conscious acknowledgement of both sexism and speciesism in any class analysis or theory of the state. Patriarchy, anthroparchy, and capitalism are systems that perpetuate the oppression of many for the benefit of few. Within the confines of these interlocking oppressions, consumption is fetishized, and feminized bodies are systemically made vulnerable to interpersonal and institutional violence. Society, in other words, is structured to disadvantage and hurt women and other animals in the process of extracting value and privilege from them. Females are made into "meat" (the commodified and butchered bodies of the feminized), and the making and selling of "meat" is a primary function of capitalism.

This chapter will examine how the female body gets caught in this grind, specifically building on Marxist critique to incorporate a vegan-centric ecofeminist analysis. Traditional approaches most often take a gender-neutral or species-neutral approach, which inappropriately conflates the privileged human male experience as the universal experience. As will be demonstrated, an intersectional lens unveils a system of oppression that is anything but even or universal in its effect. Only through an examination of the suffering of those who are generally made invisible in the narrative can the true mechanics of the system be revealed.

MISOGYNISTIC SCRIPTS

It is useful to clarify that sex and gender are distinct categories, and gender, not sex, is typically the primary focus of feminist critique. Gender refers to the socially constructed expectations ascribed to individuals based on their biological sex. In Western culture, masculinity is a performance of domination, while femininity is a performance of subordination. Thus, any force or entity of domination, control, and violent power can be said to be masculinized, whereas any display or entity of subordination, powerlessness, or vulnerability can be said to be feminized. Importantly, anything and anybody that exhibits feminine gender role characteristics can be considered feminized. Women are feminized, nature is feminized, Nonhuman Animals are feminized, and even proletariats in the Marxian sense are feminized. Femininity is defined by its powerlessness in relationship to masculinity, which in turn is defined by its domination of the feminine. The entire capitalist system in this sense is a patriarchal one, as Nonhuman Animals, women, and exploited workers are all feminized through subordination.

In the anthroparchal-patriarchal capitalist system,[3] Adams (1996) suggests that feminized bodies are both literally and figuratively butchered to facilitate their oppression in a culture of consumption. Among human women, dozens of misogynistic words are regularly employed in the English language (Lakoff 2004), and women are heavily sexually objectified across all mass media (Collins 2011). Both linguistically and figuratively, women are fragmented as legs, breasts, and bottoms; they become a collection of parts and orifices. In such a system, women's bodies are for sale, and the language lands the sale. This may be relevant from an ecosocialist perspective, which acknowledges a societal hyperfocus on production and capital accumulation that is detrimental to the natural world (Löwy 2015), as well as an ecofeminist perspective (which more specifically focuses on gendered exploitation in the natural world) (Adams and Gruen 2014). Like women, Nonhuman Animals are objectified, butchered, otherized, and offered for consumption. Making "meat" is a profitable endeavor.

By way of an example, I pass a small New Jersey restaurant known as Cluck-U Chicken on the way home from work each evening. Located on a major intersection in town, Cluck-U specializes in "fried chicken" and "chicken wing" products. Its mascot is both highly masculinized and humanized with an exaggerated chest and bulging biceps. Advertising materials include cartoons depicting him as "Chicken Man" or "Super Chicken" in the style of popular comic superheroes. Although the chickens bought, sold, and eaten here are predominantly female-bodied, this mascot speaks instead to a perceived male consumer. The relationship here is highly gendered. Males consume, while non-males are consumed; males fuck, while non-males are fucked. Although the eatery's mascot is a chicken in a college basketball uniform (insinuating that "Cluck-U" could be short for "Cluck University"), the double entendre is clear. "Cluck-U" reads similarly to "fuck you," a common expression of aggressive derogation and sexualized depredation among English speakers. This meaning is in all likelihood intentional, as Cluck-U's branding is meant to be interpreted in the context of consuming the feminized body parts of dead chickens. This is a man's marketplace.

In addition to the connotations conjured by Cluck-U's name and mascot, its slogan, "It's an addiction," further exemplifies the masculinization of capitalism. Consumption is framed as sexualized, insatiable, and *uncontrollable*. Men just cannot help but to use women and eat other animals. To be sure, capitalists willfully nurture this addiction. Cluck-U is only one example of many. Addiction ensures continued consumption (it also keeps the citizenry in a state of powerlessness and dependency) (Schaef 1987).[4] Arousal addiction is also thought to disempower and depoliticize, especially so for targeted male consumers (Zimbardo and Coulombe 2012). Addiction terminology surfaces in the context of other gendered relationships of consumption, specifically in men's narratives of rape or pornography use. Framing male violence as "uncontrollable" ideologically masks the fact that it is actually agential and deliberate (Adams 1996).

Misogyny, in other words, becomes a script of oppression in a capitalist system. Gender is difference, and difference is conjured to stimulate market growth. For instance, advertisers carefully craft particular foods as feminine or masculine in hopes of increasing sales (Parkin 2004). This advertising is so thoroughly effective that a physiological reaction can be cued in consumers based on their gender identification (research demonstrates that men's esophagi will dilate at the mention of "steak" and women's to the mention of salad). This capitalist-driven psychology ensures that Nonhuman Animal products remain firmly in the privileged realm of masculinity, securing their profitability in the androcentric (male-oriented) marketplace. Consumers learn a sexist script that translates across anthroparchal, patriarchal, and capitalist systems. Men are positioned as privileged consumers and free agents with interests to speak of in the marketplace, while women and other animals are simply traded goods in that marketplace. They are objects of resource and highly vulnerable in an economy that relies on their relative powerlessness.

CAPITALISM AS AN AFFRONT TO NATURE

Patriarchy and capitalism are inherently linked as they are both hierarchical systems of domination that rely on force and control in their maintenance and growth. In the simplest sense, capitalism relies on class oppression, whereas patriarchy relies on gender oppression. Oppression in both systems is the logic of production. What it means to occupy a particular class or gender will more or less depend on the inclinations of elites occupying the top levels of the social hierarchy. Feminist theory, however, specifically identifies gender as the basic qualifier in the formation and maintenance of social stratification (Marxist analysis instead envisions a relatively genderless class framework). That is, feminism suggests that all systems of oppression (speciesism and capitalism included) are fundamentally products of a more ancient form of sexism. With imperfect research implements and cloudy or adulterated historical record, it is difficult to determine which oppression takes precedence in the larger history of humanity's evolution, be it sexism, speciesism, classism, or something else entirely. Perhaps they are best understood as interlocking systems. The script of misogyny does, however, appear to guide speciesism and other forms of capitalist oppression in several ways. In *Toward a Feminist Theory of the State*, Catharine A. MacKinnon (1989, xi) observes that state power, under closer inspection, ultimately emerges as *male* power. Most importantly, she also identifies gender distinction as a fundamental inequality that is intentionally exploited by the state. As she explains it, "Sexuality is to feminism what work is to Marxism: that which is most one's own, yet most taken away" (1989, 3).

This mechanism was mostly lost on Marx, whose theory views women as defined by nature, not by society as are men (MacKinnon 1989, 13). It is this sexist underpinning (that some social inhabitants are defined by nature and are thus more subordinated than others in society) that immediately conjoins the experiences of women and other animals. This connection necessitates that a feminist critique of capitalism also acknowledges the plight of other beings excluded from the social structure narrative, those who are objectified nonpersons in the "natural world."[5] Just as Marx views women's role-taking as bound to the natural (whereas men's roles in the class system are considered more of an accident that became institutionalized), a human-centric society understands the roles of other animals as "natural." Nonhuman Animal roles are thought a result of social Darwinism or nutritional necessity. Sociobiological explanations of this kind (the same that work against women, disabled persons, persons of color, and poor persons) form an ideology that naturalizes and normalizes socially constructed relationships. As Marx himself has emphasized, ideologies support a false consciousness; they distract and mislead economic participants from the true and actual mechanisms of oppression. The traditional Marxist understanding of work as a male behavior exacerbates the invisibility of others, as it inaccurately paints women and other animals as things of nature who are uninvolved in the creative manipulation of their environment.

Indeed, Marx's understanding of women's plight in the capitalist system (that capitalism is seen as an affront on the "natural" role for women in the home) is quite sexist by modern standards (MacKinnon 1989).[6] With many women pulled into factory work in the nineteenth century, Marx suggests that woman's absence from the home is responsible for "denaturalizing" them, a process that creates significant harms for children.[7] This same logic appears in liberal understandings of Nonhuman Animals in the capitalist system, as evidenced in the hyperfocus on factory farming. As many activists and nonprofits will attest, the goal of the anti-speciesism movement is not necessarily to liberate Nonhuman Animals entirely, but only to return to earlier forms of oppression that are deemed to be more "natural" or "humane." That is, the capitalist system is "denaturalizing" Nonhuman Animals: it is disrupting the "natural" order of things and the "natural" role of other animals. The emphasis is not on the exploitation of women or Nonhuman Animals, per se, but rather on the disruption or distortion of traditional exploitations that were idealized in an anthroparchal-patriarchal system.

What this suggests is that, if the capitalist system were to be replaced or significantly modified in some way, the prevailing social order of male rule and human supremacy would remain supported. The problem is not that women and other animals are being exploited. It is that they are being exploited in ways that challenge older, more established institutions of oppression which are perhaps romanticized as a result of their harms being more carefully concealed within the fabric of social life. The human factories of Marx's era and the factory farms of today's industrialized speciesism erode these illusions and force the consumer to confront the discomforting realities of oppressive social relations.[8]

Certainly, the oppression of women and other animals existed outside of capitalism, but capitalism is nonetheless thought to prevent women and other animals from reaching their "true potential" as doting housewives and "happy meat."[9] Welfare capitalism has subsequently emerged as a means to alleviate this affront to the dignity of sentient beings. Capitalists take the lead (with state encouragement) in the support of social services and charities. In tending to the overall well-being of laborers in this way, control over the means of production need not be relinquished. Laborers thus remain especially disempowered and dependent upon the paternalistic benevolence of their employer. This also aggravates social stratification by creating a hierarchy of need among those who may or may not qualify for assistance (Esping-Andersen 2006). Though human and nonhuman welfare may be marginally improved, the logic of domination thus remains the same so long as hierarchies remain intact.

WHEN FEMINISM BUTCHERS VEGANISM

Critical feminist theories of the state are thus actively engaged in recentering gender in the socialist dialogue. The status of Nonhuman Animals, however, remains inadequately addressed. They are persons who are not readily identified as men, women, or proletariats, and this leaves their inclusion tenuous and their position highly vulnerable. Unfortunately, many of those who are married to the neoliberalized incarnation of feminism see meaningful acknowledgement of Nonhuman Animal interests (hitherto referred to as veganism) as a matter of personal choice and can seem bothered when asked to examine their own role in exploitation.[10] For her part, MacKinnon (2004) fails to grant the attention warranted to the nonhuman experience given the magnitude of species-based oppression, though she does explore the relationship between human and nonhuman oppression in pornography, as evidenced in her publication on "crush" films and the failure of civil rights legislation to protect women and other animals alike.

Feminists such as MacKinnon have criticized traditional critiques of capitalism as androcentric and insensitive to the unique experiences of women, but the feminist critique itself shows itself to be hierarchical in its anthropocentrism. Indeed, much feminist theory erases the Nonhuman Animal experience entirely. If feminism is to fully acknowledge that capitalism is not a gender-neutral phenomenon, it must become species-inclusive in scope. The unpaid or underpaid labor of women undergirds capitalism, but the experience of nonhuman females is no different in this regard. Female cows labor in "dairies" where they undergo repeated sexual assaults, forced pregnancies, and separation from their children before eventually being shipped to slaughterhouses, their still adolescent bodies having become "spent" in the process. Hens are genetically manipulated and physically tortured with starvation, dehydration, and sensory deprivation to coax hundreds of eggs out of each animal until their weakened bodies, too, will be shipped to slaughterhouses. Other species such as pigs, sheeps,[11] horses, turkeys, dogs, and rabbits are similarly confined, assaulted, and killed by the millions as standard practice in capitalist production.

The female body is especially valued in the capitalist system, as it is the machine that creates product (such as breast milk and eggs), but also maintains the system through reproduction (in producing offspring). Sexism and social discrimination against the female body erase this great value and also cheapen its labor. In other words, while female bodies are extremely profitable and integral to the capitalist functioning, they are ideologically devalued as a means of naturalizing the oppressive conditions females endure and extorting more production for less cost. For instance, one survey estimates that American housewives on average work 94 hour weeks, which, if paid, would be worth a salary of more than $133,000 (Woodruff 2013). Yet, housewifery is neither salaried nor especially prestigious. It is this same devaluation which applies to nonhuman labor. Each pregnancy carried by a "dairy cow," for instance, earns her "owner" approximately $278 in milk sales (De Vries 2006). She also provides value in carrying the pregnancy to term, birthing the calf, and becoming "meat" when she is "culled" after her reproductive abilities wane. In wider culture, however, the roles of housewives, "dairy cows," and other feminized positions carry little prestige and might even be stigmatized.

In fact, the female body is so integral to the Nonhuman Animal industrial system that non-females are apt to destruction soon after birth in a number of different industries. In the capitalist system, value is tied to productivity, so the reproductive capacities of female-bodied animals of various species are fundamental to economic functioning, while unproductive and nonproducing bodies decrease in value to the point of worthlessness. Sick, feeble, older, and infertile bodies with low production value and little or no hope of future production value are made vulnerable to violence (jones 2014a). For instance, male chicks in the egg industry are subject to immediate suffocation or mincing in industrial grinders, while male calves exiting the "dairy" industry face infanticide in the production of "veal."[12] The same holds true for nonproducing human bodies who frequently find themselves socially ostracized and victims of institutionalized discrimination.

Vegan feminism acknowledges a speciesist economic system that is not only capitalistic but also patriarchal. Flesh consumption, for instance, is linked to strength and thus believed integral to men's success in the capitalist system. As a "marker of nationhood, social status, and gender"

(Cudworth 2011, 84), "meat" is the embodiment of oppressive power. Throughout history, colonizers have understood a plant-based diet to be an indicator of economic inferiority and poverty (Adams 1990). Sometimes the act of colonization itself creates this poverty, and Nonhuman Animals vanish from the colony's diet as a consequence, as was the case with Ireland pre-independence (Wrenn, forthcoming). Subsequently, vegetarians and vegans come to represent failures in a capitalist worldview. Flesh consumption is a marker of power, and those who are less able to engage it are disproportionately women, children, persons of color, elderly persons, infirm persons, and impoverished persons. These groups all become feminized in this powerlessness; they can neither consume vulnerable bodies nor adequately contribute to a capitalist system through production.

A vegan feminist theory of the state, however, is specifically concerned with making visible the plight of Nonhuman Animals in their fueling of human economy. The invisibility of Nonhuman Animals' oppression in the anthroparchal-patriarchal capitalist system is such that few take notice of the cows, chickens, pigs, and other animals killed to produce the "hamburgers," sandwiches, and snacks that sustain proletariats and bourgeoisie alike, women and men alike, and labor activists and feminists alike. Little notice is given to those animals killed or displaced to facilitate both labor exploitation and sexual exploitation. As is the case with women's oppression, the unrecognized exploitation of Nonhuman Animals makes possible the exploitation of proletariats. Just as women's unpaid work in the home as manifest in cooking, cleaning, childcare, and elder care allows men to go forth into the public sphere to sell their labor for many hours a day, so too does the unpaid work of Nonhuman Animals in the provision of clothing, food, transportation, and supervision of the home allow the proletariat, regardless of gender, to conduct their work.

By way of an example, the industrialization of cows' milk in the nineteenth century freed working class women to leave babies and young children in the care of others during work hours (Allen 2009). Cows' milk also formed the basis of women's care work in tending not just to their children but also to sick, disabled, and elderly persons who were thought to benefit from the believed high digestibility and healthfulness of milk (Boland 1906). In other words, the capitalist exploitation of male laborers relies on the exploitative domesticity of women, but human exploitation, regardless of gender (or perhaps *because of* gender), relies on the exploitation of other animals. Gender *and* species, as categories of difference, maintain the hierarchy of oppression necessary for capitalism's functioning.

Of course, I am not the first to take notice of these intersections. Vegan socialists have been advocating for the recognition of other species in the class struggle (Nibert 2013), and vegan feminists understand that the oppression of Nonhuman Animals is patriarchal in nature and closely mirrors that of women (Adams 2013; Hall 2010). However, ecosocialist theory displays shortcomings similar to that of nonvegan socialism. It assumes a gender-neutral approach, which either diminishes the unique trials of the female body or incorrectly predicts a trickledown effect, whereby the liberation of the (male) proletariat will also liberate other oppressed groups such as women and other animals. This oversight has much to do with the gender identity of prominent vegan socialist theorists, who, as predominantly male-identified, generally fail to notice how misogynistic scripts order human-nonhuman relations. Sociologist Erika Cudworth (2011) has been more explicit in exploring the intersections of gender and species within the confines of capitalism. Nonhuman Animals, she insists, are gendered in the agricultural system, and the institution of human dominance itself is gendered as well.

For many sociologists of the Marxist tradition, the prevailing economic means of production is thought to determine a society's structure and stratification. In a capitalist economy reliant upon endless production and consumption, women and other animals become the raw materials and vital labor in a society already following misogynistic scripts for many centuries prior. A feminist theory of social structure becomes invalid should it stop short of Nonhuman Animals' vital role in this formula. By focusing only on women's experience, it remains individualist in scope. This individualism obscures the collective condition of oppression and serves to maintain a false consciousness.

WHERE DOES CAPITALISM GET ITS PROTEIN?

Females feed and nourish the economy in many ways. The feminization process facilitates patriarchal exploitation of many kinds of bodies regardless of sex, but it is the female body (with the understanding that there is considerable variation across biological sex characteristics) which is disproportionately exploited. Capitalism runs on females. Females produce the next generation of laborers who will toil in factories and farms, soldiers who will monger for more resources, police officers who will control unrest, and leaders who will maintain ideologies of oppression. Females also tend to the hearth. They ensure that laborers, soldiers, officers, and leaders are well fed and their heirs attended to, so that men can fully focus their efforts in the public sphere.

Women's devalued status in the capitalist system is also functionally important in regard to the role they play in consumption. Food in particular plays a key role in economic relations, though it is often overlooked in its deceptive mundanity. As early socialist feminists such as Charlotte

Perkins Gilman attested, women restricted to the domestic sphere not only support men's ability to participate in the public sphere in caring for men's home, children, food, and clothing, but men are also supported when women become consumers of the products he creates (Allen 2009).[13] This consumption role comes full circle when women are made responsible for food purchasing and preparation, often purchasing adulterated or poor quality foods to the extreme profit of capitalist producers (a particular issue before food safety laws took effect in the early twentieth century).

Women's individualized experience in the home is a more extreme form of individualism experienced by men in the public sphere. Within the confines of domesticity, Victorian and Edwardian feminists identified that women were quite literally isolated from outside processes and other women as potential comrades. Accessing information or mobilizing for social change became all the more difficult.[14] Gilman (1911) was also insistent that women's role as cook kept her in a perpetual state of wage-slavery. It was a form of drudgery that, inefficient as it was for women themselves (women of her time spent the better part of the day busied with food preparation), served an important function in upholding androcentrism. More recent research demonstrates that women's home magazines and cookbooks further uphold anthroparchy and patriarchy in that they tend to emphasize women's place in the home and other animals' place on the dinner plate (Cudworth 2011). As such, cooking is an intensely political act.

The physical bodies of these females feed as well, nourishing capitalist functioning. Be it breast milk, eggs, or the production of edible offspring, females are the literal fodder of capitalism. As Adams (1990) identifies, Nonhuman Animal products for consumption can be understood as "feminized protein" in this regard. First, animal protein is frequently a product of the female reproductive system, as is true of eggs and breast milk. Second, many flesh products butchered for human consumption come from female bodies. For instance, "hamburger" and chicken "meat" derives largely from expended Nonhuman Animals who labored in "egg" and "dairy" industries. Third, these nonvegan products, regardless of make or origin, come from Nonhuman Animal bodies that were dominated and exploited in the production process. This inevitability ensures that *all* nonvegan products are thus feminized. In this way, the capitalist system is not simply carnivorous but also patriarchal in its design.

It is not only domesticated (or *domesecrated*) Nonhuman Animals who are vulnerable in an anthroparchal-patriarchal capitalist system. Free-living animals, too, are subject to systemic oppression on a number of fronts. First, these feminized communities can be displaced, either through habitat destruction or through intentional extermination, to make way for disproportionately male-led, male-owned, and male-profiting farms, resource extraction, or other such industries. Secondly, these free-living communities can be harassed and subjected to a number of violent executions at the hands of "hunters" equipped with guns, traps, and high-powered crossbows. As are farm "owners" and agricultural elites, "hunters," too, are overwhelmingly male (Luke 2007).

The institution of "hunting" is justified in a number of additional ways that work in the service of an anthroparchal-patriarchal capitalist system.[15] First, it is considered a way to affordably supplement a family's food supply. The killing of free-living Nonhuman Animals is understood, in this context, as another means for the male "breadwinner" to offer added value to the home. In the United States, where food security is tenuous for many (generally a result of the exploitative economic system and capitalism's facilitation of poverty), the ideology of "hunting" as a matter of thriftiness or economic necessity is a popular one. In any event, it lacks empirical truth. For the most part, "hunting" is actually a rather expensive enterprise. In addition to the high license fees (state and national "game" management entities solicit many millions of dollars in revenue from licensing each year) (Anderson 2012), participants will likely need to purchase highly expensive weapons (which require regular maintenance), ammunition, camouflaged clothing, and many other crutches or advantages designed to improve their kill rate such as packaged pheromones or tree stands. Kill limits mean that the price of each corpse can be many times that of one produced in the agricultural system when the costs of licenses and equipment are considered. Participants may also need to take time off work, potentially eating into their paid employment (a particular problem for workers with part-time or precarious employment). Despite the enormous advantage given to men with high-powered rifles, camouflage, tree stands and the like, the success rate is not especially high.[16] Time invested into stalking Nonhuman Animals has a much lower return than other solutions for economic supplementation. Furthermore, in those instances when a participant is successful in killing others, time must be invested in the butchering of their bodies. There is also the financial expense required to both store and preserve the flesh. Lastly, the risk is also considerable. "Hunting"-related accidents are responsible for hundreds of injuries and deaths to the participants themselves (2,891 Americans between 2002 and 2007 alone) (IHEA 2016) but also to nonparticipating citizens and nontarget Nonhuman Animals (Anderson 2012). Those who are seriously injured might be hampered in their ability to engage in paid employment. For those killed, they leave their families in an even greater compromised position.

"Hunting" is not only engaged to survive poverty under capitalism, it may also work to satiate frustrated proletariats. Ecofeminists observe that "hunting" is sometimes framed as a way for men to achieve sexual release (Kheel 1995) or "let off steam" to the benefit of wives left at home who are spared his abusive behavior (Adams 1990). Whether as a means to supplement income or deflect aggression, the fragility of capitalism is artificially pro-tected through the outsourcing of costs to vulnerable feminized groups, namely free-living animals. In doing so, an additional level of oppression is implemented with "hunting." A system reliant on male rule and economic exploitation will only compound suffering, allowing for few rational or life-affirming strategies of survival.

MOTHERHOOD AND MISSING CHILDREN

Although capitalism heavily relies on female bodies, this reality is relatively obscured from popular consciousness. The capitalist system is thus deg-endered. Advertisements selling hens' eggs or cows' milk exemplify this phenomenon. Although hens and cows are often anthropomorphized as "girls" or "ladies," their mother status is frequently concealed. In a typical advertisement for Bregott[17] "dairy products," a cow stands in a sunny field under a bright blue sky. The image reads "Girl Power." On Bregott's Insta-gram social media page, dozens of portraits capture these "girls" as they graze, relax, and play. Very rarely are the children of these "girls" pictured. Indeed, the invisibility of childbirth, nursing, and parenting is a consistent theme. Consider also the "Happy Cows Come from California" television campaign for Real California Cheese or Laughing Cow's advertising imagery. These cows are shown as giggling, trivial, and carefree. These are not depictions of ideal mothers or even competent mothers. Depicting these cows as mothers would disrupt the fantasy presented to the human con-sumer; the presence of calves forces the viewer to acknowledge the intended purpose of cows' breast milk. Instead, *farmers* are more frequently pictured nurturing calves when calves are visible at all. In this way, farmers are pre-sented as caring stewards, while the bovine mothers are dematernalized as silly and immature good-time girls. Characterized as such, they are not to be taken seriously as willing participants in this seemingly harmless, live-and-let-live industry.

It is worth considering that "girl" language encourages consumers to only superficially conceptualize "dairy cows" as female. Subsequently, the audi-ence will not be invited to acknowledge that they are actually mothers. Motherhood reminds the audience that these animals do not exist solely for the pleasure of the consumer. It is a reminder of their connectedness in complex social relationships, their responsibilities for others, their love for others, and others' love for them. Motherhood is essential to the reproduc-tion of the capitalist system, but it must be hidden from the public sphere lest its sentimentality interfere with business. That said, it is also true that characterizing mothers as "girls" is certainly accurate in the sense that these are immature cows who are still juveniles themselves. While bovines live an average of two decades, their average age at slaughter is just four or five years.[18] In this way, their own childhoods are erased as well.

Chicks, too, are generally absent from egg commercials. Even in those advertisements that seek to amplify the "naturalness" of the farms from which the eggs are sourced, industry fails to depict the most natural aspect of egg production: the creation of chicks. Hens are shown frolicking in open yards, chasing bugs, and chatting away as though existing in an enclosed, childless, monogender society for the express purpose of ceaselessly producing eggs for another species to consume is the epitome of nature's intention. It is this same seamless idyll of "natural order" that normalizes human oppression, nonhuman oppression, and, under capitalism, a number of other oppressions. "Nature" as an ideology facilitates a false consciousness that disempowers and protects the system as is. Chicks are replaced by the sterile imagery of crisp, clean white eggs that seem to appear almost by magic. The raw emotion and organic mess of egg laying and childbirth are rendered invisible in speciesist advertising, presumably so as not to spoil the consumer's appetite. The birds' eggs humans are invited to dine on only vaguely refer to the femaleness of the hens involved in creating them.

As with cows' breast milk, hens' eggs are degendered. Gendering eggs and egg production would create an awareness unconducive to consumption. As is the function of advertising, this strange fantasy fashioned by capitalist elites is taken for granted as "normal" and "natural" by the audience. It is facilitating consumption by obscuring the unpleasantries of production. Subsequently, the absence of children goes unnoticed. Pornography also engages this approach by encouraging the viewer to consume without emotional attachment (Dines 2010). The omnivore is thus encouraged to become a "playboy," enjoying the pleasures of nonhuman bodies with no ethical qualms and no strings attached. Like playboys who are subscribing to pornography "for the articles," nonvegan consumers also mask the crass consumption of vulnerable bodies with narratives of admirable moral behavior (this is one reason why consumption of "organic" or "free-range" products is linked with class).[19] Eating higher welfare products of speciesism is thought of as a means of treating Nonhuman Animals to a "good life," and nonvegans are reframed as good shepherds of sustainability and community health.

The irony of erasing nonhuman mothering and childhood is especially poignant in the American "milk carton kids" affair. Missing children notices were memorably printed on milk cartons for a time in the 1980s in a campaign to locate the disappeared. When a boy went missing on his newspaper route one morning in Iowa, desperate relatives turned to their family business and began printing his image on the back of their product (99% Invisible 2015). In addition to its primary purpose of spreading awareness, the campaign's latent function was evidenced in its ability to bond, connect, and repair the human community in a time of crisis. What began with one local "dairy" would soon spread to the cartons of competitors seeking similar altruistic recognition. The pretense of caring helps a brand to stand out, and capitalizing on missing children cases would be no exception. "Dairy cows" thus extended their maternalism beyond the baby bottles of infants and the lunchboxes of school children. Now it embraced motherless children scattered to the winds, suffering unimaginable violence at the hands of presumably male perpetrators. Historian Paul Mokrzycki-Renfro comments, "There is a sense of familial unity that I think milk helps to offer; maternal nurturance. And also being this item around which people gather" (99% Invisible 2015). Like the frantic human mothers, "dairy cows," too, seemed to be calling the milk carton kids back to their bosom.

Of course, the nonhuman children of these milking mothers—the calves—were never themselves considered worthy of notice. *Their* abduction and *their* assault are only a matter of course. The violence that these nonhuman children endure is unsettling and is strategically hidden from view. Hundreds of "dairies" volunteered their services to the milk carton campaign, and their participation served as a gesture of good will, but more than a civic duty, these missing children notices also humane-washed the product. In the process, nonhuman children were further invisibilized, and the exploitation of their mothers was further romanticized.

Ultimately, the milk carton campaign was not successful in bringing missing children home, but the campaign *did* raise awareness about violence against children. That is, it brought light to male violence. As a result of this uncomfortable exposure, the campaign was deemed depressing and traumatizing; it began to foster negative responses from consumers. Humane-washing and maternalism, having been employed with the intention of selling more product, were thus subsumed by the overpowering reminder of patriarchal violence. As a result, the "dairies" ceased participation. Drawing attention to missing children of any species is bad for business.

MILKING THEM FOR ALL THEY'RE WORTH

Vegan feminism seeks to make visible that which is made invisible in humane-washed industry narratives, and the 2014 film release *The Herd* exemplifies a graphic attempt to enact this strategy. The film's plot rests on the captivity and torture of several young women who are exploited for their breast milk (and one prepubescent girl who will presumably replace the older captives in maintenance of the system). Viewers are encouraged to consider how the normalized, institutional captivity and torture of female bodies is a horror show in the human context but entirely routine in the nonhuman context. The film subsequently bills itself as a vegan feminist project, but vegan feminist theory is not so simplistic. Indeed, the film actually presents itself as an example of important shortcomings in single-issue veganism.

Veganism, too, can be complacent in obscuring the experiences and the suffering of vulnerable groups by more privileged media producers and storytellers. Most, if not all, of the women featured in *The Herd*, for instance, appear to be white-identified. This invisibilizes the experiences of many women of color who already feel the strain of embodied institutionalized exploitation. These experiences are no fantasy of film production; what is unthinkable for privileged women is a strategy of survival for destitute women. *The Herd*, in other words, asks the audience to think critically about the female suffering involved in food production, but it fails to acknowledge how this feminized oppression is endured by nonhuman *and* human bodies. Indeed, while vegan spaces enjoy a female majority and are generally presumed inclusive, they are notoriously white- and Western-centric (Wrenn 2016). The presumably privileged location of the filmmakers likely accounts for the film's failure to acknowledge how very normalized the exploitation of breastfeeding mothers actually is within the capitalist system, regardless of species. Vulnerable groups are subject to systemic violation, which is otherwise thought a sacred or fundamental right to more privileged mothers. To have autonomy over one's own lactation and custody over one's own young is a marker of social privilege, humans included. Many poor women are pressured into adoption at incredible profit to charities and governments (Joyce 2013), or coerced into using unhealthful infant formulas at the behest of the large food corporations that produce them (Gaard 2013). Wealthier women, in the meantime, are privileged enough to purchase the breast milk of other women for their children if they so desire, and it is disproportionately poor women who will feel compelled to sell their milk to satisfy this demand.[20] Indeed, women of color—colonized, enslaved, or otherwise oppressed—have long acted as wet nurses to more privileged women (Joshel 1986). Today, they continue this tradition in a patriarchal capitalist system that commodifies their milk. As *The New York Times* reports: "Breast milk, that most ancient and fundamental of nourishments, is becoming an industrial commodity [. . .]" (Pollack 2015). While male-owned corporations stand to profit, vulnerable women, especially women of color, are apt to exploitation. In response to one company's attempt to target African American women in Detroit, for example, the Black Mothers Breastfeeding Association in solidarity with a number of other similar organizations penned an open letter that urged: " [. . .] African American women have been impacted traumatically by historical commodification of our bodies. Given the economic incentives, we are deeply concerned that women will be coerced into diverting milk that they would otherwise feed their own babies" (Green 2015).

Eggs and wombs, too, are increasingly commodified. Poor women are encouraged to "donate" eggs for a compensation of a few thousand dollars. Besides the potential psychological consequences of doing so, there are a number of physical risks involved, including an inability for donors to have their own children afterwards (Pearson 2006). The surrogacy industry is another affront to women's well-being. While women in the United States also act as surrogates for hire, increasingly childbirth is being outsourced to developing nations, namely India, China, and the Ukraine (Twine 2015). Through this control of reproduction, patriarchy and anthroparchy thus serve similar functions in the capitalist system:

> [...] both daughters and dairy cows were the property of males who presumed the right to force females—whether they be called wives, slaves, or livestock—to bear more or different offspring than they would otherwise choose. [...] both require fairly relentless preoccupation with and control of reproduction [...] (jones 2014b, 98)

This legacy harkens to the shared word origin of "husband" and "husbandry," terms that imply patriarchal mastery and control over both wives and "livestock." The commodification of female bodies is not only a vegan issue but also a feminist one.

It would be a mistake for vegan feminist theory to overlook this visceral shared experience between human and nonhuman females. Forced sex and impregnation was and *is* a lived reality for many women. As with unproductive nonhumans in speciesist institutions, women can also face neglect or death for failing to produce an heir. Henry VIII famously ordered the public execution of Anne Boleyn and several other wives for failing their duties in this regard. However, many women in India and other developing nations face disfigurement or execution in "accidental fires" and acid attacks for failing to produce adequate capital for their husbands, be it sufficient dowry, adequate servitude in the home, or the production of a male heir (Stone and James 1995).

BUYING AND SELLING BODIES

In early 2016, beachgoers in Argentina spied and captured a newborn Franciscana dolphin,[21] pulling her from the water and releasing her to the mercy of dozens of grabbing hands hoping to use her as a photo prop. As the story went viral and made international news, audiences were horrified by the cruelty this infant endured. Outside of the normalizing confines of capitalist industry, her death was seen as tragic, and yet, there was nothing necessarily unexpected about her treatment. The Kimmela Center for Animal Advocacy (2016) explains:

> It is difficult not to see the connection between how this young dolphin was used and what happens at the institutionalized versions known as zoos, aquariums and circuses. The only difference is that one has to pay for a ticket to gawk at, touch or ride on the animals at one of these facilities. But the psychology is the same.

As this incident demonstrates, anthroparchal-patriarchal capitalism facilitates a social structure that normalizes the exploitation of vulnerable bodies for the entertainment of those in power.

Here, again, the connection to women's struggle is strong. Prostituted women endure comparable debasement and violation, their bodies treated as commodities to be bought, sold, and used. Much of the abuse she endures (groping, hitting, or aggressive penetration) is not included in her price and is certainly not consented to. Once commodified, however, her abuse becomes institutionalized and sanctioned. The cruel violation and violence inflicted on the infant South American dolphin who passed away in a state of terror as she was passed through the hands of so many excited and entitled humans highlights how vulnerable feminized bodies of all make remain in a society where the owning and consuming of bodies is a culturally valid practice. Rates of assault, rape, and murder are high for prostituted girls and women (Moran 2013). Nonprostituted women, too, are endangered in a society that normalizes the entitlement to feminized bodies. Research demonstrates that the legalization of prostitution, for instance, creates a sharp increase in demand (Jeffreys 2008). Sex trafficking increases as a result, as does the likelihood of experiencing sexual assault for all women in the community, prostituted or not. Likewise, research also demonstrates that the arrival of slaughterhouses in a community increases the prevalence of rape against female citizens (Jacques 2015). The commodification of some female bodies, even if comprising only a particular subset of the larger population, spells danger and degradation for *all* female bodies.

Women and Nonhuman Animals are the original proletariats. They are less likely (or not likely at all) to own land or any means of production. To survive, they rely only on their labor. In many ways, however, this contract with the state (the exchange of labor for survival in society) is not consensual. As survivor of prostitution Rachel Moran (2013, 159) explains, "[. . .] choice and consent are erroneous concepts here. Their invalidity rests on the fact that woman's compliance in prostitution is a response to circumstances beyond her control, and this produces an environment which prohibits even the possibility of true consent." In other words, an extremely exploitative economic system severely reduces or even eliminates agency. It is a system that predisposes feminized bodies for entry into exploitative industries. Moran (2013, 183) presses us to consider that, so long as prostitution is deemed an acceptable institution in some areas of society and entry into the industry depends on one's social vulnerability, women *as a class* are oppressed in this context. "The acceptance of prostitution," she offers, "makes all women potential prostitutes in the public view [. . .]." The ideology of misogyny thus normalizes the buying and selling of bodies and degrades the status of women in general. Moran's logic can be expanded to suppose that, so long as the consumption of Nonhuman Animals is deemed acceptable, no feminized group will be safe. In a system that normalizes the exploitation, ownership, and consumption of female bodies, all manner of feminized persons are made vulnerable. Misogynistic scripts can be enacted on anyone in almost any context, so long as they are deemed legitimate in the culture.

Because so much of the work undertaken by human and nonhuman females is nonconsensual, undercompensated, and unpaid in capitalist societies, a discussion of the relationship between the capitalist system and the slave system is also warranted. Slave and capitalist systems are often conceptualized as distinct systems, with the rationalized capitalist system (boasting a supposed equality of opportunity) overtaking the irrational slave system (wherein social mobility and consent are privileges enjoyed only by the owning class). The victory of the industrialized American North over slavery in the South is one popular narrative that depicts capitalism as prevailing in the name of democracy. It is, however, a misnomer that slavery ended with abolition in the United States (Baptist 2014). Capitalism, in fact, continues to foster the systematic ownership of vulnerable groups. It *necessitates* nonconsensual use of others' bodies and labor in a number of ways. The American North profited considerably from slavery before emancipation in the 1860s. For that matter, many institutions of the North were made possible or at least viable by the original boost of wealth and labor provided by slavery. By way of an example, many prestigious northern universities such as Yale, Brown, and Harvard were launched with donations made by wealthy slave "owners" in the community (Wilder 2013). Some of the grounds were built and maintained by enslaved persons as well.

The feminist perspective understands the slave system as a patriarchal one (Wertz 1984). As a dominated group, enslaved persons can be understood as feminized. When slavery as an institution is conceptualized as inclusive of Nonhuman Animals, this gendering becomes stronger. Rarely, however, is the nonhuman experience considered in the Western or global historical narrative of progress. Millions upon millions of horses were and still are purposefully bred, broken, and driven to their deaths after years in the harness pulling humans and cargo in the name of commerce (Nibert 2013). Many whale populations were brought to the brink of extinction as millions drowned or exsanguinated at the end of a harpoon to fuel the lamps that lit streets and factories. Billions and billions of animal bodies were born, killed, processed, and consumed by workers of all industries. Again, these relationships are not only anthroparchal but also patriarchal, as they demonstrate male power over feminized, vulnerable nonhumans.

When the critical lens is explicitly gendered, the enslavement of female bodies becomes visible as foundational to a viable capitalist system. Slavery as a mode of production may predate the capitalist system, but it does not exist outside of it. Slavery was only absorbed and masked by ideologies of free markets and equality of opportunity. Indeed, there are more slaves toiling in today's economy than at any other point of human history, including the era of the transatlantic slave trade (U.S. Department of State 2013). Most of these slaves are girls, women, and other animals (Free the Slaves 2015).[22]

INTERSEX AND GAY ANIMALS ON THE MARGINS

While this chapter has argued that the state relies extensively on the exploitation of the female body, it is important to acknowledge that other bodies, thus feminized, are also necessary for the state's function. Importantly, transfeminist theory recognizes that the "female body" in the strict biological sense is inconsistent; bodies vary tremendously across species and resist clear categorization (Noble 2012). It also recognizes that one need not possess a vulva, vagina, or cervix in order to be feminized. Recall that gender refers to role, not biology. Femininity as a category depends on subservience in relation to masculinity. In other words, anybody of any make or shape can be feminized if they are oppressed under patriarchal conditions.

Nonetheless, female bodies in possession of wombs that are capable of biological reproduction are especially prized under capitalism. Those bodies which are thought "incomplete" in this regard may be especially endangered. As with the human species, intersexuality exists among farmed animals as well at about the same rate of 1 in 2,000 (Abdel-Hameed 1971; Davis 2015). Like their human counterparts, intersex farmed animals (referred to as "free martins" by speciesist industries) are pathologized. This is evident when "farmers" speak to the difficulty in "diagnosing" this "abnormal" (read: infertile and unproductive) body type. While intersexuality cannot be prevented, the genitals of baby animals are inspected for quality assurance, and defectors are presumably destroyed. The Oklahoma Cooperative Extension Service explains: "The cattleman [sic] can predict the reproductive value of this heifer calf at birth and save the feed and development costs if he is aware of the high probability of freemartinism" (Lyon 2007). As with male-bodied "dairy calves," male-bodied chicks, and other undesirables in the capitalist system, intersex animals are not deemed valuable enough to warrant nourishment and care. They are denied the right to exist.

The treatment of intersex farmed animals mirrors closely that of intersex human animals, many of whom have undergone painful and impairing, nonconsensual surgeries by medical practitioners who likewise understand the intersex body as deviant and problematic in a binary society. The intersex community has protested these "corrective" surgeries, as well as the hormonal treatments that are often administered as an act of state violence (Davis 2015). For humans and nonhumans in the capitalist system, a body that cannot produce is a body that is not valued.[23] This lack of productive value is at once a site of extreme vulnerability.

The intersex body, both human and nonhuman, disrupts a gender-based hierarchical society and is apt to state manipulation, control, and extermination. Ecofeminist pattrice jones (2014b) suggests that a gendered capitalist system, so thoroughly reliant on reproduction for its sustenance and growth, also mandates a "compulsory heterosexuality" whereby homosexual or asexual animals are forced into heterosexual relationships. While much of this systemic violence is associated with the horrors of factory farms in "breeding" practices, even innocuous animal businesses engage in compulsory heterosexuality. jones (2014b, 97) explains: "Dog lovers who decry puppy mills still feel free to decide whether, when, and with whom the canines under their control will partner." A gendered capitalist system is thus inherently exploitative of heterosexuality and the female body, but it also exists as a source of immeasurable violence and marginalization for nonconforming bodies and orientations.

FEMALE LABOR IN THE NONHUMAN ANIMAL RIGHTS INDUSTRIAL COMPLEX

While the industries of capitalism hold considerable blame in the exploitation of female bodies, it is interesting that similar misogynistic mechanisms also surface in the efforts to disrupt them. A primary reason for this occurrence springs from the tendency for social movements to themselves become agents of capitalism (Chasin 2000; Smith 2007). Care, empathy, love, and even sex are vulnerable to commodification in social justice industries. As movements raise social awareness to inequalities, they also inspire new markets when emerging concerns can be monetized and activism can be bought and sold. Furthermore, gender difference and sexism lubricate market processes, and, unfortunately, this relationship does not cease to be relevant in the confines of social change spaces. As capitalism infiltrates movements, scripts of misogyny simply transfer to resource mobilization efforts. This happens in at least two ways. First, the bodies of human women are exploited to provide free or meagerly compensated labor, sexually or otherwise.[24] Adams (1996) observes that women's caregiving roles are invisibilized in anti-speciesism spaces, largely a result of a patriarchal culture that is also unacknowledged. Secondly, the bodies of feminized nonhumans (and disproportionately female-bodied nonhumans at that) are exploited without consent to the benefit of activists or organizations.

Researchers have noted that social movements fundamentally rely on gender in both emergence and outcome (Taylor 1999). This reliance has not always developed from an equitable relationship. To name just a few examples, the abolitionists of the nineteenth century (Davis 1981), the Civil Rights movement of the mid-twentieth century (Robnett 1997), and the gay liberation movement of more recent times (Chasin 2000) have documented histories of exploiting women's labor in the service of more visible male leaders. The Nonhuman Animal rights movement, too, while estimated to be 80 percent female-identified, is predominantly led by men and disproportionately celebrates male contributions (Gaarder 2011).[25] In the patriarchal and hierarchical structure of a corporatized social movement space, the threat to female integrity is *inherent*. More and more Nonhuman Animal rights organizations rely on female labor for efficient and economic operations. Much of this work is voluntary, while the rest is extremely underpaid (Coulter 2016).[26] In addition to the drudgery work relegated to women in Nonhuman Animal advocacy, women are also disproportionately engaged in emotional labor (Adams 1996; Coulter 2016; Gaarder 2011), a pattern that is especially pertinent in the affecting and psychologically taxing space of protest (Jasper 2011).

Increasingly, this exploited labor comes in the form of prostitution. That is, women are recruited to enter public spaces adorned with little or no clothing to attract passersby. This attraction is expected to translate into social, cultural, and economic capital such as notoriety, membership, or donations. While some of these prostituted women are admirably attempting to raise awareness to Nonhuman Animal suffering, it is an important distinction that these activities almost always take place within the confines of the organizational identity. Women may be holding signs featuring the organization's name or logo (sometimes the branding is as prominent as the anti-speciesist message itself), or the participants may be distributing leaflets or fliers that are heavily decorated with the organization's information. Women's bodies are thus sold on street corners to the advantage of "nonprofit" pimps. The oppression of female bodies is as much a matter of securing wealth as it is a matter of securing male privilege. Nonhuman Animals, whose bodies are pictured in this protest imagery, are also used for organizational gain in this way. They, too, are feminized, and their participation in campaigns are not consensual. Indeed, the sexist exploitation of women and other animals blend seamlessly in protest, protecting the very hierarchies of domination they were designed to dismantle.

LIBERATORY VEGAN FEMINIST FUTURES

A vegan feminist theory of the state identifies a species-inclusive patriarchal social structure that is dependent upon hierarchy and domination. Male violence flourishes under capitalism, while powerful misogynistic ideologies naturalize or invisibilize feminized oppression. Capitalism's false promise of equality in opportunity is a privilege enjoyed only by groups in power and has little meaning for most women and other animals. Feminist scholars have suggested a reconfiguring of society in general but also the domestic sphere in particular, so that all genders can experience liberation (Allen 2009). If Nonhuman Animals are not accounted for in the feminist vision for the future, however, the scripts of misogyny will remain viable, and oppression will remain ever present. The redesigned home front would need to ensure the elimination of Nonhuman Animal products from the closets, cabinets, and dinner table. As ruling classes gain in power, their consumption of animal foods and nonhuman labor increases. The process applies to entire societies as they rise in the global system and begin to amass wealth (Sans and Combris 2015). Speciesism is as integral to upholding capitalism as is sexism, and speciesism is made possible by the same misogynistic scripts. A feminist approach to dismantling capitalism must include a vegan component, or it is rendered impotent.

Capitalism systematically exploits feminized bodies for smooth and efficient functioning. To do so, it engages class oppression, it stigmatizes and devalues disabled and intersex bodies, and it aggravates sexism and racism in human communities, in addition to the billions of nonhumans also impacted. The strength of vegan feminist theory lies in its intersectional consciousness to these processes (Kemmerer 2011). That is, it recognizes that oppression under capitalism directly impacts the life chances and well-being of various marginalized identities, human *and* nonhuman. Intersectionality theory, born of Black feminism, notes that racism, sexism, classism, and other systems exist in a matrix of domination (Collins 2003). Ecofeminist theory grounds this matrix in the larger natural environment, ensuring that Nonhuman Animals and ecosystems are included in the framework. In turn, vegan feminism emerges from this ecofeminist dialogue to distinguish species as an identity in its own right. While it acknowledges that barriers of access can make participation difficult for some, it also positions veganism as a more or less obligatory expression of political solidarity for other species. In the Marxian tradition, vegan feminists nurture an imagination for change and employ consciousness-raising as a regular tactic. This is an approach promoted by MacKinnon (1989) as well, prized for its power to subversively challenge an oppressive system.

As a juggernaut of oppression, capitalism will require collectively engaged disruption in a number of ways in addition to shared awareness. First, those with the means of doing so can discontinue the consumption of Nonhuman

Animal products, *all* of which are sourced from a relationship of domination. This is important as a political matter, and, to a lesser extent, an economic one. Politically speaking, veganism represents solidarity with oppressed nonhumans. It sends a message of dissatisfaction with a speciesist social structure and desire for justice. Veganism educates, and it leads by example. As an economic matter, anti-speciesist consumption can also contribute to the struggle in the promotion of vegan companies. However, nonvegan industries are intensely powerful and politically protected. Vegan research does not reliably indicate that purchasing-power can significantly manipulate the structure of the food system given the immense control that industry lobbyists wield over the state (Simon 2013; Wrenn 2011, 2016). In other words, activists may be disappointed should they presume to fight capitalism with capitalism. A more sophisticated strategy will be required.

A vegan feminist theory of the state offers not only a critique of the anthroparchal-patriarchal capitalist system but also an imagination for a just future. Upturning capitalism will necessitate, at the very least, a disruption of misogynistic scripts. It will necessitate the abolition of prostitution, pornography, nonvegan food systems, and other institutions that involve the commodification and domination of feminized groups. It also requires an egalitarian approach to social justice activism, one that does not compromise women's integrity in order to "sell" concern for Nonhuman Animals. In short, a species-inclusive critique of the capitalist state will be incomplete if it remains gender-neutral in its scope.

As Kendra Coulter (2016) insists, an "inter-species solidarity" is imperative. It is the *hierarchical structure* of anthroparchy, patriarchy, and capitalism that must be dismantled. The very concepts of "gender," "species," and "class" must ultimately be questioned as these are categories known to serve hierarchies. Hierarchies are themselves social constructions and are thus vulnerable to radical change. In the socialist tradition, Gilman (1911) envisions a society where work is communally conducted, not disproportionately burdened on the lowest classes (Allen 2009). Silvia Federici (2012) also suggests that recreating the commons is one important feminist means of resisting the alienating nature of capitalism. As such, moving away from a corporatized nonprofit structure that monetizes activism to instead embrace a structure that is grassroots and community-based might be appropriate. Values that characterize nonprofitization (privatization, concentrated power, hierarchies of authority, allegiances to industry and the state, copyrighting, and controlled resources) are contrary to vegan feminist goals. The commons is community-centered, not capital-centered.

In said commons, the interests of *all* persons must be accounted for. Gilman (1911) imagined a vegetarian society[27] in her utopian novel *Moving the Mountain*, where "hunting," zookeeping, and even predation ceased to exist. More recently, Federici (2012, 145) continues this species-inclusive approach, insisting that overcoming our "state of constant denial and irresponsibility" in regard to our consumption patterns is a vital first step for reconstructing the commons. In this regard, veganism is feminist resistance. It rejects the legitimacy of powerful groups that dominate and consume less powerful groups. Veganism imagines a society grounded in respect for the autonomy and dignity of all bodies.[28] Subsequently, veganism may speak specifically to the plight of Nonhuman Animals, but it holds genuine implications for other feminized bodies as well. The forced domination of feminized bodies constitutes an injustice. As a consequence, veganism must be absorbed into the repertoire for change, as it explicitly acknowledges that consumption is socially constructed and, at present, hierarchical. MacKinnon (1989, 140) writes of sexual objectification, "To be sexually objectified means having a social meaning imposed on your being that defines you as to be sexually used, according to your desired uses, and then using you that way. Doing this is sex in the male system." It is a mistake to ignore the plight of Nonhuman Animals in the context of socialist or feminist analysis. Nonhuman Animals experience sexual objectification as the designated nonhuman other; they, too, are feminized and sexually exploited by a patriarchal capitalist system.

ACKNOWLEDGMENTS

The author wishes to thank Brian Snead for his assistance in proofreading the original manuscript, offering critical feedback on *The Herd*, and suggesting a number of recent publications in Marxist theory that were helpful to the arguments herein. The author also thanks Carol J. Adams and Dr. Johanna Foster for providing literature suggestions utilized in this chapter, Lucas Hayes for his critical thoughts on parent citizenship and ecosocialism, and Emma Tumilty for her generous proofreading assistance.

NOTES

1. This is a term developed by Erika Cudworth (2011) which refers to the institutionalization of human domination.

2. Language that is speciesist, sexist, or euphemistic will be placed in quotation marks to denote its contested meaning.

3. Adams (1996) refers to this as the "sex-species system."

4. Schaef actually understands addiction and patriarchy to be mutually supporting.

5. This term is meant to encompass urban-dwelling and domesecrated animals who are often invisibilized by the natural/"man-made" binary (Noske 1989).

6. Some scholars disagree with this interpretation and instead understand Marx's scant writings on women's condition to be much more feminist in nature (Brown 2012).

7. Modern sociological research demonstrates that women's employment outside of the home does not damage children and may actually advantage them (Barnett and Rivers 2004).

8. Some of Marx's writings acknowledge the capitalist exploitation and genetic manipulation of Nonhuman Animal bodies (what he describes as "disgusting") already well underway in Victorian England and Ireland (Saito 2016).

9. "Happy meat" is the colloquial term used in vegan spaces for Nonhuman Animal products that are purportedly produced in humane conditions.

10. As one common example of this response, please see the video, *Does Feminism Require Vegetarianism or Veganism?* by popular feminist project, *Everyday Feminism* (Edell 2016).

11. "Sheeps" here is used intentionally to avoid mass terms, which work to objectify other animals.

12. Information on agricultural practices is derived from fact sheets produced by nonprofits such as Farm Sanctuary.

13. While women's work plays an important function, this importance should not negate the inherent conflict to the arrangement. Given the opportunity, many women might opt for greater agency and independence in their economic condition.

14. Wives and mothers have never been universally isolated or completely powerless. As Schirmer (1989) identifies in women's collective action against institutionalized violence, motherhood can be political. Mothers may also be deeply committed to civic engagement in the public sphere, as evidenced in the influence of the National Parent-Teacher Association (Crawford and Levitt 1999). Mothers (and house-husbands/stay-at-home fathers) certainly utilize public spaces to engage in parenting and other collective behaviors, and binary notions of public and private realms can invisibilize this citizenship (Prokhovnik 1998).

15. Sociologist Gail Dines (2010) notes that pornography magazines enjoy levels of popularity comparable to "hunting" magazines and other publications themed in violence, demonstrating an important intersection of sexism and speciesism in the marketplace.

16. Only 48 percent of killers stalking deer in 2011 were successful. This number is double that of the mid-twentieth century before the industrialization of "hunting" (Dougherty 2013). The success rate for killing other "food" animals such as turkeys is much lower (Prettyman 2010).

17. Bregott is a Swedish "dairy" company.

18. Information on agricultural practices is derived from fact sheets produced by nonprofits such as Farm Sanctuary.

19. Dines (2010) argues that the *Playboy* enterprise explicitly appeals to an imagined upper class ideal to encourage consumption. Lower class persons who desire social mobility may consume *Playboy* pornography to attain a sense of being higher classed, while higher class persons who consume the decidedly less "classy" *Hustler* material can do so without an affront to their identity as a sort of "slum-diving." Speciesist industries engage this play on class identity in the marketing of Nonhuman Animal products as well.

20. Some mothers exchange breast milk freely as a community service online or through milk banks. Having access to networks of this kind or the leisure time to donate, however, will also reflect the social privilege of participants (Azema and Callahan 2003; Lindemann et al. 2004).

21. Also known as the La Plata dolphin, the Franciscana dolphin is an endangered species native to South American oceans and estuaries.

22. Reports on trafficking and slavery do not generally include the plight of Non-human Animals.

23. Cis-women, too, who are childfree, involuntarily childless, or infertile can experience stigma (Miall 1986).

24. Lauren Ornelas, founder of the Food Empowerment Project, discusses the gender disparities in compensation in a panel presented at the Resistance Ecology Conference 2015 titled "Critiquing Privilege in Animal Advocacy Circles." It is available on Vimeo at https://vimeo.com/131004617.

25. As of early 2016, 66 percent of the inductees to the Animal Rights Hall of Fame operated by Farm Animal Rights Movement (FARM) are male. As of March 23, 2016, 60 percent of the best-selling books on Amazon in the category of "Animal Rights" are male-authored.

26. According to the HSUS 2013 990 IRS form, the average salary for its highest compensated male employees is $166,080, while the average salary for its highest compensated female employees is only $90,526. This is a difference of 54 percent and partially reflects the absence of women in more prestigious, better-compensated positions in the organization. As further evidence, the 2014 990 IRS form filed by Farm Sanctuary reports only one female employee as highly compensated; Vegan Outreach's 2014 form reports none. These figures do not include the litany of other affiliates who are not reported on IRS documents. These organizations, however, rely heavily on female volunteers. For instance, Vegan Outreach's street team (available at http://www.teamvegan.biz/team) is, at the time of this writing, approximately three-fourths female-presenting.

27. This utopian society is not wholly vegetarian. Gilman (1911, 74) imagines that "meat" could be available on request in the now familiar "happy meat" vein. One character in the novel explains, "The way we manage about meat is this: A proper proportion of edible animals are raised under good conditions—nice, healthy, happy beasts; killed so that they don't know it!—and never kept beyond a certain time limit."

28. Ecofeminists in particular promote social relations that are based on care-giving and community (Adams 1996), which directly challenges the exploitative and conflict-focused domination approach favored by capitalism.

REFERENCES

Abdel-Hameed, M., H. Neat, and W. Briles. 1971. "Differences in Erythrocyte Measurements of Intersex and Normal Adult Chickens." *Poultry Science*, 50(6): 1847–1854.

Adams, Carol. 1990. *The Sexual Politics of Meat: A Feminist-Vegetarian Critical Theory*. New York: Continuum Publishing.

Adams, Carol. 1995. "Toward a Feminist Theology of Religion and the State." In C. Adams and M. Fortune (eds.), *Violence Against Women and Children: A Christian Theological Sourcebook*. New York: Continuum, pp. 15–35.

Adams, Carol. 1996. "Caring About Suffering: A Feminist Exploration." In J. Donovan and C. Adams (eds.), *Beyond Animal Rights: A Feminist Caring Ethic for the Treatment of Animals*. New York: Continuum, pp. 170–196.

Adams, Carol, and Lori Gruen. 2014. "Groundwork." In Carol Adams and Lori Gruen (eds.), *Ecofeminism: Feminist Intersections with Other Animals & the Earth*. New York: Bloomsbury Academic, pp. 7–36.

Allen, Judith. 2009. *The Feminism of Charlotte Perkins Gilman: Sexualities, Histories, Progressivism*. Chicago: University of Chicago Press.

Anderson, Will. 2012. *This Is Hope: Green Vegans and the New Human Ecology*. Hants, UK: Earth Books.

Azema, E., and S. Callahan. 2003. "Breast Milk Donors in France: A Portrait of the Typical Donor and the Utility of Milk Banking in the French Breastfeeding Context." *Journal of Human Lactation*, 19(2): 199–202.

Baptist, Edward. 2014. *The Half Has Never Been Told: Slavery and the Making of American Capitalism*. Philadelphia: Basic Books.

Barnett, Rosalind, and Caryl Rivers. 2004. *Same Difference: How Gender Myths are Hurting Our Relationships, Our Children, and Our Jobs*. New York: Basic Books.

Boland, Mary. 1906. *A Handbook of Invalid Cooking: For the Use of Nurses in Training-Schools, Nurses in Private Practice and Others Who Care for the Sick*. New York: The Century Co.

Brown, Heather. 2012. *Marx on Gender and the Family: A Critical Study*. Boston: Brill.

Chasin, Alexandra. 2000. *Selling Out: The Gay and Lesbian Movement Goes to Market*. New York: Palgrave Macmillan.

Collins, Patricia. 2003. *Black Feminist Thought: Knowledge, Consciousness, and the Politics of Empowerment*. New York: Routledge.

Collins, R. 2011. "Content Analysis of Gender Roles in Media: Where Are We Now and Where Should We Go?" *Sex Roles*, 64(3): 290–298.

Coulter, Kendra. 2016. *Animals, Work, and the Promise of Interspecies Solidarity*. New York: Palgrave Macmillan.

Crawford, Susan and Peggy Levitt. 1999. "Social Change and Civic Engagement: The Case of the PTA." In T. Skocpol and M. Fiorina (eds.), *Civic Engagement in American Democracy*. Washington, DC: Brookings Institution Press, pp. 249–265.

Cudworth, Erika. 2011. *Social Lives with Other Animals: Tales of Sex, Death, and Love*. New York: Palgrave Macmillan.

Davis, Angela. 1981. *Women, Race, & Class*. New York: Random House, Inc.

Davis, Georgiann. 2015. *Contesting Intersex: The Dubious Diagnosis*. New York: New York University Press.

De Vries, A. 2006. "Economic Value of Pregnancy in Dairy Cattle." *Journal of Dairy Science*, 89: 3876–3885.

Dines, Gail. 2010. *Pornland: How Porn Has Hijacked Our Sexuality*. Boston: Beacon Press.

Dougherty, Craig. 2013. "Deer Hunting: A Success Story." *Outdoor Life*. Retrieved March 26, 2017, from http://www.outdoorlife.com/blogs/big-buck-zone /2013/10/deer-hunting-success-story.

Edell, Celia. 2016. "Does Feminism Require Vegetarianism or Veganism?" *Everyday Feminism*. Retrieved March 26, 2017, from http://everydayfeminism .com/2016/02/feminism-and-vegetarianism/.

Esping-Andersen, Gøsta. 2006. "Three Worlds of Welfare Capitalism." In Christopher Pierson and Francis Castles (eds.), *The Welfare State Reader*. Cambridge, UK: Polity Press, pp. 160–174.

Federici, Silvia. 2012. *Revolution at Point Zero: Housework, Reproduction, and Feminist Struggle*. Oakland: PM Press.

Free the Slaves. 2015. *Trafficking and Slavery Fact Sheet*. Retrieved March 26, 2017, from https://www.freetheslaves.net/wp-content/uploads/2015/01/FTS_fact sheet-Nov17.21.pdf.

Gaard, Greta. 2013. "Toward a Feminist Postcolonial Milk Studies." *American Quarterly*, 65(3): 595–618.

Gaarder, Erica. 2011. *Women and the Animal Rights Movement*. Piscataway, NJ: Rutgers University Press.

Gilman, Charlotte. 1911. *Moving the Mountain*. New York: Charlton Company.

Green, Kiddada. 2015. "Open Letter to Medolac Laboratories from Detroit Mothers." *Black Mothers Breastfeeding Association*. Retrieved March 26, 2017, from http://blackmothersbreastfeeding.org/2015/01/open-letter-to -medolac-laboratories-from-detroit-mothers/.

Hall, Lee. 2010. *On Their Own Terms: Bringing Animal-Rights Philosophy Down to Earth*. Darien, CT: Nectar Bat Press.

International Hunter Education Association. 2016. *Incident Reports 2002 to 2007*. Retrieved March 26, 2016, from http://www.ihea.com/news-and-events /news/incident-reports?id=147.

Jacques, Jessica. 2015. "The Slaughterhouse, Social Disorganization, and Violent Crime in Rural Communities." *Society & Animals*, 23: 594–612.

Jasper, James. 2011. "Emotions and Social Movements: Twenty Years of Theory and Research." *Annual Review of Sociology*, 37: 285–303.

Jeffreys, Shelia. 2008. *The Industrial Vagina: The Political Economy of the Global Sex Trade*. New York: Routledge.

jones, pattrice. 2014a. *The Oxen at the Intersection: A Collision*. Brooklyn, NY: Lantern Books.

jones, pattrice. 2014b. "Eros and the Mechanisms of Eco-Defense." In Carol Adams and Lori Gruen (eds.), *Ecofeminism: Feminist Intersections with Other Animals & the Earth*. New York: Bloomsbury Academic, pp. 91–106.

Joshel, S. 1986. "Nurturing the Master's Child: Slavery and the Roman Child-Nurse." *Signs*, 12 (1); 3–22.

Joyce, Kathryn. 2013. *The Child Catchers: Rescue, Trafficking, and the New Gospel of Adoption*. New York: Public Affairs.

Kemmerer, Lisa. 2011. "Introduction." In Lisa Kemmerer and Carol Adams (eds.), *Sister Species: Women, Animals and Social Justice*. Chicago: University of Illinois Press, pp. 1–44.

Kheel, Marti. 1993. "From Heroic to Holistic Ethics." In Greta Gaard (ed.), *Ecofeminism: Ethics and Action*. Philadelphia: Temple University, pp. 243–271.

Kheel, Marti. 1995. "License to Kill: An Ecofeminist Critique of Hunters' Discourse." In Carol Adams and Josephine Donovan (eds.), *Animals and Women: Feminist Theoretical Explorations*. Durham, NC: Duke University Press, pp. 85–125.

Kimmela Center for Animal Advocacy. 2016. "A Mob by Any Other Name." Retrieved March 26, 2017, from http://www.kimmela.org/2016/02/18/a-mob-by-any-other-name.

Lakoff, Robin. 2004. *Language and Woman's Place: Text and Commentaries.* New York: Oxford University Press.

Light, Melanie. 2014. *The Herd.* Eat Your Heart Out Films, UK.

Lindemann, P., I. Foshaugen, and R. Lindemann. 2004. "Characteristics of Breast Milk and Serology of Women Donating Breast Milk to a Milk Bank." *Archives of Disease in Childhood,* 89(5): F440–F441.

Löwy, Michael. 2015. *Ecosocialism: A Radical Alternative to Capitalist Catastrophe.* Chicago: Haymarket Books.

Luke, Brian. 2007. *Brutal: Manhood and the Exploitation of Animals.* Champaign, IL: University of Illinois Press.

Lyon, Laurie. 2007. "What Is a Freemartin?" *The Cattle Site.* Tulsa, OK: Oklahoma Cooperative Extension Service. Retrieved on March 26, 2017, from http://www.thecattlesite.com/articles/975/what-is-a-freemartin/.

MacKinnon, Catharine. 1989. *Toward a Feminist Theory of the State.* Cambridge, MA: Harvard University Press.

MacKinnon, Catharine. 2004. "Of Mice and Men: A Feminist Fragment on Animal Rights." In Cass Sunstein and Martha Nussbaum (eds.), *Animal Rights: Current Debates and New Directions.* Oxford, UK: Oxford University Press, pp. 263–274.

Miall, C. 1986. "The Stigma of Involuntary Childlessness." *Social Problems,* 33(4): 268–282.

Moran, Rachel. 2013. *Paid For: My Journey Through Prostitution.* New York: W. W. Norton & Company.

Nibert, David. 2013. *Animal Oppression and Human Violence: Domesecration, Capitalism, and Global Conflict.* New York: Columbia University Press.

99% Invisible. "Milk Carton Kids." Episode 181. Retrieved from http://99percentinvisible.org/episode/milk-carton-kids/.

Noble, Bobby. 2012. "Trans. Panic. Some Thoughts toward a Theory of Feminist Fundamentalism." In Anne Enke (ed.), *Transfeminist Perspectives: In and Beyond Transgender and Gender Studies.* Philadelphia: Temple University Press, pp. 45–59.

Noske, Barbara. 1989. *Humans and Other Animals: Beyond the Boundaries of Anthropology.* Winchester, MA: Pluto Press.

Parkin, Katherine. 2004. "The Sex of Food and Ernest Dichter: The Illusion of Inevitability." *Advertising & Society Review,* 5(2).

Pearson, H. 2006. "Health Effects of Egg Donation May Take Decades to Emerge." *Nature,* 442: 607–608.

Pollack, Andrew. 2015. "Breast Milk Becomes a Commodity, with mothers Caught Up in Debate." *The New York Times.* Retrieved March 26, 2017, from http://www.nytimes.com/2015/03/21/business/breast-milk-products-commercialization.html.

Prettyman, Brett. 2010. "Spring Hunt: Wild Turkey, Something to Gobble About." *Salt Lake Tribune.* Retrieved March 26, 2017, from http://archive.sltrib.com/story.php?ref=/outdoors/ci_14976677.

Prokhovnik, R. 1998. "Public and Private Citizenship: From Gender Invisibility to Feminist Inclusiveness." *Feminist Review,* 60(Autumn): 84–104.

Robnett, Belinda. 1997. *How Long? How Long? African-American Women in the Struggle for Civil Rights.* New York: Oxford University Press.

Saito, Kohei. 2016. "Marx's Ecological Notebooks." *Monthly Review,* 67(9). Retrieved March 26, 2017, from https://monthlyreview.org/2016/02/01/marxs-ecological-notebooks/.

Sans, P., and P. Combris. 2015. "World Meat Consumption Patterns: An Overview of the Last Fifty Years (1961–2011)." *Meat Science,* 109: 106–111.

Schaef, Anne. 1987. *When Society Becomes an Addict.* New York: HarperCollins Publishers.

Schirmer, J. 1989. "'Those Who Die for Life Cannot be Called Dead:' Women and Human Rights Protest in Latin America." *Feminist Review,* 32: 3–28.

Selders, A. n.d. "Artificial Insemination Breeding Chute." *Dairy Integrated Reproductive Management,* IRM-13. The Cooperative Extension Service.

Simon, David. 2013. *Meatonomics.* San Francisco: Conari Press.

Smith, Andrea. 2007. "Introduction." In INCITE! Women of Color Against Violence (ed.), *The Revolution Will Not Be Funded: Beyond the Non-Profit Industrial Complex.* Cambridge, MA: South End Press, pp. 1–20.

Stone, Linda and Caroline James. 1995. "Dowry, Bride-Burning, and Female Power in India." *Women's Studies International Forum,* 18(2): 125–134.

Taylor, Verta. 1999. "Gender and Social Movements; Gender Processes in Women's Self-Help Movements." *Gender & Society,* 13(1): 8–33.

Twine, France. 2016. *Outsourcing the Womb: Race, Class, and Gestational Surrogacy in a Global Market,* 2d ed. New York: Routledge.

U.S. Department of State. 2013. *Trafficking in Persons Report.* Retrieved March 26, 2017, from http://www.state.gov/j/tip/.

Wertz, Dorothy. 1984. "Women and Slavery: A Cross-Cultural Perspective." *International Journal of Women's Studies,* 7(4): 372–384.

Wilder, Craig. 2013. *Ebony and Ivy: Race, Slavery, and the Troubled History of America's Universities.* New York: Bloomsbury Press.

Woodruff, Mandi. 2013. "Here's How Much It Would Cost to Replace Your Mom." *Business Insider.* Retrieved March 26, 2017, from http://www.businessinsider.com/value-of-stay-at-home-moms-2013-5.

Wrenn, Corey. 2011. "Resisting the Globalization of Speciesism: Vegan Abolitionism as a Site for Consumer-Based Social Change." *Journal for Critical Animal Studies,* 9(3): 9–27.

Wrenn, Corey. 2016. *A Rational Approach to Animal Rights: Extensions in Abolitionist Theory.* London: Palgrave Macmillan.

Wrenn, Corey. Forthcoming. "The Land of Meat and Potatoes? Exploring Ireland's Vegan and Vegetarian Foodscape." *Encyclopedia for Cultural and Social Studies on Vegetarianism and Veganism.* Vienna: University of Vienna.

Zimbardo, Philip. and Nikita Coulombe. 2012. *The Demise of Guys: Why Boys Are Struggling and What We Can Do About It.* Amazon.

10

Nonhuman Animal Metaphors and the Reinforcement of Homophobia and Heterosexism

Luis Cordeiro-Rodrigues

Homophobia and heterosexism are two phenomena present in most contemporary societies. In this article, *homophobia* is understood as "fear, unreasonable anger, intolerance or/and hatred towards homosexuality" (ILGA–Europe 2013). *Heterosexism* is defined as the discriminatory system that targets gays, lesbians, and bisexuals; this includes, for example, unequal marriage laws that allow different sex couples to marry but not same-sex couples. Portugal is an example of a country where many individuals are homophobic and that operates a heterosexist system. Even though it has made some advances in institutionalizing the rights of sexual minorities, there is still significant discrimination towards gays, lesbians, and bisexuals (A. C. Santos 2012). In this article, I have two objectives. The first objective is to describe a representational schema that predominates in homophobia towards gay and bisexual men in Portugal. I will defend that this representational schema strongly relies on casting gays and bisexuals in the image of nonhuman animals. This is noticeable in the kind of metaphors used to insult gay and bisexual men in Portugal. Hence, my argument is that homophobia towards gay and bisexual men is expressed through images of nonhuman animality. The parallel is insulting for gay and bisexual men to the extent that it aims to dehumanize them. The second objective is to argue that the homophobic metaphors used reinforce a heterosexist system in relation to gay and bisexual men in the areas of family law, health, and violence. The reason why they do so is because these metaphors express the same kind of prejudice that is used to justify discrimination in these aforementioned areas.

By defending this, I do not mean to claim that homophobia and heterosexism in Portugal can be reduced to nonhuman animal imagery of gays and bisexuals. The point is rather to demonstrate that images of nonhuman animality have been largely neglected in the conceptualization of homophobia and heterosexism in Portugal, even though these images play an important role in homophobia in the Portuguese context.

A question that may come up is why I do not also focus on lesbians and transgendered individuals, as most LGBT social movements address the struggles of these individuals as a group, and there does seem to be a connection between these forms of oppression. The reason why I do not include lesbians is because the kind of nonhuman animal slurs used to insult them in Portugal are, broadly speaking, the same as those used to denigrate heterosexual women. This suggests that the conceptualization of discrimination towards lesbian women is more akin to the sexism women suffer than in general than the case of discrimination here. In fact, the kind of discrimination men and women suffer, independent of their sexual orientation, is fundamentally different (Benatar 2012). There are, of course, similarities, but my point is that given the distinct form of insults used against gay and bisexual men, for which a different case study is needed .

There are at least two reasons why I do not include transgender individuals in this article. First, while the normative challenges arising for gays and bisexuals are related to having a sexual orientation towards the same-sex, in the case of transgender, the normative challenges result from a gender identity conflict. Second, in general terms, the interests of transgender individuals are distinct from the interests of gay and bisexual men. Some of these interests include an interest in changing one's official name, having aesthetic operations, changing one's own sexual organ, among other interests (ILGA-Europe, 2013). As a consequence of these different demands, the sentiment against transgender individuals is different from those against bisexual and gay men.

This chapter is organized as follows. In the first section, I contend that in capitalist societies, such as Portugal, nonhuman animals are valued for their utility value for human beings. This generates a tripartite typology of other animals: "domesticated," "wild," and "liminal." In this typology, the ones at the top of the rank with the highest utility value are "domesticated animals," then comes "wild animals," with "liminal animals" situated at the end. In the second section, I defend the idea that metaphors are not only revealing of how individuals perceive social reality, but they also have cognitive functions; that is, they influence how individuals perceive the world. In the third section, I contend that using nonhuman animal metaphors is a way to dehumanize and "other" individuals, and I explain how such metaphors are used in Portugal to refer to gay and bisexual men. Finally, in the fourth section, I demonstrate how the nonhuman animal metaphors mentioned in the previous section perpetuate instances of homophobia and heterosexism towards gay and bisexual men in the areas of family law, health care, and physical and psychological violence. In short, my argument is that metaphors are a form of legitimizing discrimination in family law, health, and a form of self-justification for acts of violence against gay and bisexual men.

A TRIPARTITE NONHUMAN ANIMAL TYPOLOGY

Capitalism is a mark of the contemporary West. Western society, Portugal included, is embedded in the economic system of capitalism (B. de S. Santos 2014; Sennett 2007). Capitalist societies have specific cultures (Gramsci 2012), and in such a culture, everything and everyone tends to become commoditized (Robbins 2004). Commodification means that the value of each person or object in a capitalist society is assigned and perceived as a utility value. In other words, in a society with a capitalist culture, the perceived value of everything—things and persons—tends to be dependent on its instrumental value. The reason why this is the case is because the incentives for action are routinely associated with the instrumental value of the goal of that action.

The same logic applies to nonhuman animals. In contemporary Western societies, including Portugal, nonhuman animals are primarily defined according to their economic relation to economic agents (human beings) and how these perceive other animals' utility value (Stewart and Cole 2009). Those nonhuman animals who are perceived as useful for humans are accorded high utility value, whereas other animals that are perceived as being somehow harmful are assigned a low value (Francione 1995; Stewart and Cole 2009).

Humans, as a result of this commodification, generate nonhuman animal typologies (Benton 1996; Stewart and Cole 2009; Donaldson and Kymlicka 2013). The dynamics of these typologies are explained below from a contemporary Western perspective. However, it is important to bear in mind that these typologies are contingent and socially constructed and therefore culturally and historically variable (Stewart and Cole 2009).

With regard to the socially assigned utility given to nonhuman animals, it can be stated that these can be categorized in a tripartite typology.

234 Animal Oppression and Capitalism

Namely, this typology divides other animals into "domesticated, wild and liminal animals" (Donaldson and Kymlicka 2013). Each category is usually assigned different levels of utility.

"Domesticated animals" are the ones that are given higher utility and are those nonhuman animals whose preferences throughout history have been manipulated by humans so they can best serve human interests. This process, involving substantial violation of other animals' negative and positive freedoms, has led these beings to have, broadly speaking, docile bodies and behaviors, which make them follow human interests rather than their own. This category of nonhuman animals includes "pets" such as cats and dogs and farmed animals such as cows, pigs, and chickens. Dogs offer the most illustrative case of how these nonhuman animals' behaviors have been manipulated. Indeed, many breeds of dog have been routinely caged, beaten, and selectively bred throughout history so that they can transform in ways that meet humans' interests (Donaldson and Kymlicka 2013). The reason why these other animals are given higher utility status is because obviously they fulfill humans' interests more often. Farmed animals meet human interests because they are used for food (Leach 1989), while "pets" have affective functions they can fulfill in a human-dominated household (Stewart and Cole 2009). Hence, due to the fact that these other animals play such important functions in contemporary Portuguese society, they are given high levels of utility.[1]

The nonhuman animals that receive, generally speaking, the second level of higher utility value are "wild animals." From a Western perspective, these are normally other animals who live in communities separate from human communities, are autonomous, and do not normally wish to mix with humans (Donaldson and Kymlicka 2013). Some examples of these nonhuman animals are lions, elephants, tigers, and giraffes. The utility attributed to these nonhuman animals in the West has to do mainly with two core ideas. Firstly, the utility resulting from the touristic value that these other animals offer; that is, they are perceived as commodities that are valuable for the aesthetic pleasure given to those who watch them in nature parks, zoos, safaris in the wild, and so forth (Cole and Stewart 2014). Secondly, utility is assigned to these nonhuman animals because they are perceived as having a close link with the highly socially valued ideology of ecological conservation. In the West, what is routinely the most socially convincing argument for protecting other animals is that this is all part of protecting the ecosystem and the diversity of species (Kim 2015). "Wild animals," like the ones mentioned above, are often socially perceived as important in the preservation of ecosystems and are valued because of this.

Finally, the nonhuman animals that are socially given less value are often "liminal animals," like rats, deer, raccoons, spiders, insects in general, and snakes (Donaldson and Kymlicka 2013). "Liminal animals" are those that live in human communities but are not "domesticated." Rather, they are "wild animals" living amongst humans. Although they share the same geographical space, they routinely avoid human contact. Thus, these other animals have an in-between status, that is, between "wild animals" and "domesticated animals" (Donaldson and Kymlicka 2013). These beings are usually victims of stigma and are often considered invaders of human territory who do not have the right to live within human communities (Donaldson and Kymlicka 2013). In fact, this can be noticed not only by the lack of legal protections in place to defend these nonhuman animals, but also through the campaigns of mass extermination carried out against them. Legally speaking, there is no legislation with regard to limiting humans harming rats, snakes, and similar nonhuman animals. This contrasts with the status of "wild and domesticated animals" that, comparatively speaking, are significantly more protected from human harm (Schaffner 2010). "Liminal animals" are thus absolute pariahs of the legal system. On top of this, humans regularly engage in campaigns including trapping, expelling, poisoning, and creating a variety of lethal barriers to constrain these other animals from entering human territory (Donaldson and Kymlicka 2013).

To sum up, in contemporary capitalist Western society, which includes the Portuguese social reality, nonhuman animals are commoditized, and this is substantiated by a tripartite typology that ranks them according to their utility value to humans. Routinely, the social value given to "domesticated animals" is quite high, that for "wild animals" is medium, and for "liminal animals," the value is low. I have contended that this typology includes, by order of higher to lower utility assigned, "domesticated, wild, and liminal animals."

CULTURE, LANGUAGE, AND CONCEPTUAL METAPHOR THEORY IN OTHERING

Human beings are cultural beings. This means that the groups with which humans socialize provide an epistemological basis on which to understand the world and a normative groundwork for acting within it. Epistemologically speaking, the cultural environment influences individuals' mode of reasoning, evaluating, and expressing (Young 2011). The way the world is perceived strongly depends on what one is taught in one's own culture. For example, a man who engages in polygamy in a Bantu culture is routinely perceived to be someone who is helping the community flourish because various aspects of such a culture encourage polygamy (Metz 2007). Contrastingly, in Western society, a man who is polygamous is likely to be considered disrespectful of women's rights, and, indeed, the practice is illegal in most Western countries (Morin 1996). By affirming that culture

provides the normative groundwork for acting, I mean that culture is important for one's practical identity, that is "those features of a person that
ground at least some of their reasons to act" (Festenstein 2005, 10). Therefore, social relations are a "source, or at least an important source, of a
person's values and commitments" (Festenstein 2005, 14). Culture is,
therefore, semiotic. As Benhabib explains (2002, 3) "affirming that culture
is semiotic means that it is a totality of social systems and practices of sig-
nification, representation and symbolism that have an autonomous logic of
their own."

A fundamental aspect of culture is language (Taylor 1992; Kymlicka
1996). In fact, there is a positive correlation between the strength of group
membership and conformity to linguistic habits. It is important to emphasize that language is not a neutral mechanism for communication, where
individuals deliver or receive straightforward and objective information
(Mitchell 2011). Rather, language always contains an element of ideology
and is inevitably embedded in understandings of the world (Dijk 2008; Fairclough 2010). Consequently, language has the capacity to construct reality
and, indeed, is one of the main means of doing so. In particular, language
can create representations of reality, thereby constructing and constituting
the world with meaning (Fairclough 2010). Thus, individuals' perceptions
and evaluations of the world are strongly shaped by language. For example,
language can stimulate moral disengagement (Bandura 1999; Bandura et al.
1996; Mitchell 2011). If one describes the same event using different words
and forms of agency, the way the message is received by the receiver dif-
fers. Imagine, for example, that the *Charlie Hebdo* attacks were described
in the two different ways:

1.   Islamic terrorists kill again in secular France.

2.   Hate speech journalists finally get what they deserve.

These two descriptions are reporting the same event, but the meaning
perceived by the reader is completely different. In proposition 1, agency is
placed with Islamic terrorism, and the word "again" signals that the agent
is someone who routinely engages in such acts, attributing the agent a certain characteristic. Proposition 2, on the other hand, has no reference to
Islamic terrorism and puts all emphasis in the kind of speech *Charlie Hebdo*
engaged with and criticizes such a posture. Hence, the same message can
be significantly different, influencing the receiver of the message in various important ways. As this example demonstrates, language shapes the
thought patterns on which actions are based and events can take on very
different appearances depending on the kind of lexicon used (Bandura et al.
1996; Mitchell 2011).

The reason why language can be so powerful is because human beings
are self-interpreting animals who form their identities dialogically (Taylor

1992). By self-interpreting animals, I mean that individuals' identities depend on the way each individual sees himself/herself. By "dialogical nature" I mean that individuals are continuously formed through conversation with their significant others, with this occurring against a wider linguistic background (Taylor 1992).

Metaphors are one of the main mechanisms of language that are not only revealing of what people think but also have the potential to shape individuals' epistemology and normative beliefs (Lakoff 1981; Deignan 2003; Rodríguez 2009; Kilyeni and Silaški 2014). A *metaphor* can be defined as a figure of speech that identifies something as being the same as another unrelated thing, with the objective of highlighting the similarities between the two.

Contemporary developments in conceptual metaphor theory (CMT) suggest, however, that metaphors are not simply a figure of speech used to add rhetorical flourishes. According to CMT, metaphors are deeply embedded in individuals' way of conceptualizing the world. Consequently, metaphorical linguistic expressions result from the underlying conceptual metaphors that structure individuals' thinking (Lakoff 1981; Kilyeni and Silaški 2014). Hence, metaphors make up part of a central cognitive and representational process. They are not only revealing of what individuals actually think, but they also construct the social reality influencing individuals' perception of the world and actions (Lakoff 1981; Nunberg, Sag, and Wasow 1994; Kilyeni and Silaški 2014).

Indeed, metaphors have been shown to be a quite effective way of othering individuals. In this article, I understand *othering* as a process of exclusion from social and economic institutions of a group that portrays the members of this group as fundamentally different or alien from the ones classifying it. Put differently, *othering* occurs when two groups are classified in juxtaposed ways and classified as opposites, using binary categories that are perceived as the defining categories of the group (Said 2003; Fanon 2008; Al-Saji 2010). In this juxtaposition, one group is classified with positive characteristics and the other with the opposite negative ones. Therefore, part of the process is to essentialize and crystallize differences between the groups by making the identities of the members of the groups inherently relational, that is, to the extent they depend on a dialectical opposition to another identity (Dossa 2002, 2005). Metaphors can participate in the othering process by offering a window into the construction of social identities (Rodríguez 2009). There are mainly two reasons why metaphors can contribute to the othering process. First, they are channels of folk beliefs and thereby convey biases in favor of particular social groups and in detriment of other groups (Lakoff 1981; Deignan 2003; Rodríguez 2009). Second, othering is primarily done through the linguistic manipulation of reality (Dijk 2008; Fairclough 2010).

NONHUMAN ANIMALITY, NONHUMAN ANIMAL METAPHORS, AND DEHUMANIZATION

Harmful conduct is not an ordinary human behavior (Bandura et al. 1996). Rather, humans tend to follow their conscience in everyday actions (Kukathas 2007). Contrastingly, if humans engage in harmful behavior to others, they tend to rationalize what they have done in moral terms. That is, harmful conduct is usually accompanied with a moral explanation of what was done to justify the harm (Bandura et al. 1996; Osofsky, Bandura, and Zimbardo 2005). One of the strategies of moral justification is the dehumanization of the individual being harmed. The reason is that if the one being harmed is perceived as similar, this usually triggers an empathetic emotional response, through perceived similarity; this in turn triggers a sense of social obligation (Osofsky, Bandura, and Zimbardo 2005). Contrastingly, the dehumanization of the individual being harmed enables the person judging to shut down their emotional response; this is due to the fact that the individual being harmed is perceived as a subject without feelings, who does not feel pain or have aspirations (Mitchell 2011; Osofsky, Bandura, and Zimbardo 2005; Osofsky, Bandura, and Zimbardo 2005).

Throughout history, nonhuman animal metaphors have proved an effective and common way to dehumanize others. This has largely happened to dehumanize those who deviate from being white, middle class and male (Rattansi 2007). In other words, women, the working class, and non-whites have routinely been dehumanized by the use of nonhuman animal metaphors. Women, for example, are very often objectified in similar ways to nonhuman animals (Adams 2010; Wyckoff 2014). Women and their body parts are very often definitionally absent through being misnamed and, therefore, objectified (Adams 2010). For example, a vagina is referred to as "pussy" or "kitty," and women are sometimes called a "cow" or bitch (Rodríguez 2009). Blacks have routinely been compared to apes, and this comparison has been used to unfairly justify slavery, discrimination, and oppression (Rattansi 2007). Equally, racists have frequently characterized Chinese culture as "animalistic," and this has been instrumental for perpetuating hatred towards Chinese (Kim 2015). In Victorian times, interactions with nonhuman animals were a critical part of a middle-class agenda to dehumanize the working class (Deckha 2013). To be precise, the upper class's treatment of "companion animals" was characterized as humane in contrast with the working class's interaction with these other animals, which was characterized as "animalistic" and, thereby, inferior (Deckha 2013).

In the Portuguese language, the dehumanization of gay and bisexual men is also, in part, substantiated through nonhuman animal metaphors. Below, I outline and explain the meanings and connotations of such metaphors used in the Portuguese language and then explain how these contribute to the perpetuation of homophobia and heterosexist injustices. As will become clear, most metaphors refer to "liminal animals," although there are two exceptions to this.

One of the most common terms by which to refer to gay men is *bicha*, which means "beast." *Bicha* means a gay man who is extremely effeminate and promiscuous. The term can also mean "bitch" (Dictionaries 2012). The metaphor seems to be motivated by the stereotypical image of dogs being promiscuous (Cacciari, Massironi, and Corradini 2004). In fact, the term "dogging" is an Anglicism used in Portuguese to refer to sexual intercourse in public. Additionally, *canzana*, which means "doggy style" is the name of a sexual position in the Portuguese language. Thus, there is a figurative meaning of connecting gays and bisexuals with promiscuity and reducing bisexual and gay identity to their sexuality (Cacciari, Massironi, and Corradini 2004).

The only non-"liminal animal" word used to describe gay men, besides the connotation of the slur *bicha*, is *porca*. *Porca* literally means pig (Dictionaries 2012). In Portuguese, *porca* is used metaphorically, implying promiscuity and dirtiness. Most likely, this idea of promiscuity derives from "the symbolism which associates cleanliness with purity and dirtiness with immorality" (Cacciari, Massironi, and Corradini 2004). Hence, a reinforcement of the stereotypical view of gays as promiscuous and same-sex intercourse as dirty is implied by means of the figurative use of the nonhuman animal name.

Another category of slurs designed to offend gay men is insect names, insects also being "liminal animals." These include "damselfly" and "butterfly." In the Western social imagination, insects are normally considered annoying and sometimes gruesome, they have little utility for humans, and usually individuals wish to simply exterminate them. Thus, the connotation is that gays are also annoying, gruesome, and useless. Hence, this latter connotation hints at the idea of displacement and despicability, therefore, reducing gays to the category of pariahs. Another two slurs used to refer to gay men are *viado* and *gazela*, which can be translated as "deer" and "gazelle,"[2] respectively (Dictionaries 2012). Once more, the terms refer to "liminal animals," those normally conceived as "pests." As a result, there is a figurative use in the metaphor trying to suggest gay individuals are also "pests."

Finally, another category of insults directed at gay men are those that over-sexualize them by simply referring to them as performers of oral sex for other men. Three terms are used like this: *chupa-cobras*, *mama-cobras*, and *chupa-lesmas*. The first two can be translated as "snake-sucker" and the latter as "slug-sucker." These descriptions over-sexualize gays to the extent that they define them simply as oral sex performers. That is, gay men are described as having a defining feature and that is performing oral sex for other men. There is, thereby, a reinforcement of this stereotypical view of the idea that gay men's actions are fully motivated by sexual desire (Sullivan 2003). On top of this, given the use of the words "snake" and "slug," there are elements of disgust and uselessness embedded in the metaphor. For in the social imagination, these nonhuman animals are "liminal animals" that are considered both disgusting and useless to humans.

Bisexual men are also victims of these slurs outlined above, but terms that refer only to bisexual men have a different element; namely, the element of characterizing bisexuals as sexually ambiguous and confused. "Caracol" which means snail is a slur used to offend bisexuals because it hints at sexual ambiguity, given that snails are hermaphrodites. Equally, the term *barata tonta*, which can be translated as "confused cockroach," also suggests sexual ambiguity. Additionally, as cockroaches and snails are usually considered disgusting by many people, the usage of this term also suggests that such men are despised for their ambiguity, bringing an element of disgust in relation to bisexual individuals.

To summarize, my aim in this section has been to describe a representational schema that predominates in hate discourses towards gays and bisexuals that is carried out in contemporary Portuguese society. It is quite common in the Portuguese language to come across metaphors presenting gays, lesbians, and bisexuals in the guise of nonhuman animals such as snakes or insects. Given that metaphors are a window on how individuals perceive social identities, it can be affirmed that speakers of Portuguese frequently understand sexual orientation differences in terms of nonhuman animal imagery. In other words, if one accepts that metaphors play a cognitive and social role in our understanding of the world, as defended in the previous section, the examples of slurs just outlined illustrate that there is a strong reference to nonhuman animality in hate speech towards gays and bisexuals.

DECODING THE HOMOPHOBIA AND HETEROSEXISM WITHIN NONHUMAN ANIMAL METAPHORS

Having described the representational schema that links hate speech towards gays and bisexuals and images of nonhuman animality, in this section I wish to contend that the use of these metaphors plays a constitutive role in many homophobic narratives in Portugal. This is because they perpetuate current forms of heterosexist injustice present in the Portuguese context. These metaphors contribute to the creation of an image of gays and bisexuals as a kind of constitutive outside (Butler 2006), which helps to sustain the exclusionary function played by this representation. Thus, the metaphors simultaneously structure the ways in which gay and bisexuals are represented and perceived, while also describing the ways in which heterosexist privilege divides bodies politically, economically, spatially, and socially in order to exploit and subvert them. In other words, these homophobic metaphors are not merely accidental, but they sustain a logic of heterosexist dominance. In advancing this argument, my claim is not that homophobia and heterosexism in Portugal are only sustained by nonhuman animal metaphors, nor do I wish to discount the roles played by other important factors. Instead, I wish to explore the role of these metaphors in heterosexist discourse in the Portuguese context. To show this, I will proceed via three steps. Firstly, I will briefly outline what homophobia and heterosexism are. Then, I will contextualize the gay and bisexual rights struggles in Portugal as carried out by LGBT social movements.[3] Thirdly, I will link these with critical metaphor theory in the previous sections.

Homophobia can be defined as hatred, fear, or unreasonable anger and intolerance towards same-sex couples. These emotions, in turn, are what often cause heterosexism. *Heterosexism* can be defined as a form of discrimination that, in a variety of ways, favors individuals with a heterosexual sexual orientation over lesbian, gay, and bisexual individuals. Hence, heterosexism places heterosexual people or relationships as superior to non-heterosexual ones. Heterosexism occurs when state institutions are organized around heterosexual sexual orientation and in a way whereby homosexual relations are outlawed or less valued. In a heterosexist society, it may be the case that legal, social, psychiatric, educational, and familial institutions directly or indirectly assume and promote heterosexual relationships (Calhoun 1994; Calhoun 1995; Calhoun 2003). I am referring to heterosexism as a phenomenon that appears at the institutional level when there are public institutions that correspond to heterosexuals' identity but not homosexuals; these institutions ensure that relationships, directly or indirectly, will be built around male-female pairing (Calhoun 1994; Calhoun 2003; Herek 2004). For example, a society where heterosexual marriage is legal but same-sex marriage is illegal is a heterosexist one. Therefore, in a heterosexist system, there is heterosexual privilege; everyday and institutional advantages and rights that systematically empower heterosexuals over homosexuals.

Even though contemporary heterosexism is widespread and often shows in broadly similar patterns across Europe, the Americas, and Australia (Herek 2004; McCann, Minichiello, and Plummer 2009), the shape of heterosexism varies slightly according to culture, geography, and historical context, among other factors (Mondimore 1996; Herdt 1998; Fone 2001). Consequently, the Portuguese struggle for gay and bisexual rights has its specificities. An informative way to understand heterosexism in the Portuguese context is by looking into the agenda of the Portuguese LGBT rights movements and what they have prioritized as urgent problems. Social movements can provide an important insight in this matter because such movements emerge as a reaction to what is perceived as injustice. Therefore, social movements can be revealing of how societies are structured (A. C. Santos 2012; Pellow 2014).

With respect to the rights of gay and bisexual men, Portuguese LGBT movements have prioritized and concentrated mainly on addressing and campaigning against three forms of heterosexism; namely, these are heterosexism in family law, in health care, and in violence against gay and bisexual individuals (A. C. Santos 2012).[4]

In the arena of family law, LGBT activist groups in Portugal have mainly focused on legalizing same-sex marriage and the access of same-sex parents to the adoption of children (A. C. Santos 2012). The former was achieved in 2010, while campaigns to achieve the latter have only been successful in 2016. A good number of the campaigns have focused on demystifying various forms of prejudice about gay and bisexual men that have the discursive function of justifying discrimination in these areas (A. C. Santos 2012). Regarding same-sex marriage, activists have been focusing on demystifying the idea that same-sex relationships are unstable, impermanent, promiscuous and non-monogamic (A. C. Santos 2012). A significant part of the objection to the institutionalization of same-sex marriage in Portugal has been that same-sex relationships, especially between males, consist mostly of sporadic sexual encounters and often with multiple partners (A. C. Santos 2012). This discourse, however, characterizes same-sex relationships in a way that sustains homophobic discourse to the extent that it justifies discrimination on the basis of affirming a radical difference in how relationships are structured.

The discourse against same-sex parents' adoption in Portugal has followed a similar arc, characterizing gays and bisexuals as too incompetent to be child caregivers. Against the right for same-sex parents to adopt, three arguments have been prominent. Firstly, it is argued that because of the instability of same-sex relationships, children adopted by gay and bisexual parents would be emotionally affected. Hence, the rationale used is that the sexual and sporadic nature of same-sex relationships is unwelcoming and unstable for children. Secondly, it has been argued that children experiencing same-sex parenting will also turn out gay or lesbian, and this is undesirable. Thirdly, those opposed of same-sex adoption in Portugal contend that children need a father and a mother, rather than two fathers or two mothers, to grow up healthy (A. C. Santos 2012). As a result of such discourse, LGBT groups have strongly focused their campaigns on demystifying the ideas that homosexual relationships are unstable, that homosexual parents will necessarily inform the creation of homosexual children, and that two fathers or two mothers cannot jointly raise a healthy child (A. C. Santos 2012).

In the area of health care relating to gay and bisexual men's rights, LGBT activists have focused on campaigning against the association of gay and bisexual individuals with health problems. In Portugal, there is a tendency to associate LGBTs, especially gay and bisexual men, with HIV (A. C. Santos 2012). Consequently, in Portugal, the law does not allow gay and bisexual men to give blood, because they are considered an at-risk group (A. C. Santos 2012). This prejudice has been accompanied and reinforced by many health professionals' prejudiced ideas that homosexuality is a pathology with special consequences for one's sexual behavior (A. C. Santos 2012). As a result, LGBT groups have focused on demystifying the idea that gay and bisexual men engage in riskier sexual behavior than heterosexuals, and that homosexual sexual orientation places individuals in an at-risk health group.

Finally, the third major issue that such campaigns have focused on is violence against these individuals. In Portugal, it is not uncommon for gays and bisexuals to suffer psychological and physical violence (A. C. Santos 2012), with verbal harassment being one of the main ways that gay and bisexual men are attacked. Thus, LGBT rights activists have campaigned strongly for creating the means to report abuse (A. C. Santos 2012).

I contend that all these forms of discrimination are sustained by the nonhuman animal metaphors mentioned in the previous section. To understand this, it is important to recall the idea that language and metaphors have the potential to reveal, sustain and reproduce the social status quo, and, for that reason, can contribute to transforming it. This potential is, of course, dependent on the social-historical context to which language and, in particular, metaphors are used (Dijk 2008; Fairclough 2010; Mitchell 2011). Hence, the metaphors here have the power to sustain heterosexism as a result of the social-historical context in which they are used. The metaphors used by homophobes in Portugal can be said to sustain and perpetuate this kind of prejudice towards gay and bisexual men to the extent that they reiterate and accentuate the forms of prejudice that homophobes use to justify discrimination in the areas of family law, health care and violence. This is done in three ways.

First, the metaphors analyzed in this paper accentuate the heterosexist system to the extent that they stimulate norms of physical disappearance and discursive silence which are prevailing ways of discriminating against gay and bisexual men (Tebble 2011). In other words, the way metaphors accentuate heterosexism is by trying to remove homosexuality from political and legal arenas. In particular, there is a silencing and physical disappearance hinted at in the figurative usage of "liminal animals." These nonhuman animals are absolutely outside the legal system and have no legal status, and this outcast status is exactly what is being pursued with the exclusion of gay and bisexual men from important social institutions, like the family. Put differently, part of what the "liminal animal" metaphors convey is that the moral status of gays and bisexuals is akin to that of these other animals, that is, situated outside the realm of the political and the legal. Also, through their figurative usage, these metaphors suggest a feeling of disgust towards gays and bisexuals. As explained, "liminal animals" are often attributed low utility value and perceived as disgusting. By the usage of slurs such as "snake-sucker," "confused cockroach," and "damselfly," the speaker is conveying a message that associates disgust with bisexuals and gays. Indeed, such a strategy is used in Western discourses to exclude homosexuals from society's legal institutions. Martha Nussbaum (2010), for example, has surveyed various American laws and identified that the rationale behind the exclusion of homosexuals from institutions is not based on reason but instead on the disgust the legislators feel in relation to homosexual acts. In particular, concepts such as dirtiness underlie the rationale for legal exclusion (Nussbaum 2010). Indeed, the exclusion of gays and bisexuals from family laws such as marriage and adoption partly has as a biased rationale, the prejudice that these relations are promiscuous and dirty. Likewise, this rationale is applied to associating them with HIV, pathologizing homosexuality and denying them the right to give blood. As an example of exclusion take the Labouchere Amendment of 1885 in the United Kingdom, where homosexuality was a crime because it was a gross indecency. Another more recent example of this is in Portugal, where gay and bisexual men were not allowed to give blood because they were considered by Portuguese authorities to be individuals who engaged in risky sexual behavior and were considered more likely to have sexually transmitted diseases.

Second, the metaphors sustain a logic of dichotomizing normal and abnormal attributes with the privileging of the former, which is a form of stigmatizing gay and bisexual men (Okin 1996; Herek 2004). They serve the function of abnormalizing gay and bisexual men via the creation of nonhuman animalistic images, with the intention of showing that they are unfit to be members of institutions that heterosexual men are entitled to join, such as marriage, adoption, and social, political, and cultural life. Thus, nonhuman animalization has the purpose of inferiorizing and classifying as abnormal (and thereby pathologizing) gay and bisexual men. This is particularly the case in the classification of gay men as "snake-suckers," as it reduces their identity to a sexual behavior. This strategy of abnormalization validates the current forms of discrimination that gay and bisexual men suffer in Portugal today. Firstly, the idea of abnormality suggests that there is a pathology, which, as explained, is still a way that fosters the discrimination of gay and bisexual men in terms of health care. In particular, the association of gay and bisexual men with abnormal sexual behavior is what is used to justify excluding them from giving blood. Secondly, inferiorization is at the heart of denying family rights to gays and bisexuals. For the reasons to exclude gays and bisexuals from marriage and adoption is that their lifestyles are inferior, and they are thus unqualified to take part in such institutions (Herek 2004).

Third, a significant part of psychological violence is made up of inferiorization through pathologization of what is and what is not normal. Hence, to the extent that these metaphors effeminize gays and bisexuals, they are engaging in psychological violence.

Thirdly, another way that these metaphors dehumanize gay and bisexual men is by degradingly singularizing these individuals to an oral sex act performed or as a solely sexual being. That is, these insults aim at oversexualizing gay and bisexual men through metaphors of nonhuman animalization, interpreting everything that they do in terms of their sexuality. This is clearly the case for the terms "snake-sucker," "slug-sucker," "snail," and "confused cockroach" for such terms reduce gay and bisexual men's agency to sexual agency. As in the previous two instances of heterosexism, this is not accidental. Rather, these slurs are ways to communicate current forms of prejudice that serve to justify exclusion from important institutions. In particular, by reducing gay and bisexual men to their sexuality, these metaphors are reinforcing various forms of prejudice in relation to family law and health care.

In family law, by reducing gays and bisexuals to existing solely as sexual beings, the metaphors substantiate the belief that they live in unstable, love-free and promiscuous sex-only relationships, which, as explained above, is the part of the justification used by heterosexists for justifying their denial of same-sex marriage. Equally, such prejudices extend to denying bisexual and gay men the right to adopt. Here, the fears that arise with regards to gays and bisexuals sexually abusing their children or influencing them into also becoming gay is based on the idea that all their behavior is sexually motivated. Hence, when, for example, a gay man is reduced to being an oral sex performer by the use of a metaphor such as "snake-sucker," the prejudice whereby all gay men's actions are motivated by their sexual orientation is reinforced because the prejudice regarding the right to adopt is the same, then this prejudice is simultaneously reinforced. Likewise, the term "confused cockroach" conveys the message that bisexuals are emotionally unstable and sexually perverse, which is the same kind of discourse as that which limits adoption rights.

Regarding health care, these metaphors reinforce the current prejudice towards gay and bisexual men because the discrimination regarding giving blood is precisely based on the idea that gay and bisexual men are promiscuous, have a pathology, and are more likely to be carrying HIV. To be more exact, metaphors like *bicha*, "snake-sucker" and "pig" convey the message that gays and bisexuals are dirty and promiscuous, which is exactly the same kind of discourse used to justify barring gays and bisexuals from giving blood, pathologizing same-sex intercourse, and associating these individuals with HIV.

To conclude this section, it is important to note the role of the typology in the perpetuation of capitalism. Effective challenges to the capitalist system are undermined by the existence of factions among the working class (Althusser and Bidet 2014; A. F. Gramsci, Hoare, and Nowell-Smith 2005). Prejudice and discrimination against gays and lesbians and their "animalization" by members of the working class serve as a distraction from capitalist-based problems while undermining worker and community solidarity.

CONCLUSION

In this article, I set two objectives. The first objective was to describe part of the representational schema of homophobia that currently exists in relation to gay and bisexual men in Portugal and demonstrate that this is intertwined with images of nonhuman animality. This was shown by using conceptual metaphor theory as a tool by which to analyze insults directed at gay and bisexual men. Owing to the fact that metaphors are a window through which to see how individuals perceive social reality, and that many insults that dehumanize gays and bisexuals are nonhuman animal insults, then I conclude that nonhuman animality, homophobia, and heterosexism, in the Portuguese context, are strongly intertwined. The second objective was to demonstrate that the use of such metaphors is not accidental. Rather, they are used because they sustain current heterosexist institutions in Portugal that disadvantage gay and bisexual men. They do this to the extent that they mirror the discourse regarding bisexual and gay men being entitled to family law, health and antiviolence rights.

Further research should be focused on the idea of total liberation, defended by philosophers like Steven Best (2014) and movements like the Earth Liberation Front (Pellow 2014). The idea of total liberation is that all forms of oppression are linked, so to effectively and consistently address one form of oppression means all others should also be addressed. The reason why this idea should be on the agenda of future research is because what the arguments in this article suggest is a link between speciesism and heterosexism. Other research has demonstrated the links between sexism and racism (hooks 1987; McClintock 1995), sexism and speciesism (Adams 2010; Wyckoff 2014), and so forth. Hence, it is important that research be carried out on a unifying theory of all forms of oppression. Moreover, it is important to find strategies that address all these forms of oppression in their totality.

NOTES

1. Arguably, farmed and "companion" animals may have some differences in utility. The point is, however, that they are at the top of utility scales.

2. These nonhuman animals may seem to be "wild animals" rather than liminal. However, these should be considered liminal because they live amongst humans.

3. These movements have also focused on transgender, intersex, and lesbian rights, but because these are outside of the scope of this paper, I do not mention them here. Hence, while I call them LGBT movements because they also focus on different areas, I only outline the campaigns regarding gay and bisexual men.

4. They have also focused on violence towards transgender, intersex, and lesbian individuals, but these are not critical to understand the point being made in this article.

REFERENCES

Adams, Carol. 2010. *The Sexual Politics of Meat: A Feminist-Vegetarian Critical Theory, 20th Anniversary Edition*. New York and London: Bloomsbury Academic.

Al-Saji, Alia. 2010. "The Racialization of Muslim Veils: A Philosophical Analysis." *Philosophy & Social Criticism*, 36(8): 875–902. doi:10.1177/01914537 10375589.

Althusser, Professor Louis, and Jacques Bidet. 2014. *On the Reproduction of Capitalism: Ideology and Ideological State Apparatuses*. G. M. Goshgarian, trans. Verso Books.

Bandura, Albert. 1999. "Moral Disengagement in the Perpetration of Inhumanities." *Personality and Social Psychology Review*, 3(3): 193–209. doi:10.1207/ s15327957pspr0303_3.

Bandura, Albert, Claudio Barbaranelli, Gian Vittorio Caprara, and Concetta Pastorelli. 1996. "Mechanisms of Moral Disengagement in the Exercise of Moral Agency." *Journal of Personality and Social Psychology*, 71(2): 364–74. doi:10.1037/0022-3514.71.2.364.

Benatar, David. 2012. *The Second Sexism: Discrimination Against Men and Boys*. Malden, MA: Wiley-Blackwell.

Benton, Ted. 1996. *Natural Relations: Ecology, Animal Rights and Social Justice: Animal Rights, Human Rights and the Environment*. London; New York: Verso.

Best, Steven. 2014. *The Politics of Total Liberation: Revolution for the 21st Century*. New York: Palgrave Macmillan.

Butler, Judith. 2006. *Gender Trouble: Feminism and the Subversion of Identity*. New York: Routledge.

Cacciari, Cristina, Manfredo Massironi, and Paola Corradini. 2004. "When Color Names Are Used Metaphorically: The Role of Linguistic and Chromatic Information." *Metaphor and Symbol,* 19(3): 169–190. doi:10.1207/s1532 7868ms1903_1.

Calhoun, Cheshire. 1994. "Separating Lesbian Theory from Feminist Theory." *Ethics,* 104(3): 558–581.

Calhoun, Cheshire. 1995. "The Gender Closet: Lesbian Disappearance under the Sign 'Women.'" *Feminist Studies,* 21(1): 7–34. doi:10.2307/3178313.

Calhoun, Cheshire. 2003. *Feminism, the Family, and the Politics of the Closet: Lesbian and Gay Displacement.* Oxford, UK: Oxford University Press.

Cole, Matthew, and Kate Stewart. 2014. *Our Children and Other Animals: The Cultural Construction of Human-Animal Relations in Childhood.* Farnham, UK, and; Burlington, VT: Ashgate Publishing Company.

Deckha, Maneesha. 2013. "Welfarist and Imperial: The Contributions of Anticruelty Laws to Civilizational Discourse." *American Quarterly,* 65(3): 515–548. doi:10.1353/aq.2013.0033.

Deignan, Alice. 2003. "Metaphorical Expressions and Culture: An Indirect Link." *Metaphor and Symbol,* 18(4): 255–271. doi:10.1207/S15327868MS1804_3.

Dictionaries, Oxford. 2012. *Oxford Essential Portuguese Dictionary.* 2d ed. Oxford: Oxford University Press.

Dijk, A. van. 2008. *Discourse and Power.* Houndmills, UK, and New York: Palgrave Macmillan.

Donaldson, Sue, and Will Kymlicka. 2013. *Zoopolis: A Political Theory of Animal Rights.* Oxford, UK, and New York: Oxford University Press.

Dossa, Shiraz. 2002. "Liberal Imperialism? Natives, Muslims, and Others." *Political Theory,* 30(5): 738–745.

Dossa, Shiraz. 2005. "Bad, Bad Multiculturalism!!." *The European Legacy,* 10(6): 641–644. doi:10.1080/10848770500254191.

Fairclough, Norman. 2010. *Critical Discourse Analysis: The Critical Study of Language.* 2d ed. London: Routledge.

Fanon, Frantz. 2008. *Black Skin, White Masks.* London: Pluto Press.

Fone, Byrne. 2001. *Homophobia: A History.* Reprint edition. New York: Picador.

Francione, Gary. 1995. *Animals Property & The Law.* Philadelphia: Temple University Press.

Gramsci, Antonio. 2012. *Selections from Cultural Writings.* Chicago: Haymarket Books.

Gramsci, Antonio, Quintin Hoare, and Geoffrey Nowell-Smith. 2005. *Selections from the Prison Notebooks of Antonio Gramsci.* London: Lawrence & Wishart Ltd.

Herdt, Gilbert H. 1998. *Same Sex, Different Cultures: Exploring Gay and Lesbian Lives.* Boulder, CO: Westview Press.

Herek, Gregory M. 2004. "Beyond 'Homophobia': Thinking about Sexual Prejudice and Stigma in the Twenty-First Century." *Sexuality Research & Social Policy,* 1(2): 6–24. doi:10.1525/srsp.2004.1.2.6.

hooks, bell. 1987. *Ain't I a Woman—Old Edition: Black Women and Feminism.* London: Pluto Press.

Kilyeni, Annamaria, and Nadežda Silaški. 2014. "Beauty and The Beast from a Cognitive Linguistic Perspective: Animal Metaphors for Women in Serbian and Romanian." *Gender Studies,* 13(1): 163–78.

Kim, Claire Jean. 2015. *Dangerous Crossings: Race, Species, and Nature in a Multicultural Age.* New York: Cambridge University Press.

Kukathas, Chandran. 2007. *The Liberal Archipelago: A Theory of Diversity and Freedom.* Oxford, UK: Oxford University Press.

Kymlicka, Will. 1996. *Multicultural Citizenship: A Liberal Theory of Minority Rights.* Reprint ed. Oxford, UK: Clarendon Press.

Lakoff, George. 1981. *Metaphors We Live By.* Chicago: University of Chicago Press.

Leach, Edmund. 1989. "Anthropological Aspects of Language: Animal Categories and Verbal Abuse." *Anthrozoös,* 2(3): 151–165. doi:10.2752/08927 9389787058055.

McCann, Pól Dominic, Victor Minichiello, and David Plummer. 2009. "Is Homophobia Inevitable? Evidence That Explores the Constructed Nature of Homophobia, and the Techniques Through Which Men Unlearn It." *Journal of Sociology,* 45(2): 201–220. doi:10.1177/1440783309103347.

McClintock, Anne. 1995. *Imperial Leather: Race, Gender, and Sexuality in the Colonial Contest.* New York: Routledge.

Metz, Thaddeus. 2007. "Toward an African Moral Theory." *Journal of Political Philosophy,* 15 (3): 321–341. doi:10.1111/j.1467-9760.2007.00280.x.

Mitchell, Les. 2011. "Moral Disengagement and Support for Nonhuman Animal Farming." *Society and Animals,* 19(1): 38–58. doi:10.1163/156853011X545529.

Mondimore, Francis Mark. 1996. *A Natural History of Homosexuality.* Baltimore: Johns Hopkins University Press.

Morin, Karen Marie. 1996. "Gender, Imperialism, and the Western American Landscapes of Victorian Women Travelers, 1874–1897." *ETD Collection for University of Nebraska—Lincoln,* January, 1–281.

Nunberg, Geoffrey, Ivan A. Sag, and Thomas Wasow. 1994. "Idioms." *Language,* 70(3): 491–538. doi:10.2307/416483.

Nussbaum, Martha. 2010. *From Disgust to Humanity: Sexual Orientation and Constitutional Law.* Oxford, UK; New York: Oxford University Press.

Okin, Susan Moller. 1996. "Sexual Orientation, Gender, and Families: Dichotomizing Differences." *Hypatia,* 11(1): 30–48.

Osofsky, Michael J., Albert Bandura, and Philip G. Zimbardo. 2005. "The Role of Moral Disengagement in the Execution Process." *Law and Human Behavior,* 29(4): 371–393. doi:10.1007/s10979-005-4930-1.

Pellow, David Naguib. 2014. *Total Liberation: The Power and Promise of Animal Rights and the Radical Earth Movement.* Minneapolis: University of Minnesota Press.

Rattansi, Ali. 2007. *Racism: A Very Short Introduction.* New York: Oxford University Press.

Robbins, Richard H. 2004. *Global Problems and the Culture of Capitalism.* 3d ed. Boston: Pearson.

Rodríguez, Irene López. 2009. "Of Women, Bitches, Chickens and Vixens: Animal Metaphors for Women in English and Spanish." *Cultura* 7: 77–100.

Said, Edward W. 2003. *Orientalism*. 25th anniversary edition, with 1995 afterword. London: Penguin Books.

Santos, Ana Cristina. 2012. *Social Movements and Sexual Citizenship in Southern Europe*. Houndmills, UK: Palgrave Macmillan.

Santos, Boaventura de Sousa. 2014. *Portugal: Ensaio Contra a Autoflegelação*. Cortez Editora.

Schaffner, Joan E. 2010. *An Introduction to Animals and the Law*. Houndmills, UK; New York: Palgrave Macmillan.

Sennett, Richard. 2007. *The Culture of the New Capitalism*. New Haven, CT: Yale University Press.

Stewart, Kate, and Matthew Cole. 2009. "The Conceptual Separation of Food and Animals in Childhood." *Food, Culture & Society*, 12(4): 457–476. doi:10.2752/175174409X456746.

Sullivan, Nikki. 2003. *A Critical Introduction to Queer Theory*. New York: New York University Press.

Taylor, Charles. 1992. *Sources of the Self*. Reprint ed. Cambridge, MA: Harvard University Press.

Tebble, Adam James. 2011. "Homosexuality and Publicness: Towards a Political Theory of the Taboo." *Political Studies*, 59(4): 921–939. doi:10.1111/j.1467-9248.2011.00884.x.

Wyckoff, Jason. 2014. "Linking Sexism and Speciesism." *Hypatia*, 29(4): 721–737. doi:10.1111/hypa.12098.

Young, Iris Marion. 2011. *Justice and the Politics of Difference*. With a new foreword by Danielle Allen. Princeton, NJ: Princeton University Press.

Workers of the World. (Copyright © 2016 Sue Coe. Courtesy Galerie St. Etienne, NY)

11

Ideological Monkey Wrenching:
Nonhuman Animal Politics
beyond Suffering

Lauren Corman

This chapter asks critical animal studies scholars, intersectional nonhuman animal advocates, and anyone who recognizes that profit drives the overwhelming majority of violence against other animals to take seriously their exploitation while refusing to reduce nonhuman animal subjectivities to representations of suffering and victimization. This kind of beyond suffering approach, which some advocates and scholars may see as fiddling while Rome burns, is a necessary antidote to capitalist objectification of nonhuman animals. That said, suffering should not be dismissed or neglected in efforts to end exploitation. Rather, we must discuss suffering, but we should do so in conjunction with other, richer versions of other animals' experiences beyond suffering.

This *including but beyond* suffering approach strongly resonates with other social justice movements that have long resisted both the homogenization and the reductionism of various subjects to pure victims. These movements, which have fought hard against dehumanization, recognize that objectification manifests as denial of full or even partial subjectivity and thus exclusion from the realm of full humanity. Objectification, and thus use and violation without recourse, is predicated on the disavowal of full subjectivity, to be rendered, as Gary Francione (2008, 103) argues, "exclusively as means to our ends."

Representations of suffering in the absence of fuller versions of nonhuman animal subjectivity allow stereotypes about other animals to persist, stereotypes necessary for the functioning of capitalism. Indeed, we know that capitalist modes of use and production cause a staggering and historically unprecedented amount of suffering for billions of nonhuman animals globally each year. While some may feel distraught and motivated to act when confronted with the nightmarish suffering endured by other animals, the representation of their suffering alone can also fail to unsettle fundamental assumptions about them, the very assumptions required for the continuation of capitalist industries.

In legal terms, the widespread industrial exploitation of nonhuman animals is predicated on their property status. When we think of "property status" as a stereotype (not just a legal category), one based on inaccurate assumptions about who other animals are and can be, it becomes clear that we must address the layered nature of this stereotyping. Public exposure and even condemnation of other animals' suffering—egregious as that suffering is—by liberationists and rightists can fall too easily into existent welfarist paradigms that concede that nonhuman animals suffer but ultimately imply this suffering is less significant than human suffering.

As many have long noted, "unnecessary suffering," which centrally informs our legal approach to other animals, suggests that some suffering is acceptable. The acknowledgment of suffering, as part of the sociocultural turn toward the recognition of nonhuman animal sentience, grants that we have a moral and ethical (and subsequently legal) obligation to minimize their suffering, yet the *diminished* significance of nonhuman animal suffering relative to human suffering is a core presupposition that underpins nonhuman animal welfare legislation, in which we recognize that other animals suffer and thus legislate the prevention of *unnecessary* suffering while their property status remains intact.

The reorientation I suggest in this chapter serves as a kind of ideological monkey wrenching[1] of nonhuman animal politics, including intersectional approaches. Intersectionality demonstrates how different forms of oppression and domination connect and reinforce each other, yet this focus means that issues of suffering, pain, and violence garner the majority attention, while other animals' experiences beyond their capacity to suffer are oddly obscured or erased; further, coalition-building through intersectionality suggests alliance across communities and identities is forged through resistance to interlocking forms oppression. The *intersections* at the heart of intersectionality demonstrate overlap between different forms of domination. As such, through intersectional nonhuman animal politics, certain forms of subjectivity are privileged (suffering), while others are minimized. This is potentially disadvantageous because the re-articulation of human and nonhuman animal suffering in the public sphere—in which subjectivity is presented as and through suffering—limits a broader challenge to objectification by concentrating on a small yet significant band of experience while neglecting the larger spectrum. In relation, our legal system, which overwhelmingly supports the capitalist exploitation of other animals, in essence claims that society has already acknowledged nonhuman animal suffering and laws (however grossly lacking) exist to minimize this.

Through my experience as a sociology professor expressly hired to teach critical animal studies (CAS), I have repeatedly witnessed that it is far more powerful to combine representations of nonhuman animal suffering with representations of their lives outside of such states and conditions. When taught this way, alongside intersectional analyses that foreground the interlocking nature of oppressions and which illuminate the economic conditions frequently driving such treatment, students are more open to engaging with the brutal realities facing humans, other animals, and the planet. In this way, the insights presented throughout the following chapter are corroborated by seven years of teaching critical animal studies courses in the department of sociology at Brock University. To date, I have taught 26 CAS classes to 1,180 students.[2]

More specifically, throughout the following chapter, I build on the work of legal scholar Taimie Bryant (2007), who offers a compelling critique of suffering-focused nonhuman animal advocacy. Additionally, I build on the research of critical disabilities and nonhuman animal scholar Sunaura Taylor, who likewise notes our preoccupation with suffering. Taylor (2014, 113) argues,

> While disability advocates have often pushed away from narratives of suffering, it is everywhere within animal ethics scholarship. A huge amount of work has been done by animal activists simply to prove that animals can suffer, and much more work has sought to explain why human beings should care about this fact. Suffering is an inevitable part of the conversation around animal industries, as well as around disability within these industries and for good reason. However, animals are too often presented simply as voiceless beings who suffer.

The arguments presented here also extend my previous scholarship (Corman 2012; Corman and Vandrovcová 2014), which centrally critiques the nonhuman animal movements' common claim that other animals are voiceless and that we are their voice, while the question of who other animals are and who they might be has often been neglected within rights and liberation efforts.[3]

This chapter suggests in particular that cognitive ethology[4] is an important complement to suffering-based scholarship, in which researchers focus on nonhuman animals' emotions, sociality, and culture. While some cognitive ethology includes studies in pain and suffering, these scientists offer more complex and specific information about other animals' inner worlds beyond the pain-based preoccupation presented within traditional nonhuman animal ethics and critical animal studies, which has not significantly incorporated this work. Pairing such research with representations of suffering deepens the sense of what is lost when other animals are harmed, extending beyond the physical (and to some extent psychological) pain that has largely been the target of nonhuman animal advocacy: As Jonathan Balcombe (2009) contends, a nonhuman animal's quality of life cannot be adequately measured by the absence of suffering, as other animals seek out and experience pleasure. When we harm and kill other animals, we deny them both current pleasure and the opportunity to experience future pleasure. Similar to Balcombe, other cognitive ethologists who study nonhuman animals' emotionality, sociality, and culturality provide crucial knowledge about their subjective experience and relational dynamics. These are also denied or disrupted when other animals are exploited and killed.

Cognitive ethology is one way to include richer versions of nonhuman animals' subjectivity within intersectional and anti-capitalist dialogue about human-nonhuman animal relations. Testimony from shelter and sanctuary workers, as well as anyone with direct, close, and equitable relations with other animals can also offer important insight into their lives. My own draw to cognitive ethology relates to the field's detailed investigation of nonhuman animal relationships, in conjunction with comparative studies, which help situate various nonhuman animal behaviors within larger ecological and evolutionary patterns. Significantly, I have witnessed the potency of cognitive ethology within my courses, as students often identify with, and are compelled by, research about other animals' lives beyond suffering, including their capacities for play, friendship, and grief, among others.

Overall, this chapter emerges at the intersections of nonhuman animal liberation, critical animal studies, and cognitive ethology, as well as the biological sciences and social sciences. Interspersed throughout this chapter are four vignettes that highlight nonhuman animals' emotionality, sociality, and culturality. The first describes the eye-poking ritual of white-faced capuchin monkeys of Costa Rica. The second considers the cultural impacts of hunting right whale elders. The third reframes humans as dogs' tools. The final vignette describes the friendship of Hope and Johnny, two pigs who lived at Farm Sanctuary. Although it might not be immediately apparent how such stories and cognitive ethology generally are relevant to anti-capitalist struggles, the field has a significant role to play in countering the current cultural hegemony that rationalizes nonhuman animal exploitation.

VIGNETTE ONE: THE EYE-POKING WHITE-FACED CAPUCHINS OF COSTA RICE

A group of white-faced capuchins in Costa Rica participate in an eye-poking game, in which they stick a finger of a partner (up to the first knuckle) into their own eye. Anthropologist Susan Perry (2011, 990) suggests that this and other risky behaviors (such as hair pulling) practiced by the capuchins reaffirm trust between individuals. These conventions signal and test social bonds. Perry argues, "Certainly, C. capucinus has one of the highest rates of coalitionary lethal aggression of conspecifics [members of the same species] found in a mammal, and coalitions are employed in a wide range of contexts. The greater importance of alliances may necessitate a richer source of information about whom to trust." She also notes C. capucinus is a "prime candidate to have social conventions, because these monkeys form coalitions in a wide variety of contexts and are highly dependent on allies to successfully migrate, acquire high rank, and defend their offspring from infanticidal males" (p. 988). Part of what makes this behavior so remarkable is that the convention persists (in low frequencies) despite the death of the innovator.

CALL AND RESPONSE: NONHUMAN ANIMAL LIBERATION AND COGNITIVE ETHOLOGY

The Western nonhuman animal rights and liberation movements have largely structured their resistance to the objectification, commodification, and exploitation of other animals through what legal scholar Taimie Bryant (2007) calls the similarity argument. These arguments attempt to demonstrate how nonhuman animals, or at least certain other animals, are similar enough to human beings in morally relevant ways.

Bryant (2007, 208) contends, "Stated generally, the [similarity] argument is that if animals are similar to humans as to capacities and characteristics of humans that define humans, then animals should receive protections equivalent to the protections of humans because a just society treats like entities alike." As law professor Gary Francione (2010) argues, the typical criteria used to exclude other animals from the sphere of moral concern, capacities such as language or the possession of a soul, are not morally relevant. In practice, the similarity argument has stressed nonhuman animals' sentience, especially focusing on their capacity to suffer.

While this fixation on similarity has made certain political advances and arguably encouraged empathy for other animals, as Bryant notes, there are a number of drawbacks to this approach. For example, when a criterion is identified, is it similar enough to humans? Disturbingly, efforts to answer this question might prompt further nonhuman animal experimentation to prove how other animals suffer in similar or dissimilar ways to people. Such an approach also has the potential to reinforce hierarchical thinking about human and nonhuman animals, with humans maintaining their status at the top of the speciesist pyramid. Despite the problems associated with the similarity argument, the approach follows the same pattern that various social justice movements have used to advance their causes, especially in their early stages (Bryant, 2007), wherein people lacking rights attempt to show how they are like existing rights holders. The similarity argument replicates the formal equality principle, to "treat like cases as like," which has been considered a moral principle of justice.

While recognizing the work that the similarity argument does and can do, it does little to "de-center" the human subject as figured through liberal humanism. As Cary Wolfe suggests, the conventional arguments for non-human animal rights suggest troubling implications for both nonhuman animals and for human beings who also do not possess, or are not perceived to possess, criteria deemed essential to what it means to be human. Wolfe (2010, 13-137) argues that while some important short-term gains can be made within liberal humanist frameworks, such as rights discourses, they do so while sacrificing a more long-term and radical goals:

> What I am suggesting is that these pragmatic pursuits are forced to work within the purview of a liberal humanism in philosophy, politics, and the law that is bound by a historically and ideologically specific set of coordinates that, because of that very boundedness, allow one to achieve certain pragmatic gains in the short run, but at the price of a radical foreshortening of a more ambitious and more profound ethical project: a new and more inclusive form of ethical pluralism that is our charge, now, to frame. That project would think the ethical force of disability and nonhuman subjectivity as something other than merely an expansion of the liberal humanist ethos to ever new populations, as merely the next room added onto the (increasingly opulent and globalizing) house of what Richard Rorty has called "the rich North Atlantic bourgeois democracies."

Cognitive ethology, in some of its manifestations, offers a response to Wolfe's call. Scholars such as Marc Bekoff (2005, 2007) and Barbara Smuts (2001, 2006) attempt to meet other animals on their own terms, in their own worlds, to centralize the ways in which nonhuman animals share certain continuities with humans. These continuities are irreducible to sameness as the similarity argument has often presented them, wherein other animals must mirror some pre-existing image of human subjectivity in order to be granted ethical consideration; comparatively, through the work of Bekoff and Smuts, we are asked to think with and outside of our own literal and metaphorical skins.

As Bekoff (2007) argues, to say that dogs feel joy is not to say that they feel joy as humans do, but instead it is more accurate to speak of "dog joy" or "rat joy" or "monkey joy." Further, not only are these forms of joy particular to the species, they are particular to the individuals within the species. This means holding together two crucial insights. On the one hand, we must recognize that evolutionary continuity implies emotional continuity (Bekoff 2007), which can encourage us not to enact the so-called "'retreat' response" (Alcoff 1991) that has plagued some forms of politics: We can so fear misrepresenting Others that we fail to engage and meet our ethical responsibilities, which I believe must include representations of nonhuman animals beyond the objectified and reductive ones that serve economic interests. On the other hand, we must challenge the tendency to assume that we know who other animals are and what they want, in absence of really paying attention to them. Postcolonial and nonhuman animal studies scholar Philip Armstrong (2002, 417) summarizes this point well when he states, "Encountering the postcolonial animal means learning to listen to the voices of all kinds of 'others' without either ventriloquizing them or assigning to them accents so foreign that they never can be understood."

Of course, cognitive ethology is only one way to pay attention, and the field is not immune from its own challenges and limitations, but it offers an important set of tools that can help us cultivate humility in relation to other animals. Indeed, fieldwork in cognitive ethology begins with the premise that nonhuman animals are worthy of our attention, and we might learn something valuable by paying attention to them. Perhaps such a suggestion seems wildly obvious—that advocacy and scholarly efforts should be informed by studies about other animals—but these sorts of studies are often missing in nonhuman animal ethics and are also chronically missing from CAS and intersectional human-nonhuman animal advocacy.

Vignette Two: When the Elders Aren't Human

After their population was decimated through hunting, the North Atlantic right whales have struggled to rebuild despite a whaling moratorium. Their lack of population resiliency is somewhat baffling if the cultural dimension of these other animals is ignored. However, whale researchers Whitehead et al. (2004) suggest the dependency of the remaining few hundred whales on a single feeding ground, the Gulf of Maine, provides a partial answer: When conditions are poor in this area, the whales lack information about alternative habitats due to a loss of traditional knowledge.

REDUCTIONISM: NONHUMAN ANIMAL SUBJECTIVITY AS VICTIMHOOD AND SUFFERING

Why do the nonhuman animal movements and CAS (their closest academic ally) largely fail to incorporate field-based cognitive ethology and, generally, richer versions of other animal subjectivities—beyond suffering and victimhood—into their work? How is it that movements dedicated to nonhuman animals, and an area informed by these movements and ethically committed to the same goals, have so often neglected a key area of inquiry that is dedicated to better understandings of other animals? As one of my mentors asked me years ago, "Where are the animals in critical animal studies?" And, conversely, as one of my CAS colleagues remarked, "Why do we need to talk about animals? We already know what they don't like."

I would like to suggest some provisional answers to my first question about this specific absence. It feels important to address because, for me, my answers to this question have prompted an overhaul of my subsequent work over the past decade. In other words, how I have answered this question has been paradigm shifting. As noted, I have also observed the positive effects of this paradigm shift on my students. I hope if we can centralize this question and open ourselves to asking these difficult questions, we might further transcend the stagnating "rights versus welfare" debates and other quagmires that currently entangle the nonhuman animal movements.

My question is answered in part through consideration of three compounding and interrelated modes of thinking that I believe work against engagement with richer versions of nonhuman animal subjectivities and associated representations. The first answer relates back to the similarity argument, which although not usually put in these terms, might be credited for launching the Western nonhuman animal welfare movements. The second relates to intersectionality, a form of analysis that predates the rise of critical animal studies. The third relates to the nonhuman animal rights and liberation movements judgments about other animal use.

Let me begin with the first provisional answer: The similarity argument and its articulation of suffering. Utilitarian philosopher Jeremy Bentham (1789, 311), considered one of the earliest proponents of nonhuman animal welfare, famously stated, "The question is not, Can they *reason*? nor, Can they *talk*? but, Can they *suffer*?" Through such proclamations, Bentham helped shift calls for nonhuman animal-related social reform away from concerns about the ill effects of nonhuman animal cruelty on human society to a marked concern with other animals themselves. In this way, nonhuman animal subjectivity enters the public and political spheres through suffering.

Through Bentham, the criteria that had been used to exclude other animals from ethical concern, specifically speech and reason, are dismissed in favor of the "humane treatment principle" (Francione, 2008), which holds that it is wrong to cause unnecessary suffering to nonhuman animals. In this sense, the way that other animals' subjectivity is made visible, and morally relevant, is through their suffering. Indeed, the Western nonhuman animal movements' central aphorism, "the voice of the voiceless," repeatedly names other animal suffering as voicelessness (Corman, 2012). Conversely, advocates' voice signals the broadcast of, and resistance to, cruelty to nonhuman animals and the suffering they endure. Thus, modern Western nonhuman animal advocacy finds its roots in an understandable preoccupation with nonhuman animal suffering and a public rendering of the subjectivity of other animals through victimhood and suffering.

While the focus on nonhuman animals' suffering signaled a vital turn towards other animals and their interests, it also set the stage for the movements' limited conceptual frame regarding their lives. Conversations outside of victimhood and suffering are sometimes understood as potential distractions from the movements' raison d'être. As Bryant argues, the nonhuman animal movements' emphasis on suffering is a form of the similarity argument. The concentration on suffering was a necessary remediation to the wanton abuse of other animals, but it could not and does not adequately disrupt the social construction of animals as lesser beings, which in turn continues to justify their use and mistreatment today.

My second provisional answer as to why richer versions of other animal subjectivities are frequently absent within the nonhuman animal movements, particularly its academic arm, critical animal studies, relates to intersectionality and its origins in feminist praxis. CAS is an interdisciplinary field founded in 2006 and forged through a commitment to intersectional analyses, in part as a response to what cofounder Steve Best (2009) calls mainstream animal studies (MAS), which was critiqued as woefully single-issued and apolitical. Instead, CAS founders sought to build on political and economic analyses that maintained that various different "social axes of difference" intersect, and that systems of domination and oppression overlap and reinforce each other. The earlier work of animal ecofeminists such as Carol Adams and Josephine Donovan, which considered species as another "axes of difference" and included nonhuman animal oppression within intersectional feminist theory, helped lay the foundation for the inauguration of CAS.

The intersectional analyses of nonhuman animal ecofeminists and CAS scholars are vital counterpoints to scholarship that considers the "question of the animal," namely our ethical and political responsibilities toward other animals, in isolation from race, gender, class, and ability. CAS offers an overtly political intervention into the study of human-nonhuman animal relations, and it demonstrates connections between speciesism and other forms of oppression, which often leverage a debased version of nonhuman animality as a means of subjugating marginalized human groups. Over the past 20 years, I have similarly been dedicated to this approach as a student, a radio host and producer, and now as a sociology professor.

Given my background in gender studies, which initiated me into the academy through intersectional theory, I continue to see its tremendous value in both scholarly and political registers. However, despite my appreciation for intersectional thought, particularly as it relates to other animals, I have grown increasingly troubled by the way it centralizes domination and oppression as the sole points of solidarity and coalition-building among oppressed groups. Within CAS and a growing contingent of the nonhuman animal movements dedicated to this approach, the nodes of intersection relate to shared forms of domination, particularly under capitalism. While this helps illuminate mutually reinforcing forms of domination, it also continues to greatly reproduce a version of nonhuman animal subjectivity indivisible from their suffering and victimization. From this orientation, it becomes difficult to imagine the relevance of other animals' lives outside of the ways they are oppressed. Through this, we witness continuity with earlier forms of nonhuman animal ethics that reduce their subjectivity to suffering.

While it might seem counterintuitive to focus on nonhuman animals' subjectivity outside of suffering, by incorporating broader understandings into our work, we are able to get at the "question of the animal" on a deeper level. In my view, not only is this ultimately more effective for unsettling speciesism, but the turn away from purely victim-based analyses is also more closely aligned with other social justice movements and associated scholarship that increasingly emphasize the agency and resistance of their subjects (Mohanty 1988; Kapur 2002; Newdick 2005; Agustín 2003). The point becomes less about saving others but more about striving for solidarity (Hribal 2007; Coulter 2016). Further, from such vantage, we can struggle for a fuller realization of other animals' lives, including their capacity for pleasure, when we highlight that in their "liberation" they deserve so much more than simply the absence of suffering (Balcombe 2009). If we are not attuned to other animals' own forms of sociality, emotionality, and in some cases culturality, we can easily fail to reckon with the complexity of their lives and inadvertently reproduce a reductionist version of other animals that smacks of the kinds we oppose.

My last provisional answer to the question of why analyses of other animal lives beyond suffering are frequently missing from the nonhuman animal movements, and overwhelmingly from critical animal studies in particular, may relate to the movements' position toward nonhuman animal use. Specifically, there is a persistent commitment to noninterference with other animals (Francione 2008), which James McWilliams (2013) aptly calls the "leave animals alone argument." That is, nonhuman animal exploitation arises from their property status and humans' associated use of them, and in an ideal world, so the thinking goes, we would stop meddling in their lives. Liberation and freedom are figured as the possibility of living one's life outside of the oppressive grip of humanity.

Cognitive ethology is a field that combines both lab research and field research, with the former roundly condemned by researchers such as Marc

Bekoff (2007) who maintain that laboratories stress other animals and generate data about their behavior that is separate from the ecological contexts where it originally evolved. Bekoff, an evolutionary biologist, asks how we can accurately draw conclusions about other animals' social behavior when that behavior is divorced from the places where it evolved. Field research, where other animals are studied in more natural environments, may be seen as straying dangerously close to its lab counterpart. Even when field research is unobtrusive, on the surface, these studies suggest use, in the sense of "using" other animals to generate data. Further, these relations, by virtue of the fact that they are *relations*, open the possibility of unequal power relationships among human and nonhuman animals. In human-nonhuman animal relations predicated on nonhuman animal use, many which are enacted through factory farming, lab experimentation, and a host of other capitalist industries, other animals fair terribly, and so some caution about cognitive ethology makes sense. Cognitive ethology is, by definition, nonhuman animal research (of a sort).

Still, the incorporation of cognitive ethology into critical animal studies and the nonhuman animal liberation movements—as one way to encourage more expansive understandings of other animals' lives and fuller representations of them—thus encounters at least three major hurdles. First, preoccupation with suffering marks the historical initiation of nonhuman animal advocacy as a movement, and we continue in that legacy today, as we are rightfully concerned with the horrific treatment of other animals. Second, intersectionality remains perhaps the most significant defining principle of critical animal studies, while intersectionality has taken domination and oppression as its main objects of analysis. Its emphasis on suffering fits lock-in-key with this orientation, and third, the nonhuman animal movements and critical animal studies tend to vehemently eschew other animal use.

Vignette Three: When We Are a Tool—Wolves and Dogs Encounter a Locked Box

A common way of thinking about dogs is that they are simply intellectually-diminished wolves. That in the great trade of evolution they gave up something vital about themselves in order to cohabitate with humans. This story appears corroborated by certain problem-solving tests in which dogs fare worse than their wolf counterparts. Yet, as Alexandria Horowitz explains in her inspiring book Inside of a Dog: What Dogs See, Smell and Know *(2009), dogs (who live in people's homes) give up more easily than wolves when confronted with a secured box containing food. According to these standard intelligence tests, dogs seem like poor problem-solvers. However, unlike wolves, dogs search for humans to perform the task. When humans are around, dogs employ a series of solicitation and attention-seeking behaviors to petition for help. Horowitz (2009, 181) declares, "By standard intelligence tests, the dogs have failed at the puzzle. I believe, by contrast that they have succeeded magnificently. They have applied a novel tool to the task. We are that tool. Dogs have learned this—and they see us as fine general-purpose tools, too: useful for protection, acquiring food, providing companionship."*

SOCIAL SCIENCES MEET THE BIOLOGICAL SCIENCES, SHAKE HANDS, AND MAKE A DEAL

I applied for tenure and promotion October 2014, and as part of that process at Brock University, I was required to submit a list of external reviewers who, in addition to the department and larger university faculty of social science committee, would evaluate my research, teaching, and service dossiers. As my research and teaching draws from the natural sciences, social sciences, and humanities, and critical animal studies was founded by interdisciplinary scholars, I generated a list of relevant academics who work across a variety of disciplines.

Keeping with Brock's strategic mandate, which explicitly values "transdisciplinarity," I assumed that my list was appropriate both to my subfield as well as to the university's expectations. This list was then voted on prior and separate to my application. I sweated in the hallway while my colleagues deliberated on my proposed list of external reviewers. When the door finally opened, I was greeted with a significant question, "Why weren't there more social scientists on my list?" Given my interest in nonhuman animal sociality, much of my work had recently been informed by the biological sciences. Unfortunately, social scientists tend not to discuss other animals' societies, yet I wanted scholars on my list who recognize nonhuman animals' own lives, including their own social relationships.

My home discipline of sociology has greatly presumed that society is, by definition, the study of human social relationships. Indeed, the notion of "the social" is indivisibly tied to humanity and what it means to be human. In other words, sociology largely begins with an anthropocentric definition of society as one of its foundational premises. When sociologists study other animals, they do so insofar as they relate to human society, such that the definition of society remains wholly undisturbed. That bias holds throughout the social sciences in which the social is assumed to be the exclusive purview of humanity.

Anthropologist Barbara Noske clearly maps the humanist biases within the social sciences and biological sciences in her groundbreaking book *Beyond Boundaries: Humans and Animals* (1989); she shows how questions regarding nonhuman animal subjectivities, societies, and culturality become largely unthinkable within either of these major academic subsets due to their a priori assumptions about humans and nonhuman animals. In the case of both the social sciences and the biological sciences, other animals are not afforded the possibility of subjectivity, let alone complex subjectivity. First, regarding the social sciences, Noske (1989, 81–21) states,

> The field of the social scientist simply does not include animals as independent beings; one does not look for the social and the cultural where it cannot be found, that is, outside of the human sphere. After all, social science is the science of man—and increasingly of woman—and so social scientists have little or not time for the non-human. And since they began by defining sociality and culturality as exclusively human phenomena, they fall victim to the circular argument that animals, not being human, can in no way be social or cultural beings, as this would be a contradiction in terms.

Second, regarding the biological sciences, she argues,

> Biologists have increasingly come to view the animal as an object to be dissected into its smallest constituent parts, and animal actions as mechanisms of living matter governed by natural laws . . . Nowadays the essential apparatus of the biological sciences consists of genes, phenotypes, genetic variation, genetic transmission and selection. Arthur Caplan has noted that the interactions of these factors are held to be adequate for explaining not only the origin but also the presence of any and all of the persistent traits in living creatures (Noske, 83–84).

Although increasingly there are exceptions, generally speaking, both the social and the biological sciences create a reductionist image of other animals and nonhuman animality. In the sense that we speak of dehumanization, Noske writes of de-animalization, in which nonhuman animal subjectivity is erased, the inner lives of other animals are considered irrelevant or nonexistent, and the kind of theoretical objectification within these academic fields replicates the objectification that factory farming and other industries enact in practice. In both cases, other animals are de-animalized. Consequently, we can think about the social sciences and the biological sciences, while generating different kinds of knowledge and often employing different kinds of methodologies, as nonetheless united in their profound humanism in a kind of academic house of mirrors, each reflecting back an objectified image of nonhuman animals to the other.

In 2011, I taught "Animals in Cross-Cultural Perspective," which was part of the course calendar, but that had not been taught before. Although I had read Noske's *Beyond Boundaries* years ago (which had piqued me to the possibility of nonhuman cultures) and I received two graduate degrees in environmental studies (in which theories of nature and human-nonhuman animal relations include intersectional analyses and complex versions of other animals' subjectivities), I nonetheless assumed that the course would take the expected form: Twelve weeks dedicated to thinking about different human cultural understandings of other animals, their practices, and human-nonhuman animal relationships. We would study different cultures, different countries, and different contexts.[5]

As I researched course material, though, I encountered the "nonhuman animal culture wars" (Kendal 2008). Some scholars within these debates argue that if we are willing to open to nonanthropocentric definitions of culture, it becomes clear that many nonhuman animal populations are cultural. Once we are willing to grant that some nonhuman animals also have cultural lives and are cultural beings, then it raises very challenging questions that seem to cause a great deal of anxiety: If certain nonhuman animals have cultures, and culture has been a key way we have defined what it means to be human, what does it mean to be human then? Consider Jane Goodall (1998), who first observed chimpanzees using sticks to fish ants out of logs. When she later reported her findings to Louis Leakey, he famously declared, "Now we must redefine 'tool', redefine 'man', or accept chimpanzees as humans." I think we are at a similar crossroads now. In light of very convincing research about nonhuman animal cultures, I teach the course in two parts: Nonhuman cultural understandings and human cultural understandings. We spend the first six weeks researching other animals' emotions, sociality, and, in some cases, cultures. Midway through the course we learn about industrial nonhuman animal exploitation as part of a transition into various human cultures and their relationships to other animals, all while employing an intersectional lens.

As critical animal studies is a new field, there are few precedents for pedagogy in this area. When I started teaching at Brock, it was the first time a professor had been hired anywhere to primarily teach and research in this area, although others (including my colleague John Sorenson) had taught CAS courses. So, while I can only speak as one person, I am in the unique position to exclusively teach CAS, and to do that over a seven-year period. What remains remarkable to me is that "Animals in Cross-Cultural Perspective" seems to inspire and motivate students about nonhuman animal issues more than any other course I teach. That may be partially due to my own particular enthusiasm for the material, but I think that at least part of that trend relates to the emotional connection the students develop with the other animals discussed through the materials.

I have come to believe, the more that I teach, that students' exposure to other animals' pain and suffering, coupled with intersectional analyses, is often not enough to thoroughly trouble their entrenched speciesism and anthropocentrism. Otherwise it is too easy to say, I intellectually agree, but still, "they're only animals." When discussions about nonhuman animals entail both descriptions of their subjectivities, including but beyond suffering, students are more greatly motivated to not only build better, multidirectional human-nonhuman animal relationships in their own lives but also to actively resist the capitalist commodification and objectification of other animals' lives. Nonhuman animals move from being seen as passive victims, to emotional, and often social and cultural subjects whose lives have inherent worth. Discussions of suffering alone, intersectional analyses alone, and anti-capitalist critiques alone do not seem to carry the weight they might otherwise when they are decoupled from broader representations of other animals' subjectivities.

The above arguments were drawn into sharper focus when I was visiting Farm Sanctuary for the first time. I had been studying industrial pig production throughout my graduate degrees, with an emphasis on the racialized and gendered dynamics of slaughterhouse labor. At the time, I had been vegan for years and had immersed myself in the nonhuman animal movements. I was hosting a nonhuman animal liberation radio show and conducting one-hour, weekly interviews with a variety of scholars and activists. I considered myself well educated about the "pork" industry and the conditions pigs and other animals endure under industrial capitalism, yet I left the pig barn at Farm Sanctuary startled. I had briefly stood among the pigs, and one rolled on her back for a belly rub. That wide-open motion and contented body language reminded me of my cat. Bending down, I hesitated to touch her. A staff member exclaimed, "They love belly rubs!" For me, this was a life-changing belly rub. It was just as possible that she was not like my cat, but my cat was like her. I had read a great deal about pigs, and nothing had affected me like this.

Given the reprehensible treatment of pigs within factory farms, in which female pigs are kept in gestation and farrowing crates so cramped they are unable to turn around, many people are fighting the industry to meet even the barest minimum of care. Pigs in factory farming conditions are often plagued by stereotypic behaviors, such as bar biting, pacing, and "vacuum chewing" (chewing with nothing present), which signal stress and boredom. Still, the Canadian National Farm Animal Care Council (2014, 5) *Code of Practice* for pigs reminds us, "The Requirements and Recommended Practices in this document represent a challenging balance between animal welfare and the abilities of producers to effect change in an economically viable way."

The "Recommendations" in The Code suggest "provid[ing] continual access to a range of novel suspended toys such as cloth strips or rubber, or straw dispensers, along with free toys on the pen floor in housing where the use of substrates may impede manure management systems" (Canadian National Farm Animal Care Council 2014, 19). They lament, "[o]bjects used for enrichment can quickly lose their novelty value, so it is unlikely that long-term use of the same object will continue to satisfy pigs' enrichment needs" (Canadian National Farm Animal Care Council 2014, 19). These industry handbook comments are distinct reminders that pigs are highly curious and have the capacity to enjoy their lives when given the opportunity, yet even if these forms of enrichment were consistently met, what chance would they have to form friendships and other relationships? Enrichment, perhaps one of the most sophisticated standards for nonhuman animal welfare—one that acknowledges other animals' psychology—seems bleak in comparison to the complexity of pigs' hearts and minds. Industrial production can never truly provide for pigs' potential.

Vignette Four: Friendship Outside of the Factory Farm— Hope and Johnny

Jeffrey Moussaieff Masson (2003) shares the story of two pigs named Hope and Johnny who lived at Farm Sanctuary in California:

Able to scoot round on the barn on her three good legs, she could not walk. Johnny, who was much younger than Hope, bonded closely with her. At night, he would always sleep right next to her, keeping her warm on cold nights. In the morning, Bauston would bring Hope bowls of food and water. Johnny would stay with her to keep the other pigs from interfering with her or taking her food. During the day, Johnny would spend most of his time hanging out in the barn with Hope. When Hope died of old age, Johnny was still a young and healthy pig. Maybe he knew about death. The death of his closest friend seemed to devastate him; he died suddenly and unexpectedly within a couple of weeks after Hope, perhaps of a broken heart.

NOTES

1. Michael Mikulak (2007) coined the term to describe the ideological impact of Earth First! activism.

2. Brock University's Department of Sociology currently houses the greatest number of CAS classes at any postsecondary institution, in addition to offering a concentration and minor in CAS. My position at Brock allows me to develop curriculum and assess its impact through direct feedback from students (either in person or through letters), from teaching assistants, and course evaluations. While I cannot claim that these observations are generalizable to all populations, my courses provide some unique understanding into what reaches students most and how certain curricular choices are more effective than others. That said, certainly my students have various privileges not afforded to everyone: The course demographics include mostly white students and tend to have more women than men. Concomitantly, the university is located in St. Catharines, a city situated within the economically depressed area of Niagara, Ontario. Students are often the first generation within their families to attend university.

3. In particular, I am indebted to Jason Hribal (2007) for his histories of nonhuman animal agency and resistance, which greatly inspired my shift from suffering to a broader approach based on solidarity.

4. According to Marc Bekoff (2005, 40), "Cognitive ethology is the comparative, evolutionary, and ecological study of nonhuman animal (hereafter animal) minds including thought processes, beliefs, rationality, information-processing, and consciousness."

5. A deeper discussion of these points can be found in my coauthored piece, "Radical Humility Toward a More Holistic Critical Animal Studies Pedagogy" (Corman and Vandrovcová, 2014).

REFERENCES

Agustín, Laura Ma. 2003. "Forget Victimization: Granting Agency to Migrants." *Development.* 46(3): 30–36.

Alcoff, Linda. 1991. "The Problem of Speaking for Others." *Cultural Critique,* 20, 5–32.

Armstrong, Philip. 2002. "The Postcolonial Animal." *Society & Animals,* 10(4): 413–419.

Balcombe, Jonathan. 2009. "Animal Pleasure and Its Moral Significance." *Applied Animal Behaviour Science,* 118(3–4): 208–216.

Bekoff, Marc. 2005. *Animal Passions and Beastly Virtues: Reflections on Redecorating Nature.* Philadelphia: Temple University Press.

Bekoff, Marc. 2007. *The Emotional Lives of Animals: A Leading Scientist Explores Animal Joy, Sorrow, and Empathy—and Why They Matter.* Novato, CA: New World Library.

Bentham, Jeremy. 1789. *An Introduction to the Principles of Morals and Legislation.* Oxford, UK: Clarendon Press.

Best, Steven. 2009. "The Rise of Critical Animal Studies: Putting Theory into Action and Animal Liberation into Higher Education." *Journal for Critical Animal Studies,* 7(1): 9–52.

Bryant, Taimie L. 2007. "Similarity or Difference as a Basis for Justice: Must Animals Be Like Humans to Be Legally Protected?" *Law and Contemporary Problems,* 70: 207–253.

Canadian National Farm Animal Care Council. 2014. *Code of Practice: For the Care and Handling of Pigs.* Retrieved on August 30, 2016, from https://www.nfacc.ca/pdfs/codes/pig_code_of_practice.pdf.

Corman, Lauren E. J. 2012. *The Ventriloquist's Burden? Animals, Voice, and Politics.* Unpublished doctoral dissertation. Toronto: York University.

Corman, L., and T. Vandrovcová. 2014. "Radical Humility: Toward a More Holistic Critical Animal Studies Pedagogy." In Anthony J. Nocella II, John Sorenson, Kim Socha, and Atsuko Matsuoka (eds.) *Defining Critical Animal Studies: An Introduction to an Intersectional Social Justice Approach to Animal Liberation.* New York: Peter Lang Publishing, 135–157.

Coulter, Kendra. 2016. *Animals, Work, and the Promise of Interspecies Solidarity.* New York: Palgrave Macmillan.

Francione, Gary Lawrence. 2000. *Introduction to Animal Rights: Your Child or the Dog?* Philadelphia: Temple University Press.

Francione, Gary Lawrence. 2008. *Animals as Persons: Essays on the Abolition of Animal Exploitation.* New York: Columbia University Press, 25–66.

Francione, G. 2010. "Animal Welfare and the Moral Value of Nonhuman Animals." *Law, Culture and the Humanities,* 6(1): 24–36.

Goodall, Jane. 1993. "Chimpanzees—Bridging the Gap." In Paola Cavalieri and Peter Singer (eds.), *The Great Ape Project.* New York: St. Martin's Griffin, 10–18.

Horowitz, Alexandra. 2009. "Noble Mind." In *Inside of a Dog: What Dogs See, Smell, and Know.* New York: Scriber, 175–208.

Hribal, Jason C. 2007. "Animals, Agency, and Class: Writing the History of Animals from Below." *Human Ecology Review,* 14(1), 101–112.

Kapur, Rama. 2002. "The Tragedy of Victimization Rhetoric: Resurrecting the Native Subject in International/Postcolonial Feminist Legal Politics." *Harvard Human Rights Law Journal,* 15: 1–28.

Kendal, Rachel L. 2008. "Animal 'Culture Wars': Evidence from the Wild?" *The Psychologist,* 21: 312–315.

Masson, Jeffrey Moussaieff. 2004. *The Pig Who Sang to the Moon: The Emotional World of Farm Animals.* New York: Random House Publishing Group, 15–53.

McWilliams, James. 2013. "The Animal's All-Knowing Gaze." Retrieved August 30, 2016, from http://james-mcwilliams.com/?p=2885.

Mikulak, M. 2007. "This Is the End: Earth First! And Apocalyptic Utopianism." *FORUM: University of Edinburgh Postgraduate Journal of Culture and the Arts,* 5.

Mohanty, Chandra Talpade. 1988. "Under Western Eyes: Feminist Scholarship and Colonial Discourses." *Feminist Review,* 30: 61–88.

Newdick, Vivian. 2005. "The Indigenous Woman as Victim of Her Culture in Neoliberal Mexico." *Cultural Dynamics,* 17(1): 73–92.

Noske, Barbara. 1997. "Human-Animal Discontinuities?" In *Beyond Boundaries: Humans and Animals.* Montreal, New York, and London: Black Rose Books.

Perry, Susan. 2011. "Social Traditions and Social Learning in Capuchin Monkeys." *Philosophical Transactions of the Royal Society,* 366: 988–996.

Smuts, Barbara. 2001. "Encounters with Animal Minds." *Journal of Consciousness Studies,* 8(5–7): 293–309.

Smuts, Barbara. 2006. "Between Species: Science and Subjectivity." *Configurations,* 14(1–2): 115–126.

Taylor, Sunaura. 2014. "Animal Crips." *Journal for Critical Animal Studies,* 12(2): 95–117.

Whitehead, Hal, Luke Rendell, Richard W. Osborne, and Bernd Wursig. 2004. "Culture and Conservation of Nonhumans with Reference to Whales and Dolphins: Review and New Directions." *Biological Conservation,* 120: 427–437.

Wolfe, Cary. 2010. *What Is Posthumanism?* Minneapolis: University of Minnesota Press.

12

Capitalism and the Commodification of Animals: The Need for Critical Vegan Praxis, Animated by Anarchism!

Richard J. White

> Not only is structural violence inherent in the capitalist system, but it results in death on a genocidal scale.
>
> (Leech 2012, 4)

> "Only 10 years ago, roughly 12% of global food and drink products carried any vegetarian or vegan claims, but now even Wal-Mart Stores are stocked with vegan labeled products. Global sales of vegan products are expected to reach $5 Billion by 2020. This trend will continue, so what's driving forward the growth of vegan businesses? There are four main reasons: Millennials are interested, entrepreneurs are working, diseases are growing, billionaires are investing."
>
> (Caldera 2016)

> "Anarchy, being as it is opposed to the many "isms" that keep groups under the dominion of a ruling class or organization (sexism, racism, nationalism) seems a logical place to ideologically position oneself as an opponent to speciesism: the belief that human needs and desires trump those of other species."
>
> (Socha 2012, 17)

Veganism doesn't solve all the world's problems, but it can offer a springboard into rethinking human-animal relationships, help resist the objectification of animals' lives, and interrupt the idea that animals exist for us.

(Corman 2014)

INTRODUCTION

In many ways, the old Dickensian adage "it was the best of times, it was the worst of times," captures the contemporary nature(s) of the relationship(s) between human and nonhuman animals. For one thing, advanced largely through animal studies, our *academic* knowledge regarding the remarkable beauty, deep intelligence, and rich emotional capabilities and capacities of nonhuman sentient beings is undoubtedly the most extensive it has ever been. Engaged within and beyond academia, these richer layers of understanding have the potential to invite more complex readings of existing human-animal relations, and articulate new, mutually empowering forms of inter-species engagement and ways of being. However, in most cases, animal studies have stopped short of explicitly problematizing the moral and ethical implications that are caught up in our existing relations with fellow earthlings. The notable exceptions here have been those activist-scholars who define the evolving spaces on which an explicitly critical animal studies (CAS) discourse stands (Nocella et al. 2014; Gillespie and Collard 2015). For it is this interdisciplinary community that has always sought to apply knowledge directly in ways that recognizes "the animal condition" (Pederson and Stănescu 2012, ix). This is largely motivated by the desire to continually expose, challenge, and reconfigure many overt forms of prejudice and bigotry that have been used to perpetuate a false "human/ animal" binary, and justify human supremacy and speciesist practices. However, *despite* our heightened consciousness concerning the complexity of other animals, and *despite* CAS acting as a tremendous source of inter-species solidarity, the promises that CAS carries—of freedom, liberation and life—will *never* be experienced by billions of human and nonhuman animals alive today and the billions that are yet to be born.

If knowledge is power, then it would seem that critical animal studies are currently nowhere near powerful enough to mount an effective challenge to dismantle those entrenched hegemonic forms of oppression experienced by other animals. This certainly appears to be the case when focusing on farming, "which has long been, and continues to be, the most significant social formation of human–animal relations" (Calvo 2008, 32), and particularly so within the immense, and increasing, capitalist exploitation of nonhuman animal bodies through industrial farming practices. In this context, it will be argued that, despite an unprecedented momentum and visibility of academics and activists directly advocating social justice and total liberation *for all*, and despite the rise of veganism in the Western world, it is without a doubt that for many nonhuman animals our *anthropogenic* epoch undoubtedly represents—or will come to represent—the worst: indeed, the most evil, dark, sadistic, and hellish of times.

Reinforcing an urgent need to envisage and usher "postcapitalist" futures of nonhuman animal liberation into being, and thereby create important new counter-power spaces for CAS to occupy, this chapter focuses both on the struggle to resist capitalism and ways to embed alternative strategies of resistance in the everyday. In particular, the chapter explores the limits of appealing to veganism, *per se,* as a means of challenging capitalist exploitations of animals, both human and nonhuman. This serves as a perfect demonstration of the power of advanced capitalism to commodify the alternative by stripping out the radical praxis of veganism and repackaging this as an "alternative lifestyle choice." The challenge then becomes one of how to envisage and enact a postcapitalist world that is consistent with the appeal for total liberation of humans, other animals, and the Earth. To these ends, the chapter invokes a spirit of anarchism; a radical praxis that has significantly animated the trajectory of critical animal studies to date. Here, a narrative focused on re-imagining of the political economy of the household and community spaces through critical vegan praxis will be outlined.

The structure of the chapter is divided into three key sections. The opening section focuses on the relationship between capitalism and industrial farming, with the intent of drawing attention to the *for-profit* rationales that underpin and legitimate the abusive treatment of "farmed" [sic] nonhuman animals. As Dominick (2015, 35) observes

> (W)e know factory farming wasn't invented as a means of mass sadism; it was established because abusing animals on a large scale is generally more profitable than mistreating them less severely on a small scale.

Indeed, the decision to use the referent "animals," rather than "nonhuman animals" in the title of this chapter was deliberate, for we must be sensitive to the reality that capitalist exploitation of nonhuman animals always overlaps and intersects with human rights violations at some significant level. Indeed, one of the particularly important and emancipatory frontiers of critical research in human-animal relations continues to be embedded in research which approaches these intersections through the prisms of class, gender, and race. The second section, having acknowledged the importance of anarchist praxis within the trajectories of critical animal studies, focuses in more detail about the limits of appealing to veganism as an effective counter-power strategy both to 1) confront the capitalist exploitation of animals and 2) bring forward postcapitalist worlds rich in anarchist narratives of freedom and social justice. In considering how to address these limits of veganism, the third section draws on the importance of bringing these postcapitalist worlds into being through harnessing a critical vegan praxis in our immediate household and broader community spaces.

CAPITALISM, COMMODIFICATION, AND THE EXPLOITATION OF ANIMALS

All societies have economies in which goods and services are produced, exchanged, and consumed. Here two things should be recognized: first, there is nothing natural or inevitable about how economies are organized; and second, there are extraordinarily diverse modes of economic organization functioning within any given society at any one time. With this understanding, though, given its centrality in the chapter, it is important to understand what is meant by capitalism. Most general definitions of a "capitalist" society would broadly agree that this is a society where goods and services are increasingly "organized around the systematic pursuit of profit in the marketplace" (Williams 2005, 13). The term *commodification*, "highlights the fact that the commodity status of a thing, object, idea, creature, person, or what-have-you is not intrinsic to it but, rather, assigned . . . it usefully connotes a process or state that is irreducible to the thing/s being commodified but which nonetheless affect them . . ." (Castree 2003, 277). Given the focus on anarchist praxis in this chapter, and particularly in this context of this present discussion of commodified relations, it is also timely to offer an understanding of anarchism:

> *Anarchism is a purity of rebellion.* A pig who struggles wildly and rends the air with his cries while he is held to be slaughtered, and a baby who kicks and screams when, wanting warmth and his mother's breast, he is made to wait in the cold—these are two samples of natural rebellion. Natural rebellion always inspires either deep sympathy and identification with the rebelling creature or a stiffening of the heart and an activation of aggressive-defensive mechanisms to silence an accusing truth. This truth is that each living being is an end in itself; that nothing gives a being the right to make another a mere instrument of his purposes. (Baldelli 1972, 17)

Baldelli's final sentence perfectly, if unintentionally, captures the ethical violations that occur when sentient life is commodified. Life caught up within the capitalist matrix is valued *instrumentally* (as means to other ends) rather than *intrinsically* (as an end in itself), and perhaps nowhere do such violations occur on such an enormous level as they do within the Animal Industrial Complex. With reference to Noske (1989), Twine (2012, 23) succinctly defines the "Animal Industrial Complex" as a partly opaque and multiple set of networks and relationships between the corporate (agricultural) sector, governments, and public and private science. With economic, cultural, social, and affective dimensions, it encompasses an extensive range of practices, technologies, images, identities, and markets.

Great effort has been made within the CAS literature to capture the multiple ways in which nonhuman animals have been cruelly, violently commodified, and exploited by overt capitalist practices (Nibert 2014; Novek 2013; Pachirat 2013; Twine 2013; Stallwood 2014; Sorenson 2014). Though the extent and nature of capitalism in contemporary Western society is subject to ongoing contestation (White and Williams 2012, 2014), there is little doubt that the practices followed by nonhuman animal industries "are embedded in a capitalistic fabric" (Noske 1989, 22). Within these spaces, hierarchical speciesist power relations are institutionalized, and human-animal relationships are transformed in ways that "treat livestock [sic] animals as tools for production and as commodities themselves, prioritizing exchange-values over use values" (Stuart, Schewe, and Gunderson 2013, 209). Even the very language used to differentiate, objectify, and value the unique nature of those nonhuman animals caught in these capitalist spaces is ugly and material. As Wadiwel (2016, 162–163) observes "For 'livestock,' value is tied to the animal's death, since value will only be fully realized when the animal has been raised, is killed, and is converted into meat."

While recognizing that the domination of nature and the capitalist commodification of nonhuman animals manifests itself in many different ways, from horse racing, zoos and circuses to exotic "pet" trades, "canned" hunts, and vivisection, the "political economy of meat production [is] a key social form in which certain species of nonhuman animal are exploited and oppressed. In turn, it is part of a wider system, the domination of nature" (Calvo 2008, 33). Here the sheer scale of nonhuman animal abuse (always culminating in a violence that will directly lead to the animal's death) within industrial farming is staggering:

> Factory farming and industrialised slaughter technologies, for examples, enable a monstrous deployment of violence and extermination. The scale of death defies imagination. One conservative estimate is that worldwide over 60 billion land animals are killed annually for food. Since these figures do not include sea animals killed for human use, they do not illustrate the full scale of death. (Wadiwel 2015, 6).

Part of the power of exploitation lies in the stupefying statistics: in the impossibility to comprehend them, let alone to formulating actions in the name of liberation. Working with an earlier estimate of 55 billion land-dwelling nonhuman animals, Les Mitchell (2011, 38) appeals to a sense of geography to try and offer connection:

> Worldwide, approximately 55 billion land-based nonhumans are killed every year in the farming industry . . . This is over 150 million individuals each day

or the equivalent of the populations of South Africa, Zambia, Zimbabwe, Malawi, Mozambique, Namibia, Botswana, and Angola . . . Except for a very tiny minority, all the nonhumans in the industry will meet with a violent death at a relatively young age; all will have been confined during their lives; many will have been mutilated; numerous females will have been repeatedly made pregnant but their young taken away shortly after birth; family structures will have been destroyed.

Today, the approximate number of land-dwelling farmed animals killed every year is closer to 70 billion. While it is a struggle to comprehend the sheer magnitude of oppression and suffering, it is important to focus on more immediate, personal human/nonhuman animal relations and actual places of exploitation in order to provide meaning, recognizable contexts, and "achievable" means of intervention.

Qualitative (ethnographic) research focused on industrial farming has time and time again indicated how barbarous practices—"where cruelty is casually dispensed on an unimaginable scale" (Gellatley and Wardle, 1996) are anything but exceptional, and indeed are indicative of normal standard practice (Regan 2004). Despite the belief that the most horrific accounts of cruelty are found within factory farms, (a self-interested idea promoted by capitalist industries keen to market and promote "free-range," "organic," or "ethically sourced" animal flesh as the "cruelty-free" alternative), as Wadi-wel (2015, 286) argues: the "idea that there is a 'humane form of killing,' a 'civilized' way to kill is already oxymoronic."

Why such systematic cruelty takes place can be understood with reference to the capitalist imperative to maximize profit, and as such, these terrible and destructive practices become *intrinsic* to capitalist logic. Commodi-fied nonhuman animal bodies are valued only in ways that serve to maximize the owner's profit, even if these fundamentally override and violate all ethical norms. As Stuart, et al. (2012, 209) argue:

> When animals become commodities or production devises they are no longer seen as beings with moral status, and to meet the demands of industry, they are subjected to conditions that do not match their living requirements . . . To maximise profits, capitalist logic squeezes as much from the animal as possible, giving the minimum attention to basic needs. This push for profit is most obvious in industrial or "factory" farms.

What has been emphasized many times by critical animal scholars, and critical research on human-animal relations more generally, is the dark reality that capitalist modes of exploitation and violence in the farming industry—its "fundamental nature" (Mitchell 2011, 9)—are never just about nonhuman animals. Notwithstanding that the treatment of other animals in industrial farms may well be "the worst crime in history" (Harari, 2015), the violence unleashed by capitalism must not be allowed to obscure those broader realities that demonstrate how this violence spans "the species divide." In this context, a significant body of critical literature has drawn attention to these entangled connections in a number of ways, particularly through exploring the intersectional and interlocking forms of oppression between speciesism, class, racism, and sexism (Cochrane 2010; Eisnitz 2006; Fitzgerald and Pellow 2014; Nibert 2003; Pachirat 2013). As Gillespie (2013, 2) points out, these connections of capitalist repertoires of human-nonhuman animal violence are not "optional" extras but are absolutely central to understanding the complex reality of these capitalist circuits of dominion and power:

> Understanding this commodification is important both for the sake of the individual animals laboring and dying within the industry and for the more extensive project of uncovering the consequences of gendered commodification of all bodies—nonhuman and human—and the violent power structures to which they are subjected. Animal bodies, and particularly farmed animal bodies, are subject to mundane, routinized forms of violence in every day agricultural practice.

Some illustrative ways in which industrial capitalist farming practices routinely violate basic human rights for those working with the slaughterhouse itself include the risk of "chronic respiratory disorders, exacerbation of asthma, cardiovascular complications, and premature death" (Food Empowerment Movement 2016); ill treatment of illegal migrants (Torres and Torres 2005); emotional distress (Leenaert 2016); low pay, physical and verbal abuse (Arrieta 2004); and so on. Focusing on North America, Spangher (2014) reported that:

> Workers in the "meat" industry make an average of $23,000 a year, work 10-plus hours a day, are pushed so hard they often defecate in their pants to avoid slowing down, and suffer a repetitive motion injury rate 30 times the national average.

To maximize profit—where time equals money—the appalling consequences witnessed in the systematic abuse of human rights are staggering.

Another connection needs to be emphasized, namely the fusion of "political" and "economic" interests. Contemporary research focused on the political economy that legitimates this industrialization and exploitation of animals continues to provide important insights into this opaque relationship, with Torres's (2007) *Making A Killing: The Political Economy of Animal Rights* being a particularly influential text here. Indeed, the fact that all of these highly profitable animal farming practices are perfectly legal is a deeply uncomfortable truth for many people; people who are otherwise:

> . . . of the opinion that animals are generally well cared for in animal industries, that laws protect animals, and that it is in the industry's best interest to treat others creature well. Nothing could be further from the truth. (Kemmerer 2011, 173).

As Garcia (2011, 143) writes, "factory farming is a government-sponsored conventional and institutionalised form of animal abuse." Thus, the desire to challenge and dismantle these key intersections of violence and to challenge the exploitation within these capitalist spaces, nonhuman animal liberationist intimately bound up with human liberation.

CHALLENGING CAPITALISM THROUGH VEGANISM
THE DANGER OF COMMODIFICATION

There are many inspiring examples of animal-rights activism that challenge and close down capitalist spaces of oppression (Best and Nocella 2006). Concentrating on industrial farming practices, a significant focus of nonhuman animal rights activists—synonymous with the rise of the Animal Liberation Front (ALF) from the 1970s onwards—has been to engage in diverse forms of illegal direct action. Here, the primary intention has been to transgress private, capitalist spaces of oppression, and certainly this has been witnessed in activism focused on factory farms and slaughterhouses. This has been undertaken at considerable personal risk and sacrifices for activists. This risk has often been perceived in terms of the danger of loss of freedom (of being arrested and incarcerated), but there has also been a great personal price to be paid for these undercover operations: a consequence of bearing witness to violence, misery, and suffering. As Ornelas (2011, 153) says:

> Animal investigations are emotionally draining . . . I was horrified watching workers hang ducks upside down on the slaughter line, while some fell off in a desperate attempt to escape. I was deeply saddened by the haunting echoes of confined pregnant pigs banging their heads against bars of crates so narrow that they couldn't turn around.

The dominant justifications for such high-risk activism may be to directly liberate nonhuman animals from these hellish spaces and/or to bring new truths to light that expose the lies and propaganda perpetuated by the animal abuse industry. Through doing so, the hope and the expectation is that this heightened awareness may change hearts and minds in ways that inform future ethical decisions, by encouraging the individual to withdraw their (financial) support for such practices and speak out against them wherever possible.

When these acts of liberation take place in societies where the government is in the thrall of capitalism, their success can perhaps be measured in the excessive legislation and enforcement measurements that follow. Nonhuman animal liberation activists, for example, continue to be among the FBI's "highest domestic terrorism priorities" (Woodhouse 2012). Within North America, some of the most draconian laws in recent years include the Animal Enterprise Terrorism Act (AETA) and other so-called "ag-gag laws," which criminalize undercover investigations of business which exploit other animals (Phelps 2013).

Another key radical form of activism within critical animal studies (Jenkins and Stănescu 2014) and beyond has been to directly appeal to individuals to act ethically in ways that minimize violence against human and nonhuman animal life. Central within this call has been the call to 'go vegan!' Nibert (2013, 261), for example, maintains that promoting veganism is an important part of a broader strategy in the struggle against entangled oppression:

> In the face of these realities, not the least of which is the exploitation and violence against growing numbers of domesecrated animals, the morally responsible position is to practice and promote global veganism.

Prima facie in a capitalist world, veganism as a counter-power strategy in which individuals refuse to financially give support to capitalist enterprises that profit from the ongoing commodification of other animals clearly makes sense. If success could be gauged from the growing number of individuals who identify as vegan, then there would be plenty of reasons to celebrate! Focusing on Western society, for example, within European countries, the number of vegetarians and vegans stands at all-time high. In the United Kingdom alone, the Vegan Society (2016b) reported that, "at least 542,000 people in Britain are now following a vegan diet," an increase of 350 percent over the last decade. Focusing on North American population, Watters (2015) notes, "In 2009, a tiny 1 percent of the U.S. population reported eating vegetarian or vegan. Now, 5 percent of the U.S. population is vegetarian, and half of those people are vegan . . . to think that 16 million people in this country eat absolutely no animal products is pretty amazing."

However, one of the key strengths of capitalism and a key factor of its resilience, fluidity, and dynamism is its ability, "to absorb and reduce all values to exchange values, to commodify everything and put a price on it, *including protest itself*" (Cohen 2015, 162). In this context the danger is that, far from being the radical and critical "alternative" that it is envisaged to be, veganism is subjected to capitalist forms of appropriation and commodification in ways that strip it of any critical intent. Ultimately, this leads to veganism re-packaged and promoted in ways that serve to function as another profitable consumer-based "lifestyle" choice. Indeed, as will be mentioned later in the chapter, there is also a disturbing failure to recognize the capitalist economic practices that potentially underpin the production and distribution of vegan foods, practices that are highly exploitative of both human labor and wider natural environments (Taylor and Sturdy 2013; Food Empowerment Project 2016). On a critical reading of the actual impacts of the rise of veganism across contemporary society, it is difficult to conclude otherwise than to see that a type of commodified veganism has prospered, one uncoupled from its radical roots and divorced from activist intent. It comes as no surprise then to observe how veganism has being marketed as a wonderful business opportunity! The following extracts, taken from *Vegetarian Means Business. Market Strategy and Research Report* (Ginsberg 2011), illustrate and illuminate this commodified reality:

> Would-be entrepreneurs as well as established professionals can benefit from understanding the market and competition in order to determine the best opportunities for success. Given that the trends driving interest in vegetarian eating appear likely to continue, savvy business people can not only profit by catering to this need but also build demand by offering plant-based foods that are delicious, convenient, and affordable (Ginsberg 2011, 3).
>
> Although vegans are a small fraction of the population, they are heavy users of products that meet their needs. They can be loyal, enthusiastic customers who generate word-of-mouth recommendations not only to other vegans but also to the full spectrum of vegetarian eaters (Ginsberg 2011, 6).
>
> A 2004 *Los Angeles Times* article noted the influence vegans have had in the automotive field. "Pleasing vegans, the theory goes, is key to reaching a wider group of consumers—affluent shoppers who worry about the environment and who are willing to pay extra for food, clothing and even automobiles, if they are made in ways that do less harm to the planet" (Ibid).
>
> As a marketer, you want to identify with the passionate group . . . The middle of the bull's-eye is where you want to focus your marketing, and then you want to expand your message around that. If you draw these concentric circles, the middle of the bull's-eye right now is the vegan.—Bob Kurilko of Edmunds.com (Ibid)
>
> Although the trend isn't yet measurable, media coverage suggests the number of vegans may be on the rise. A 2011 article in the *Chicago Sun-Times* reported, "Veganism is moving from marginal to mainstream in the United States." Kathryn Peters of SPINS, a market research and consulting firm for the natural products industry, was quoted in *Natural Foods Merchandiser* as saying, "We're seeing more celebrity endorsements. It's becoming chic" (Ibid).

Thus, far from bringing the industries that profit from nonhuman animal abuse to their knees, veganism has become a handmaiden to capitalism, yet another lucrative way to increase profit margins. That vegan food products are "big business" can be seen in the incredible growth this sector has enjoyed. For example, the Vegan Society (2016a) reported that:

> The Mintel Meat-Free Foods U.K. Report for 2012 shows that meat-free and free-from sales are expected to reach a total of £949 million in 2012, with meat-free sales set to reach £607 million, and free-from market sales expected to reach £342 million. Almost four in 10 (38 percent) Britons have bought vegetarian or meat-free food, while one in five (20 percent) has bought free-from food. The growth of the soya, rice, and other alternatives to dairy milks

as well as the dairy-free margarine market show the potential for this segment of the market.

More recent U.K. figures attest to this trend:

> In 2013, the U.K. meat-free food market hit £625 million in sales, a figure forecasted to rise to £657 million in 2014. Today, some 12 percent of the U.K. population identify as either vegan or vegetarian, and 20 percent of 16- to 25-year-olds self-identify this way. Jennifer Pardoe, founder of London plant-based food consultancy Zest says businesses are slowly recognising the "mega trend." Recently, we have seen brands like Birdseye introduce plant-based meal options and Sainsbury's create clearer vegan and vegetarian product labelling.
>
> "With more people becoming plant curious, restaurants and supermarkets are realizing they need high-quality, plant-based food options to satisfy consumer demand," explains Pardoe. (Clarkson, 2014)

The inconvenient and unpalatable truth to be told here is that of all the vegan meals consumed, of all the many brave and uncompromising forms of nonhuman animal activism and activists campaigns that have drawn attention to the atrocities of farmed animals, of all the thousands of words written in the name of CAS, when taken individually or collectively, would seem to have had little tangible impact on preventing the rampant acceleration and intensification of global capitalist farming practices. The Worldwatch Institute (2013), for example (I include this quote directly not only to illustrate the figures but also to draw attention to the speciesist language used, where individual sentient beings are aggregated into tonnage), reported that:

> In 2007, meat production remained steady at an estimated 275 million tons; in 2008, output is expected to top 280 million tons. Experts predict that by 2050 nearly twice as much meat will be produced as today, for a projected total of more than 465 million tons. For more than a decade, the strongest increases in production have been in the developing world—in 1995 more meat and dairy products were produced in developing than in industrial countries for the first time, and this trend has continued ever since. In fact, in 2007 at least 60 percent of meat was produced in developing nations.

Indeed, within European countries the trend and future projection is similar:

> Beef and poultry production in the European Union (EU) has been growing steadily this year, putting the sectors on track for further growth in 2015, said a new European Commission (EC) report, released on October 8. (Lange-Chenier, 2014)

Finally, in North America, despite consuming less red "meat," the demand for "poultry" continues to expand. So too does the industrial farm, as "the meat industry lurches on, consolidating operations and stuffing its factory-scale facilities ever tighter with animals . . ." (Philpott 2015). All of this evidence supports the underrepresented critiques that are emerging within critical animal studies, exemplified by Dominick's (2016, 27) conclusion: "Veganism is not a counter-power movement. It involves at most a hint of a strategy and lacks even the pretense of an institutional alternative to decrease human impact on nonhuman animals."

In the face of these deeply alarming trends, how can the cutting edge of critical animal studies be sharpened and strengthened in meaningful ways to challenge capitalism and build new counter-power spaces? What would it be to envisage and enact a postcapitalist world where, at a minimum, nonhuman animal abuse and exploitation were uncoupled from the profit-motive and not subjected to capitalist process of commodification? What role would veganism play both in and as a means of achieving a postcapitalist world? The chapter responds to these questions by emphasizing the centrality of anarchist praxis within critical animal studies and focuses on "the household" as an overlooked but crucial site of vegan praxis and intersectional activism.

TOWARD A CRITICAL VEGAN PRAXIS, ANIMATED BY ANARCHISM

". . . I see evidence every day of my life that anarchism's core principles and promises make a lot of sense to those of us who are committed to total liberation—ideas, scholarship, artistic expression, and action aimed at challenging all forms of oppression."

(Pellow 2015, 1)

To date, the theory and practice (praxis) of anarchism has enjoyed great influence within CAS (Nocella et al. 2014; White 2015, a, b; White and Cudworth 2014). Indeed, through its commitment toward direct action and prefigurative praxis as a means of challenging domination, exploitation, and oppression, anarchism has long been a significant inspiration for nonhuman animal liberation activists, and social justice movements more generally (Colling et al. 2014; Kinna 2012). It is little surprise to note then that understanding, challenging, and confronting capitalism has been a keen and consistent focus within the rich and diverse canon of anarchist literature (Shannon et al. 2012). What must be stressed again here, not least to challenge deliberate misreading's of anarchism, is that anarchist praxis: (1) is concerned with addressing *all* forms of dominion, and as such "is not reducible to economics—or even economics and political life" (Shannon, et al. 2012, 13); and (2) anarchism emphases the importance of nonviolence as means of achieving social justice (Franks and Wilson 2010).

These two crucial points are perfectly captured by the vegan anarchist geographer Simon Springer (2012, 2016), who argued that the core of anarchist thought should be:

> properly understood as the rejection of all forms of domination, exploitation, and "archy" (systems of rule), hence the word "an-archy" (against systems of rule). Anarchism is a theory and practice that seeks to produce a society wherein individuals may freely co-operate together as equals in every respect, not before a law or sovereign guarantee—which enter new forms of authority, imposed criteria of belonging, and rigid territorial bindings—but before themselves in solidarity and mutual respect. Consequently, anarchism opposes all systems of rule or forms of archy (i.e., hierarchy, patriarchy, monarchy, oligarchy, anthroparchy, etc.) and is instead premised upon co-operative and egalitarian forms of social, political, and economic organization, where ever evolving and autonomous spatialities may flourish. Although it has often been said that there are as many anarchisms as there are anarchists, my contention is that anarchism should embrace an ethic of nonviolence precisely because violence is recognized as both an act and process of domination.

It is this recognition of the intersectional nature of violence and oppression—and the way these transgress species boundaries—that enables anarchism, of all the radical and dissident traditions, to offer particularly timely, and critical interventions. Indeed, a common interspecies sense of freedom, suffering, and resistance has often been woven together by anarchists' critiques of cruelty and brutality. The Baldelli (1972) quote highlighted earlier in the chapter was one example of this; here the French anarchist geographer Élisée Reclus (2009), in *The Great Kinship of Humans and Fauna* wrote this striking—and poignant passage:

> The poet sees in [cats] magicians; it is that in fact they do seem at times more intelligent than their human friends, in their presentiment of the future. And such and such "happy family," exhibited by showmen in the fairs, does it prove to us that rats, mice, guinea pigs and so many other little creatures, only desire to enter, with man, into the great kinship of gladness and kindness? Every prison cell is soon transformed—provided the warders do not impose "good order"—into a school of lower animals, rats and mice, flies and fleas. The story of Pelisson's spider is well known. The prisoner had begun again to take interest in life, thanks to the little friend whose training he had undertaken, but a guardian of order appears on the scene, and avenging official morality with his boot, crushes the creature which had come to console the unfortunate man!

What I want to impress upon is the importance of taking a critical look at anarchist (vegan) praxis through acknowledging the revolutionary potential that is present within the everyday (household/postcapitalist) spaces we occupy. This emphasis is entirely consistent with an anarchist desire to focus on engaging the complex realities of the here and now, thereby resisting the temptation to indulge in excessively utopian visions of a postcapitalist future. Similarly, the delusional way of thinking that the total liberation we desire will be achieved by either adopting a politics of waiting, or by desiring other people to create the changes in the world we wish to see, is also refused. For, as Dominick (2015, 39) argues, "It's not enough to behave as if the world were different; we have to make the world different."

Here we must also be mindful of another question: would a postcapitalist society, one in which there were no capitalist spaces of nonhuman animal abuse and exploitation, be free from animal oppression? Unfortunately, and not dismissing the fact that, "the abolition of capital . . . would eliminate the most profoundly disproportionate incentive to establish mass-scale apparatus of animal exploitation" (Dominick 2015, 36) the answer is surely, *no*, for the geographies of violence toward (all) animals are far from limited or reducible to capitalist relations. There is still a broader speciesist tapestry of oppression that would need unpacking much further, and one, it must be said, that an anarchist reading of the intersectional natures of oppression is particularly well positioned to do. Moreover, focusing singularly on "the economic," when read as an increasingly influential mode of organizing within the global economy, neoliberal capitalism is still a recent phenomenon, no more than 40 years old. Of course, economies have been around as long as people have lived together, and the configuration of each has allowed specific forms of domination and subjugation to emerge. As Nibert (2003, 11) argues:

> The economic factors that primarily cause the oppression of humans and other animals can be traced to the latter stages of hunting and gathering society. Systematic stalking and killing of other animals contributed to other inequalities, such as the devaluation of women. Hunting shaped relations between female and male humans largely because the bodies of other animals became a prized asset and killing them enhanced male prestige and privilege.

> Capitalism largely continued the 10,000-year-old tradition of exploiting humans and other animals to create wealth and privilege for the few, exploitation that continued to bind the fate of devalued humans and other animals. (Nibert 2003, 12)

With this in mind, we should also be aware (and thankful for!) the fact that there are no off-the-shelf, made-to-order, "anarchist economic blueprint" waiting to be cut and pasted onto society. Far healthier to recognize that:

> . . . Anarchism, in fact, cannot be linked to a particular economic system. Justice is social rather than economic, and injustice and oppression are compatible with any economic system so far devised. There can be no freedom where the modes of production and consumption are decided on any grounds

other than a particular society's needs and resources . . . The economic system acceptable to anarchists is one free from coercion; its name and particular modes of operation are of secondary importance. Economy subordinated to ethics and not controlled by power—that is the anarchist formula. (Baldelli 1972, 21)

That said, it is possible to try and determine the relative presence or absence of anarchy in action within economic modes of organization (White and Williams 2014). For example, we can ask how consistent is an economic system with anti-capitalist sentiment? How far does this economic system embody the social principles of anarchism, in particular by emphasizing mutuality, reciprocity, voluntary association, self-determination, horizontality, and experimentation (Shannon et al. 2012; Springer et al. 2016; Ward 1982)?

At the beginning of this chapter, attention was drawn toward the multiple possibilities about how economies could be—and are—organized in society. Embedded in a critical economic geography literature, a great deal of research highlights the pervasive nature of noncapitalist spaces of work and organization in contemporary society. Here, many important findings have focused explicitly on the household and related forms of community self-help. Within this context, research has shown how many of these daily coping practices are consistent with anarchist principles and modes of organizing (White and Williams 2014, 2016). The following section, will argue for the importance of explicitly locating vegan praxis firmly within the household, and radiating intersectional forms of activism outwards from this space. Thus, as well as acknowledging the importance of challenging the commodification of animals through popular direct forms of activism "out there," what overlooked possibilities for vegan praxis can be found by embedding these firstly in our ordinary everyday domestic environments? In many ways, this acts first an invitation to unleash a new radical imaginary that politicizes "the household." As Byrne, et al. (1998, 16) argued:

> We can view the household as hopelessly local, atomized, a set of disarticulated and isolated units, entwined and ensnared in capitalism's global order, incapable of serving as a site of class politics and radical social transformation. Or we can avoid conflating the micro logical with the merely local and recognize that the household is everywhere, and while it is related in various ways to capitalist exploitation, it is not simply consumed or negated by it. Understanding the household as a site of economic activity, one in which people negotiate and change their relations of exploitation and distribution in response to a wide variety of influences, may help to free us from the gloom that descends when a vision of socialist innovation is consigned to the wholesale transformation of the "capitalist" totality.

If critical attention is paid to the social organization of our household economies, mindful of how this can be done in ways that undermine the intersectional, interspecies natures of oppression and violence, then, rooting vegan anarchist geographies within the household holds great transformative and liberatory potential.

There are several strategic advantages gained by choosing to focus attention on the household, and a few indicative examples will be attempted here. The first is that, for many people, the household is often the space where affirmative and caring relations between humans and other animals can be found, epitomized by the presence of nonhuman companion animals. To encourage new empowered connections between this life-affirming space—which recognizes and values the uniqueness of companion animals (e.g., dogs, cats, and rabbits) therein—in ways to challenge the violent (farming) spaces that distance "us" from of other (farmed) animals (pigs, cows, and sheep) is important. As both Owen (2011) and DeVries (2012) suggest:

> The moving away from "face-to-face" positioning of nonhumans to making them "faceless" things must contribute to the cruelty many face today . . . Any possible switch from relating to nonhuman others as collectives to relating to them instead as individuals has profound implications for how we live on this planet and may have a significant narrative for the future. (Owen 2001, 281)

> The idea is that the more closely situated we are to animals and/or the more valued, cherished, and familiar that they are to us, the less likely we are to exploit them. One way of doing this is to form an emotional bond with an animal, something that frequently occurs with dogs, cats, horses, and other animals with which human beings often share close quarters. Another way would be to visit . . . the factory farms. . . . (DeVries 2012, 135)

Second, a focus on the household would encourage critical attention to be paid toward demonstrably "anarchist" modes of organization of the home and, in doing so, encourage further recognition that the household is a legitimate and central crucible of activism. Indeed, focusing on just 'the kitchen' space and the question of "food" itself comes loaded with potential, unjustifiable examples of "archy" that must be recognized and confronted: Who gets the food? Who prepares the food? Who cooks the food? Who sets the table? Who washes the dirty plates? Who puts away the plates? Where does the uneaten food go? Who empties the dustbin? What, if any, are the gendered divisions of labor here? Again, the intersections between class, gender, race, and speciesism are part of this tapestry of household work practices, and these questions are relevant when attempting to articulate and embody a resurgent critical vegan praxis. Crucially here, and always, "veganism" should neither be seen in isolation, nor as an end in itself. Rather, it is an integral part of broader liberatory currents.

Third, in terms of harnessing a critical vegan praxis within the household, the ability and the responsibility to actively seek out information in order to make better informed ethical choices about food and the production of that food is essential. Where real choices exist (and where they do not then 'how to help address this' becomes the challenge), households could be encouraged to engage in DIY food production. Not only would this allow households to participate in what is for many a pleasurable and cathartic activity, but by ensuring further self-provisioning of food, this directly avoids the need to purchase these and engage directly with the capitalist economy. Any surplus food could be distributed to the wider community, particularly aimed at those who are most in need, and done so via a myriad of not-for-profit forms of exchange. Valuable knowledge, experiences, and skills acquired in growing food could also be shared with others in the local community.

There is also, as mentioned earlier, a great need to raise awareness in ways that challenge the uncritical reflection that all vegan food is cruelty-free. Again, there is a responsibility to be active in learning about the (exploitation of) labor and the environment, in the production and distribution of "vegan" foods. It is this attitude, based on the awareness that genuine *choices* are possible, that explains why a critical vegan gaze should always look to question the conditions of which the food was produced and harvested.

Fourth, in what ways can the practice of freedom enacted in the household be connected and informed by other noncapitalist social and economic spheres, particularly in the wider community? This is the key challenge of reclaiming veganism as a radical praxis, as articulated by Corman (2014):

> The vegan challenge for many animal advocates has been to build coalitions across social justice and environmental movements, develop a stronger analysis of capitalism as a key driver of animal exploitation, and centralize the analyses of those who have always made the connections. In absence of these understandings, veganism is destined to stay a fringe activity of those who want their soy lattes free of animal products, and thus "cruelty-free," but saturated with other forms of misery.

Here direct support and/or expressions of solidarity for grassroots and community organizing groups such as *Food Not Bombs,* local food banks, rescue centers and shelters, and so on could be engaged meaningfully. Ultimately these spheres of freedom, building in size and momentum, are powerful affirmations of the ability to move ever closer toward a post-capitalist politics based on total liberation and freedom for all. To these ends:

> Vegan praxis must incorporate a discourse and affect that reflect not only animal liberation but also total liberation. Vegan praxis must be orientated toward challenging all oppressive power structures, externally—in the realm of material institutions—and internally—in discourse/ perception/ affect . . . A

vegan praxis, ideally, is an ever-changing way of understanding and relations to oneself and all other beings based on empathy, authenticity, reciprocity, justice, and integrity—the principles that underscore true freedom. (Weitzenfeld and Joy 2014, 25)

Recognizing the ever fluid and dynamic nature of society, this ongoing unfolding spirit of freedom and change is important within anarchist sentiments of a (postcapitalist) world, considered by Socha (2012, 15):

It [an anarchist society] is not a perfect society free from violence, hierarchy, and oppression; rather, it is an evolved society whose abiding objective is freedom from violence and oppression, not capital gain . . . .

This recognition should also be liberating for scholars and activists who central focus is intent on eradicating capitalism and all its represents. The paths toward freedom are many, as conversely are the paths toward violence, domination, and oppression. Thus, a rejection of dogmatic strategies to tackle the capitalist exploitation of other animals, and a turn toward embracing diversity and difference in strategies of resistance, all the better to reflect and respond to specific and contextual values and opportunities should be encouraged. As Dominick (2015, 27) argued:

What if veganism and anarchism weren't do-or-die, go-for-broke ideologies but rather constellations of values and principles helping us plot our way to a better future?

What if, indeed! What wonderful new horizons and opportunities for liberation and freedom could yet emerge and prosper?

CONCLUSIONS

In countless ways, the exploitation of animals rebounds to create crises within the human world itself. The vicious circle of violence and destruction can end only if and when the human species learns to form harmonious relations—nonhierarchical and nonexploitative—with other animal species and the natural world. Human, animal, and Earth liberation are interrelated projects that must be fought for as one (Best 2006).

A key aim of the chapter has been to better understand the ways in which capitalism commodifies both nonhuman and human life and seeks to appropriate potentially radical postcapitalist alternatives that are present in activist calls to "go vegan." The focus has been necessarily partial, particularly in the choice to concentrate exclusively on industrial farming practices: to the neglect of other examples of animal abuse done so for profit. Focusing on anything from the "pet" industry, zoos and circus, to hunting and vivisection would have been equally legitimate. The chapter ends, though, as it began, by recognizing that critical animal studies itself is in need of a critical appraisal: how far is the perception of the positive impacts CAS has had—and is having—in the world, reflected in actual lived realities?

In many ways, the challenge for critical animal studies seems to be greater than it has ever been. However, I would suggest that there exists, often in the most unexpected of places, wonderful examples and encounters of interspecies solidarity in the here and now; examples from which we can hopefully draw new depths of inspiration and strength from. In this context, while the need to reflect on the relative success and limits of critical animal studies is an ever present one, there must also be a willingness to push forward into new and increasingly radical directions, *if* this serves to effectively challenge the structural genocide of capitalism and other forms of oppression and domination. Fundamentally, though, these challenges will stand the most chance of success by taking the line of *greater* resistance; that is to say by changing those hearts and minds that are currently unaware of, or resistant too, appeals for a nonviolent, critical praxis of total liberation animated by anarchism. Of course, this challenge also demands that we take an honest look at where we (personally) are now in terms of our own activism and in our future ability "to be" an effective part of the wider change that we wish to see. Goodman (2011, 34) argued that:

> A free society cannot be the substitution of a "new order" for an old order; it is the extension of spheres of free action until they make up most of the social life.

Where better to begin then by focusing more critically on the prefigurative anarchist praxis within the household? How can a more conscious awareness of the everyday activism that takes place work to challenge ongoing, intersectional speciesist and capitalist relations "out there"? How can we strive to ensure that demonstrably anarchist spaces of freedom found within (our) households are always out there and everywhere in (our) worlds? Responding to this challenge, we should always be mindful that our deepest and greatest freedom will always be that which is intimately tied up with the freedom of our fellow beings:

> This is what anarchists mean by freedom. Left to our own devices, freed from the control of rulers and exploiters, we individuals would co-operate and combine in the way that we were intended to, in the same way as our fellow creatures, plants, insects, fungi, and microbes (Cudenec 2014).

If this chapter has served to generate some further insight and reflection, in ways that encourage constructive discussion—and activism—around questions of capitalism and the commodification of animals, vegan praxis, anarchism, and the importance of recognizing the household as an important site of activism, then it will have served an important and timely purpose.

REFERENCES

Animal Liberation Front. "Going Underground for Animal Liberation." Accessed on August 18, 2016, from http://www.animalliberationfront.com/ALFront/Activist%20Tips/GoingUnderground.htm.

Arrieta, R. M. 2004. "Hidden Horrors: California Dairy Workers Face Danger and Abuse." *Dollar & Sense*, Issue 255. Accessed on August 18, 2016, from http://www.dollarsandsense.org/archives/2004/0904arrieta.html.

Baldelli, Giovanni. 1972. *Social Anarchism.* London: Penguin Books.

Best, Steve. 2006. "Rethinking Revolution: Animal Liberation, Human Liberation, and the Future of the Left." *The International Journal of Inclusive Democracy*, 2(3). Accessed on August 18, 2016, from http://www.inclusivedemocracy.org/journal/vol2/vol2_no3_Best_rethinking_revolution.htm.

Best, Steve, and Anthony J. Nocella (eds.). 2006. *Igniting the Revolution: Voices in Defense of the Earth.* Edinburgh, UK: AK Press.

Byrne, Ken, R. Forest, J. K. Gibson-Graham, S. Healy, and G. Horvath. 1998. "Imagining and Enacting Noncapitalist Futures." Rethinking Economy Project Working Paper No. 1. Accessed September 9, 2016, from http://www3.nd.edu/~econrep/papers/graham.html.

Castree, Noel. 2003. "Commodifying What Nature?" *Progress in Human Geography*, 27(3): 273–297. doi: 10.1191/0309132503ph428oa.

Clarkson, Damien. 2014. "Business and Entrepreneurs Seize Opportunities in Rise of Veganism." *The Guardian*, November 28. Accessed on August 18, 2016, from https://www.theguardian.com/sustainable-business/2014/nov/28/business-and-entrepreneurs-seize-opportunities-in-rise-of-veganism.

Colling, Sarat, Sean Parson, and Alessandro Arrigoni. 2014. "Until All Are Free: Total Liberation through Revolutionary Decolonization, Groundless Solidarity, and a Relationship Framework." In Anthony J. Nocella, John Sorenson, Kim Socha, and Atsuko Matsuoka (eds.), *Defining Critical Animal Studies.* New York: Peter Lang Publishing, 28–48.

Caldera, Perla Vasquez. 2016. "Why Vegan Is Big Business." Accessed on August 18, 2016, from https://www.linkedin.com/pulse/why-vegan-big-business-perla-vasquez-caldera

Cudenec, Paul. 2014. "Anarchy Is Life!" Accessed on August 18, 2016, from https://network23.org/paulcudenec/2014/12/10/anarchy-is-life/.

Cochrane, Alasdair. 2010. *An Introduction to Animals and Political Theory.* Basingstoke, UK: Palgrave MacMillan.

Cohen, Richard A. 2016. "A New Economic Order Without Violence." In Vicente Berdayes and John W. Murphy (eds.), *Neoliberalism, Economic Radicalism, and the Normalization of Violence.* New York: Springer International.

Corman, Lauren. 2014. "Capitalism, Veganism, and the Animal Industrial Complex." Rabble.ca blogs. Accessed on August 18, 2016, from http://rabble.ca/blogs/bloggers/vegan-challenge/2014/04/capitalism-veganism-and-animal-industrial-complex.

Dominik, Brian. 2015. "Anarcho-Veganism Revisited." In Anthony Nocella, Richard J. White, and Erika Cudworth (eds.), *Anarchism and Animal Liberation:*

Essays on Complementary Elements of Total Liberation. Jefferson, NC: McFarland.

DeVries, Scott M. 2012. *Creature Discomfort. Fauna-Criticism, Ethics, and the Representation of Animals in Spanish American Fiction and Poetry.* Leiden, the Netherlands: Brill.

Eisnitz, Gail, A. 2006. *Slaughterhouse: The Shocking Story of Greed, Neglect, and Inhumane Treatment Inside the U.S. Meat Industry.* New York: Prometheus Books.

Faith. 2016. "My First Day at Work at the Slaughterhouse." Accessed on August 18, 2016, from http://www.veganaustralia.org.au/my_first_day_at_work_at_the_slaughterhouse

Food Empowerment Project. 2016. *Slavery in the U.S.* Accessed on August 18, 2016, from http://www.foodispower.org/factory-farm-workers/.

Fitzgerald, Amy F., and David Pellow. 2014. "Ecological Defense for Animal Liberation." In Anthony J. Nocella, John Sorenson, Kim Socha, and Atsuko Matsuoka (eds.), *Defining Critical Animal Studies.* New York: Peter Lang Publishing, 28–48.

Franks, Benjamin, and Matthew Wilson. 2010. *Anarchism and Moral Philosophy.* New York: MacMillan.

Garcia, Christine L. 2011. "Isn't Justice Supposed to Be Blind? Practicing Animal Law." In Lisa Kemmerer (ed.), *Sister Species: Woman, Animals, and Social Justice.* Chicago: University of Illinois Press, 141–151.

Gellatley, Juliet, and Tony Wardle. 1996. *The Silent Ark.* Glasgow, UK: Thorsons.

Gillespie, Katie. 2013. "Sexualized Violence and the Gendered Commodification of the Animal Body in Pacific Northwest, U.S. Dairy Production." *Gender, Place, and Culture.* doi:10.1080/0966369X.2013.832665.

Gillespie, Kathryn, and Rosemary-Claire Collard (eds.). 2015. *Critical Animal Geographies. Politics, Intersections, and Hierarchies in a Multispecies World.* London: Routledge,

Ginsberg, Caryn. 2011 Vegetarian Means Business: Market Strategy and Research Report. The Market for Vegetarian Foods. Arlington: Priority Ventures Group LLC. 1–16.

Harari, Yuval Noah. 2015. "Industrial Farming is One of the Worst Crimes in History." *The Guardian.* September 25. Accessed on August 18, 2016, from https://www.theguardian.com/books/2015/sep/25/industrial-farming-one-worst-crimes-history-ethical-question.

Hawthorne, Mark. 2013. "The Problem with Palm Oil." *Veg News.* May 22. Accessed on August 18, 2016, from http://vegnews.com/articles/page.do?pageId=5795&catId=1.

Jenkins, Stephanie, and Vasile Stănescu. 2014. "One Struggle." In Anthony J. Nocella, John Sorenson, Kim Socha, and Atsuko Matsuoka (eds.), *Defining Critical Animal Studies.* New York: Peter Lang Publishing, 76–85.

Kemmerer, Lisa. 2011. "Appendix: Factory Farming and Females." In Lisa Kemmerer (ed.), *Sister Species: Woman, Animals, and Social Justice.* Chicago: University of Illinois Press, 173–186.

Kinna, Ruth. 2012. "Preface." In Deric Shannon, Anthony J. Nocella, and John Asimakopoulos (eds.), *The Accumulation of Freedom: Writings on Anarchist Economics.* Oakland, CA: AK Press, 5–19.

Lange-Chenier, Hanna. 2014. "EU Beef and Poultry Sector Growing, Pork Expected to Shrink." Accessed on August 18, 2016, from http://www.globalmeatnews.com/Industry-Markets/EU-beef-and-poultry-sector-growing-pork-expected-to-shrink.

Lawrence, Felicity. 2016. "The Gangsters on England's Doorstep." *The Guardian.* Accessed on August 18, 2016, from https://www.theguardian.com/uk-news/2016/may/11/gangsters-on-our-doorstep.

Leech, Gary. 2012. *Capitalism: A Structural Genocide.* London: Zed Books.

Leenaert, Tobias. 2016. "Interview with Kristina Mering." Accessed on August 18, 2016, from http://veganstrategist.org/2016/08/05/slaughterhouse-workers-the-meat-industrys-other-victims/.

Mitchell, Les. 2011. Moral Disengagement and Support for Nonhuman Animal Farming. *Society & Animals,* 19(2011): 38–58. doi: 10.1163/1568530 11X545529.

Nibert, David. 2003. "Humans and Other Animals: Sociology's Moral and Intellectual Challenge." *International Journal of Sociology and Social Policy,* 23(3): 4–25. http://dx.doi.org/10.1108/01443330310790237.

Nibert, David. 2013. *Animal Oppression and Human Violence: Domesecration, Capitalism, and Global Conflict.* New York: Columbia University Press.

Nibert, David. 2014. "Foreword." In Anthony J. Nocella, John Sorenson, Kim Socha, and Atsuko Matsuoka (eds.), *Defining Critical Animal Studies.* New York: Peter Lang Publishing, ix–xii.

Nocella, Anthony J., John Sorenson, Kim Socha, and Atsuko Matsuoka (eds.). 2014. "The Emergence of Critical Animal Studies." In Anthony J. Nocella, John Sorenson, Kim Socha, and Atsuko Matsuoka (eds.) *Defining Critical Animal Studies.* New York: Peter Lang Publishing, xix.

Noske, Barbara. 1989. *Humans and Other Animals.* London: Pluto Press.

Novek, Joel. 2012. "Disciplining and Distancing: Confined Pigs in the Factory Farming Gulag." In Aaron Gross and Anne Valley (eds.), *Animals and the Human Imagination: A Companion to Animal Studies.* New York: Columbia University Press.

Ornelas, Lauren. 2011. "An Appetite for Justice." In Lisa Kemmerer (ed.), *Sister Species: Woman, Animals, and Social Justice.* Chicago: University of Illinois Press, 152–160.

Pachirat, Timothy 2011. *Every Twelve Seconds: Industrialized Slaughter and the Politics of Sight.* New Haven, CT: Yale University Press.

Pellow, David N. 2015. "Foreword." In Anthony J. Nocella II, Richard J. White, and Erika Cudworth (eds.), *Anarchism and Animal Liberation: Essays on Complementary Elements of Total Liberation.* Jefferson, NC: McFarland.

Phelps, Norm. 2012. *The Dominion of Love: Animal Rights According to the Bible.* New York: Lantern Books.

Phelps, Norm. 2013. *Changing the Game: Why the Battle for Animal Liberation Is so Hard and How We Can Change It.* New York: Lantern Books.

Philpott, Tom. 2015. "We're Eating Less Meat—Yet Factory Farms Are Still Growing." *Mother Jones.* June 3. Accessed on August 18, 2016, from http://www.motherjones.com/tom-philpott/2015/06/factory-farms-keep-getting-bigger.

Reclus, Élisée. 2009. *The Great Kinship of Humans and Fauna*. Accessed on March 27, 2017, from http://theanarchistlibrary.org/library/elisee-reclus -the-great-kinship-of-humans-and-fauna.

Regan, Tom. 2004. *Empty Cages: Facing the Challenge of Animal Rights*. Lanham, MD: Rowman & Littlefield.

Rudy, Kathy. 2011. *Loving Animals: Towards a New Animal Advocacy*. Minneapolis, MN: University of Minnesota Press.

Shannon, Deric, Anthony J. Nocella, and John Asimakopoulos. 2012. "Anarchist Economics: A Holistic View." In Deric Shannon, Anthony J. Nocella, and John Asimakopoulos (eds.), *The Accumulation of Freedom Writings on Anarchist Economics*. Oakland, CA: AK Press.

Sorenson, John (ed.). 2014. *Critical Animal Studies: Thinking the Unthinkable*. Toronto: Canadian Scholars Press.

Spangher, Lucas. 2014. "The Overlooked Plight of Factory Farm Workers." August 18 (updated October 18). *Huffington Post*. Accessed on August 18, 2016, from http://www.huffingtonpost.com/lucas-spangher/plight-of-factory -farm-workers_b_5662261.html.

Springer, Simon, Marcelo Lopes de Souza, and Richard J. White. 2016. "Transgressing Frontiers through the Radicalization of Pedagogy." In Simon Springer, Marcelo Lopes de Souza, and Richard J. White (eds.), *Radicalization of Pedagogy*. London: Rowman & Littlefield, 1–26.

Springer, Simon. 2012. "Anarchism! What Geography Still Ought to Be!" *Antipode*, 44(5): 1605–1624.

Stallwood, Kim. 2014. "Animal Rights: Moral Crusade or Social Movement?" In John Sorenson (ed.), *Critical Animal Studies: Thinking the Unthinkable*. Toronto: Canadian Scholars Press.

Stuart, Diana, Rebecca Schewe, and Ryan Gunderson. 2013. "Extending Social Theory to Farm Animals: Addressing Alienation in the Dairy Sector." *Sociologia Ruralis*, 53(2). doi:10.1111/soru.12005.

Taylor, Jo, and Julian Sturdy. 2013. "Fens migrant workers 'exploited.'" *BBC News*. Accessed on August 18, 2016, from http://www.bbc.co.uk/news/uk-england -24108665.

Torres, Bob. 2007. *Making a Killing: The Political Economy of Animal Rights*. Oakland, CA: AK Press.

Torres, Bob, and Jenna Torres. 2005. *Being Vegan in a Non-Vegan World*. Oakland, CA: Tofu Hound Press.

Twine, Richard. 2012. "Revealing the 'Animal-Industrial Complex'—A Concept & Method for Critical Animal Studies?" *Journal for Critical Animal Studies*. 10(1): 12–39.

Twine, Richard, 2013. "Addressing the Animal–Industrial Complex." In Raymond Corbey and Annette Lanjouw (eds.), *The Politics of Species Reshaping our Relationships with Other Animals*. Cambridge, UK: Cambridge University Press, 77–92. doi: http://dx.doi.org/10.1017/CBO9781139506755.009.

Vegan Society. 2016a. "Sale Figures for Vegan Food Products." Accessed on August 18, 2016, https://www.vegansociety.com/about-us/key-facts.

Vegan Society. 2016b. "There are Three and Half Times as Many Vegans as There Were in 2006, Making It the Fastest Growing Lifestyle Movement."

Accessed on August 18, 2016, from https://www.vegansociety.com/whats
-new/news/find-out-how-many-vegans-are-great-britain.

Wadiwel, Dinesh. J. 2015. *The War Against Animals*. Leiden, the Netherlands: Brill.

Watters, Nadine. 2015. "16 Million People in the U.S. Are Now Vegan or Vegetarian! The Raw Food World." Accessed on August 18, 2016, from https://news
.therawfoodworld.com/16-million-people-us-now-vegan-vegetarian/.

Weitzenfeld, Adam, and Melanie Joy. 2014. "An Overview of Anthropocentrism, Humanism, and Speciesism in Critical Animal Theory." In Anthony J. Nocella, John Sorenson, Kim Socha, and Atsuko Matsuoka (eds.), *Defining Critical Animal Studies*. New York: Peter Lang Publishing, 3–25.

White, Richard J. 2015a. "Critical Animal Geographies and Anarchist Praxis: Shifting Perspectives from the Animal 'Question' to the Animal 'Condition.'" In K. Gillespie and R. C. Collard (eds.), *Critical Animal Geographies: Power, Space, and Violence in a Multispecies World*. London: Routledge, 19–35.

White, Richard J. 2015b. "Following in the Footsteps of Élisée Reclus: Disturbing Places of Inter-Species Violent That Are Hidden in Plain Sight." In *Anarchism and Animal Liberation essays on Complementary Elements of Total Liberation*. Jefferson, NC: McFarland Press, 212–230.

White, Richard J., and Erika Cudworth. 2014. "Taking It to the Streets: Challenging Systems of Domination from Below." In A. Nocella, J. Sorenson, K. Socha., and A. Matsuoka (eds.), *Critical Animal Studies Reader: An Introduction to an Intersectional Social Justice Approach to Animal Liberation*. New York: Peter Lang, 202–220.

White, Richard J., and Simon Springer. (forthcoming). "For spatial emancipation." In J. Sorenson and A. Matsuoka (eds.), *Critical Animal Studies*. Lanham, MD: Rowman & Littlefield.

White, Richard J., and Colin C. Williams. 2014. "Anarchist Economic Practices in a 'Capitalist' Society: Some Implications for Organisation and the Future of Work." *Ephemera: Theory and Politics in Organization,* 14(4): 951–975.

White, Richard J., and Colin C. Williams. 2012. "The Pervasive Nature of Heterodox Economic Spaces at a Time of Neoliberal Crisis: Towards a 'Post-Neoliberal' Anarchist Future." *Antipode.* 44(5): 1–20.

Williams, Colin C. 2005. *A Commodified World? Mapping the Limits of Capitalism*. London: ZED.

Woodhouse, Leighton. 2012. "How the Pursuit of Animal Liberation Activists Became Among the FBI's 'Highest Domestic Terrorism Priorities.'" *Huffington Post*, October 5 (updated December 24). Accessed September 9, 2016, from http://www.huffingtonpost.com/leighton-woodhouse/animal
-liberation_b_2012426.html.

Worldwatch Institute. 2013. "Meat Production Continues to Rise." Accessed on August 18, 2016, from http://www.worldwatch.org/node/5443.

Liberator or Terrorist? (Copyright © 2004 Sue Coe. Courtesy Galerie St. Etienne, NY)

13

The Business of Revolution is Counterrevolutionary

Roger Yates

In a video entitled *Understanding Sociology: Making Sense of Sociological Theory*,[1] Anthony Giddens explains what he regards as the chief defining characteristic of the capitalist economic system: *Everything can be bought and sold*. The narrator adds, "including people."

What's up with your vegan animal rights people? They just don't get capitalism.[2]

The quote here comes from a presentation in Dublin, Ireland, entitled "Challenging Racism and Ableism within the Animal Liberation Movement and Fighting for Total Liberation" by Anthony Nocella II, which took place on March 2014. He was describing an "animal movement problem:" that other social justice movements do not take the modern-day nonhuman animal advocacy movement seriously. Nocella (2014) says they have good reason not to:

> We have to acknowledge, right off the bat, that animal rights people are very single-issue, maybe not the people in this room. But there are a lot of other people like P*e*TA that gives you all a bad name. So the moment you walk into a room, they think you are a member of P*e*TA, right, so they think you are sexist, ableist, and racist. Right off the bat, they think you're vegan, and you

don't get any other issue. They might even think that you are a republican, a conservative, or neo-Nazi.

Nocella argues that "there are so many organizations [in the nonhuman animal movement] who are saying, oh, you can have green capitalism: all we need is the CEO of Whole Foods to go vegan, and the world is a better place," and maintains that social justice movements tend to regard the nonhuman animal advocacy movement as a naïve apolitical single-issue mobilization. The advocacy movement for other animals displays a shockingly shallow understanding of the importance of the most powerful structural elements of society, namely the capitalist economic system and mindset, even though they represent the main block to the achievement of its aims.[3]

In *Making a Killing: The Political Economy of Animal Rights* (Torres 2007), Bob Torres describes a common view of students in his first-year university class when the issue of poverty comes up. He says: "In many of my introductory sociology classes, I often begin discussions about poverty by asking students why people are poor. Inevitably, people tell me that poor folks are lazy or unintelligent, that they are somehow deserving of their poverty" (Torres 2007, 7). Torres prefaces this remark by noting that we live embedded into capitalist societies run by capitalist economies; that our very thoughts have the ideology that upholds capitalist domination as a central constituent; that we are *utterly familiar* with the norms and values of capitalism, and we come to know through socialization processes its fundamental explanatory "scripts."

Therefore, for Torres, his students were severely hampered by their individualistic view of the world, and a fuller understanding of structural elements of society, especially of structural capitalism, is beneficial. Therefore, he tells them that the sociological literature on poverty reveals a complex picture, a picture that includes understanding that issues such as poverty, unemployment, and reserve armies of labor are simply part and parcel of the capitalist economic order. The sort of structural analysis missing in these sociology students' accounts of poverty is also absent, by and large, in the modern nonhuman animal advocacy movement.

In this chapter, drawing from social movement theory and recent developments within the advocacy movement for other animals, I argue that the modern movement's shallow understanding of social structure, and what it means to exist in—and not challenge—and even attempt to "use" the capitalist mode of production is a serious impediment to it succeeding. Further, its shallowness acts to reduce down the original radical justice-for-all vision of the vegan nonhuman animal advocacy movement. Just as "animal rights" so often slides into some form of nonhuman animal welfare, the modern individualistic conception of "vegan" regularly reduces it to a diet or to some consumer health fad.

Casey Taft (2016) argues that things are so confused within the movement that, ". . . what it really means to be vegan is not well understood, as popular culture and mainstream animal advocacy organizations promote the view that veganism is simply a diet" (Taft 2016, 13). This chapter calls for a radical recapturing of the original vision of veganism, best expressed by sociologist Matthew Cole (2014, 233):

> The vegan telos [end/purpose/goal], therefore, combines compassionate non-exploitation of other animals with an emancipated vegan self and a more compassionate human society. Vegan ethics, from the beginning, was directed towards these interconnected goals of transforming human beings and transforming human society, with both flowing from the foundational reconfiguration of human-nonhuman animal relations.

This must be read as an anti-capitalist venture. Citing Benton 1993, Fox 1999, Nibert 2002, and Torres 2007, Angus Taylor (2009, 183) notes that, "As a number of philosophers and observers have remarked, the animal liberation movement is unlikely to succeed in its goals unless it joins forces with other movements challenging the assumptions in industrial society . . . [in which] capitalism has succeeded in creating an increasingly integrated world economy."

Other academic voices continue to explore these issues. For example, Alex Plows and I (1997, cited in Yates 2009) explored the role of the "activist-researcher" or "bridge person" who could not only explain a social movement to the academy but also teach social movement participants about capitalist social forces that impact on what they do. Rob White (2002) explores how capitalism assigns value to profitable use. Maxwell Schnurer (2004) notes that the creation of industrial capitalist power was essential in enabling "mechanized animal exploitation." Piers Beirne (2007) explores the issue of other animals' use in the context of green criminology and harms to the environment, humans, and other animals. Gaarder (2011) speaks about women in the nonhuman animal advocacy movement, anti-globalization, and the issue of "cross-movement alliances." David Nibert (2013) identifies the use of other animals as violence integral to the rise of corporate capitalism, and Sue Donaldson and Will Kymlicka (2014) note that "as a result of capitalism, we now have very powerful vested corporate interests in the exploitation of animals, who will resist any concerted social movement to challenge supremacist ideologies," while arguing that the rise of nonhuman animal exploitation cannot be laid solely at capitalism's door, and neither will the dismantling of capitalism alone be enough to liberate other animals from human tyranny (Taylor 2014).

A few voices within the advocacy movement for other animals itself have made the case for seeing the struggle for nonhuman animal rights within its structural economic constraints. For example, Juliet Gellatley and Tony

Wardle (1996) describe the role of multinationals, colonization, and the depopulation of Ireland, in an exposé of "meat—the global killer;" Mark Gold (1998, 4) describes the life and work of Henry Salt, "a self-confessed 'rationalist, socialist, pacifist, and humanitarian'" whose position on human and nonhuman animal rights, in the twenty-first century, would be called "intersectional." Both Jim Mason (2005) and Will Tuttle (2005) provide critical accounts of humanity's "herding culture." While Mason focuses on his concept of *misothery* (defined as hatred and contempt for other animals), Tuttle's more radical exposition sees generationally transmitted human culture embedding humans as "modern inhabitants of a herding and animal-consuming capitalist culture" (Tuttle 2005, 22). Richard Kahn (2010) provides a radical, vegan-relevant, exploration of "critical pedagogy" and "ecoliteracy;" Travis Elise (2013) writes an anti-capitalist critique of recent books, debates and issues in the movement; Steven Best's (2014) vision of "Total Liberation" explores crises under the impact of global capitalism, human overpopulation, species extinction, and runaway climate change; and critical sociologists, "opposed to the exploitation of other animals," Matthew Cole and Kate Stewart (2014), explore the capitalist commodification of other animals and how that is reflected in cultural artifacts.

Many radical nonhuman animal advocates came into the movement—or its periphery at least—through punk music, radical feminism, anti-capitalism, and forms of anarchy. A great deal of this often zine-based literature is, naturally enough, staunchly anti-capitalist in outlook. Examples include *From Animals to Anarchism* by Kevin Watkinson and Dónal O'Driscoll (2014), *Beasts of Burden: Capitalism—Animals—Communism*, in Do or Die.[4] The "Anti-Capitalist Meet-Up: An Anti-Capitalist Case for Animal Rights,"[5] contains a critique of private property and labor inequalities. *Humans, Animals and Nature in The Crisis: On the Need for an Anti-Capitalist Critique of Animal Exploitation*[6] is a call to action against the "daily barbarity of capitalism." The Talon Conspiracy[7] (formerly Conflict Gypsy) provides an extensive archive of anti-capitalist, pro-nonhuman animal liberation, materials dating back to the 1940s.

Finally, and most surprising perhaps, is the rather anarchic, anti-capitalist vision created by the Movement for Compassionate Living, an offshoot from the British Vegan Society. They suggest a "new world order" which is based on self-reliant, tree-based, autonomous, vegan villages. They oppose voting, declaring that the "present money-dominated, profit-motivated, competitive civilization" is unsustainable, arguing that workers work long hours at the behest of managers who themselves are trapped into the profit-driven system in which politicians are beholden to corporations. They suggest a radical alternative built on a system of self-governing vegan villages based on frequent decision-making meetings in which issues such as "deviant behavior" is dealt with at "village consensus meetings" (Movement for Compassionate Living, 1997).

Other more prominent and mainstream movement for other animals' names are not so helpful in identifying capitalism as a major cultural and economic engine of nonhuman animal exploitation. David Nibert (2002, 237), for example, underlining his own central position that the exploitation of "others" has capitalist economic self-interest as its chief motivational base, explains that, "Some powerful advocates for other animals—such as Regan, Stallwood, and Spiegel . . . suggest either overtly or implicitly that economic systems, capitalism in particular, are not primary in the causation of oppression." Kim Stallwood (1996, 195) regards the nature of different economic systems as rather irrelevant in terms of the use and exploitation of other animals. Therefore, be it in a communist, capitalist, or a "developing" world, "the labor of nonhuman animals is used." Law professor and animal advocate Gary Francione's view on this subject was outlined in a 2014 Facebook post[8] and is essentially a mirror image of Stallwood's 1996 view.

As a general matter, however, and certainly in terms of the general day-to-day discourse of the mainstream nonhuman animal advocacy movement, this subject is hardly ever mentioned, let alone discussed at length: it is certainly not a major part of claims-making in the movement. Moreover, just as we see that some mainstream voices deny the importance of an anti-capitalist analysis, some also defend capitalist consumerism as a means of ending the exploitation of other animals. Some nonhuman animal advocates believe that "animal rights" and/or veganism can be sold as in the selling of ethics and ethical ideas. Recent developments in the nonhuman animal advocacy movement are quite disturbing in this regard. The last few years have seen a growth in advocates, suggesting the nonhuman animal cause can benefit by becoming familiar with sales psychology and some elements of the data from "pop" psychology. One consequence of this attempt to "sell ideas" as if they are commodities themselves has been a moderation of views, a change in campaigning attitudes, with notions of "effectiveness" as the new clarion call, and moves away from the early radical vision of the vegan pioneers (Cole 2014), for example, in the name of research-informed "strategy" (Taft 2016). Efforts and pressures to moderate views within social movement organizations are predicted in some social movement theorizing.

SOCIAL MOVEMENT DYNAMICS

Social movements "move" and can be lively entities. As early as the 1960s, it was recognized by Herbert Blumer that social movements are, "made by the agents who are involved in them" (quoted in Tovey 2007, 83). However, Blumer (1969) described a career path or "stages" that may apply to social movements (Mauss 1975; Tilly 1978). There is an increasing complex literature on this, but the stages of social movements can be summarized as follows: 1. emergence; 2. coalescence; 3. bureaucratization, and 4. decline. John Macionis and Ken Plummer (2008, 526) note that stage 4, *decline*, does not necessarily mean the death or the total demise of a social movement, precisely because of the dynamism inherent in them. It may mean that a movement may wither, but it may also lead to a new phase, a rebirth, a recapturing of an original radical vision—social movement theorists speak of movement "cycles" (Staggenborg 1998) and "waves." (Freeman and Johnson 1999).

The "stages" of most interest to the thrust of this chapter are 3 and 4. Bureaucratization, as Jonathan Christiansen notes, was called "formalization" by Blumer and is "characterized by higher levels of organization and coalition-based strategies" (Christiansen 2009). Moreover, "SMOs will come to rely on staff persons with specialized knowledge that can run the day-to-day operations of the organization and carry out movement goals."

Doug McAdam (1999, 325), in a critical evaluation of resource mobilization theory, describes the overall process of stage 3 using the following characteristics: "oligarchization," "conservatization," and "institutionalization." McAdam suggests that oligarchization involves

> the emergence of an elite that comes to exercise disproportionate control over the movement organization. These "leaders" share an interest in the organization's survival as a prerequisite of maintaining their privileged position within the organization, *even* when this survival requires the subordination of the movement's original goals. (McAdam 1999, 325–326, emphasis in original)

McAdam is essentially describing phenomena social movement theorists have called "goal displacement" (Warner and Havens 1968)[9] when the original goals of an organization are replaced by more conservative ones. Elizabeth West (2000, 120) suggests that goal displacement is what happens when an organization takes its "eyes off the ball." When it comes to institutionalization, McAdam (1999, 326) says that this

> involves the development of a hierarchical organization, an explicit division of labor, and established administrative procedures. While created to facilitate organizational function, these inevitably dampen member enthusiasm and creativity in favor of predictability and organizational stability. Thus, institutionalization encourages movement organizations to shift resources from achieving their original goals to maintaining their current structure.

As suggested, this is something that *may* happen to social movements and social movement organizations. It is not inevitable, and indeed McAdam (1999, 344) says that the movement he looked at, the civil rights movement, grew progressively more radical over time.

In a similar vein, Suzanne Staggenborg (1988, 585) offers a critical examination of the impact of "professionalization" in the pro-choice movement.

She says that, "Resource mobilization theorists have argued that profession-
alized social movements emerge as more sources of funding become available
for activists who make careers out of being movement leaders." Staggenborg argues that there is an important difference between waged professional
managers and "movement entrepreneurs"[10] Thus, while John McCarthy
and Mayer Zald (1977) suggest that movement entrepreneurs create "professional" social movement organizations (SMOs), Staggenborg argues
that they may prefer to keep things informal and resist the formalization of
organizations. Where organizations *are* formalized, then we see the rise of
the "professional"—"the rise in career leadership" (Staggenborg 1988, 594)—
who tend to emphasize management issues, and formulization may occur
in the social movement organizations "that have the resources to hire professional managers" (Staggenborg 1988, 594). Building on William Gamson's (1995) insight that bureaucratic or formalized organizational structure
is associated with organizational maintenance, Staggenborg (1988, 595)
says that, "professional leaders have a strong motivation to promote formalization: ongoing resources are needed to pay the salary of the professional
manager." Thus, professional managers are interested in the expansion and
long-term survival of the social movements they lead because their careers
are entangled with such developments.

Recent members of the modern advocacy movement for other animals
are likely to be aware of criticisms of Greenpeace International from the
film *Cowspiracy*.[11] However, those longer in the tooth will know that Paul
Watson, who founded the Sea Shepherd marine conservation organization,
was expelled from Greenpeace International and has been a critic ever since.
In 2016, Watson complained that Greenpeace International had gone over
to "the dark side" and "sold out" on its seals campaigning, writing, "I initiated and led the first Greenpeace campaigns against sealing from 1975 until
1977. I really never thought I would see the day when Greenpeace would
sell out to the sealing industry."[12] Ronald Shaiko (1993) wrote about Greenpeace International in terms relevant to this chapter. For example, he mentions that Paul Watson co-founded Greenpeace International in 1971 but
"left" six years later to set up Sea Shepherd. Shaiko says that, "dissatisfied
with what he perceived to be a betrayal by Greenpeace organizers of the
group's original direct-action mission, Watson criticizes Greenpeace for
shifting the focus toward fund-raising and media baiting" (Shaiko 1993, 90).
Shaiko (1993, 96) reports that a 1990 study found that the largest proportion
(23.1 percent) of Greenpeace International's budget was spent on fundraising,
compared to an 11.6 percent average of 11 other groups surveyed, while
the organization became increasingly hostile to some direct-action tactics
such as "monkeywrenching" and "ecotage:" "In fact, some of the recent
activities of the leadership indicate a greater willingness to act in concert
with the mainstream reform organizations" (Shaiko 1993, 98). Pressure to

engage in reformism is ever present. Political scientist Robert Garner (2004) speaks about the benefits of campaigning groups achieving "insider status," and Shaiko (1993, 98) suggests that Greenpeace International, seen as radical by some other conservation organizations and as a sellout by others, is left to attempt an "insider-outsider" approach.

CAPITALISM AND THE NONHUMAN ANIMAL ADVOCACY MOVEMENT

The Selling (out) of A Revolutionary Idea

Rejecting speciesism requires the rejection of the exploitation of *all* who are oppressed under capitalism, and those on the left who reject the oppression of all human animals need to start asking themselves why they draw the line so as to exclude the other sentient beings with whom we share the planet. Conversely, those in the animal rights movement *must* understand that a coherent animal rights position *needs to* provide justice for all beings. Any other position leads to a valid criticism that our movement is misanthropic. (Charlton et al. 1993, emphasis in original)

David Nibert (2002, 243) argues that, "those active in the movement for the liberation of other animals must examine their tendency to view capitalism as a largely benign social force." Unfortunately, the mainstream advocacy movement for other animals does not have a good track record in terms of thinking critically about the structural forces in our lives. If anything, the very structural forces *within* the movement acts against critical thinking and drives towards moderation, as some social movement theorizing suggests. The funding structure and the "faulty giving culture"[13] of the nonhuman animal movement also block what would arguably be the most revolutionary development possible: a growth in grassroots nonhuman animal activism that seeks to join forces with other social justice movements acting and organizing locally. Such a development would inevitably create a reflexive movement culture that would eliminate the racist, sexist, and even fascist factions in the advocacy movement for other animals.[14]

Recent developments in the movement seem to indicate that it is now more corporatized than ever, with several national and international organizations competing in the nonhuman animal campaigning marketplace. The movement is still largely focused on "social transformation largely through changed perceptions and priorities on the part of individuals and through welfarist reforms" (Nibert 2002, 243), with a recent counterrevolutionary push towards developing a capitalist market for new vegan food technologies and a phenomenon known as *reducetarianism*.

A 2016 Orcas and Animals blog entry about nonhuman animal movement matters spells out the problem, and although understated, it can be read as based on an anti-capitalist position:

> The present animal movement contains many groups with approaches that rely on privilege and inequality as a strategy to alter treatment for nonhuman animals in such a way that animals may suffer less. This approach neglects the vast system that is responsible for subjugating nonhuman animals while it maintains the supply and demand for exploited bodies, and this is one consequence of an approach that has prioritized an appeal to the elite in society.[15]

And:

> This conventional campaigning approach from mainstream groups has allowed the fundamental issue of power to remain largely unchallenged. Indeed, it purposefully neglects to examine the issue in order to encourage and reassure those potential "allies," while concurrently promoting such methods of advocacy in the grassroots movement, commonly articulated around the dichotomy of "professionals" (bearers of "knowledge" and "wisdom") and the "civilians" (those that have not thought through their approach to advocacy).[16]

This is a radical statement given the current state and funding structure of the advocacy movement for other animals. For example, this particular essay links to Tom Regan's rights-based nonhuman animal rights position. The very fact that it is necessary to describe the nonhuman animal rights position as "rights-based animal rights" points to a long-standing philosophical problem in the movement. Few people in the movement—even though it often uses the term "animal rights" to describe itself in a rhetorical manner—have much knowledge and thus little or no adherence to rights-based theorizing about human relations with other sentient beings.

The corporate organizations in the movement—to the extent that they are interested in philosophical foundations or anything "theoretical"—subscribe to Peter Singer's utilitarian perspective. The most popular, most widely advertised, and most frequently sold philosophy book in the movement for other animals is Singer's *Animal Liberation* (Singer 1995).[17] *The Case for Animal Rights* by Tom Regan (1983) gets much less publicity and attention.[18] There is some resistance to Regan's position even in the movement's grassroots because people claim that explaining a rights-based position is more difficult than one based on welfarist principles like the opposition to "cruelty," and because there are numbers of misanthropists in the movement's ranks, and for mainstream organizations, nonhuman animal rights in the sense of based on rights-based theorizing is not easy to "sell."

The idea that an ethical position can be "sold" has come to the fore in the vegan community in recent times. Moreover, if the philosophy of veganism cannot be sold *as a philosophy*, especially a far-reaching radical philosophy embedded into the original vision of veganism, then sales psychology research may suggest forms of "repackaging," or at least this is what the rank and file of the movement for other animals are being told by most of the national organizations (Taft 2016). Meanwhile, in terms of the structure of the nonhuman animal advocacy movement, as suggested above, a "dichotomy of 'professionals' (bearers of 'knowledge' and 'wisdom') and the 'civilians' (those that have not thought through their approach to advocacy)"[19] has developed with greater emphasis in recent years. Indeed, there are currently one or two powerful cartels running the mainstream, corporatized, "business side" of the nonhuman animal advocacy movement. Based on the data from "pseudoscience" (Taft 2016), a fairly large segment of the careerist nonhuman animal advocacy movement has backed away from regarding veganism as the moral baseline (Francione and Garner 2010) and embraced the new "effective strategies" of *reducetarianism*[20] and *reducetarian* initiatives such as "Meat Free Monday."[21]

Tobias Leenaert gained prominence in the advocacy movement for other animals in 2013 and is now a leading light and rising star of the *reducetarian* movement, yet going under the name of "The Vegan Strategist."[22] This choice of name is as interesting as it is odd. The fact that Leenaert calls himself The Vegan Strategist is bizarre and counterproductive according to his *own* theory. He outlines a two-phase model. Society, he says, is currently in phase one, and there is no sign of phase two. Phase one is a "pre-vegan stage" in which talk about veganism, nonhuman animal rights, and speciesism should be discouraged and severely restricted. Leenaert's own ideas suggest that the last name he should go under during the "pre-vegan" period is "The Vegan Strategist." In a series of videoed talks to vegans relatively new to the vegan community, Leenaert insists that the vegan movement is "about food," and he is one of those who seeks to reduce the meaning of veganism to its dietary component—in other words, the "sellable" part of veganism. Furthermore, Leenaert openly mocks the philosophy of veganism in his presentations, while constructing a number of bizarre "thought experiments" designed to get the new vegan activists in his audiences to agree that they would be willing to consume nonhuman animal products for some "greater good." He also regularly propagated the myth of the "crazy vegan," a "purist" extremist who furiously waives her arms around in the street screaming and shouting at members of the public.[23] Leenaert's account of the "crazy vegan" stereotype dates back to when he was informed by politicians who provided financial support to the vegetarian organization he founded that they believed vegans to be "crazies."

Leenaert is an enthusiastic supporter of the research he says is designed to reveal "what works" in terms of advocacy for other animals. This research data is widely disseminated on social media by the mainstream nonhuman animal advocacy corporations. Casey Taft (2016), a professor of psychiatry at Boston University, an internationally recognized researcher and methodology expert who has consulted with the United Nations on preventing violence and abuse, claims that the data *reducetarians* and others rely to justify their slide away from veganism is seriously flawed and scientifically unreliable. He is particularly critical of current activities that seem to be set in place to assist a reformist agenda and maintain a system of waged nonhuman animal advocates. Taft (2016, 25) says

> I have witnessed a new cottage industry of advocacy research seeking effective approaches for helping animals. While this is a worthy goal, these groups are conducting and promoting flawed, pseudoscientific research that doesn't really tell us anything about effective animal advocacy. Data from this research are being used by Animal Charity Evaluators (ACE) to determine the most "worthy" charities to donate to, which is problematic because we end up with a "garbage in/garbage out" scenario where flawed data are input to generate flawed recommendations. Unfortunately, ACE regularly rates the organizations conducting this research as top charities, and ACE top charities are overwhelmingly (perhaps exclusively) professionalized organizations that do not promote veganism as a moral imperative, which has contributed to questions about bias in their rating system.

As well as promoting the "data" that the nonhuman animal organizations insist suggests that a moderate, don't-ask-too-much approach is the best, Leenaert argues that technological developments are crucial in increasing the numbers of people who reduce their intake of nonhuman animal produce or became "vegan eaters." The biggest asset of the movement right now, he insists, is the money being spent by rich capitalists and capitalist businesses that are in the process of discovering and exploiting new plant-based food and drink markets.[24]

> I'm happy to see that lately, we've seen another factor at our side: **money**. Not that the vegan movement didn't have any money at all before, but today it's kind of a whole new ballgame. For the first time, **big money** is being bet on vegan products. Companies like Hampton Creek, Beyond Beef, and Impossible foods have raised literally **hundreds of millions of dollars in venture capital** (emphases in original) (Leenaert 2015).[25]

THE MARKETIZATION OF VEGAN NONHUMAN ANIMAL RIGHTS

For Tobias Leenaert (2015) and other *reducetarians*, pragmatism is the key: "I'm a pragmatist. I don't tell people that veganism is the moral baseline or that they should go vegan, but suggest that they take whatever steps in that direction that they are comfortable with."[26] If one merely wants to *sell* a plant-based diet rather than a justice-for-all ethic, one has to be pragmatic, moderate, and *inconsistent*.[27]

> I get a quite a bit of criticism from some people for my blogposts and videos. I'm being told that I'm telling people not to be vegan and that hence I'm an anti-vegan. I'm being told I'm not vegan myself because I'm not picky about

wine because I would eat a steak for $100 (which I can use for animals), or because I would make small exceptions if I thought it was better for people's idea of vegans and veganism and, therefore, for the animals.[28]

Those in the movement for rights for other animals who have "tactically" moved away from talking about consistent veganism, nonhuman animal rights, and speciesism in the name of bringing about veganism, nonhuman animal rights, and defeating speciesism insist that *they too* are abolitionists. Indeed, in the original formulation of the concept of the "new welfarist" (Francione 1996),[29] such people were seen as ultimately reaching for the abolition of use of other animals but through the use of problematic theories (such as utilitarianism) and flawed methodology (nonhuman animal welfarism). Reformists and *reducetarians* claim that "abolitionists" are asking for too much and certainly asking for it too soon, that "baby steps" are necessary incremental steps, and the alleged abolitionist "all-or-nothing" approach is unworkable and off-putting to the very people the movement is trying to influence. The better "strategy," they say, is to go easy—be moderate—don't ask for much. Tell people that all they need to do is make step-by-step changes in their diet, that they can eat their way to a less cruel world. This world will be chock full of new yummy vegan foods developed by capitalist entrepreneurs who have no interest and need no interest in justice-for-all veganism that, for sure, would look critically at how these new vegan products are produced.

In relation to editorial freedom and self-regulation by the press, journalist Will Hutton (1996, 9) warned against hoping for too much given the "transient preoccupations of editors and proprietors." Similarly, hanging one's hat on the profit-driven wants and wishes of capitalist entrepreneurs in relation to bringing about a vegan world—even in the slimmed down, ethics-free, "food only" sense currently in vogue—seems equally problematic. As David Nibert (2013) writes:

> Today, capitalism promotes domesecration[30] on an enormous level. Tens of millions of animals are tortured and brutally killed every year to produce growing profits for twenty-first-century elites, who hold investments in the corporate equivalents of Genghis Khan. (Nibert 2013, 266)

Nibert warns the transcending of capitalism may not automatically end *domesecration of other animals* or bring about global justice, but he says transcending capitalism, rather than trying to bring about a capitalist vegan world, is a necessary precondition to real and meaningful change. Huge numbers of humans have been impoverished by capitalism, and the World Bank acknowledges that more than 1 billion humans around the world live on less than $1 a day (Nibert 2013, 269). How such people are to take part in the new vegan consumerism remains a mystery. *Reducetarian* theorists do not concern themselves with such weighty matters. Their position is itself elitist, and that makes their rejection of the original vegan ethos of justice-for-all internally logical. They seem able to sell *small* to one another.

Steve Best (2014) insists that the advocacy movement for other animals is a left-wing movement.[31] He, like Nibert, says that capitalism must be abolished if other animals are to be liberated. We need to critique hierarchical domination and realize that "capitalism absorbs our critique," he states. Best is scathing about what he calls "vegan porn." He says veganism is being "marketized." He argues that veganism is being sold to the nonhuman animal movement as vegan capitalism. He says that "capitalism loves veganism" because of its reformist nature—thus modern-day veganism is easily co-opted. The vegan movement, with no economic analysis, doesn't advocate economic change. He says that capitalism is predatory, violent, and its values oppose the very world that vegans want.

Therefore, Best (2014) argues, as a way to move forward and see the problems it faces, "this movement is a left-wing movement." He encourages us to look at and fully understand the common values that many vegan advocates for other animals embrace: equality, democracy, inclusivity, nondiscrimination, nonhierarchy, rights, justice, peace, and nonviolence. These are left-wing values, he says, while right-wing values are hierarchy, military, family, nation, borders, war, and security. Right wing values are *not* our values, Best states—in fact, "we talk about the opposite."

This chapter has examined a worrying development within the modern vegan nonhuman animal rights social movement. The original justice-for-all vision of veganism is being neutered, while the concept of rights-based nonhuman animal rights is totally ignored by an increasingly corporatized hierarchical movement run by a careerist cartel of waged advocates for other animals who, as we have seen, have their jobs bound up in making their cause a business enterprise. The structural effects of capitalism in furthering both human and other animal oppression are also ignored as it is too "big picture" to be *sellable*. Not only is capitalism not problematized by the corporate movement "professionals," many believe that changes in *shopping habits* can bring about an end to one of the most violent, widespread, and profitable capitalist enterprises ever developed. The original radical vision of veganism needs to be recaptured and re-centered in a movement that has almost completely lost its way in modern day consumerism and shallow celebrity culture.

NOTES

1. Marx's Theory. https://youtu.be/6RDRfkEMoF4.

2. Anthony Nocella II. 2014. "Challenging Racism and Ableism within the Animal Liberation Movement and Fighting for Total Liberation." Talk given for the

Vegan Information Project in Dublin, Ireland, March 26, 2014. Accessed September 25, 2016, from https://gaming.youtube.com/watch?v=3iZAZYJTUss&list=PL3Ez-HNLsjFyxsJhM4pjQbYSE0l12BDsU.

3. This tendency extends to the way in which the nonhuman animal movement's core concepts are conceived. For example, Nibert (2002, 7–12) explains that the movement's conception of the term *speciesism* "hampers somewhat the analysis of the social structural causes of the oppression of other animals" (Nibert 2002, 7).

4. See the review of the online work titled "Beats of Burden: Capitalism, Animals, and Communism." Accessed September 23, 2016, from http://www.eco-action.org/dod/no9/beasts_review.htm.

5. *Daily Kos*. "Anti-Capitalist Meet-Up. An Anti-Capitalist Case for Animal Rights." June 5, 2011. Accessed September 25, 2016, from http://www.dailykos.com/story/2011/6/5/982050/-.

6. Red, Black, Green. An Anti-Capitalist Critique of Animal Exploitation. January 24, 2014. Accessed September 25, 2016, from http://www.tierbefreiung-hamburg.org/wp-content/uploads/Capitalism_Englisch_CMYK.pdf.

7. Visit: http://thetalonconspiracy.com/. Accessed September 25, 2016.

8. See Gary L. Francione's August 24, 2014, Facebook post: "On Capitalism and Animal Exploitation." Accessed September 25, 2016, from https://www.facebook.com/abolitionistapproach/posts/840379032648519.

9. There are conflicting accounts as to the origins of the concept of "goal displacement." For example, Gordon Marshall (1994, 203) claims that Robert Michels first noted the idea in his classic study in 1911 of the German Social Democratic Party. Marshall argues that Michels was "particularly interested in the ways in which organizational dynamics inhibit the realization of radical objectives," quoting Michels: "Who says organizations, says oligarchy" (Marshall 1994, 327). On the other hand, David Jary and Julia Jary (1995, 267) claim that Michels was clearly speaking about goal displacement without using the term, which was coined by Robert Merton in 1949. Also in 1949, Philip Selznick published *TVA and the Grassroots*, about the Tennessee Valley Authority, which led a number of researchers to describe how the original goals of organizations can be changed, subverted, and undermined.

10. Understandably, both Peter Singer and Tom Regan have been named as movement entrepreneurs of the nonhuman animal advocacy movement.

11. The film *Cowspiracy: The Sustainability Secret,* which was made by Kip Andersen and Keegan Kuhn, can be accessed at http://www.cowspiracy.com/. Accessed September 25, 2016.

12. This January 26, 2016, commentary by Captain Paul Watson titled "Greenpeace Has Gone over to the Dark Side with Their Endorsement for the Sealing Industry" can be read at http://www.seashepherd.org/commentary-and-editorials/2016/01/26/greenpeace-has-gone-over-to-the-dark-side-with-their-endorsement-for-the-sealing-industry-752. Accessed September 25, 2016.

13. This January 22, 2016, blog post by Roger Yates, titled "The Faulty Giving Culture in the Animal Advocacy Movement," can be read at http://onhumanrelationswithothersentientbeings.weebly.com/the-blog/the-faulty-giving-culture-in-the-animal-advocacy-movement. Accessed September 25, 2016.

14. For a discussion of such a development, see the talk by Steve Best: "Total Liberation—Revolution for the 21st Century," given at the International Animal Rights Conference 2013 in Luxembourg. https://youtu.be/Pr7Ax_p7ocw.

15. "A Few Thoughts on Elitism in the Animal Movement." A March 26, 2016, blog from orcas and animals. https://network23.org/orcasandanimals/2016/03/25/a-few-thoughts-on-elitism-in-the-animal-movement/. Accessed September 25, 2016.

16. Ibid.

17. Singer's status as an applied philosopher is controversial. People opposed to nonhuman animal rights—including many in organized countermovement mobilizations—*want* Singer to be seen as the "leader" of the "animal rights movement" because they believe that brings advocacy for other animals into disrepute as a general matter (Yates 2007).

18. There was a brief moment (the late 1980s) in the history of the modern nonhuman animal advocacy movement when Regan's rights-based position was prominent, leading sociologists James Jasper and Dorothy Nelkin to declare that, "it is Regan's rights argument—not Singer's utilitarianism—that has come to dominate the rhetoric of the nonhuman animal rights agenda, often pushing it beyond reformism and pragmatism" (Jasper and Nelkin 1992, 97).

19. See note 15: "A Few Thoughts on Elitism in the Animal Movement."

20. For a description of the reducetarian movement, go to: http://reducetarian.org/. Accessed September 25, 2016.

21. See 2016 website established by the Meat Free Mondays Foundation: http://www.meatfreemondays.com/. Accessed September 25, 2016.

22. See related blogs by Tobias Leenaert at: http://veganstrategist.org/. Accessed September 25, 2016.

23. For an example of a related talk by Tobias Leenaert, see the video: "Attacking Veganism One Talk at a Time." https://youtu.be/GiEpWaJhUWE. Accessed September 25, 2016.

24. See the blog post by Tobias Leenaert titled "Our Movement's Biggest Asset: Big Money." August 4, 2015. http://veganstrategist.org/2015/08/04/our-movements-newest-asset-big-money-2/. Accessed September 25, 2016.

25. Ibid.

26. http://veganstrategist.org/2015/08/12/can-abolitionists-and-pragmatists-ever-trust-each-other/.

27. In some of Tobias Leenaert's presentations, he tells his audiences that "consistency is overrated."

28. See the August 12, 2015, blog post by Tobias Leenaert titled "Can Abolitionists and Pragmatists Ever Trust Each Other?" http://veganstrategist.org/2015/08/12/can-abolitionists-and-pragmatists-ever-trust-each-other/. Accessed September 25, 2016.

29. Francione (1996, 34) writes, "Many modern animal advocates see the abolition of animal exploitation as a long-term goal, but they see welfarist reform, which seeks to reduce animal suffering, as setting the course for the interim strategy."

30. Nibert (2013, 12) describes his concept of *domesecration* thus: "The emergence and continued practice of capturing, controlling, and genetically manipulating other animals for human use violates the sanctity of life of the sentient beings

involved, and their minds and bodies desecrated to facilitate their exploitation: it can be said that they have been *domesecrated*. *Domesecration* is the systematic practice of violence in which social animals are enslaved and biologically manipulated, resulting in their objectification, subordination, and oppression."

31. See note 14: "Total Liberation—Revolution for the 21st Century."

REFERENCES

Beirne, Piers. 2007. "Animal Rights, Animal Abuse, and Green Criminology." In Piers Beirne and Nigel South (eds.), *Issues in Green Criminology: Confronting Harms Against Environments, Humanity, and Other Animals.* Cullompton, UK: Willan, 55–83.

Best, Steven. 2014. *The Politics of Total Liberation: Revolution for the 21st Century.* London: Palgrave Macmillan.

Benton, Ted. 1993. *Natural Relations: Ecology, Animal Rights, and Social Justice.* London: Verso.

Blumer, Herbert. 1969. "Collective Behaviour." In Alfred McClung Lee (ed.), *Principles of Sociology*, 3d ed. New York: Barnes & Noble, 65–121.

Charlton, Anna. E., Sue Coe, and Gary Francione. 1993. "The American Left Should Support Animal Rights: A Manifesto." *The Animals Agenda,* Jan/Feb: 28–34.

Christiansen, Jonathan. 2009. "Four Stages of Social Movements." In EBSCO Research Starters. EBSCO Publishing. Accessed September 25, 2016, from https://www.ebscohost.com/uploads/imported/thisTopic-dbTopic-1248.pdf.

Cole, Matthew. 2014. "'The Greatest Cause on Earth': The Historical Formation of Veganism as an Ethical Practice." In Nick Taylor and Richard Twine (eds.), *The Rise of Critical Animal Studies—From the Margins to the Centre.* Abingdon, UK: Routledge, 203–224.

Cole, Matthew, and Kate Stewart. 2014. *Our Children and Other Animals: The Cultural Construction of Human-Animal Relations in Childhood.* Farnham, UK: Ashgate.

Elise, Travis. 2013. "Anti-Capitalism and Abolitionism." In Kim Socha and Sarahjane Blum (eds.), *Confronting Animal Exploitation: Grassroots Essays on Liberation and Veganism.* Jefferson, NC: McFarland & Company, 22–43.

Fox, Michael A. 1999. *Deep Vegetarianism.* Philadelphia: Temple University Press.

Francione, Gary L. 1996. *Rain Without Thunder: The Ideology of the Animal Rights Movement.* Philadelphia: Temple University Press.

Francione, Gary L., and Robert Garner. 2010. *The Animal Rights Debate: Abolition or Regulation?* New York: Columbia University Press.

Freeman, Jo., and Victoria Johnson. 1999. *Waves of Protest: Social Movements Since the Sixties.* Oxford: Rowman & Littlefield.

Gaarder, Emily. 2011. *Women and the Animal Rights Movement.* London: Rutgers University Press.

Gamson, William A. *The Strategy of Social Protest.* Homewood, IL: Dorsey.

Garner, Robert. 2004. *Animals, Politics, and Morality.* 2d ed. Manchester, UK: Manchester University Press.

Gellatley, Juliet, and Tony Wardle. 1996. *The Silent Ark: A Chilling Expose of Meat— The Global Killer.* London: Thorsons.

Gold, Mark. 1998. *Animal Century: A Celebration of Changing Attitudes to Animals.* Charlbury, UK: Jon Carpenter Publishing.

Hutton, Will. 1996. *The State We're In,* London: Vintage.

Jary, David, and Julia Jary. 1995. *Collins Dictionary of Sociology,* 2d ed. Glasgow, UK: HarperCollins.

Jasper, James M., and Dorothy Nelkin. 1992. *The Animal Rights Crusade: The Growth of a Moral Protest.* New York: Free Press.

Macionis, John J., and Ken Plummer. 2008. *Sociology: A Global Introduction,* 4th ed. Harlow, UK: Pearson Education.

Marshall, Gordon. 1994. *The Concise Dictionary of Sociology.* Oxford, UK: Oxford University Press.

Mauss, Armand. 1975. *Social Problems of Social Movements.* Philadelphia: Lippincott.

McAdam, Doug. 1999. "The Decline of the Civil Rights Movement." In Jo Freeman and Victoria Johnson (eds.), *Waves of Protest: Social Movements Since the Sixties.* Oxford: Rowman & Littlefield, 325–348.

McCarthy, John D., and Mayer N. Zald. 1977. "Resource Mobilization and Social Movements: A Partial Theory." *American Journal of Sociology,* 82: 1212–1241.

Movement for Compassionate Living: The Vegan Way. 1997. *A New World Order of Self Reliant, Tree Based, Autonomous, Vegan Villages.* Leatherhead, UK: MCL.

Nibert, David. 2002. *Animal Rights/Human Rights: Entanglements of Oppression and Liberation.* Lanham, MD: Rowman & Littlefield.

Nibert, David. 2013. *Animal Oppression & Human Violence: Domesecration, Capitalism, and Global Conflict.* New York: Columbia University Press.

Plows, Alexandra, and Roger Yates. 1997. *Break the Rules: Breaking the Stereotype of the "New Age Traveller."* Unpublished MA research project. Department of Sociology, University of Wales, Bangor, UK.

Regan, Tom. 1983. *The Case for Animal Rights.* Berkeley, CA: University of California Press.

Schnurer, Maxwell. 2004. "At the Gates of Hell: The ALF and the Legacy of Holocaust Resistance." In Steven Best and Anthony Nocella II (eds.), *Terrorists or Freedom Fighters: Reflections on the Liberation of Animals.* New York: Lantern Books, 106–127.

Shaiko, Ronald G. 1993. "Greenpeace U.S.A.: Something Old, New, Borrowed." *Annals of the American Academy of Political and Social Science,* 528(1): 88–100.

Singer, Peter. 1995. *Animal Liberation.* 2d ed. London: Pimlico.

Staggenborg, Suzanne. 1988. "The Consequences of Professionalization and Formalization in the Pro-Choice Movement." *American Sociological Review,* 53(4): 585–605.

Staggenborg, Suzanne. 1998. "Social Movement Communities and Cycles of Protest: The Emergence and Maintenance of a Local Women's Movement." *Social Problems,* 45(2): 180–204.

Stallwood, Kim. 1996. "Utopian Visions and Pragmatic Politics: Challenging the Foundations of Speciesism and Misothery." In Robert Garner (ed.), *Animal Rights: The Changing Debate.* New York: New York University Press, 194–208.

Taft, Casey. 2016. *Motivational Methods for Vegan Advocacy: A Clinical Psychology Perspective.* Danvers, MA: Vegan Publishers.

Taylor, Angus. 2009. *Animals & Ethics: An Overview of the Philosophical Debate.* 3d ed. Plymouth, UK: Broadview.

Taylor, Angus. 2014. "An Interview with Sue Donaldson and Will Kymlicka." *Between the Species,* 17(1), June: 140–165.

Tilly, Charles. 1978. *From Mobilization to Revolution.* Reading, MA: Addison-Wesley.

Torres, Bob. 2007. *Making A Killing: The Political Economy of Animal Rights.* Oakland, CA: AK Press.

Tovey, Hilary. 2007. *Environmentalism in Ireland: Movement and Activists.* Dublin: Institute of Public Administration. Accessed September 25, 2016, from http://www.aughty.org/pdf/environ_book07.pdf.

Warner, W. Keith, and A. Eugene Havens. 1968. "Goal Displacement and the Intangibility of Organizational Goals." *Administrative Science Quarterly,* 12(4): 539–555.

Watkinson, Kevin, and Dónal O'Driscoll. 2014. *From Animals to Anarchism.* Leeds, UK: Dysophia. Accessed September 25, 2016, from http://dysophia.org.uk/wp-content/uploads/2014/10/ARzineweb.pdf.

West, Elizabeth. 2000. "Organisational Sources of Safety and Danger: Sociological Contributions to the Study of Adverse Events." *Quality in Health Care,* 9: 120–126.

White, Rob. 2002. "Environmental Harm and the Political Economy of Consumption." *Social Justice,* 29(1–2): 82–102.

Yates, Roger. 2007. "Debating 'Animal Rights' Online: The Movement-Countermovement Dialectic Revisited," In Piers Beirne and Nigel South (eds.), *Issues in Green Criminology: Confronting Harms Against Environments, Humanity, and Other Animals.* Cullompton, UK: Willan, 140–157.

Yates, Roger. 2009 "From Dock to Doctor." In Chris Powell (ed.), *Critical Voices in Criminology.* New York: Lexington Books, 109–124.

Afterword: Animals, Capitalism, and Liberation

John Sorenson

This edited collection provides compelling evidence of the influence of David Nibert's invaluable work on the entangled oppression of humans and other animals and his insistence on the need for structural analysis and an understanding of the role of capitalism. These matters could not be more urgent. In her contribution to this volume, Julie Andrzejewski provides an overview of how the plight of other species, including their mass extinction, is directly linked to the operations of global capitalism, its assault on the entire planet, and why these issues should attract our most urgent concern and active engagement. Yet despite the fact that the issues are of fundamental importance and that this approach offers the best understanding of nonhuman animal exploitation today, few have welcomed it, and it has faced much opposition.

As Marcel Sebastien points out in this work, the significance of capitalism as the economic framework for the exploitation of nonhuman animals and human workers is typically ignored, while Peter Li reminds us that ending the exploitation of the former is unlikely to be achieved without transforming the conditions of the latter. Liberal theorists who have written about nonhuman animal rights focus on ethical, individualistic, or psychological terms rather than examining the social structural aspects of their oppression and exploitation and recognizing these as foundational for the operations of capitalism. Clearly, there are individual ethical choices to be made in terms of one's own involvement in how other animals are used and treated, but that is also true of other types of injustice, and it does not preclude the understanding of broader structural features. Our feelings, ideas, and ethical decisions all develop in particular material conditions and are

313

historically constructed; a system in which nonhuman animals are regarded as resources, property, and commodities is not conducive to analyses in which their use and treatment will be understood as matters of social justice.

In this book, Roger Yates criticizes the shallowness that characterizes some of the nonhuman animal advocacy movement. None of the large, conservative nonhuman animal organizations are willing to undertake the necessary structural analysis, but instead they solicit donations for their efforts to ameliorate some of the most egregious forms of abuse while maintaining partnerships with the very industries that perpetuate those abuses on a regular basis. While failing to analyze and oppose the systemic nature of the abuse of other animals as well as the fundamental significance of the capitalist framework in which it occurs, these organizations do not advocate for veganism as a boycott of such institutionalized abuses. The Humane Society of the United States provides an unfortunate example with its sponsorship of events such as "Hoofin' It" in Denver, where "humanely slaughtered" other animals of various species are served at local restaurants, as does the marketing of "high welfare" pig-flesh by the Royal Society for the Prevention of Cruelty to Animals (RSPCA). Citing such spectacles, Francione (2013) condemns them as forms of "happy exploitation" in which nonhuman animal welfare organizations present themselves as working for other animals but collaborate with the industries that exploit them for mutual benefit. Earlier, Marx (1977, 343–344) criticized the hypocrisy of these reformist organizations. However, as Gunderson (2011) points out, his target was not the welfare of nonhuman animals themselves. Rather, in the only references that Marx made about nonhuman animal welfare issues, in Volume 1 of *Capital* and in the *Communist Manifesto*, both concerning the RSPCA, Marx uncovered the hypocrisy of reformists who expressed sympathy for oppressed other animals but not oppressed humans and criticized them seeking to change certain social relations while preserving the social structure that provided them with advantages.

Given such shortcomings, it is unsurprising that many on the left see no radical potential in these mainstream organizations. Of course, some leftists who wish to continue consuming nonhuman animal products themselves find this lack of radical commitment on the part of mainstream welfarist organizations a convenient excuse for evading their own ethical responsibilities to refrain from supporting exploitation as much as possible, but as Tracey Harris and Corinne Painter argue in their chapters here, food choices are part of a genuine politics of liberation.

In contrast to the reformist efforts of conservative welfare organizations, many grassroots activists are making determined and sustained efforts to advance the truly radical agenda of the nonhuman animal rights movement and advocate for a project of total liberation rather than reformism. That project of total liberation has a history going back to nineteenth-century nonhuman animal advocates in Britain and France. They were also socialists, anarchists, and feminists who recognized the intersectionality of these struggles and criticized reformists; for example, socialist and vegan Lewis Gompertz was expelled from the SPCA for his radical views, even though he was one of the organization's founders. Today, critical animal studies (CAS) avoids such omissions and employs structural analysis to investigate the intersectionality of oppressions and academics working in this field support activists' efforts to promote total liberation.

In spite of nonhuman animal advocacy's historical roots in the political left, the current political left has failed to be as visionary as these early radicals and has been unsympathetic and dismissive, even contemptuous, of the nonhuman animal rights movement (Sorenson 2011). Failing to recognize our relations with other animals as a fundamental aspect of our social structure, or the intersectionality of various forms of injustice, many on the left dismiss nonhuman animal rights and veganism as forms of lifestyle politics or matters of individual choice and as less significant than mobilization around other issues than concern only humans. One of the most notorious denunciations was that of Michael Albert, cofounder of *Z* magazine and Z-Net, who told *Satya* magazine (2002) that he did not regard nonhuman animal rights as being "remotely as urgent as preventing war in Iraq, winning a 30-hour workweek, or overthrowing capitalism." Albert rejected analogies between the oppression of human and nonhuman animals and dismissed rights for other animals as a serious issue. Albert, like many others on the left, rejects any suggestion that the oppression of other animals is not only analogous to the oppression of humans but that these forms of oppression are intertwined. He, therefore, assumes that the latter constitutes a serious political issue, while the former does not. However, as Peter Singer pointed out, all animals are equal in the sense that their interests have to be considered, and Tom Regan has argued all animals who are self-aware subjects of a life have inherent value and cannot be used as instruments to further the ends of others. Thus, there is no justification for Albert's position beyond the assertion of prejudice. David Nibert and the contributors to this collection challenge such narrow views of social relations. They demonstrate not only that human and nonhuman animals are exploited in similar ways under capitalism, but these processes are historically interconnected and remind us that we have ethical obligations to oppose all forms of oppression and exploitation.

Astonishingly, Albert's dismissive comments were made in the course of an interview that concerned efforts to build social movements and incorporate diversity of political concerns; his remarks were unlikely to have encouraged any feelings of solidarity from nonhuman animal activists, who he depicted as hypocrites and dilettantes. One might expect such a dismissal of concern for the suffering of others, including that of other animals, from those who embrace the most vulgar ideas of neoliberalism, such as Margaret Thatcher's claim that "there is no such thing as society" (Keay 1987), an assertion still promoted as if it contained some particular insight. It is more disappointing to find such sentiments among progressives on the left where one expects empathy, concern for others, solidarity, and a sense of the common good, none of which should be limited only to humans. In fact, ideas of speciesism and human exceptionalism are as deeply rooted on the left as elsewhere in society. Albert did vaguely suggest that the success of his own anthropocentric priorities might establish conditions that could be "beneficial to any animal rights commitments that emerge," much as some Marxists once claimed that a socialist revolution would automatically resolve issues of women's oppression. However, Albert's failure to recognize the exploitation of nonhuman animals as a fundamental pillar of capitalism is an indication of both how radical and how necessary Nibert's analysis of entangled oppression was, in his *Animal Rights/ Human Rights*, published that same year.

To the extent that many on the left have considered nonhuman animals at all, it is mainly to view them as part of "the environment," which is itself imagined as existing for human benefit. Other animals are not regarded as being of concern in themselves but only as peripheral matters and mainly as resources to be owned and used. The extent of most leftists' concern is to join in the general chorus of what is misleadingly called "animal welfare." Reformist, welfare initiatives suggest the idea that contemporary societies are evolving towards ever more humane ways of treating nonhuman animals, without questioning the fundamental issue of using them in the first place. Rather than progress in the treatment of other animals, what we see are simply ever more efficient ways of exploiting them, as corporations adopt methods and practices that allow them to process huge numbers of other animals faster and at lower costs.

The "animal welfare" chorus mingles the voices of virtually every operator of a factory farm, slaughterhouse, or vivisection laboratory, all calling for these other animals to be tortured and killed "humanely." The left's contribution to the overall performance, exemplified by Michael Albert's case, has been to add the refrain that a future socialist society will offer something better, all the while sneering at those who would attempt to actually establish such conditions. Like Albert, most leftists today have accepted the general view, pervasive in our speciesist society, that there is a qualitative and hierarchical distinction between humans and other animals (to the extent that humans are even recognized *as* animals). They have failed to recognize that similar processes of alienation, exploitation, and oppression have affected *all* animals.

For example, Noske (1997, 18–21) has outlined how the Marxist concept of alienation applies to nonhuman animals. Under capitalism, other animals are not considered individuals with their own interests but as property; used as raw materials or instruments of production, they are forced to work and die for the benefit of the humans who enslave them. They are alienated under capitalism in the sense that they are prevented from realizing their own nature in environments that would allow them to fully develop those capacities. For all the exploitation endured by human workers, Torres (2007, 38) argues that nonhuman animals are oppressed and suffer misery to an even greater extent because they do not receive compensation in the form of wages and are confined within the cage of capitalism for the entire duration of their prematurely shortened lives. This is most obviously apparent in those industries that transform other animals into food.

Nonhuman animals are alienated from the products of their labor, which include their own flesh, eggs, and milk as well as their offspring, who are taken from them soon after birth. While corporations mask these atrocities with images of contented cows, activists remind us that "milk comes from a grieving mother" (Peaceful Prairie Sanctuary, nd), and the abduction of children causes anguish both for the mother whose natural desire to care for her child is thwarted and for the child who needs care, love, and security. These other animals are also alienated from productive activity. They are forced to labor in completely unnatural ways, with their entire being made to serve a single productive function, in factory farms, for example, where they are immobilized, isolated, or overcrowded, repeatedly and forcibly impregnated before they are all killed. "Not only has the animal been dispossessed of its productive activity, the *total* animal is being subordinated to this one activity" (ibid., 19), a process that Noske identifies as deanimalization, which operates to subdivide them and transform them into machines (ibid., 12).

Perhaps, this process has reached its most dreadful and shameful apogee in the transformation of the bodies of chickens, as they are produced for a division of labor as egg-laying machines in the case of females and "broilers," "fryers" or "roasters" in the case of males engineered for "meat" production, all kept in intensive confinement and physically constructed to meet the profit-seeking needs of industry; Davis (2014, 175–176), too, describes this as alienation. Other animals are also alienated from their fellows, either by removing them from the families and societies they would naturally share or distorting their social existence by forcing them into unnaturally close proximity, which stimulates anxiety and aggression. Nonhuman animals are alienated from their natural environments, removing them from the ecosystems they would normally inhabit and forcing them to live in artificial and alien conditions to which they are not adapted and which create physical and psychological stress. Noske (1997) concludes that these all constitute alienation from species life as nonhuman animals are subsumed by capitalism, while Davis (2014, 176) emphasizes that we have stripped the lives of these other animals of everything that provides any pleasure in living, forcing them to inhabit "an existential void" until we see fit to kill them. They are further victimized by the alienation of human workers, such as those in slaughterhouses who are forced to perform their tasks of killing and eviscerating other animals at ever-increasing speeds to enhance efficiency and profits and who violently take out their frustration on nonhuman animals who struggle, resist, or attempt to escape. Such violence is facilitated not only by the horrific conditions that prevail in these institutions but also by speciesist ideology that devalues other animals and often denies their ability to suffer. As Kimberley Ducey demonstrates in her powerful chapter that opens this collection, both chickens and human workers are exploited simultaneously by the institutionalized system of domination that serves the interests of a small elite, which is predominantly male and white.

In general, not only have other social justice movements been uninterested in the nonhuman animal rights movement, but they have resisted efforts to demonstrate the intersection of various forms of oppression when these involve nonhuman animals. Lara Drew and Corey Wrenn provide examples here in discussions of the intersecting and mutually supporting systems of capitalism and hegemonic masculinity. We should be clear that it is not the fact that these forms of oppression are interrelated that makes them relevant for those on the left; rather, it is simply an additional factor that should be taken into account in one's analysis of their operation. The instrumental use and suffering of other animals in itself should be of ethical and political significance for those on the left. It may be possible that, for some, their lack of concern reflects a lack of awareness of the extent of nonhuman animal suffering. That would seem strange, given the fact that nonhuman animal advocates have worked for decades to expose the use and treatment of other animals in factory farms, vivisection laboratories, zoos, circuses, rodeos, and other sites of institutionalized abuse. By providing a glimpse into the inferno to which we have consigned other animals, the striking illustrations by artist Sue Coe used throughout this volume provide a sobering counterpoint to the comforting illusions of industry propaganda. For those who are involved in nonhuman animal rights issues, it does seem inconceivable that anyone could remain unaware of these realities. Nevertheless, some do remain ignorant of how other animals are used or even of basic biological facts, such as that cows produce milk to feed their children. As Kadri Aavik notes, such ignorance about other animals and the myth that humans must consume products derived from their bodies are perpetuated by government and industry propaganda. Such harmful disinformation is disseminated in societies where the idea that other animals exist for us has come to saturate our lives and shape the construction of personal, gendered, and national identities

While many on the left dismiss the significance of the nonhuman animal rights movement, it is true that some advocates for other animals maintain that an understanding of capitalism is not significant for their work. They point out that nonhuman animal exploitation existed before capitalism and has occurred in all types of economic systems, ranging from indigenous hunting and gathering societies to industrial states and socialist countries. Indeed, it is true that the exploitation of other animals has been ubiquitous throughout the whole course of human history, and all societies have developed various means to justify these practices. These ideological justifications have ranged from claims that other animals allow themselves to be hunted and killed because they pity the weakness of humans who would otherwise starve to death, to assertions that other animals are only machines who lack awareness, the capacity to think, or the ability to feel pain. In their contributions to this collection, Lauren Corman, Taichi Inoue, pattrice jones, and Mary Trachsel point out how the consistent disregard of other animals' subjectivity and cultural lives helps to perpetuate their exploitation, while Luis Cordeiro-Rodrigues adds that the institutionalized contempt for other animals has provided a useful mechanism that facilitates the oppression of various groups of humans. Usefully, Richard White reminds us that the goal of an interdisciplinary CAS is to recognize "the animal condition" and to create interspecies solidarity.

While it is certainly true that speciesism predates capitalism, the latter's imperative for ceaseless growth has expanded and intensified the exploitation of other animals and their suffering. In his incisive chapter, John Sanbonmatsu identifies speciesism as a mode of production and, indeed, as a fundamental form of oppression and argues that capitalism is speciesism in its most developed form. In his major historical studies, Nibert (2002, 13) pointed out that capitalism perpetuates nonhuman animal suffering through economic exploitation, unequal power, and ideological control. This is most obvious in the case of the "meat" industry and agribusiness. Although based on horrendous suffering and massively inefficient in terms of energy use, the "meat" industry has been able to expand globally to unprecedented levels while making consumption seem both natural and indispensable. As consumption has increased, so have many associated diseases and dangerous health conditions, environmental destruction, climate change, biodiversity loss and extinction, displacement of rural human populations, use of pesticides and other chemicals, mismanagement of water resources, pollution, and threats to the effectiveness of essential antibiotics. Neoliberal policies accelerated processes already underway: concentration of ownership, vertical integration, and control of entire supply chains, including fertilizers, pesticides, genetically modified seeds, trading companies, farm machinery, "livestock" sales, transportation, slaughterhouses, and super-markets. A very small number of massive corporations control these indus-tries, supported by public subsidies awarded as corporate welfare by compliant politicians, while paying their employees minimum wage for extremely hazardous work in conditions that brutalize and desensitize them, encouraging them to commit acts of deliberate sadism towards the other animals they kill, and contributing to substance abuse and domestic vio-lence in their own homes. The suggestion that nonhuman animal exploita-tion is merely a personal matter, unrelated to the most urgent problems of our time, is entirely mistaken, as is the suggestion that it is something that exists and operates outside capitalism. The industries that exploit other animals are operated by some of the world's largest and most powerful corporations, and historically the oppression of other animals has been consistently intertwined with human violence (Nibert 2013).

As Nibert demonstrates, capitalism perpetuates these intertwined forms of exploitation through ideological means. The foundation of these ideologi-cal operations includes the fervently held convictions of human exception-alism and speciesism, which insist that only humans count morally, and the suffering of other animals (if it is even acknowledged to exist) is of no, or at least far less, consequence. The system that Ariana Ferrari identifies here as biocapitalism does not recognize the oppression of nonhuman animals as a problem but treats these other beings as living machines to be increas-ingly exploited by ever more sophisticated technology. While these atti-tudes are deeply rooted in Western history and culture, they have been intensified and amplified under capitalism in the construction of fantasy worlds through advertising. Wealthy and powerful corporations control mainstream media and use them to disseminate propaganda about their products, including those derived from nonhuman animal exploitation. The global "meat" industry is the most obvious example, although as Núria Almiron, Carol Glasser, Rob Laidlaw, and Michelle Pickover demonstrate here, the commodification of other animals takes endless forms in a wide variety of industries. However, keeping to the case of the "meat" industry, we see how commodity fetishism operates through advertising to transform the flesh of other animals into an object of intense desire and prime value, able to provide unparalleled pleasures. Activists' efforts to present the facts about the suffering of nonhuman animals are often ignored, censored or blocked. Even if information about the suffering and killing of other ani-mals, environmental damage, and dangers to human health caused by "meat" consumption is available, it is swept aside by the torrent of paid advertising that is engineered to stimulate desire and present these prod-ucts as exciting and essential, far removed from suffering and death. Beyond the advertisements themselves, there is an overwhelming preponderance of journalistic support for the "meat" industry in the form of restaurant reviews, nutrition advice, columnists who denounce nonhuman animal activist as extremists and fanatics, and stunts by celebrity chefs and their denunciations of vegans (e.g. Anthony Bourdain compared vegans to Hezbollah, and more recently Italian television chef Gianfranco Vissani described vegans as "members of a sect," saying "I'd kill them all"). Overwhelmingly, veganism is presented as a difficult and austere form of self-denial in which, inexplicably, one deprives oneself of all of life's pleasures. Not only do corporations spend billions of dollars to ensure that these sorts of messages are conveyed, but they also fund propaganda and lobby groups such as the Center for Consumer Freedom to attack nonhuman animal rights groups and veganism. As Mathew Cole demonstrates in his chapter, ethical concerns about the use, commodification, and killing of other animals are swept aside by advertising that creates false needs and conceals exploitation through propaganda constructions about "animal welfare" consisting of minor reforms. As noted, industry propaganda has responded to activists' efforts to end other animals' suffering through the creation of fantasies about "humane meat." In this volume, Livia Boscardin and Jana Canavan reveal the hollowness of these "green capitalist" fantasies, with Vasile Stănescu characterizing them as biopolitical myths and emphasizing the significance of veganism as a revolutionary ethical/political strategy. However, as Richard White warns here, capitalism stands ready to undermine any alternative, including veganism, in this case presenting it merely as an alternative lifestyle or consumer choice and jettisoning its radical praxis that challenges all forms of domination.

As well as being targeted by such corporate propaganda efforts, the nonhuman animal rights movement is subject to corporate-funded repression. Because of their economic power, corporations involved in the exploitation of other animals are able to call upon all of the resources of the state's police and legal apparatus to repress their critics. Tactics deployed to defend nonhuman animal-exploitation industries include infiltration and provocation by undercover police agents, manufacture of evidence, the design of new laws and harsher punishments specifically for nonhuman animal and environmental activists, the use of the "terrorism" label to demonize activists and justify their repression, libel and ag-gag laws that make it a criminal offence to criticize or expose the institutionalized cruelties inflicted on nonhuman animals, and the direct use of physical violence, including murder, against activists (the organization Global Witness designated 2015 the deadliest year for activists so far, with 185 murders). That these efforts are directed against nonviolent activists whose objective is to prevent the suffering of other animals and protect the environment in which they live is a powerful indication of the determination to protect corporate profits against opposition from citizens.

Compassion itself is seen as dangerous and as intolerable interference with the operation of business as usual, even when that business is murderous. For example, in June 2015, Anita Krajnc, of the now-international activist group Toronto Pig Save, was charged with mischief and faced possible imprisonment for giving water to dehydrated pigs being trucked to their doom at (the aptly named) Fearmans Pork, Inc., a slaughterhouse in Burlington, Canada. The case demonstrates how the industry's relentless drive for profit makes a mockery of its claims to be concerned about "animal welfare." Obviously, an industry based on killing other animals so that their flesh can be consumed cannot be interested in the welfare of its victims, but even within the obfuscatory framework of industry discourse, which construes welfare as meaning only that other animals will be kept in saleable condition until they are killed for maximum profit, it is clear that crowding nonhuman animals in overheated trucks with other panicked beings is a form of torture. The fact that Krajnc could be charged for providing such small mercy to these helpless and terrified individuals provides a stark example of the debasing effects of capitalist production on both human and nonhuman animals.

Not only are the oppression of human and nonhuman animals intertwined, but Nibert (2002) and Patterson (2002) argue that the exploitation of other animals provides a useful model for the exploitation of humans. The construction of nonhuman animals as a category of beings who can be exploited legitimately provides a serviceable tool by which to denigrate other humans and justify their exploitation and oppression. Most of those on the left, like the majority of the population generally, have failed to examine these practices and these serviceable tools, rejecting only the inclusion of humans within such a despised category without challenging the category itself. Nonhuman animals are constructed as mere objects, denying their subjectivity so that we can continue to profit from their exploitation in various sites of institutionalized violence.

Speciesism has its own history, but capitalism has supercharged its scale of operations. Overthrowing capitalism will not automatically eliminate speciesism, although to give Michael Albert his due, by providing greater material security for the majority of people and promoting a more democratic system, it may facilitate a context in which more enlightened ideas can flourish. However, it would be a serious mistake to assume that these developments will happen automatically without the determined efforts of nonhuman animal advocates to transform the dominant anthropocentric values and ideas that still persist among the left. What is needed is a social movement that hearkens back to the expansive and encompassing vision of the nineteenth-century radicals in the sense of calling for total liberation and that brings socialism and nonhuman animal liberation into coalescence (Sanbonmatsu 2011, 31).

As a contribution to these worthy objectives, this work is vitally important. David Nibert and the contributors to this edited collection have furthered the goal of total liberation by calling on readers to reconceptualize our relations with other animals. They remind us that our oppressive relations with other animals are not natural, and our commodification and exploitation of their bodies and minds, indeed, their entire lives are not matters of personal preference or lifestyle choice but matters of social justice. This monumental edited collection demonstrates the need to recognize that our use and treatment of other animals is not simply unjust, exploitative, and violent but that it is systemically so, and what is required to break with this system is a rejection of both speciesism and capitalism.

REFERENCES

Davis, Karen, 2014. "Anthropomorphic Visions of Chickens Bred for Human Consumption." In John Sorenson (ed.), *Critical Animal Studies: Thinking the Unthinkable*. Toronto: Canadian Scholars Press, 169–185.

Francione, Gary, 2002. "Gary L. Francione on the State of the U.S. Animal Rights Movement." Interview by Lee Hall. Friends of Animals. Summer. Accessed September 26, 2016, from http://www.friendsofanimals.org/programs/animal-rights/issues-ideas/gary-l-francione-state-us-animal-rights-movement http://www.friendsofanimals.org/programs/animal-rights/issues-ideas/gary-l-francione-state-us-animal-rights-movement.

Francione, Gary, 2013. "Animal Welfare Regulation, 'Happy Exploitation,' and Speciesism." The Abolitionist Approach. August 27. Accessed September 26, 2016, from http://www.abolitionistapproach.com/animal-welfare-regulation-happy-exploitation-and-speciesism/#.V8H8y1d4PVo.

Global Witness, 2016. *On Dangerous Ground*, June 20. Accessed September 26, 2016, from https://www.globalwitness.org/en/reports/dangerous-ground/.

Gunderson, Ryan, 2011. "Marx's Comments on Animal Welfare." *Rethinking Marxism*, 23(4): 543–548.

Keay, Douglas, 1987. "Aids, Education and the year 2000." *Women's Own*, October 31, 8–10. Accessed September 26, 2016, from http://www.margaretthatcher.org/document/106689.

Marx, Karl, 1977. *Capital*. Volume 1. New York: Vintage.

Marx, Karl, and Friedrich Engels. 1978. *Manifesto of the Communist Party*. In R.C. Tucker (ed.), *The Marx-Engels Reader*. New York: W.W. Norton. 469–500

Nibert, David, 2002. *Animal Rights/Human Rights: Entanglements of Oppression and Liberation*. Lanham, MD: Rowman & Littlefield.

Nibert, David, 2013. *Animal Oppression and Human Violence*. New York: Columbia University Press.

Noske, Barbara, 1997. *Beyond Boundaries*. Montreal: Black Rose.

Patterson, Charles, 2002. *Eternal Treblinka*. New York: Lantern

Peaceful Prairie Sanctuary. Nd. "Milk Comes from a Grieving Mother." Accessed September 26, 2016, from http://www.peacefulprairie.org/outreach /grievingMother.html.

Satya, 2002. "Progressives: Outreach Is the Key." September. Accessed September 26, 2016, from http://satyamag.com/sept02/albert.html.

Sorenson, John, 2011. "Constructing Extremists, Rejecting Compassion: Ideological Attacks on Animal Advocacy from Right and Left." In John Sanbonmatsu (ed.), *Critical Theory and Animal Liberation*. Lanham, MD: Rowman & Littlefield, 219–238.

Torres, Bob, 2007. *Making A Killing*. Oakland, CA: AK Press.

Index

About the Contributors

DAVID NIBERT is professor of sociology at Wittenberg University in Springfield, Ohio. He is the author of *Animal Rights/Human Rights: Entanglements of Oppression and Liberation* and *Animal Oppression and Human Violence: Domesecration, Capitalism, and Global Conflict.*

SUE COE is one of the foremost political artists working today. While her work covers a variety of subjects, she has spent years documenting the atrocities committed by people against animals and continues to generate art on that subject. Her published collections include *Dead Meat* (1996), *Cruel: Bearing Witness to Animal Exploitation* (2012), and *The Ghosts of our Meat* (2013).

NÚRIA ALMIRON is an associate professor of communication at the Universitat Pompeu Fabra, in Barcelona, Spain. Her main research topics merge the field of critical animal studies (CAS) with the political economy of communication, the ethics of mediation, and interest groups. She is also the codirector of the UPF Centre for Animal Ethics, a multidisciplinary think tank focused on promoting nonspeciesist views.

JULIE ANDRZEJEWSKI is professor emeritus at St. Cloud State University, in St. Cloud, Minnesota. Her publications include *Social Justice, Peace, and Environmental Education* (coeditor) and book chapters: "Urgent Global Problems Require Teacher Agency," "The Sixth Mass Extinction" (with John Alessio), and "War: Animals in the Aftermath."

LUÍS CORDEIRO-RODRIGUES holds a PhD from the University of York and is currently a postdoctoral fellow at the Center for Leadership Ethics in Africa (CLEA) at the University of Fort Hare, in Alice, South Africa. He has published in various journals, including the *Journal for Critical Animal Studies, Theoria*, and *Critical Studies on Terrorism.*

LAUREN CORMAN, an associate professor of sociology at Brock University, St. Catharines, Canada, teaches critical animal studies (CAS) and contemporary social theory. She hosted and produced Toronto's *Animal Voices* radio show and podcast (animalvoices.ca) from 2001–2009. She publishes in the areas of intersectional feminist theory, critical pedagogy, and critical animal studies.

LARA DREW obtained a PhD from the University of Canberra (Australia) in Adult Education. Lara's other research and writing interests include radical adult education, anarchism, feminism and the body, and anticapitalist positions. Lara is a project director for the Oceania Institute for Critical Animal Studies chapter, on the executive board for the Institute for Critical Animal Studies, co-runs and co-writes for Veganarchy and participates in various grassroots campaigns for animal liberation.

CAROL L. GLASSER is an assistant professor of sociology at Minnesota State University, Mankato. She is a cofounder of Progress for Science, an antivivisection group currently focused on ending experiments on non-human primates in the public university system. Her research examines social movements, critical animal studies, and gender inequality.

pattrice jones is a cofounder of VINE Sanctuary, an LGBTQ-led farmed animal sanctuary, as well as the author of *The Oxen at the Intersection* and *Aftershock.* A former tenant organizer and antiracist educator, she has also contributed chapters to numerous books, including *Ecofeminism, Sister Species, Sistah Vegan*, and *Contemporary Anarchist Studies.*

ROB LAIDLAW is founder and director of the international "wildlife" protection charity Zoocheck and the writer of nine nonfiction children's books about "wildlife" protection. He has been involved in a broad range of successful nonhuman animal protection initiatives across Canada and around the world, including investigative and legislative campaigns, public awareness programs, litigations, and nonhuman animal rescues.

MICHELE PICKOVER is the author of *Animal Rights in South Africa* and a cofounder of Animal Rights Africa (ARA). She is director of the EMS Foundation, a South African NGO that works for social justice and to make the connection between human and nonhuman oppression.

JOHN SANBONMATSU is an associate professor of philosophy at Worcester Polytechnic Institute, in Worcester, Massachusetts. He is the author of the book *The Postmodern Prince* and editor of *Critical Theory and Animal Liberation*. He currently writes a blog for the Huffington Post.

JOHN SORENSON is professor of sociology at Brock University, St. Catharines, Canada. His books include *Ape, About Canada: Animal Rights*, and *Constructing Ecoterrorism: Capitalism, Speciesism and Animal Rights*, and he is the editor of *Critical Animal Studies: Thinking the Unthinkable*.

RICHARD J. WHITE is a reader in human geography at Sheffield Hallam University, in Sheffield, United Kingdom. He is particularly interested in deconstructing the ways in which exploitation of humans and animals intersects in society and developing a new geographic imaginary based on peace and nonviolence.

COREY WRENN is director of gender studies and a lecturer of sociology at Monmouth University, in West Long Branch, New Jersey. In July 2013, she founded the Vegan Feminist Network, an academic-activist project engaging intersectional social justice praxis. She is the author of *A Rational Approach to Animal Rights: Extensions in Abolitionist Theory*.

ROGER YATES has been an ethical vegan since 1979, an animal rights prisoner, and an academic with a research interest in social movements. He is currently an organizing volunteer for the Dublin-based Vegan Information Project and a regular speaker at VegfestUK.